Getting It Right
From the Start

The Principal's Guide to Early Childhood Education

Marjorie J. Kostelnik
Marilyn L. Grady

A JOINT PUBLICATION

naesp National Association of Elementary School **Principals**

CORWIN
A SAGE Company

For information:

Corwin
A SAGE Company
2455 Teller Road
Thousand Oaks, California 91320
(800) 233-9936
Fax: (800) 417-2466
www.corwinpress.com

SAGE Ltd.
1 Oliver's Yard
55 City Road
London EC1Y 1SP
United Kingdom

SAGE India Pvt. Ltd.
B 1/I 1 Mohan Cooperative Industrial Area
Mathura Road, New Delhi 110 044
India

SAGE Asia-Pacific Pte. Ltd.
33 Pekin Street #02-01
Far East Square
Singapore 048763

Printed in the United States of America

Library of Congress Cataloging-in-Publication Data

Kostelnik, Marjorie J.
Getting it right from the start: the principal's guide to early childhood education/
Marjorie J. Kostelnik, Marilyn L. Grady.
　　　p. cm.
"A joint publication with the National Association of Elementary School Principals."
Includes bibliographical references and index.
ISBN 978-1-4129-4949-1 (cloth)
ISBN 978-1-4129-4950-7 (pbk.)

　　1. Early childhood education—Handbooks, manuals, etc. 2. Elementary school principals—Handbooks, manuals, etc. I. Grady, Marilyn L. II. National Association of Elementary School Principals (U.S.) III. Title.

LB1139.23.K675 2009
372.21—dc22　　　　　　　　　　　　　　　2008044785

This book is printed on acid-free paper.

09　10　11　12　13　10　9　8　7　6　5　4　3　2　1

Acquisitions Editor:	Debra Stollenwerk
Editorial Assistant:	Julie McNall
Production Editor:	Amy Schroller
Copy Editor:	Alison Hope
Typesetter:	C&M Digitals (P) Ltd.
Proofreader:	Wendy Jo Dymond
Indexer:	Sylvia Coates
Cover Designer:	Rose Storey

Contents

Preface

To do:

- Appoint task force to study half-day versus full-day kindergarten.
- Approve preschool teacher candidate list.
- Meet with Even Start and Head Start directors.
- Read curriculum committee report on High Scope and Mastery Learning programs.
- Attend mayor's summit on school readiness—birth to age five.
- Check on state licensing requirements for three-year-olds.

Today, more and more principals are finding early childhood items like these on their "to-do" lists. This has come about for two reasons: First, large numbers of children in the United States are currently enrolled in some kind of early education program. Children's participation in preschool, childcare and kindergarten has grown steadily over the last fifty years. Whether accessing private or public services, today's families eagerly seek early education for their children, which has resulted in approximately half of all the three- and four-year-olds in the country (4 million children) now being enrolled in "school."

Second, schools and school districts are more active players in the early childhood enterprise than was true in the past. Their roles vary from serving as the administrative agent for early childhood programs; to providing space for nonschool administrated programs; to partnering with local agencies and providers to enhance children's school readiness. In any case, schools are not standing on the sidelines. They are becoming more central to the world of early childhood education every day.

With this increased activity comes additional responsibilities for principals. Yet, many school administrators have little or no training in how to design, implement, and evaluate programs for very young children. *Getting It Right From the Start: The Principal's Guide to Early Childhood Education* addresses this dilemma.

PURPOSE

Getting It Right From the Start: The Principal's Guide to Early Childhood Education is a practical, well-referenced manual especially created for busy principals who want to know what effective early childhood programs look like and how to achieve them in their schools and communities. Filled with useful information, it offers an insider's view of the field, by touching on key areas of operation and discussing ways to avoid the pitfalls that can derail effective school-based early childhood initiatives. Most important, the *Guide* provides the kind of information principals need to recognize and create effective programs, to "talk the talk," to provide the kind of feedback staff need to improve, and to become key players in educating our nation's youngest students.

USING THE GUIDE

Getting It Right From the Start: The Principal's Guide to Early Childhood Education can be read straight through or used as a reference manual as issues arise. In either case, it is meant to be a book you will return to again and again—one you will keep close at hand supporting your work in early childhood education.

CHAPTER ORGANIZATION

Getting It Right From the Start: The Principal's Guide to Early Childhood Education is divided into fifteen chapters. Our goal is to cover chapter topics thoroughly, by providing critical information that is immediately useful, without drowning readers in detail. Since topics vary in how much a principal needs to know, the length of each chapter varies accordingly. Thus, there are short chapters and long ones, depending on the breadth of the topic under discussion. In Chapter 1, we provide an overview of the current state of the field, and in Chapter 2, we consider the importance of quality in doing what is best for young children. How principals can become credibly involved in early childhood learning communities is the subject of Chapter 3. The full array of early childhood stakeholders is described in Chapter 4. In Chapter 5, developmentally appropriate practice, a key early childhood educational concept, is explored, including both pluses and minuses. Chapter 6 discusses how very young students learn and what they should be learning in school. Chapter 7 provides descriptions of effective curricula. Chapter 8 follows up with information about learning centers and daily routines as vehicles for translating curricula into practice. Chapter 9 focuses on relevant assessment strategies. How early childhood programs are funded is the subject of Chapter 10. Classroom teachers are the topic of Chapter 11. Next, Chapter 12 describes how to find and maintain highly qualified staff. Effective indoor and outdoor early childhood environments provide the content for Chapter 13. Family engagement is the focus of Chapter 14. We close with Chapter 15, a summary of the actions principals typically carry out in early childhood education.

SPECIAL FEATURES

Each chapter offers a blend of research-based content as well as implications for administrative practice. Numerous examples, charts, checklists, and resources are included to make key information clear and useable. All chapters end with a Principals' Roles section that summarizes key strategies the successful early childhood leader will likely implement. In some cases, more extensive checklists and rating scales are necessary to promote and monitor high-quality early childhood programs. These are provided in a special tools section at the end of the book. We intend for these tools to be duplicated and distributed as needed. An index has also been provided for easy reference.

Acknowledgments

This book came about at the request of principals searching for an easy-to-use, thorough, but not overly detailed reference book for early childhood decision making. We are grateful to many individuals who gave of their time, expertise, and experience to make the idea a reality. Special thanks go to the following individuals:

Sherry Aldrich
National Arbor Day Foundation
Nebraska City, Nebraska

Suzanne K. Becking
University of Nebraska–Lincoln
Lincoln, Nebraska

Jeremy Christiansen
Fairbury Public Schools
Fairbury, Nebraska

Marcia Corr
Nebraska Department of Education
Lincoln, Nebraska

Peggy Croy
Holy Family School
Danville, Illinois

Carolyn Edwards
University of Nebraska–Lincoln
Lincoln, Nebraska

Harriette Egertson
Temecula, California

Joan Erickson
Aurora University
Aurora, Illinois

Carol Fichter
Nebraska's Early Childhood Training Center
Omaha, Nebraska

Kris Friesen
York Public Schools
York, Nebraska

Harriet Gould
Raymond Central Schools
Raymond, Nebraska

Ruth Heaton
University of Nebraska–Lincoln
Lincoln, Nebraska

Sharon Cole Hoffman
University of Nebraska–Lincoln
Lincoln, Nebraska

Russ Inbody
Nebraska Department of Education
Lincoln, Nebraska

Barbara Marchese
St. Vincent de Paul
Omaha, Nebraska

Kyle McGowan
Crete Public Schools
Crete, Nebraska

Judy McKee
Eastern Michigan University
Ypsilanti, Michigan

Ramona Miller
Mahnomen Public Schools
Mahnomen, Minnesota

Kaye Peery
Zuni Public Schools
Zuni, New Mexico

Guy Trainin
University of Nebraska–Lincoln
Lincoln, Nebraska

Sandra Rosenboom
Crete Public Schools
Crete, Nebraska

Kathy Wilson
University of Nebraska–Lincoln
Lincoln, Nebraska

Henry Sanoff
North Carolina State University
Raleigh, North Carolina

Steve Wilson
Cairo Public Schools
Cairo, Nebraska

Deila Steiner
Lincoln Public Schools
Lincoln, Nebraska

Ginger Zierdt
Minnesota State University
Mankato, Minnesota

We are especially grateful to Anne K. Soderman, professor emeritus, Michigan State University, who contributed Chapter 9, Assessing Children's Learning. Anne has worked with schools all over the world, helping them to create authentic assessment strategies for children from preschool through middle school. We are pleased she is sharing her expertise with you. Finally, special thanks to the many principals, teachers, and children with whom we worked to make this book a reality. Their ideas, observations, questions and insights challenged our thinking and motivated us to share the story with others.

About the Authors

Marjorie J. Kostelnik, PhD, began her career in early childhood education as a Head Start teacher and has been involved in educating children and teachers ever since. Following several years in the classroom, she received her master's degree and doctorate in human development and family studies from Penn State. She was on the faculty at Michigan State for twenty-two years, serving twelve years as program supervisor of the Child Development Laboratories and then as chair of the Department of Family and Child Ecology. During her time in Michigan, she worked with early childhood educators in more than one hundred programs, by developing curricula, enhancing children's school readiness, and working with teachers to develop positive child guidance strategies. An author of sixteen books, Dr. Kostelnik arrived at the University of Nebraska–Lincoln in 2001, where she now serves as dean of the College of Education and Human Sciences. A former vice president of the National Association for the Education of Young Children (NAEYC), Dr. Kostelnik currently serves on the Lincoln Public Schools Community Learning Center Advisory Board and the State of Nebraska Early Childhood Interagency Coordinating Council.

Marilyn L. Grady, PhD, is professor of educational administration at the University of Nebraska–Lincoln. She has been a teacher and an administrator in the K–12 schools, and a faculty member and administrator at the college and university levels. She received her bachelor's in history from Saint Mary's College, Notre Dame, Indiana, and her PhD in educational administration with a specialty in leadership from The Ohio State University.

Her research specialties are leadership, the principalship, and superintendent–school board member relationships. She is the author or coauthor of twenty-three books, including *20 Biggest Mistakes Principals Make, 194 High-Impact Letters for Busy Principals, Launching Your First Principalship, Principals in Transition,* and *From First Year to First Rate.*

Early Childhood Education

An Expanding Enterprise!

Evan's big brother is in the third grade at Darwin Elementary. Evan goes to Darwin too. He is four years old and is enrolled in the district's state-funded prekindergarten program.

It used to be that most young children began their association with the public schools when they entered kindergarten. Today, however, we are seeing large numbers of prekindergarten-aged children coming through the schoolhouse doors. Many of them are involved in early childhood programs, such as Head Start or childcare services that are housed in or work in partnership with local schools. Increasingly, schools are also administering their own preschool classes.

During the 2006–07 school year, thirty-eight states funded preprimary education programs, investing $3.7 billion in the enterprise (National Institute for Early Education Research [NIEER], 2008). This nationwide infusion of state dollars into early childhood education has prompted more than twenty thousand public schools to offer voluntary preprimary programs, including special education prekindergarten, general prekindergarten, and Head Start. It has also expanded school collaborations with other early childhood partners. As of 2007, approximately 35 percent of the public schools in the United States offered state-funded preschool classes, enrolling a total of 1 million children. That accounts for one in four of all the three- and four-year-olds participating in early learning settings nationwide; there is every reason to believe that these numbers will continue to rise.

This means that if you are an elementary principal, odds are, you will have some responsibility for educating three- and four-year-old children sometime in your career. To carry out these responsibilities effectively, it is important to understand **why** very young children are coming to "school" in such high numbers.

1

WHY THE PUSH FOR PREKINDERGARTEN?

The following news items are among hundreds that appeared in last year's press.

Governor Advocates for Early Childhood Education

Enrollment of 4-Year-Olds Hits 90% in Oklahoma

Billions at Stake in Expansion of PreK

Headlines like these underscore a growing trend in the United States: the number of young children attending early childhood programs (preschool, child care, kindergarten) is increasing dramatically. Whereas preprimary enrollments in the United States were only about 0.3 million in 1970, by 2002 they topped 2.8 million. Today, approximately half of all the three- and four-year-olds in the country (4 million children) are enrolled in formally organized early childhood settings. The number of five-year-olds in prekindergarten and kindergarten programs is even higher, reaching up to 80 percent of the total five-year-old population (Hodgkinson, 2006). By age six, nearly every child in the United States is involved in some type of formal early learning program ranging from preschool through first grade.

The boom in early childhood enrollments is happening for several reasons:

- Large numbers of families need and want out-of-home care and education for their preschool-age children.
- Research has demonstrated that early childhood experiences strongly influence children's later development and learning.
- Evidence is mounting that quality early childhood education improves the chances for success of children who would otherwise be at risk for school failure.
- There is growing proof that early education provides a good return on investment to taxpayers.

Each of these factors is worth considering further.

INCREASING FAMILY DEMAND

My neighbor used to look after my daughter, but I really wanted Taylor in a learning environment. I moved her here because I didn't want her watching TV all day. When it comes time for kindergarten, I want her to be prepared. (Parent of a child in a prekindergarten program)

We have eight sections of one kind of preschool program or another spread out over three elementary buildings and still we haven't met family demand. I have my eye on a "big box store" that just went out of business—that building might make a great early childhood center for our PreK classes. (District superintendent)

Many families today see benefits in their children having some kind of school experience prior to starting the compulsory grades. Although infants and toddlers are mostly cared for at home by a mother, father, grandparent, or some other in-home provider, by three years of age, large numbers of young children are involved in out-of-home care and education. See Figure 1.1 for descriptive data on these family arrangements.

Figure 1.1 Descriptive Data on Type of Care

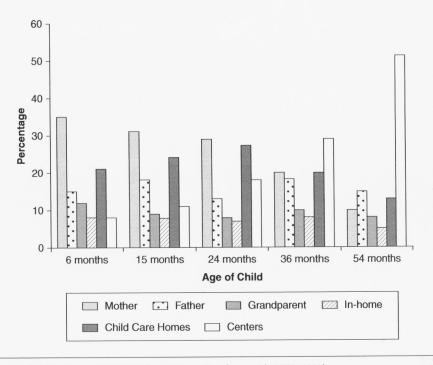

Source: National Institute of Child Health and Human Development (NICHD; 2002).

Note: Centers refer to formal early childhood education programs including state prekindergarten, Head Start, preprimary special education, and other private programs such as childcare and preschool programs. These may be housed in schools or in other community facilities.

Initially, most families seek outside programs for their children so adult family members can work, go to school, or engage in some other form of training. This involves both mothers and fathers. However, the increase in working mothers has been the single biggest demographic shift to influence the demand for early care and education. According to recent labor statistics, 56 percent of American women with infants are in the labor force. By the time their children are age six, the percentage of employed mothers goes up to 64 percent (National Women's Law Center, 2008). These high figures are precipitated by personal choice, fiscal necessity (mothers' earnings contribute approximately 35 percent to families' incomes), and welfare reform policies that require single mothers to work to continue receiving benefits.

More recently, recognition that preprimary programs can enhance children's learning has also fueled the demand for greater access. By age three, education rather than child care alone is the primary reason families cite for having their children participate in early learning settings prior to kindergarten (Barnett & Yarosz, 2007). They hope that their children will not only be safely cared for, but that they also will benefit socially and academically from going to preschool.

EARLY LEARNING IMPERATIVES

There is no question that the early years are learning years.

> From the time of conception to the first day of kindergarten, development proceeds at a pace exceeding that of any subsequent stage of life. Although there have been long-standing debates about how much the early years really matter in the larger scheme of lifelong development, our conclusion is unequivocal: What matters during the first months and years of life matters a lot, not because this period of development provides an indelible blueprint for adult well-being, but because it sets either a sturdy or fragile foundation for what follows. (Shonkoff & Phillips, 2000, p. 384)

Children come into the world biologically programmed to learn. Everything they do, every interaction they have with a person or object, and everything they see, hear, smell, taste, or touch is a source of stimulation and potential learning. From the very beginning, a healthy child is an active participant in her own learning: exploring the environment, responding, communicating, and, in a relatively short time, constructing ideas and theories about how the world works (Bowman, Donovan, & Burns, 2001). During the first five years of life, tremendous growth occurs in intellectual, linguistic, social, emotional, and physical competence. It is during this period that the basic groundwork is laid for adolescent and adult dispositions and skills in every developmental domain. That covers a lot of territory. See Table 1.1 for a few highlights of the significant competencies children potentially develop in the early years.

Table 1.1   Early Competencies That Undergird Future Learning

Developmental Domain	*Examples of Significant Competencies Grounded in Early Childhood*
Cognitive	• Number concepts • Problem-solving strategies • Concepts of time, space, order, patterns, and categories
Linguistic	• Language • Communication skills • Associating meaning and print • Emergent literacy
Social	• Social awareness • Work habits and attitudes • Prosocial understandings • Development of conscience • Understanding expectations and rules
Emotional	• Emotional awareness of self and others • Empathy • Coping strategies
Physical	• Body awareness • Attitudes toward food • Nutritional habits • Body image • Physical mastery (fine motor and gross motor)

The competencies listed in Table 1.1 are just a few of the numerous and remarkable accomplishments that develop during early childhood. All of these are influenced by what is happening in young children's brains.

THE MARVEL OF EARLY BRAIN DEVELOPMENT

At one time, we thought children were born with fully formed brains. Now we know better. Because of technological advances in neuroscience, today we can literally "see" brain activity we once knew very little about. As a result, scientists have learned that although babies are born with all the brain cells they will ever have, the connections among those cells are relatively sparse and immature. During early childhood, children's brain cell connections multiply in number and grow in strength. Basic circuits within the brain are established first. As certain connections are made over and over again, those connections become stronger (e.g., a child's repeated experiences of interacting with the same caregiver eventually lead the child to recognize and form attachments to that caregiver). With each variation in experience, new circuitry is created (e.g., the infant begins to differentiate between mom and dad). These more complex circuits create the foundation for increasingly complex skills. See Figure 1.2 for examples of how children's neural connections become more numerous and more complex from birth through two years of age.

Figure 1.2   Brain Growth Birth to Age Two

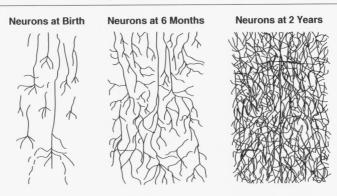

Source: From Marjorie J. Kostelnik, Anne K. Soderman & Alice Phipps Whiren *Developmentally Appropriate Curriculum: Best Practices in Early Childhood Education,* 4/e. Published by Allyn and Bacon/Merrill Education, Boston, MA. Copyright © 2007 by Pearson Education. Reprinted by permission of the publisher.

Both biology and experience play a role in brain development. Consider how the simple act of reading a storybook prompts important neural action in a young child's brain.

> A child care provider reads to a three-year-old. In a matter of seconds, thousands of cells in the child's growing brain respond. Some brain cells are "turned on," triggered by this particular experience. Many existing connections among brain cells are strengthened. At the same time, new connections are formed, adding a bit more definition and complexity to the intricate circuitry that will remain largely in place for the rest of this child's life. (Shore, 1997, p. ix)

Some experiences lead to stronger, more prolific neural connections, and some experiences hinder brain development. For young children, nurturance and stimulation are literally "brain food." Thus, children's brain development is **enhanced** when they experience the conditions outlined in Box 1.1.

Box 1.1

Day-to-Day Care of Young Children's Brains

Children's brain growth is enhanced when adults

- ensure children's health and safety,
- provide appropriate nutrition,
- establish close relationships with children,
- encourage exploration and play,
- offer a stimulating environment,
- establish routines, and
- minimize stress (Shore, 1997, pp. 26–27).

Sometimes, though, neural connections are **inhibited** when children experience deprivation and neglect, when they are habitually overstimulated (as happens in chaotic environments), and when they encounter repeated failure. Environmental assaults such as starvation, alcohol, drugs, or abuse can actually **damage** neural connections, leading to impairments that cannot be undone later in life.

By six to eight years of age, children achieve about 90 percent of their mature brain growth. If you were to compare children's brains at this age, the number and strength of the neural connections from one child to the next might vary by as much as 30 percent (Bjorklund, 2005). Those differences would be directly related to the kinds of environments the children experienced. Optimal experiences provide benefits that last a lifetime. Lost opportunities and negative experiences are difficult to overcome. Unfortunately, many children do not receive the supports they need to enhance optimal brain development. These youngsters are the ones most at risk for school failure.

CHILDREN AT RISK OF SCHOOL FAILURE

I have children come to my class who have never handled a book, never drawn with a crayon, and who are constantly worried about whether or not they will get supper each night. This puts them behind from day one. Years later, I see these same kids and they have never caught up. (Kindergarten teacher)

Kindergarten teachers report that one out of three children comes to school lacking the basic abilities they need to succeed. Most often, these children come from families living close to or below the poverty line (National Center for Education Statistics [NCES], 2000). Poverty is the single biggest predictor of low birth weight, malnutrition, poor dental and physical health, stress related to food insecurity and physical safety, homelessness, and child abuse and neglect (American Humane Association, 2006). None of these conditions contributes to healthy development or school achievement. Additional risk factors in early childhood (also associated with poverty) include having parents who have not graduated from high school, living in a single-parent family, and having parents who do not speak English at home. Consider the following statistics:

- Twenty-four million children under the age of six live in the United States.
- Ten and a half million (43 percent) of them live in low-income or poor families ($20,650 = the federal poverty level for a family of four).

Unfortunately, in this country—the richest country in the world—the proportion of children living in poverty is high and rising. Between 2000 and 2006, the number of preschoolers who were poor increased by 18 percent. We cannot afford to lose a single child to poverty, not only because it is unjust, but also because we cannot sustain ourselves in the new global economy without a huge reservoir of "brainpower." That brainpower will come from our children.

The Burden of Poverty

Growing up in a low-income family does not guarantee school failure, but children from poor families are more prone to poor achievement than are children from more-advantaged homes. At kindergarten entrance, they are twice as likely as more-advantaged children to score in the lowest quartile in reading, math, and general knowledge. Many come to school nineteen months to two years behind their peers. This creates an achievement gap that can last throughout children's school careers and that is difficult to amend (Lee & Burkham, 2002).

Although children living in low-income families share a common lack of adequate resources, they vary along many other dimensions such as family structure, race or ethnicity, country of birth, parents' education, parents' employment, and the communities and areas of the country in which they live. There is no single demographic profile that describes all children who are economically deprived. See Box 1.2.

Box 1.2

U.S. Child Poverty Snapshot

- A child in the United States has a better than two in five chance of beginning life in a poor or low-income family.
- Young children who are poor may live in single-parent families (51 percent) or in two-parent families (49 percent).
- Children living in poor or low-income families may have two working parents (54 percent), one working parent (27 percent), or no working parents (20 percent) at home. One-third of the parents in the "no parents working" category have disabilities that prevent them from entering the workforce.

(Continued)

(Continued)

- Sixty percent of young children who are poor have immigrant parents; 40 percent have parents who are native born.
- Children of every race are among the poor and struggling. Although Native American, Latino, and black children are disproportionately low income, whites compose the largest single group of low-income children under age six. See the bar graph that follows.
- A significant number of young children who are poor live with parents who have less than a high school education (26 percent). Some have parents who have earned a high school diploma (36 percent), and some live with parents who have some college or more (38 percent).
- Children living in poverty can be found in urban environments (37 percent), in the suburbs (41 percent), and in rural areas (21 percent).
- Young children live in poverty in every region of the country. See the bar graph that follows.

Figure A Percentage of Low-Income Children by Race/Ethnicity

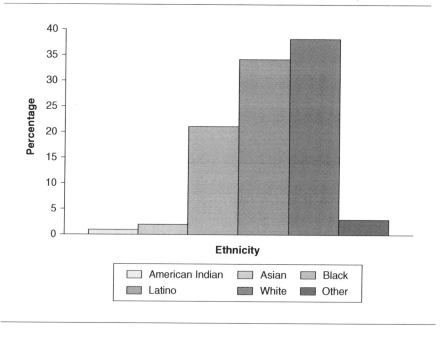

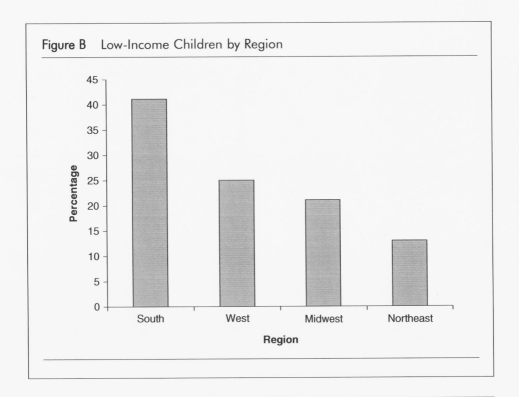

Figure B   Low-Income Children by Region

Source: Adapted from Douglas-Hall & Chau, 2007, pp. 1–4.

As the facts in Box 1.2 attest, many young children in the United States live in disadvantaged circumstances. This does not bode well for their immediate academic success or their long-term ability to break the cycle of poverty. See Box 1.3.

Box 1.3
The Consequences of Childhood Poverty Are Generally Long Term

Poor children are at greater risk of

- raising their own children in poverty,
- dropping out of high school,
- teen parenthood,
- emotional and behavioral problems,
- exposure to family violence,
- working at a low-wage job as an adult, and
- serious and chronic health problems (Rosman, Kass, & Kirsch, 2006, p. 8).

Uneven Playing Field for Poor Children

Poor families struggle to support their young children. Love and effort taken into consideration, it is hard for them to meet their children's basic physical, cognitive, and social needs. Thus, from the earliest days of life, there are essential differences between the environments experienced by children from low-income families and those experienced by other children. These differences have a significant impact on children's developing cognitive skills (numeracy, literacy, problem solving, language) and noncognitive abilities (socioemotional skills, physical and mental health, perseverance, attention, motivation, and self-confidence). For instance, research shows that in families living below the poverty line children and adults read stories together only about half as often as happens in higher-income families. This contributes to the fact that by the time children from low-income families enter first grade, many of them have only one-fourth of the vocabulary words of children from families who are better off financially (B. Hart & Risley, 1995; Vandivere, Moore, & Zaslow, 2000). Similar gaps in achievement are evident in every facet of development. These trends are depicted in Figures 1.3 and 1.4.

Figure 1.3   Cognitive Skill Accumulation of Children Born in Families Below and Above the Poverty Line

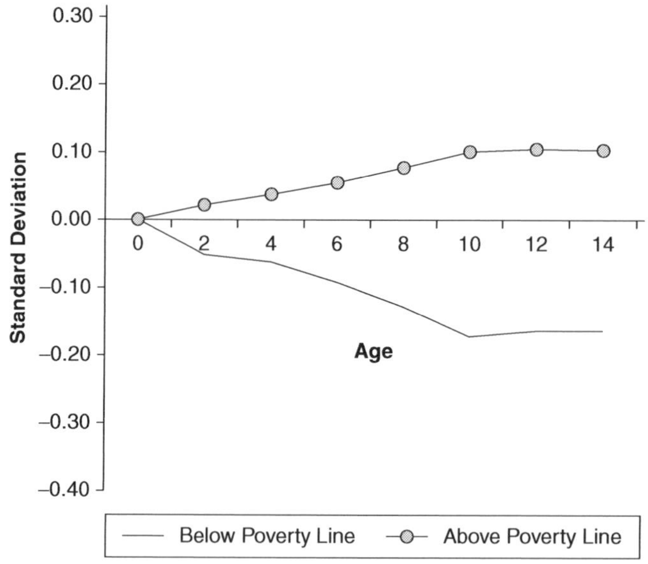

Source: Cunha & Heckman, 2007, p. 5.

Note: Cognitive skills = numeracy, literacy, problem solving, language.

By the time children reach first grade, it becomes increasingly difficult to reverse trends that began at birth. Current skills lay the foundation for new skills and contribute to expanding abilities. Lack of skill impedes new skill development and makes it harder to catch up. This explains why the trend lines in Figures 1.3 and 1.4 grow farther apart over time. Awareness of these trends has led many people to advocate for high-quality education that begins long before formal schooling starts.

Reducing the Achievement Gap Early

Formal education that begins at age five is TOO LATE. . . . While our state continues to spend more and more money correcting problems that occur later in children's lives through remediation, special education, alternative schools, and the criminal justice system, we ignore the front end of their lives, where it would truly make a difference . . . preschool will make more of a difference than anything else we can do to improve the lives of our children and our state. (C. J. Picard, former superintendent of education, Louisiana; Picard, 2006)

Figure 1.4 Noncognitive Skill Accumulation of Children Born in Families Below and Above the Poverty Line

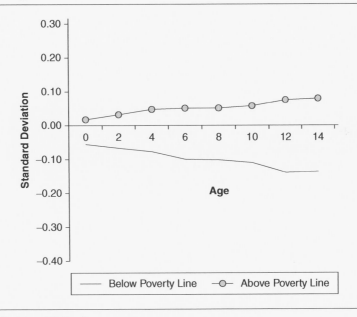

Source: Cunha & Heckman, 2007, p. 6.

Note: Noncognitive abilities = socio-emotional skills, physical and mental health, perseverance, attention, motivation, and self-confidence.

Box 1.4

Common Program Elements of Three Early Learning Projects: High Scope/Perry Preschool, Abecedarian, and the Chicago Child-Parent Centers

- Intervention started early in children's lives.
- Children and families were involved at least two years.
- The curriculum was whole-child focused.
- Curricula were tailored to the developmental characteristics of young children.
  - Programs included play, hands-on learning, and focused instruction.
- Teachers had undergraduate degrees in early childhood education.
- Teachers were relatively well paid.
- Children were taught in small classes.
- Parental involvement was a priority.

What was initially an assumption has become documented fact—high-quality early child-hood education can help children succeed. Three important studies that began in the 1960s, 1970s, and 1980s and are ongoing provide the strongest evidence in this regard. These are the High/Scope Perry Preschool Project, the Abecedarian Project, and the Chicago Child-Parent Centers Project (Karoly, Kilburn, & Cannon, 2005). Although the specific interventions and geographic locations of the projects varied, all three projects shared the characteristics outlined in Box 1.4.

The research-evaluating program effectiveness for all three projects was well designed and methodologically sound. This led to credible results. All three evaluations

- focused on young children identified as at-risk for school failure,
- utilized research designs that included both intervention groups and control groups,
- were longitudinal (followed children from preschool into adulthood),
- used a variety of academic and life success measures to compare children over time, and
- calculated academic, social, and fiscal benefits of program participation both to the child and to society.

The overall outcomes of these studies show that children at risk for school failure profit from high-quality early childhood programs. This is vividly illustrated in Figure 1.5, which provides a composite view of the impact of early intervention on children from low-income families.

Figure 1.5   The Effects of Early Intervention on Children Living in Families Below the Poverty Line

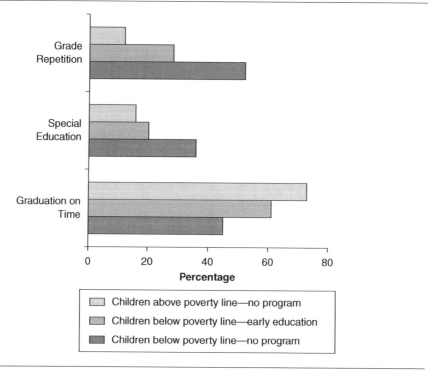

Source: Cunha & Heckman, 2007, pp. 16–17.

The findings documented in Figure 1.5 underscore the fact that **all** children born into families below the poverty line are more at risk for school problems than children living more affluent lives. The risks are greatest when no early intervention occurs, however. Poor children with no preschool experience are the most likely to repeat a grade, be referred to special education, and fail to complete high school on time. Those negative outcomes are significantly reduced when children experience a high-quality early childhood program.

A meta-analysis of state-funded preschool programs shows improved achievement test scores for children from low-income families over time as well as impressive gains (ranging from 16 percent to 54 percent) in disadvantaged children's language, mathematics, reading, and general knowledge skills (Public Policy Forum, 2007; Rosman et al., 2006). Additional results from the High/Scope study indicate that by the time students reached high school, only 15 percent of the children in the no-early-intervention group were performing at a level considered "high achieving," whereas 49 percent of the early-learning group were performing that way (Cunha & Heckman, 2007).

As we can see, children benefit developmentally and academically from participating in high-quality early childhood programs. A recent analysis of school results indicates that schools benefit, too.

Positive Impact of Prekindergarten Programs on K–12 Schools

Children who are ready for school perform better in school and the schools they attend achieve greater success as well.

> [T]he primary value of the [Perry Preschool Program] was that it improved children's readiness for school so that when they entered school, they performed better; and because they had more success, they got more committed to school; and because they got more committed to school, they had even greater success. (Schweinhart, quoted in Karoly et al., 2005, p. 9)

Investigators at the National Institute for Early Education Research (NIEER) documented significant academic, social, and economic benefits to school systems when children arrive having gone to preschool first. The NIEER (2008) findings are based on data collected through the Early Childhood Longitudinal Study (a long-term follow-up of a cohort of kindergartners who were in the fifth grade) and the Schools and Staffing Survey (teacher and administrator perceptions of their work environments).

According to the research, children's preschool attendance is associated with the following positive elementary school outcomes:

- Children score higher on standardized reading and math tests causing overall school scores to improve.
- Schools have fewer children who fail a grade.
- Fewer children are referred to special education.
- Children exhibit more "order and self-discipline" in kindergarten.
- Children exhibit fewer behavioral problems and more self-control throughout the elementary grades.
- Children's health problems are detected earlier, leading to improved performance over time.

- Incidents of risky behavior among children are reduced.
- Absenteeism among students is lower.
- Teacher absenteeism and turnover is reduced.
- Teachers report higher work satisfaction.

Based on the findings outlined above, researchers calculated the potential dollar savings that could come about as a result of reduced special education costs for children and improved working environments for teachers (i.e., lower turnover and absenteeism, and reduced teacher recruitment and retention expenses). They determined that schools would save between $2,600 and $4,400 for each "preschool" child over the time of that child's K–12 experience (Wat, 2007).

Economists and members of the business community echo the idea that early childhood education can actually save money over the long run from coast to coast. A variety of economic experts have demonstrated that preprimary education yields significant economic returns not only to school districts, but also to child participants and to society overall.

EARLY CHILDHOOD EDUCATION: A SOUND INVESTMENT

Just as public and private entities take an active interest in the construction and maintenance of roads, public transportation, utilities, housing, and educational facilities to support economic development, quality ECE should be considered essential to [the nation's] economic health. (Gruendel, 2004)

The preschoolers in the three landmark early childhood projects described earlier in this chapter are all adults now. Researchers have continued to follow their progress and have found strong evidence that, as a group, those who participated in the early childhood programs are better off financially today than those who did not. Preschool alumni are less frequently on welfare. They are more likely to own their own home, to earn higher wages, are more often employed, and are more likely to establish savings accounts. See Figure 1.6 for examples of the economic effects at age forty of former participants the Perry Preschool Program.

There is further evidence that those who went to preschool were less likely than the nonprogram subjects to engage in criminal behavior as youth and as adults. See Figure 1.7.

Looking to the Bottom Line

Results like those just described have excited the early childhood community as well as economists, business leaders, and public policy makers. Reducing the number of people on welfare and lowering the crime rate represents a substantial savings to taxpayers. Conversely, higher earnings through wages and savings dividends contribute to the tax base. As noted by James Heckman, a Nobel Laureate in economics,

The effects of high-quality preschool for disadvantaged children have been studied extensively. The programs improve student outcomes, increasing their educational attainment, decreasing their criminal activity, and improving their employment and earnings as adults. These changes in behavior reduce the burden on public resources by

Figure 1.6   Economic Effects of Participants at Age Forty

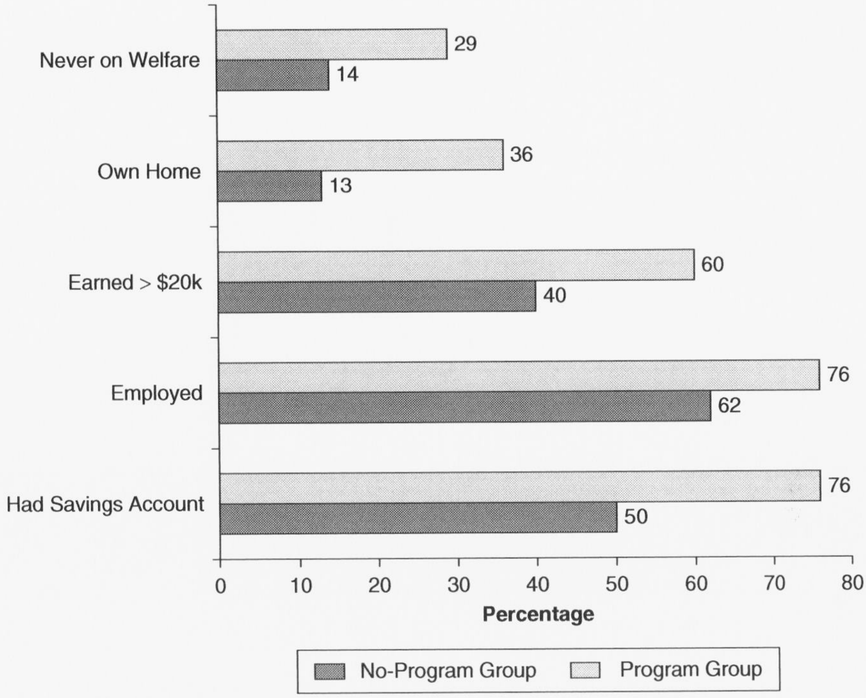

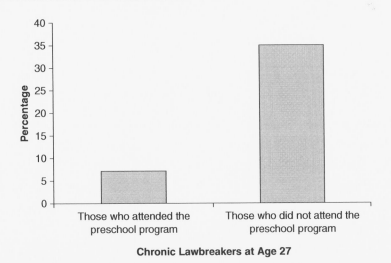

Source: Schweinhart et al., 2005.

Figure 1.7   Quality Preschool Cuts Future Crime

Source: L. J. Schweinhart, H. V. Barnes, and D. P. Weikart (1993). Significant Benefits: The High/Scope Perry Preschool Study through Age 27. (Monographs of the High/Scope Educational Research Foundation, 10). Ypsilanti, MI: High/Scope Press. PS 021 998

decreasing spending on special education, incarcerations, and public assistance; and by increasing future tax revenue. Such changes produce a substantial return on investment. Studies have estimated that these programs produce as much as $17 in social benefits for every dollar invested. (Heckman & Masterov, 2007, p. 1)

Heckman also points out that the economic return on preschool intervention is much higher than the return on later interventions such as reduced pupil-teacher ratios, public job training, convict rehabilitation programs, tuition subsidies, or tax expenditures on police. This is because there is economic efficiency to getting involved early on with a focus on building new skills that will lead to further skill development. Remedial programs in adolescence and adulthood are much more costly and much less likely to yield positive results. The difference in the rate of return on investment across the lifespan is illustrated in Figure 1.8.

Figure 1.8   Rates of Return on Human Capital Investment Across the Life Span

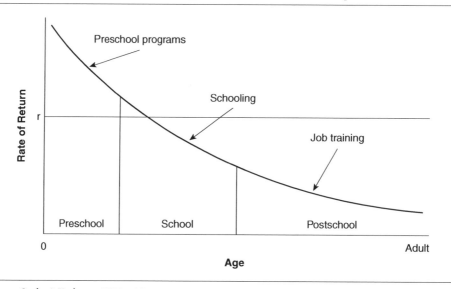

Source: Cunha & Heckman, 2007, p. 18.

Economic models such as the one presented in Figure 1.8 add to the belief that it is better to get things right the first time than to try to fix them later (Galinsky, 2006). This message is being echoed throughout the country and has led some economists to propose universal preschool for all three- and four-year-old children, especially for children from poor families.

Potential Economic Benefits of Universal Preschool for Low-Income Children

Based on findings from the Chicago Child-Parent Centers project, economist Robert G. Lynch has projected the long-term savings and benefits that would come about if high-quality early childhood programs were extended to all three- and four-year-old children in the United States whose families fall in the lowest quarter of income distribution (Lynch, 2007). His calculations are based on a program that would operate three hours a day, five days a week during the traditional school year. Teachers would be certified in early childhood education and would be paid in line with K–12 salaries. There would be at least two teachers per classroom and the curriculum would focus on whole-child learning. He assumes that the initial cost per child would be $6,300. The report includes specific cost-benefit data for each state as well as the nation overall for 2008 and for 2050 (to demonstrate the benefits accrued as the 2008 children reach middle adulthood). Sample findings at the national level are presented in Box 1.5.

Box 1.5
Projected Economic Costs and Benefits of Universal Prekindergarten for All Children Living in Poverty in the United States

Number of children served	Approximately 7 million nationwide in 2008
When the program would begin to pay for itself	Six years
Annual costs in 2008	$8.2 billion
Annual costs in 2050	$26 billion
Net benefit in 2050	$289 billion
Ratio of total benefits to costs	$12 in benefit for each dollar spent in 2050

Source: Lynch (2007).

Similar positive outcomes would be garnered at the state level. See Figure 1.9.

Figure 1.9   State Costs Versus Potential Benefits of Universal Preschool

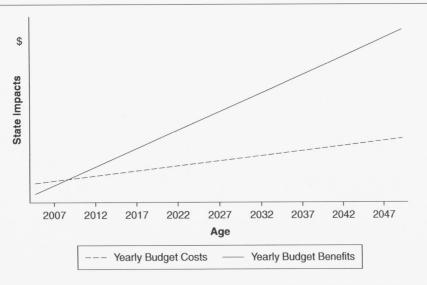

Source: Lynch, 2007.

Some Communities Moving Toward "Preschool for All"

The potential benefits of early education have proven so compelling that entire states (e.g., Florida, Georgia, Illinois, New Jersey, and Oklahoma) as well as many local communities are beginning to implement voluntary (parents may choose if they want to enroll and with whom to enroll their children), universal (available to all children regardless of income) preschool systems for four-year-olds. In each case, these systems have included significant participation by public schools as well as other public and private providers. In 2006, Illinois became the first state to legislate voluntary early education to all three- and four-year-old children in the state whose families want them to participate. In time, the program could serve as many as 190,000 children. Similar proposals are being examined in hundreds of communities throughout the United States.

As a result of initiatives like these, elementary school "principals across the country are becoming more involved with early childhood programs—leading comprehensive pre-K programs in their school buildings or creating new links with many types of pre-K programs in their communities" (National Association of Elementary School Principals [NAESP], 2005 p. v). Here are some preliminary steps you can take to contribute to this important work.

PRINCIPALS' ROLES

Laying the Groundwork

Public and private demand for high quality early childhood education is growing, and principals of elementary schools need to be ahead of the trend. (NAESP, 2005, p. v)

1. Know the benefits of early childhood education—academic, social, and fiscal. Examine the rationale for initiating high-quality early learning programs as offered in this chapter. Consider this information in terms of your own experiences. Use this as a basis for becoming more involved in early education.

2. Rethink K–12 education to include prekindergarten programs as the foundation for later learning. Talk with others about the critical nature of children's prekindergarten experiences.

3. Make a conscious decision to create a school culture that values early childhood education. Use this text as one tool to help you make this ideal a reality.

4. Provide others with information about the value of early childhood education. Use the data presented in this chapter to talk with teachers, staff, administrator colleagues, school board members, and community leaders about early childhood education. Explore the implications for your school and community.

Quality Makes *All* the Difference!

Quality is job one.

Quality first!

Quality goes in before the name goes on!

Classic advertising slogans like these underscore a fundamental belief held in our society that quality is worth pursuing and worth investing in. This belief is also paramount in early childhood education. Proponents of initiatives like "Preschool for All" (described in Chapter 1) are banking on the premise that early childhood education can make a significant difference in young children's lives. That premise comes with a caveat—only certain prekindergarten (preschool) programs are up to the task. Those programs are distinguished by their high quality. Quality affects what children learn, how well they learn it, and what long-term benefits they derive from what they learn. All the positive outcomes attributed to early education come about **only** when children experience **high-quality** programming. Mediocre and poor quality programs yield far different results. Thus, **quality is the single most important factor in determining whether or not children benefit from participating in early learning settings**.

DISTINGUISHING QUALITY IN EARLY CHILDHOOD SETTINGS

It would be wonderful if all early childhood education programs were automatically high quality. Unfortunately, that is not the case. Today's early learning settings vary widely on the quality dimension. Examples of high-, medium-, and low-quality classrooms are described in Box 2.1.

Box 2.1
Examples of Differentiated Quality in Early Learning Programs

In a recent study of early learning settings, researchers asked, "What do we mean when we characterize classrooms as high, medium, or low in quality?" Ratings were developed based on observations of a variety of different aspects of the early childhood environment that affect children's learning and experiences in that setting. The following examples describe the interactions, activities, materials, and configurations one might expect to see in classrooms at each level.

High Quality

In a classroom described as high quality, teachers interact frequently with children and provide guidance to enhance their learning. There is a buzz of talk among children in a friendly, respectful atmosphere. The teacher has close relationships with the children, talks with them about what they are doing in the classroom and about their lives outside the classroom, and is enthusiastic about the children's activities and their learning. The classroom is well organized and has a variety of age-appropriate materials for a range of hands-on activities, including art (e.g., crayons, paints, clay), science (e.g., plants and animals, magnets, science books), music (e.g., simple instruments, CDs, and tapes), language (e.g., books, flannel-board stories, picture card games), mathematics (e.g., tape measure, objects to count), manipulatives (e.g., puzzles, sewing cards), dramatic play (e.g., dress-up clothes, pretend office, housekeeping area), and building (e.g., blocks of different sizes and materials). Activities and materials are changed frequently according to children's interests and abilities. Children have many opportunities throughout the day to choose hands-on activities and use materials to experiment and create, both independently and in small, often self-selected, groups. Teachers have a planned but flexible schedule of indoor and outdoor activities that are interesting to children. Nutrition and other personal care are provided in a flexible way designed to meet children's individual needs and encourage the development of self-help skills.

Medium Quality

In a classroom described as medium quality, adults pay little positive attention to individual children, and supervision of the group is often divided with other tasks, such as preparing food or doing paperwork. Adults often do not provide educational guidance to support children's learning (i.e., teachers do not encourage children to try new things with materials or do not ask children questions to encourage them to think and talk about what they are doing). Children have some opportunities for choices. For example, they may be assigned to activities, but are able to choose how they use the materials. The classroom is organized into interest areas (centers) to support play and learning, with some materials for a variety of hands-on activities, such as art (e.g., crayons and paint), language (e.g., books), manipulatives (e.g., puzzles), dramatic play (e.g., a housekeeping area), and building (e.g., blocks). There might not be enough materials for all of the children, or some of the materials may be in disrepair. Children spend a lot of time as a whole group and have limited opportunities for small group or individual activities. Adults are generally attentive to children's safety during activities and typically meet children's basic nutritional and other personal care needs.

Low Quality

A classroom described as low quality is generally characterized by either disorganization and chaos or an overly strict atmosphere, both of which prevent children from engaging in productive learning activities. Adults are often inattentive and unresponsive or overly harsh with children. Conversations between teachers and children are infrequent, and teachers do not regularly encourage positive peer interaction or help children develop positive solutions to problems. Children are often kept together as one large group, with little attention to their individual needs. The teacher makes most decisions about activities rather than allowing children to make their own choices, which may result in activities that are not of interest to children and therefore dampen their normal enthusiasm for learning. Materials and activities may be lacking altogether or may be inappropriate for the ages of the children in the group. Basic nutritional, health, and sanitary needs are not met, and children's indoor and outdoor play spaces may be dangerous.

Source: Reprinted with permission from Peisner-Feinberg et al., 2000, p. 13.

THE CORROSIVE IMPACT OF POOR QUALITY

> *When we see poor quality in the United States, we are not generally seeing abuses or hostile caregivers. Rather, we are seeing the absence of positive and supportive interactions— caregivers who more often than not fail to respond to children's bids for attention and affection and who make few attempts to engage the children in social or learning activities.* (Cox, Phillips, & Pianta, 2002)

Every day, thousands of young children in the United States spend long hours subjected to poor quality practices and environments. Studies conducted over the past decade note that 40 percent to 50 percent of the programs observed did **not** exemplify high- or medium-quality standards (Cox, et al., 2002; Helburn, 1995; Raikes et al., 2004). These results have serious ramifications for children and for society.

At one time, we thought that programs that were less than optimal might not improve children's learning, but we did not think they would do any real harm. Now we know better.

Medium-quality programs are not strongly associated with optimal childhood learning and therefore represent lost opportunities for high cognitive or social achievement. Poor-quality programs sometimes threaten children's immediate health and safety and actually hamper their long-term development and progress (Children's Defense Fund, 2006; Raikes et al., 2004). For instance, young children who have poor-quality early learning experiences tend to demonstrate

- increased behavior problems;
- poorer social skills;
- more-frequent displays of aggression;
- delays in cognitive development, language development, prereading skills, and other age-appropriate behaviors; and
- poorer academic progress over time.

These negative effects are long lasting, with evidence of poor quality remaining apparent up to five years later. Such results have been reported for children from a wide range of family backgrounds (United Nations Educational, Scientific and Cultural Organization [UNESCO], 2005). However, children who have been traditionally at risk of not doing well in school are the ones most affected by poor quality (Vandell & Wolfe, 2000). Unfortunately, due to issues of cost and access, it is precisely these children who are most likely to be enrolled in poorer quality programs. In this way, poor-quality compounds the challenges at-risk children already face. To avoid these outcomes, it is important to understand what constitutes high-quality early childhood education.

There Is Bad News and Good News on the Quality Front

The bad news is that the least-advantaged young children are the ones most negatively affected by poor-quality early childhood programming. The good news is that these same children benefit the most from high-quality child care, early education, and afterschool experiences that provide them with opportunities to develop academic, social, and emotional skills.

HIGH QUALITY DEFINED

Quality is never an accident; it is always the result of high intention, sincere effort, intelligent direction and skillful execution; it represents the wise choice of many alternatives. (William A. Foster, U.S. Medal of Honor recipient, personal communication)

Knowing that quality makes such a difference, people worldwide are asking the question, "What constitutes high quality in early childhood education?" Fortunately, we have a strong research base from which to derive answers (Biddle & Berliner, 2002; Stronge, 2002; UNESCO, 2007; Whitebook, Sakai, & Howes, 1997). Based on the research, most early childhood experts agree that the ten variables listed below represent essential components of high-quality early learning programs. In such programs, the following are true:

**Teachers and staff are well prepared
and appropriately compensated.**

- Teachers and staff have specific training in child development, early childhood education, and relevant subject matter content such as literacy, mathematics, science, social studies, physical education, and the arts.
- Teachers and staff have appropriate background and access to resources related to cultural diversity and gender equality; mother tongue learning; and children with disabilities and other special needs.
- Teachers and staff engage in continuing professional development.
- Teachers and staff in higher-quality programs are paid reasonable wages and receive relevant benefits.

Staffing is stable.

- Adults remain with the program and the same group of children long enough for children to develop a trusting relationship with an adult outside the home.

**Group sizes are small, and a small number
of children are assigned to each adult.**

- The group size and adult–child ratios are small enough that children can engage in first-hand interactions with adults, and receive individualized instruction and personal feedback about their learning experiences.

Adults establish warm, attentive relationships with children.

- Adults are warm, respectful, understanding, and friendly toward children.
- Adults listen to children. They comfort, support, and guide them in ways that make sense to children and help children become more successful in their social interactions.

Environments are well organized, safe, and healthy.

- Children and adults know what is expected and can participate with ease and confidence.
- Instructional time is used effectively; there is enough time for children to become absorbed in learning, and there is little time in which children are not productively engaged.
- Health and safety provisions are in place to support children's well-being.

**Environments are stimulating and
geared to the unique ways in which
young children learn.**

- Children have access to adequate, appropriate materials to promote exploration and development of more advanced knowledge and skills.

> A high quality program, no matter what its name or style is proud of the youngness of its children. It is geared to honest, real-life children, the noisy, messy, active, dirty kind. . . . A good program enjoys youngsters as they are: imaginative. Full of ego. Animal lovers. Devotees of mud and water. Gigglers, fast-riders, wrestlers, talkers. (James L. Hymes, 1994, p. 23)

- The curriculum is designed to promote "whole child" learning.
- Teachers stimulate children's use of language through conversation, singing, reading to children, asking children relevant questions, and inviting children to describe things aloud or elaborate on what they are thinking.
- Teachers and staff have high expectations for children, establish appropriate goals for children and the program, and employ intentional strategies to promote continuous learning.

Teachers understand and address the needs of diverse learners.

- Teachers and staff vary their pace and teaching strategies to correspond to what is age appropriate, individually appropriate, and socially and culturally appropriate for each child.
- Teachers and staff use classroom-based assessment to guide learning improvement.

Families are involved in their children's education.

- The program is designed to support and complement families in their child-rearing role.
- Family members are welcome to observe, discuss, and recommend policies and to participate in the program's activities.

There is continuity between home, the early childhood program, and the primary school.

- Children and families experience seamless transitions from one system to another.
- Professionals interact and plan in concert across program boundaries.

There are links to comprehensive community services.

- Families are referred and have access to a wide array of services necessary to support their child-rearing responsibilities.

LEADERSHIP AND HIGH QUALITY

The indicators of high quality listed above set the stage for children to live, learn, and earn productively in the twenty-first century. All of them are more likely to happen in well-organized, well-led programs and schools. Thus strong educational leadership is another key ingredient in the high-quality equation (UNESCO, 2005). The administrative role is so important that the National Association of Elementary School Principals (NAESP) has declared early childhood education to be a significant responsibility for elementary principals. In conjunction with this responsibility, the Association has identified six standards that characterize leadership for early learning (NAESP, 2005).

Effective principals

- embrace high-quality early childhood programs, principles, and practices as the foundation for education throughout the school community;
- engage families and community organizations to support children at home, in the community, and in prekindergarten and kindergarten programs;
- provide appropriate learning environments for young children;

- ensure high-quality curriculum and instructional practices that foster young children's learning and development in all areas;
- use multiple assessments to strengthen student learning and improve the quality of programs; and
- advocate for universal opportunity for children to attend high-quality early childhood education programs.

These principles capture the essence of early childhood education and represent essential steps in creating high-quality early learning communities. You could play a major role in this enterprise.

BECOMING AN EARLY CHILDHOOD LEADER

You may be reading this chapter already knowing a great deal about early childhood education. On the other hand, this may be your first foray into the field. In either case, becoming an early childhood leader as described by the NAESP does not happen overnight. Most principals find themselves somewhere on a continuum that ranges from minimal awareness to leadership. This continuum is depicted in Figure 2.1, the Early Childhood Administrative Pyramid. Moving from an initial state of unawareness, the pyramid begins with early awareness at the base and builds to leadership as the most advanced phase of administration.

ONE PRINCIPAL'S EXPERIENCE

Principals today—more than ever before—are critical leaders in the effort to improve America's public schools. (Secretary of Education Rod Paige, speaking at the National Distinguished Principal Awards, October 5, 2001)

Steve Wilson, a 2001 winner of the National Distinguished Principal award, is principal of Centura Elementary School. The school, with a preschool–6 enrollment of about three hundred students, is located in Cairo, Nebraska, a sparsely populated rural community in the U.S. heartland. Today, Centura's early childhood programs are touted throughout the state as models of best practices in every aspect of their early childhood operations. Three- and four-year-old children attend daily preschool classes at the school. These classes are characterized by holistic hands-on learning activities. Teachers engage in research-based teaching and assessment strategies to support student progress. Children's families have access to a variety of early learning and social supports, with particular emphasis on parent education and early literacy strategies. It was not always this way.

Steve first arrived at Centura twenty years ago. When he got there, he found a school hard hit by falling enrollments and a high poverty rate (one out of every two families lived below the poverty line at that time, and this continues to be true today). He also found children entering kindergarten, who had never seen a book, who had poor language skills, and who had never been to a dentist (Wilson, 2008). Recognizing that many children were already "behind" their first day in kindergarten, Steve began to explore the feasibility of creating early learning programs for three- and four-year-olds at the school. His journey from these initial beginnings to becoming a leader for early learning communities statewide is depicted in Table 2.1.

Figure 2.1   Early Childhood Administrative Pyramid

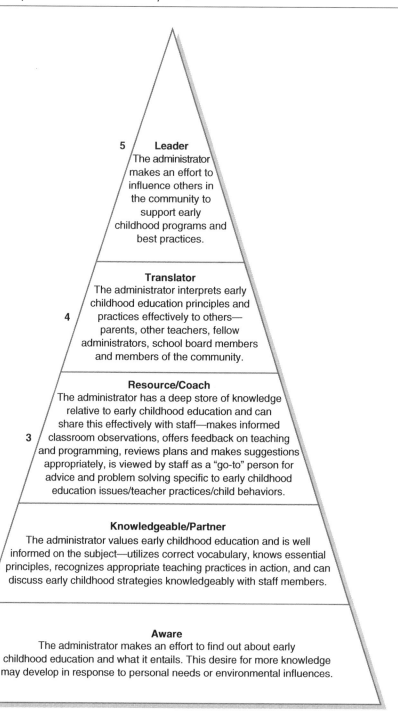

5   Leader
The administrator makes an effort to influence others in the community to support early childhood programs and best practices.

Translator
The administrator interprets early childhood education principles and practices effectively to others—parents, other teachers, fellow administrators, school board members and members of the community.
4

Resource/Coach
The administrator has a deep store of knowledge relative to early childhood education and can share this effectively with staff—makes informed classroom observations, offers feedback on teaching and programming, reviews plans and makes suggestions appropriately, is viewed by staff as a "go-to" person for advice and problem solving specific to early childhood education issues/teacher practices/child behaviors.
3

Knowledgeable/Partner
The administrator values early childhood education and is well informed on the subject—utilizes correct vocabulary, knows essential principles, recognizes appropriate teaching practices in action, and can discuss early childhood strategies knowledgeably with staff members.
2

Aware
The administrator makes an effort to find out about early childhood education and what it entails. This desire for more knowledge may develop in response to personal needs or environmental influences.
1

Unaware
0   The administrator is uninformed about and uninvolved in early chilhood education.

Table 2.1 Steve Wilson's Journey to Becoming an Early Education Leader

Phase on the Pyramid	*Examples*
Early Childhood Leader "It's very powerful when organizations start talking together about the same thing. You can really make things happen (in your district, in the state, even nationally) that you can't do if you're just out there on your own."	• Steve is completing his term as president of the Nebraska Association for the Education of Young Children. He is working closely with the Nebraska Council of School Administrators and the Nebraska Association of Elementary School Principals to help expand preschool funding opportunities for schools across the state.
Translator "When this all started, we had to convince everybody—families, teachers in the lower elementary grades and teachers in the upper grades, school board members and other people in the community. It was hard work; it took a long time. What made sense to people was when we talked in terms of school improvement, what we wanted to achieve as a learning community, and how certain ideas related to our common values."	• Steve has included early childhood education in school improvement plans required by the district. • He is adept at explaining to parents, school board members, and principals of other schools what young children and their teachers need to have initial school success.
Resource/Coach "Besides basic resources, what teachers want most from me is to know that I trust them as professionals in their classrooms. They also want to know that I believe in what they are trying to do, letting young children be children and letting them learn in the classroom the way we know young children learn best."	• Steve shares what he has learned about best practices in early education by disseminating early learning literature to staff and by promoting professional development activities that give teachers common reference points for discussion about the needs of young children. • This principal makes sure that all teachers are trained in a range of assessment strategies, including observation. Part of their training involves learning to use spreadsheets and other assessment tools to disaggregate information in a way that helps improve both student learning and classroom instruction. • Steve encourages teachers to use three days of professional development leave each year. The school pays $300 per year for teachers to take up to three credit hours of professional development at local colleges.
Knowledgeable Partner "It's a give and take world. To partner, you have to be willing to listen as well as tell. I found I wasn't always the one in control or the one who had all the answers. At times I facilitated discussions, at times I was just another participant, and a teacher led the conversation. Generally, when I ran into a really tough problem, I found I hadn't taken enough time to really listen. I also learned as much from teachers who weren't on board as from those	• Steve was a visible presence in the K–3 classrooms in his school. He used his first-hand observations to deepen his understanding of young children and to initiate conversations with teachers about best practices in early education. • Steve met regularly with teachers and team leaders to explore how to create developmentally appropriate classrooms that also addressed early learning standards. He made clear he was committed to a research-based approach with an eye toward linking prekindergarten to Grade 3 learning with the Grades 4–6 curriculum and beyond. Curriculum alignment continues to be a major focus of staff meetings.

(Continued)

Table 2.1 (Continued)

Phase on the Pyramid	Examples
who were. At times, after taking in their point of view, I had to say to myself, Wow, what do I need to do to bridge this? The answer often led to breakthroughs everyone could live with and we could use to move forward."	• Steve became involved in Nebraska Department of Education conversations about ways public schools might finance early childhood programs by braiding together dollars from Title I, Head Start, and federal special education. Within a year, Centura Public Schools became the first school district in Nebraska to try out this funding model. • Centura Elementary has partnered with Central Nebraska Community Services Head Start to expand services to children and families and to align curriculum and performance standards in both programs.
Aware "Building my own awareness of appropriate practice in preschool–3 classrooms was very valuable in knowing what needed to take place, so I could facilitate the right discussions and provide leadership and opportunities for my faculty."	• Based on what he was learning about early childhood, Steve required new preschool–3 teachers to have specific training in early childhood as well as elementary certification. • To increase his understanding of early childhood education, Steve began attending early education workshops and reading literature about best practices for young learners.
Unaware "As I observed in kindergarten and first grade and listened to what the teachers were saying about children's needs—not just academic needs, but social and health and family needs—I began to realize we needed to do more than we were doing for the youngest children in our school."	• Watching children in the kindergarten and listening to teachers talk about their students made Steve realize that many kindergartners were unprepared for school. • When Steve Wilson became an elementary school principal, he had many administrative skills, but little background in child development or early childhood education.

Source: NAESP (2006); personal communication with Steve Wilson (January 2008).

USING THE EARLY CHILDHOOD ADMINISTRATIVE PYRAMID TO REFLECT ON YOUR OWN PRACTICES

The Early Childhood Administrative Pyramid is a useful tool for considering where you might fit along the administrative continuum relative to early education overall or in terms of individual program components. Such components might include the following:

- History and traditions relative to early learning programs for children
- Stakeholders and community partners
- Developmentally appropriate practices
- The educational needs of young children
- Early childhood curriculum

- Assessment in early childhood
- Funding early childhood programs
- Early childhood teachers and staff
- Classrooms for young children
- Family involvement strategies
- Unique facets of the principal's role in early childhood

No matter where you are on the continuum regarding any of these elements, *Getting It Right From the Start: The Principal's Guide to Early Childhood Education* is designed to help you move farther up the pyramid. Each of the following chapters covers one of the components listed above. By Chapter 15, we guarantee that you will have the information you need to be a more effective leader of the early learning programs in your school and district!

PRINCIPALS' ROLES

Achieving High Quality

Each principal brings a unique set of skills and personal strengths to the task of creating PK-3 programs. Leading by doing, principals are spurring (early education) reforms in communities across the country. (NAESP, 2006d, p. 8)

1. Seek out examples of high-quality early learning classrooms and programs from which to learn. Visit early education settings in your community (including your own school) that have a reputation for high quality. Identify which of the following high-quality criteria these programs have achieved and talk with administrators and teachers about how they were accomplished. Also, discuss challenges and how they might be addressed.

- Teachers and staff are well prepared and appropriately compensated.
- Staffing is stable.
- Group sizes are small, and a small number of children are assigned to each adult.
- Adults establish warm, attentive relationships with children.
- Environments are well organized, safe, and healthy.
- Environments are stimulating and geared to the unique ways in which young children learn.
- Teachers understand and address the needs of diverse learners.
- Families are involved in their children's education.
- There is continuity between home, the early childhood program, and the primary school.
- There are links to comprehensive community services.

2. Observe the early learning classrooms for which you are responsible, using quality as your focus. Ask yourself to what extent each classroom represents the examples of high-, medium-, or low quality practices identified in Box 2.1. Identify teachers or other staff in your own school who might help you in your quest to achieve high-quality early childhood education in your school. Enlist their support.

3. Remember that early childhood education goes through third grade and apply principles of high quality to all P–3 classrooms. Provide support for staff from preschool through third grade to learn about and maintain high-quality early learning settings.

4. Use quality as a constant guide for program decision making. Ask yourself, "Will this practice or decision maintain or improve the quality of our program?" If the answer is "yes," proceed. If the answer is "no" or "not sure," reconsider.

5. Use the Early Childhood Administrative Pyramid to support your progress in becoming an early childhood leader. Reflect on your current practice. Where are you on the pyramid regarding early childhood education overall? Where are you relative to individual elements associated with early childhood education as described above? Use this self-understanding to guide your own professional development toward higher levels on the pyramid. Assist others in doing the same.

Breaking New Ground

Getting Involved in Early Childhood Education

When asked why they had an interest in early childhood education, elementary principals attending a professional development workshop gave a variety of answers:

This summer I had a delegation of teachers in my office with a proposal for starting a pre-kindergarten program They saw advantages to getting to kids early. I do too.

My children never went to preschool, but my granddaughter does and I've visited her class. She loves going and I can see that she is learning a lot that will help her in kindergarten and first grade. We have plenty of kids in our community who could use this same boost.

The state is offering early childhood grants to districts and ESUs [Educational Service Units]. We're a county with few early childhood programs. This is an opportunity to change that.

Our elementary enrollments have been declining. We have empty classrooms in a couple of buildings. PreK classes might give us a "value added" dimension that would attract or at least keep families in our (rural) community.

We've had Head Start and a CLC [Community Learning Center] in our district for years. It's been a good partnership for them and for us. Those programs are an important part of our school reform plans.

The number of children who don't speak English in our district has doubled three years in a row. I hope a preschool will help us get things on track so the transition to kindergarten and first grade is better for everyone.

As you can see, principals embrace early childhood education for many reasons:

- In response to parental or teacher requests for early childhood services
- As a result of personal experience
- To align with state mandates to expand the K–12 curriculum to include prekindergarten (preschool)
- To take advantage of new funding sources
- To use space more effectively
- As a corollary to option enrollment strategies and marketing efforts
- Because they think preschool will improve children's school readiness

No matter the reasons, becoming involved in early childhood education often requires principals to navigate new territory. As part of this journey, they quickly learn that leading early childhood learning communities involves more than simply finding space, developing RFPs, or revising curricula. It requires a whole set of sensibilities, knowledge, and skills that complement but do not duplicate what they already bring to the job. Without this additional background, success is less likely. The purpose of this chapter, then, is to give the reader an insider's view of early childhood education—what the field entails, significant aspects of the culture, current trends, issues people are talking about, and ideas on how to make the most out of being a school principal or district administrator who is leading or supporting early learning initiatives.

WHAT EXACTLY IS EARLY CHILDHOOD EDUCATION?

Consider the following settings:

- The toddler room in an employer-sponsored childcare center
- A Head Start classroom
- The three-year-old program at a private preschool
- A state-funded prekindergarten program
- A second-grade classroom

Although they vary in many ways—ages of children served, duration and types of services offered, location and sponsor—these programs have one thing in common: they are all examples of early childhood education. Early childhood education involves "any group program in a center, school, or other facility, that serves children from birth through age eight" 2009. That means early education programs address the needs of infants, toddlers, preschoolers, kindergarteners, and school-age children through the third grade.

The current definition of early childhood is more expansive and more scientifically based than was true in the past. Until the late 1980s, the term *early childhood period* referred to children five years of age and younger. Using this traditional designation, people thought that children's entry into first grade served as the dividing line between early development and later childhood. Preschoolers and kindergartners were categorized as one group, and the rest of the elementary school-age population was categorized as another (Smart & Smart, 1982). This demarcation was based on the assumption that first and second graders are more like fifth graders than they are like preschoolers. However, research over the past twenty years has caused us to rethink that conventional wisdom. The evidence suggests that children learn more holistically from infancy through age eight than at any other time in their lives. This makes early childhood a unique phase in the life span. Moreover, studies regarding children's cognitive, social, and physical abilities now indicate that significant shifts occur in children's development closer to seven or eight years of age, and not at age five, as previously assumed. Consequently, psychologists and neuroscientists have reconceptualized early childhood as starting at birth and lasting into the midprimary grades (Gullo, 2006; Kostelnik, Soderman, & Whiren, 2007).

Based on this redefinition, the early childhood period crosses traditional programmatic boundaries that once separated community-based early childhood programs and elementary schools. To address these realities effectively, the National Association of Elementary School Principals (NAESP, 2005) suggests that elementary principals treat early childhood as a continuum of learning that links prekindergarten, kindergarten, and early elementary programs. As it stands now, education from preschool to Grade 3 involves multiple providers. Of course, elementary schools are an important part of the mix, but they do not play a solo role.

Early Education Variations in Structure and Function

There is great diversity among programs designed to serve children and their families throughout early childhood. Programs that provide education and care operate through different fiscal entities (public or private) and vary in location and size (private homes; churches, temples or synagogues; small centers; large schools). They embrace a wide range of educational philosophies and curricula. Children may be grouped closely in age or be assigned to mixed-age groups that span two to three years. Early childhood programs also vary in their target audience, their scope (full day to half day, full year to partial year, every day to some days), and the training and background of key personnel. An overview of the wide array of early childhood learning settings that might be available in a given community is presented in Table 3.1.

Table 3.1   A Sampling of Early Education Programs in Communities

Program	Children Served	Ages	Purposes	Source of Funding
Family child care homes	All	Six weeks to twelve years	Comprehensive care of children, addressing all areas of development	Varies. Sources include employer subsidies; parent fees; state agencies; Title XX funds; USDA Child and Adult Care Food Program; child care tax credits; private and charitable organizations
Group child care homes	All	Six weeks to twelve years	Comprehensive care of children, addressing all areas of development	Varies. Sources include employer subsidies; parent fees; state agencies; Title XX funds; USDA Child and Adult Care Food Program; child care tax credits; private and charitable organizations
Center-based child care	All	Six weeks to twelve years	Comprehensive care of children, addressing all areas of development, includes full-day and part-time care	Varies. Sources include employer subsidies; parent fees; state agencies; Title XX funds; USDA Child and Adult Care Food Program; child care tax credits; private and charitable organizations
Preschools	Mostly middle class	Two to five years	Enrichment and early learning experiences focused on whole-child development and school readiness	Parent fees
Parent cooperative preschools	Children of participating parents and parents of participating children	Two to five years	Enrichment and early learning experiences focused on whole-child development and school readiness; parent education	Parent fees; parent-contributed labor
Faith-based preschools	Children of church, temple, or mosque members	Two to five years	Enrichment experiences focused on whole-child development and spiritual training	Parent fees; church, temple, and mosque subsidies

Program	Children Served	Ages	Purposes	Source of Funding
State-funded preschools	Children identified as at risk for school failure for economic, developmental, or environmental reasons; in some states, all three- or four-year-old children whose families wish to enroll them	Three to four years	Development of school readiness skills	State taxes and special allocations
Laboratory schools	Children associated with a high school, vocational school, college, or university	Birth to five years	Enrichment experiences focused on whole child development; training of preservice teachers or teen parents	State taxes; parent fees
Early Head Start	Pregnant women; infants and toddlers from low-income families	Prenatal to three years	Promote healthy prenatal outcomes for pregnant women, enhance the development of very young children, and promote healthy family functioning	Federal funds
Even Start	Children and parents from low income families	Birth to seven years	Supports local family literacy projects that integrate early childhood education, adult literacy, parenting education, and interactive parent and child literacy activities for low-income families with parents who are eligible for services under the Adult Education and Family Literacy Act and their children	Federal funds

(Continued)

Table 3.1 (Continued)

Program	Children Served	Ages	Purposes	Source of Funding
Head Start	Children from low income families; children with disabilities	Three to four years	Provides comprehensive education, health, nutrition, and parent involvement services to low-income children and their families	Federal funds
Title I	Children who are educationally disadvantaged (poor, migrants, disabled, neglected, or delinquent)	Four to twelve years	Supplemental education for children and parents	Federal funds
Kindergarten	All	Five to six years	Introduction to formal schooling; may be full day or half day	State and local taxes; some federal funds; in the case of private schools, parent tuition
First, second, and third grades (grades may stand alone or children may attend multigrade classrooms)	All	Six to eight years	Transmission of society's age-appropriate accumulated knowledge, values, beliefs, and customs to the young; development of academic skills necessary for further education	State and local taxes; some federal funds; in the case of private schools—parent tuition

Source: Caruso & Fawcett (2007); Kostelnik, Soderman, & Whiren (2007).

What's in a Name?

People new to early childhood education quickly notice that besides kindergarten, first, second, and third grades, the field includes a wide array of programs that go by many different names. Some of these are

- preschool,
- prekindergarten,

- nursery school,
- preprimary special education,
- child care, and
- day care.

There is no one lexicon to which everyone subscribes. Instead, a variety of designations are used, depending on what program characteristics are being emphasized. For instance, early childhood practitioners, policy makers, and grantors often differentiate among programs based on the age of the children involved:

- Infant-toddler programs—serving children from birth to thirty-six months
- Preschool programs—serving three- and four-year-olds
- Kindergarten programs—serving five- and six-year-olds
- Primary or school-age programs—serving six- through eight-year-olds

Although all such programs focus on children in the early childhood period, they may vary considerably in location, size, duration, sponsorship, cost, and availability.

Other names are used to distinguish where a program takes place (with implications about size, formality, and adult training), as is the case for family child care versus center-based programs.

- Family child care occurs in the home of a nonrelative provider for up to twelve hours a day, five or more days a week. In most states, licensed family childcare homes are limited to serving six children at a time (including the provider's own children). In forty-four states, there are regulations that allow seven to twelve children to be enrolled in family group homes operated by a primary caregiver and an assistant.
- Center-based programs are generally licensed to provide full-day, full-year care for eight or more children at a time. However, children may participate full-time or part-time, depending on family needs and goals. These programs may serve children of any age, birth to eight years, including older school-age children in before- and afterschool programs.

Some early education labels are interchangeable. The terms nursery school, preschool, preprimary, and prekindergarten are often used in reference to programs with similar functions and relatively common structures. Some words are more distinctive and are less frequently used as synonyms. This has become the case for the terms *preschool* and *child care* (Howes & Sanders, 2006). At one time, early childhood professionals were loath to differentiate between the two labels, hoping instead to blend the notion of education with the need for safe reliable care. In fact, some experts invented a new term, *educare*, to exemplify this hope (A. Smith, 1992). However, the word never caught on very broadly in the field or with the public. Today, there is a growing community perception that preschool is an educational and developmental service for children, whereas child care is a custodial service for working parents with less emphasis on cognitive and social stimulation. Although this distinction does not always hold up in practice, it has become common for early childhood practitioners who want to emphasize the educational aspects of their programs to highlight the preschool connection (no matter what the program is called or how many hours children attend). Likewise, the current trend is for states to fund early childhood education within a preschool context, rather than promoting programs focused on child care. As a result, states mandate that state-funded prekindergarten programs have strong education components. At the same time, many of these programs operate only part-time each day, which poses significant challenges to the working poor, who need a combination of developmental programming for their children as well as long hours of care in order for parents to remain employed. We discuss these challenges further in Chapter 4.

At this time, it is important to point out that the vocabulary a program uses to describe itself does not automatically indicate its level of quality. For example, a preschool is not always of higher quality than a childcare center, and different preschools may offer programs that fall in very different places on the quality continuum. Because early childhood programs have the option of choosing whether they will call themselves a childcare center, preschool, or nursery school, every program must be evaluated on an individual basis using the quality criteria outlined in Chapter 2.

Keeping these caveats in mind, from now on-we use the term preschool (and its synonyms, such as prekindergarten) to represent educational, center-based programs (versus home-based programs). Such programs may be full-time or part-time, may operate year round or not, and be located in a school or somewhere else in the community. Although at times we consider the entire age range from birth to eight years, we concentrate on preschool programs for three- and four-year-olds as well as linkages to kindergarten and the lower elementary grades. Regardless of their particulars, all the programs we discuss will be ones striving to achieve high quality. In addition, they all have their roots in early childhood culture.

BECOMING FAMILIAR WITH EARLY CHILDHOOD CULTURE

A graphic designer from central administration was showing his idea for a brochure to advertise the district's new state-funded preschool program. He was proud of the beautiful photograph that graced the cover, a smiling four-year-old child filling in shapes in a coloring book. The teachers from the preschool were not so pleased. They asked for a different photo to represent the program. They suggested one showing a child painting at an easel or one of a child working at the art table with collage materials. The designer was confused. The new images didn't seem that different from the one he had submitted. He couldn't understand why his great cover shot was being rejected.

Without realizing it, the designer had violated a cultural belief commonly held among early childhood practitioners—that children should be free to work with art materials in their own way rather than filling in prescribed designs in a coloring book. What he interpreted as a great photo of a happy child was viewed by the preschool teachers as sending the wrong message about the curricula in their classrooms. The teachers wanted to emphasize creativity, not fine motor skills. They associated free art with high-quality programming, and coloring books with lesser-quality programming. Although this was not a serious incident, it underscores the misunderstandings that can occur when individuals unfamiliar with early childhood values, beliefs, and customs become involved in early learning programs.

The Role of Culture in Early Education

Whether aware of it or not, every person and every group has a culture. (Nieto, 2007, p. 16)

As a school administrator, you know that each school has a culture all its own. You can feel it when you walk into the building, when you see and hear students in the hallways, or when you enter a classroom or the cafeteria. Likewise, various levels of education have certain cultural characteristics that distinguish one from the other. The differences in culture that characterize elementary, middle, and secondary schools are palpable. Early childhood education has a distinctive culture, too.

Culture serves two important functions in human society. First, it defines the accepted behaviors, roles, interpretations, and expectations people have within a particular group. Second, culture gives people a sense of identity (Robles de Melendez, 2007). The sharing of essential cultural dimensions such as values, beliefs, attitudes, customs, artifacts, and common language gives human beings a feeling of connectedness with one another. These same cultural dimensions also provide a sense of distinctiveness among group members. You will notice this immediately among the early childhood personnel with whom you come in contact.

For instance, talk to the head teachers in any high-quality early childhood program and they will likely know about

- scaffolding;
- unit blocks;
- learning centers;
- developmentally appropriate practice;
- circle time;
- the estimation jar;
- *Brown Bear, Brown Bear*;
- participation charts;
- word walls;
- people paint;
- home visits;
- universal precautions;
- NAEYC;
- antibias curricula;
- the Project Approach;
- ring-a-majigs;
- the Reggio Emilia approach;
- ants on a log; and
- what age groups of children need to avoid popcorn and hotdogs cut in circles.

Teachers will not only be familiar with most of these ideas, strategies, materials, routines, and people but also will have strong opinions about their relevance and the extent to which they will be incorporating them into their classrooms. Such elements and more represent essential aspects of the field.

The shared understandings that early childhood practitioners generally acquire are the result of more than one experience, such as reading a particular book or taking a single course. They come about through an amalgamation of many elements including training, experience, discussion, and years of acculturation in the profession. As a result of all this, certain ideas gradually come to feel like the natural way of thinking, acting, and viewing the world—in other words, the early childhood way. When this happens, we say that people have acquired a "thick cultural understanding of the field." Although individuals with such understandings are not identical to one another, members of the group share a common cognitive map that guides their beliefs, actions, judgments, and ethics (Katz, 1994). It is this thick understanding that one must begin to penetrate in order to successfully lead an early learning community.

Getting Beyond Cute

When first becoming involved in early childhood education, it is normal to see it primarily in terms of its surface features—small furniture, tables low to the ground, toys, childish songs, big books, and little toilets. These are the first things one notices, but they are not the essence of the field. Preoccupation with these elements results in what is best described as a "thin understanding of early childhood culture" (Geertz, 2000). Thin definitions focus on superficialities, not the deeper intellectual underpinnings that distinguish high-quality programs from those of lesser quality and substance. The danger in maintaining a thin understanding is that one is susceptible to misinterpreting or trivializing practices and programs rather than accurately understanding the world view they represent. Failing to recognize essential elements for what they are can lead to missteps when putting programs together or maintaining them over time.

> First thing, go sit in that early childhood classroom and listen to your teachers. Do not go in and do an evaluation on them or an observation for contract purposes. Go for your own benefit, see what they're doing, listen to what they have to say. You have some great resources right in your own building. (Principal, K–6 building)

A word of clarification is necessary here: it is not feasible for principals to become experts in every facet of every initiative for which they are responsible. However, delving beyond the surface makes it easier to interpret what is happening with children, families, teachers, and programs and can ultimately lead to greater success. To help readers move in this direction, what follows is a quick crash course in early childhood education. It includes information about core beliefs, heroines and heroes whose work has shaped the field, a few insights as to how early education has evolved to date, and a brief description of hot button issues that you and your staff will likely encounter. Familiarity with all these things will "get you beyond cute."

Core Beliefs Among Early Childhood Educators

Every profession has core beliefs that anchor it. These beliefs have historic roots and represent fundamental values that permeate the field. One can trace the evolution of core beliefs in the literature, through professional presentations at conferences, and around the table in the break room at a center or school. They provide a common set of ideals that drive members' actions and decision making. Knowledge of these beliefs helps to distinguish people in the know from individuals who are professional outsiders. These beliefs also help to explain some of the conflicts that arise when individuals sense that a core belief has been violated. Here are eight core beliefs that early childhood educators commonly espouse (Bredekamp, 2006; NAEYC, 2009).

Belief 1. Early childhood is a unique time of life that warrants respect in its own right. A bedrock belief within the early childhood community is that young children are unlike older children and adults in many ways. The differences that distinguish this period from other times in life are both qualitative (e.g., children think and interact with the world in different ways than adults do) and quantitative (e.g., children have less experience than adults do). A corollary of this belief is that children are fully functioning human beings who deserve to be valued for whom they are today, not just for whom they might become tomorrow.

Belief 2. Early education needs to take into account the whole child. Early childhood educators think about children as whole human beings. They believe it is their responsibility to nurture all aspects of children's development (aesthetic, cognitive, emotional, language, physical, and social) and to address the multiple dimensions of childhood learning (knowledge, skills, dispositions, and feelings). An outgrowth of this belief is the notion that children benefit from holistic experiences in which they can integrate development and learning across multiple domains and dimensions.

Belief 3. Play is integral to young children's learning and development. To have a serious conversation about early learning, one must eventually talk about children and play. Most early educators see play as a significant means (although not the only means) through which children gather and process information, learn new skills, and practice old ones. This belief extends to every young child, no matter his or her race, ethnic background, financial status, gender, or home language. The centrality of play to early childhood learning is substantiated by reams of research. It is also one of the least understood and accepted ideas by individuals outside the field.

A Kindergarten Teacher Expresses His Values

I've been teaching for 20 years, so I've seen kindergarten curricula and fads come and go. I've lived through talking toys, computer wars, science kits and math tools.

I want the public and policy makers to recognize the legitimacy of play as a means for young children to learn and to achieve standards. I want curiosity, motivation, creativity, socialization and task persistence recognized not merely as legitimate but as the primary goals of kindergarten.

I want the freedom to create my own classroom dynamic and to be as unfettered as possible by extraneous paperwork and requirements. Finally, I want and need to work in an environment where my knowledge and credentials as an early childhood educator are recognized and respected. (Kagan & Kauerz, 2006, p. 162)

Belief 4. Children are individuals. Each child is a unique being, with individual needs, abilities, understandings, preferences, and developmental attributes that must be considered in every aspect of the early learning program. As a result, early childhood education is not a "one-size-fits-all" proposition.

Belief 5. Relationships are the foundation on which learning builds. A fundamental premise in early childhood circles is that children need close personal relationships with caring adults in order to thrive. Peer relations are also critical. Thus, children benefit when they experience a sense of belonging and community in the classroom. Early childhood educators believe that if these ingredients are missing, it is less likely children will do well socially, intellectually, and academically.

Belief 6. Children's language and culture are fundamental to who they are. Language and culture are considered primary contributors to children's self-identity. In order to demonstrate respect for individual differences while building community in the classroom, early educators make a concerted effort to carry out programs that incorporate elements of children's home culture and home language into the program.

Belief 7. Families are children's first teachers and are important partners in children's education. Programs for young children emphasize the importance of the family as a primary context for childhood development and learning. Strong efforts to support families in their child-rearing responsibilities and to involve them in their children's education are typical dimensions of early childhood education regardless of what other theories or curriculum models an individual program might employ.

Belief 8. Early childhood educators are decision makers. A fundamental belief among early childhood professionals it that skilled decision making lies at the heart of good teaching. In accordance with this belief, teachers are viewed as decision makers in the classroom—deciding what to teach and how to teach and gauging what children are learning. Teachers observe, evaluate, adapt, and make choices all the time to enhance children's knowledge, skills, and dispositions. The choices they make take into account what they know about individual children, groups of children, teaching methods, developmental expectations, and program content.

A Principal Expresses Her Values

I'm the principal of a K–6 school in an urban setting. . . . I want teachers who see parents and the community as rightful partners in children's education. I want per diem funding that treats kindergarteners as full-fledged members of the school community and funds them on an equivalent basis to older children. . . . I want kindergarten standards, curriculum and assessments that are appropriate and aligned with those or preschool and first grade. I want to create a learning community in school where teachers have the opportunity and desire to grow and lead. (Kagan & Kauerz, 2006, p. 162)

Take a moment to consider the core beliefs outlined above. Which of these ring true to you? Which of these might you question? What implications do you see these beliefs having for the children, teachers, and programs for which you are responsible?

Keep these beliefs in mind as you read the rest of this chapter. They help to explain why early childhood education is structured as it is and why early childhood educators act as they do.

Heroines and Heroes

Every profession has its "stars"—people who have shaped current thinking and whose accomplishments have led to new ways of carrying out the work. Some of them are "famous"—people in the field know their names and refer to them often. Others are not as widely known but have had a strong influence on how professionals think and do things today. Early childhood education is no exception. Here is a brief "who's who" of important people who have influenced the field. These figures come from many backgrounds. Some will likely be familiar to you already; others may be names you are hearing for the first time.

Historic Figures	*Contributions*
Robert Owen (1771–1858) Welsh industrialist and social reformer "Physical punishment in a rationally conducted infant school will never be required and should be avoided as much as giving children poison on their food."	• Created an employer-sponsored infant school that was a forerunner of the North American preschool • Introduced multiage grouping • Used hands-on learning and field trips as primary methods of instruction • Championed positive discipline
Elizabeth Peabody (1804–1894) American educator "Let a child himself hammer out some substance with a mallet, and he will never forget the meaning of malleable."	• Opened the first American kindergarten in Boston in 1860 • Emphasized the value of firsthand experiences with real objects
Lev Vygotsky (1896–1934) Russian psychologist "The teacher must orient his work not on yesterday's development in the child but on tomorrow's."	• Described how language, culture, and social experience influence children's learning early in life • Emphasized the active role of the adult in early instruction
Maria Montessori (1870–1952) Italian physician "We cannot know the consequences of suppressing a child's spontaneity when he is just beginning to be active. We may even suffocate life itself. That humanity which is revealed in all its intellectual splendor during the sweet and tender age of childhood should be respected with a kind of religious veneration. Education cannot be effective unless it helps a child to open up himself to life."	• Advocated active, self-directed learning through play and freedom within limits • Created child-sized furnishings and classroom materials especially designed for young children

(Continued)

(Continued)

Historic Figures	Contributions
John Dewey (1859–1952) American educational reformer "Failure is instructive. The person who really thinks learns quite as much from his failures as from his successes."	• Emphasized learning by doing, projects, child-centered instruction, and integrated curricula • Highlighted value of play and attention to learners as individuals
Jean Piaget (1896–1980) Swiss psychologist and biologist "The principle goal of education in the schools should be creating men and women who are capable of doing new things, not simply repeating what other generations have done; men and women who are creative, inventive and discoverers, who can be critical and verify, and not accept, everything they are offered."	• Described ways in which children's thinking is functionally different from adults' thinking • Emphasized that children learn by acting on and experimenting with objects
David Weikart (1931–2003) American researcher and founder of the High/Scope Cognitively Oriented Curriculum "High-quality programs provide lifetime benefits."	• Identified key experiences children should have in preschool • Developed the "plan-do-review" sequence of early instruction • Emphasized the importance of research to document the impact of early education over time
Current Champions	**Contributions**
Sue Bredekamp "To keep the promise of preschool, educational leaders must know what to look for in a good pre-K curriculum and also recognize it when they see it."	• Early childhood educator and author • Driving force behind the creation of a national accreditation system for early childhood programs in the United States • Coauthor of Developmentally Appropriate Practice in Early Childhood Programs (on behalf of NAEYC)
Marion Wright Edelman "If we don't stand up for children, then we don't stand for much."	• Lawyer; founder and president of the Children's Defense Fund (CDF) • CDF works to influence public policy on behalf of children and families, with particular attention to the needs of poor and minority children and those with disabilities
Lillian Katz "Each of us must come to care about everyone else's children. We must recognize that the welfare of our children is intimately linked to the welfare of all other people's children. After all, when one of our children needs life-saving surgery, someone else's child will perform it. If one of our children is harmed by violence, someone else's child will be responsible for the violent act. The good life for our own children can be secured only if a good life is also secured for all other people's children."	• Early childhood teacher educator • Identified stages of teacher development in early childhood education • Proponent of children using projects to integrate learning across disciplines and developmental domains

Current Champions	Contributions
Samuel J. Meisels "Accountability should be seen as a system, not as a test."	• The nation's leading authority on early childhood assessment today • Describes the uses and abuses of developmental screening and school readiness testing • Has created assessments of young children's learning that are in widespread national and international use, including the Early Screening Inventory—Revised and The Work Sampling System
Bonnie Neugerbauer **and Roger Neugerbauer** "In the very best programs, the directors have an unflagging commitment to high performance. Even when crises seem to be breaking out all over, these directors do not allow these frustrations to serve as an excuse for letting up on quality."	• Publishers of *Exchange: The Early Childhood Leaders'* Magazine (a management publication for child care directors) • Founders of the World Forum on Early Care and Education (a biannual gathering of early childhood professionals from around the world designed to promote a global exchange of ideas on the delivery of quality services for young children in diverse settings)
Edward Zigler "Reading is just one aspect of cognitive development, and cognitive development is just one aspect of human development . . . a child's curiosity and belief that he or she can succeed are just as important to reading as knowing the alphabet. I am urging that we broaden our approach to literacy by focusing on the whole child."	• Father of Head Start, program founded in 1965 that focuses on comprehensive education, health, nutrition, and parent involvement services to low-income children and their families • Originator of Schools of the 21st Century, a comprehensive program with more than 1,300 schools currently involved that incorporates child care and education from preschool through the elementary grades

These giants in the field have blazed new trails, sparked debate, and shaped ideas that permeate early childhood education today. As you read the rest of this text, you will notice their influence many times and in many ways.

A Brief History of Early Childhood Education in the United States

It's hard to know where early childhood education is going, until you know where it has been. (Eliason & Jenkins, 2007, p. 3)

Early childhood education in the United States has its roots in five distinct traditions—(1) child care, (2) nursery schools, (3) kindergartens, (4) compensatory education, and (5) compulsory education at the elementary level. For many years, these initiatives proceeded along relatively separate paths. Today, however, they are converging. That convergence has been gradually taking place for many years, but is now moving at a rapidly accelerated pace. This has brought new energy as well as challenges to the field. The different philosophies and historic perspectives associated with each tradition sometimes complement one another and sometimes clash. All of them influence today's conversations about early childhood education and the role of the schools in this effort. As you read each synopsis, consider how the tradition it represents may be playing out in the early learning programs with which you are familiar.

Child Care

Historically, childcare centers came about in the United States to provide secure environments for children during parents' working hours. (One of the first centers was founded in Chicago in the early 1890s. It was administered by the Hull Settlement House to provide daily supervision for children of working immigrant families who might otherwise have been left at home alone.) Many childcare practices and routines are rooted in public health and child protection traditions. These origins have fostered the emphasis on children's health and safety, which is still reflected in licensing regulations for childcare programs in all states.

Nursery Schools

Nursery schools were originally created to supplement the learning experiences children received at home. They were also designed to prevent both mental and physical illness (Eliason & Jenkins, 2007). From the earliest days, nursery schools encouraged children's problem solving in the classroom, child choice, and conflict negotiation as strategies to support democratic values. The curriculum addressed children's total development as well as child nurturance. In fact, the term *nursery school* was adopted to describe a place in which children would be nurtured socially, emotionally, physically, and intellectually (Gordon & Browne, 2007). The nursery school teacher's responsibility was to know children well and to provide activities centered around children's interests. Project work, the use of natural materials, and opportunities for creative expression were fundamental to the nursery school tradition. These ideas continue to permeate early learning philosophy.

Kindergartens

The kindergarten ("children's garden" in German) was founded in Germany by Friedrich Froebel in 1837. At the time, it was a revolutionary concept, bucking the learning by rote tradition that typified nineteenth century schooling. Froebel (1887) believed that children had innate gifts that needed to be developed through play and the use of specially designed objects that could be manipulated by small hands. This child-centered approach became the hallmark of the kindergarten movement and remains important in modern times.

In 1860, the first private kindergarten was opened in the United States. Its students were children from the middle and upper classes. By World War I, however, kindergartens could be found throughout America, mostly sponsored by philanthropic organizations and targeted at children living in poverty. In these charity kindergartens, classroom practices remained play centered, but programs were also supplemented with daily medical inspections of the children and the provision of hot lunches. Teachers worked with children in the mornings and made home visits to families in the afternoons (hence, the half-day sessions still associated with many kindergarten programs today). Programs employed physicians, nurses, and social workers to offer various forms of assistance to children and their parents. These efforts ushered in an era characterized by a whole child—whole family approach that lasted several decades.

Over the years, kindergartens slowly made their way into elementary schools (Hill, 1941). At first, they occupied rooms that would otherwise be vacant, with no further obligations on the part of the school. As kindergartens became more popular, schools took on more of the financial responsibility of providing programs to the children in their communities. Welfare activities continued as long as philanthropic organizations could support them, but as those dollars subsided so did services—no more hot lunches, no more medical and dental clinic support, no more afternoon home visits by teachers, no more routine interactions between social workers and parents. As these services faded, the double class session was introduced so more children could be educated in a day.

By the end of World War II, kindergarten was a fixture in elementary schools nationwide. For many years, it served as a gentle transition between home and more formal schooling. School readiness was gauged mostly in social and emotional terms. The traditional kindergarten focus on active play, social cooperation, self-expression, and independence served this purpose well. In the 1970s, however, concern about children's subsequent academic success resulted in increasingly academic kindergarten programs. School readiness was redefined in terms of content knowledge and skills in math, language, and reading; the kindergarten curriculum changed to match. Material that once was the domain of first and second grades is now found in the kindergarten. This trend has elicited strong debate, not yet resolved, about what constitutes the appropriate function of kindergarten for children and for schools. We revisit this debate later in the chapter.

Compensatory Education

Compensatory programs such as Head Start and preprimary special education have been mandated federally to compensate for unfavorable developmental or environmental circumstances experienced by young children, particularly those from low-income families. Efforts to address poverty through federally funded early childhood education began in the 1960s and continue to evolve. More recently, the states also have begun to fund programs for young children and their families to reduce the burden of poverty (Morrison, 2007; Warner & Sower, 2005). A quick review of significant legislation highlights how compensatory programs have become a significant facet of early childhood education. These programs both influence and are influenced by the other traditions described in this chapter.

1964   The Economic Opportunity Act of 1964 was passed. This began the war on poverty and laid the groundwork for Project Head Start.

1965   Head Start was launched, serving more than 560,000 disadvantaged children and families in an eight-week summer preschool program. Over time, Head Start expanded to provide more school days and more comprehensive services to children and families.

1966   The Follow Through Program was created to extend Head Start into the early primary grades. This program continued until 1995.

1967   The federal government created the Handicapped Children's Early Education Program to fund model preschool programs for children with disabilities.

1972   The Economic Opportunity Act was amended. It mandated that at least 10 percent of the national enrollment of Head Start consist of children with handicapping conditions.

1975   Public Law 94–142, the Education for All Handicapped Children Act, was passed mandating a free and appropriate education for all children with disabilities and extending many rights to their parents.

1977   Head Start was expanded to serve bilingual and migrant children.

1981   The Head Start Act of 1981 was passed to extend Head Start to more children, to expand the scope of services (education, physical health, mental health, and family support), and to provide for more effective delivery of these services through community partnerships.

1986   Public Law 99–457 (the Education of the Handicapped Act Amendments) established a national policy on early intervention that recognized the benefits of getting to children early, provided assistance to states for building systems of service delivery, and recognized the unique role of families in the development of their children with disabilities.

1990   The Americans with Disabilities Act (ADA) and Public Law 101–476, the Individuals with Disabilities Education Act (IDEA) were enacted. ADA established civil rights for the disabled, including equal access to facilities, job opportunities, and education. IDEA added autism and traumatic brain injuries to the list of disabilities public schools should accept. It also provided funding to improve services to infants and toddlers and promoted programs that would allow children with severe disabilities to be included in general education classrooms.

1995   Head Start Reauthorization established a new program, Early Head Start, for low-income pregnant women and families with infants and toddlers.

1997   IDEA 1997 was passed. This legislation requires school districts to participate in transitional planning for toddlers with disabilities about to enter preschool. It clarifies how Individual Education Plans for young children are to be developed and mandates that the progress of children in special education classrooms be formally assessed using methods similar to those employed with the general student population.

1998   Head Start Reauthorization mandated Head Start expansion to full-day, year-round programming. Today, the program reaches about 20 percent of the eligible population. It has served more than 22 million children and families since its inception.

Compulsory Education

It may seem as if we have always had public schools in the United States that children have been required to attend, but that is not so. From colonial times until the mid-nineteenth century, American schooling relied on a jumble of mostly private institutions: church-sponsored schools, local schools created by a specific group of parents, tuition schools set up by traveling school masters, charity schools for poor children run by churches or other philanthropic organizations, boarding schools for children from wealthy families, dame schools run by women in their homes, and private tutors (Center on Education Policy, 2007). This disjointed approach resulted in limited access and inequities. Apart from boys from families who could afford tuition, many children did not go to school regularly, if they went at all. Those most likely to be left out were girls, poor children, immigrant children, children with disabilities, African American children, and Native American children. Even when children who were marginalized by economics, gender, or ethnicity got to school, the facilities they experienced were often substandard and their teachers poorly prepared.

As the country grew and immigration increased the diversity of the population, educational reformers such as Horace Mann proposed a universal system of publicly funded, locally governed schools to advance the common good. By the mid-1800s, public schools were viewed as an investment in the future whose purpose was

- to prepare children for citizenship in a democratic society,
- to help students acquire knowledge and skills to become economically self-sufficient,

- to unify a diverse population, and
- to help the nation address social problems related to poverty, violence, class conflict, and ethnic differences.

In the two centuries that have followed, these notions have remained central to compulsory schooling in the United States (Center on Education Policy, 2007).

Range of What States Require as Compulsory	
Number of years children must attend school	Nine to thirteen years total
Minimum age for compulsory education	Five to eight years of age
Maximum age for compulsory education	Sixteen to eighteen years of age
Number of instructional days per school year	173 to 186 days

Source: Center on Education Policy (2006).

More recently, issues of equal access and equal opportunity have dominated our thinking about compulsory education. Court decisions such as *Brown v. Board of Education* (1954) and federal laws enacted since the 1960s around the rights of poor children, migrant children, children with disabilities, children with limited English proficiency, women and girls, and, most recently, the No Child Left Behind Act (2001) are all aimed at raising standards and making a high-quality education available to every child. All of these ideas and events have shaped our schools and are having a major impact on what awaits young children when they begin first grade as required by law.

Early Childhood Education Is a Potpourri of Many Subcultures

Because early childhood education draws on so many traditions, it is not a monoculture. Although its members tend to share the core beliefs outlined earlier in this chapter, ideas about young children and classroom practices that are more specific vary widely within the field. Practitioners involved in Head Start for example, often see the world quite differently from those involved in child care or the primary grades. In addition, some people view teachers as active agents in the classroom; others believe a more passive teacher role is appropriate. Some practitioners believe we need to slow things down for children, while some think we need to speed things up. Differences in perspective like these can be attributed to variations in the preparation associated with each tradition, different philosophies about development and learning, and people's varying ideas about the essential nature of young children. All of these variables contribute to how early childhood practitioners conduct themselves professionally and to the kinds of programs they believe are best for young children. In Table 3.2, we provide examples of how differences in philosophical orientation sometimes manifest themselves in practitioner's thoughts and actions.

> ## Merging Traditions Yield New Trends
>
> As the five traditions described in this chapter continue to merge, new trends are becoming evident in early childhood education. Most significantly, we are seeing
>
> - greater public school involvement in preprimary education of all kinds,
> - a national movement toward universal voluntary preschool programs for three- and four-year-old children,
> - increased demand for highly qualified teachers in preschool programs,
> - stronger emphasis on curriculum development, early learning standards, and performance-based outcomes in early learning programs,
> - requirements for greater accountability within early childhood programs, and
> - more calls for seamless early childhood programs that are appropriate and aligned from preschool through third grade.

Each of the perspectives outlined in Table 3.2 has dominated the early childhood scene at one time or another. As people have debated the relative merits and drawbacks of emerging philosophies, and as research has accrued, certain notions have faded and others have remained. This has resulted in an accumulation of ideas that have contributed to our current notions of best practice in the field. For instance, practitioners who pay attention to the developmental progression of children's speech or fine motor skills are drawing on the legacy of maturationism. Those who use verbal cues to capture children's attention before beginning to read a story and those who use logical consequences when children break a rule are making use of behaviorism. Teachers who ask children to give a verbal rationale for why they grouped certain objects as they did or offer children real leaves to examine rather than relying on pictures of or words about leaves are putting cognitive developmental ideas into action. When adults challenge children to work beyond their current capacities through cooperative learning activities, heterogeneous groupings, or peer coaching, we are seeing applications related to social constructionism.

Current Perspectives

Over the years, in an effort to improve educational practices, people have tried to determine if one philosophical orientation is more correct than all the others. Arguments have raged at all levels of the profession trying to settle this matter. Although social constructivism is widely associated with the field overall, in reality no one perspective is accepted by everyone. Instead, different segments of the field tend to rely more heavily on certain perspectives than on others. For instance, many childcare providers demonstrate professional behavior that corresponds most closely to a maturational philosophy. Early childhood special education and many grade-school programs tend to be more behaviorally oriented. The preschool tradition is commonly associated with the cognitive developmental philosophy and social constructionism. The upshot of all this is that early childhood practitioners do not all speak in a single voice. This can make conversation and collaboration difficult. Exacerbating the problem is the tendency for people to see their own perspectives as appropriate, and other perspectives as inappropriate or even unethical, not just different. These conclusions can lead to serious misunderstandings and conflict among staff, between staff and principals, and between individuals with roots in one tradition and those with roots in another. When this happens, your role as an administrator may have to shift from supervisor or instructional leader to culture broker.

Table 3.2 Major Philosophical Orientations That Have Influenced Early Childhood Education

Orientation	Basic Beliefs About Child Development and Learning	Main Message	Origins	Primary Teacher Role	What Teachers Do
Maturational	Child development is an orderly process governed by a "biological clock." Development determines all that can be learned. New abilities emerge gradually and cannot be accelerated. Watchwords: "ages and stages" and "the gift of time"	*Wait for readiness.*	Most influential from the 1940s through the 1970s Strongly influenced by the work of Arnold Gesell, Frances Ilg, Erik Erikson, and Anna Freud	Observer	Create emotionally supportive and healthy environments. Look for readiness to manifest itself. Provide open-ended materials that match children's readiness to learn and that enable children to work out internal issues.
Behavioral	Child learning is primarily governed by external variables such as how instruction is designed and monitored. All children have the potential to learn. Knowledge is acquired through instruction. Learning is adult-initiated. Watchwords: cuing, shaping, reinforcement, extinction, instructional sequences.	*Get children ready* by instructing them early and formally.	Most influential from the 1960s through the present day Strongly influenced by the work of E. L. Thorndike, B. F. Skinner, and Albert Bandura	Leader	Transmit knowledge and skills directly using relevant instructional sequences. Provide external reinforcements and rewards. Maintain high expectations for classroom learning. Establish consistent rules for acceptable behavior.

(Continued)

Table 3.2 (Continued)

Orientation	Basic Beliefs About Child Development and Learning	Main Message	Origins	Primary Teacher Role	What Teachers Do
Cognitive Developmental	Children's cognitive development proceeds through a universal sequence of stages.	*Support* children's construction of new understandings through child-centered experimentation.	Most influential from the 1960s through the present day	Facilitator	Provide a rich array of hands-on materials with which children can experiment, and which are relevant to their stage of cognitive development.
	Much knowledge cannot be instructed. It must be constructed by the learner himself.		Strongly influenced by the work of Jean Piaget, Barbel Inhelder, and Constance Kamii		Focus on process over products.
	Development drives learning.				Focus on how and why children think as they do more than the correctness of their answers.
	Learning is child initiated.				
	Learning is the result of interaction between children's internal cognitive structures and their experiences with physical objects.				
	Watchwords: physical, logico-mathematical, and representational knowledge; equilibrium and disequilibrium; assimilation and accommodation				

| Social Construction | Learning and development are dynamic and interactive.

Learning drives development.

Children's mental, linguistic, and social powers are developed and enhanced through social interactions with peers and adults.

There is a strong emphasis on the people in children's environments.

Watchwords: scaffolding, zone of proximal development, intentional teaching | *Guide children* to higher levels of conceptual development through interactions with objects and people. | Came to prominence in the 1990s and continues to the present day

Strongly influenced by the work of Lev Vygotsky and Jerome Bruner | Sometimes facilitator, sometimes leader | Offer first-hand experiences for children. Do not rely on having children merely observe, listen, or deal with problems abstractly.

Provide play-based problems for children to solve.

Begin where children are then provide materials, experiences and supports that challenge them to stretch beyond what they already know and can do to gradually achieve more-independent learning. (This is called scaffolding.)

Utilizes forms of assisted learning such as cooperative learning, joint problem solving, coaching, mentoring, and collaborating.

Includes child-initiated and adult-directed experiences. |

Source: McKee, 1990; Morrison, 2007.

SCHOOL PRINCIPALS AS CULTURE BROKERS

A culture broker is a person who acts to bridge or mediate cultural differences in order to increase mutual understanding and reduce conflict (Jezewski, 1995). Cultural brokers function in a variety of ways. They

- advocate for people to work together,
- guide individuals in their attempts to cross cultural boundaries safely,
- offer useful information and correct misinformation,
- interpret ideas and perspectives,
- intervene to promote respect for subcultures and cultural mores,
- introduce people to cultural beliefs and practices,
- mediate cultural conflicts as they arise,
- model practices and attitudes congruent with cultural norms,
- negotiate agreements to help members of various subcultures find common ground,
- network with individuals across cultural boundaries,
- sensitize people to one another's points of view, and
- translate ideas and practices from one cultural perspective to another.

Anyone can become a culture broker if they are willing to work hard to establish trusting relationships with people across cultures and to learn more about cultures with which they are less unfamiliar (Pipher, 2002). Sometimes, school principals play this role themselves. If that is not feasible (especially at first), they may find someone else to assume the responsibility. In some schools, different people function as culture brokers at different times depending on the circumstances. In any case, the most effective culture brokers reflect the qualities outlined in Box 3.1.

Box 3.1

Tips From Principals on How to Be an Effective Culture Broker

Listen carefully: listen more than you talk.

Make sure many voices are heard around the table.

Model respect for different points of view.

Be patient with the process.

Commit for the long haul.

Pull people in rather than push people out.

Figure you won't know everything all the time.

Be willing to grow and to change your mind.

Let others be in the driver's seat sometimes.

Realize you can be a guru in the district twenty-five miles down the road and still meet resistance in your own backyard.

Some Hot Button Issues Culture Brokers Will Have to Navigate

Nowhere are the divides among educationally defined culture groups more evident than in the hot button issues that characterize early childhood education today. These issues are fueled by societal pressures for achievement and accountability and by misperceptions among various groups inside and beyond the field of early education. Here is a sample of some of the hottest issues people are striving to overcome.

1. Early childhood programs often view each other as competitors for limited resources (Hinkle, 2000). Head Start and many school-based preschool programs seek enrollments from the same populations and both must justify their budgets with full enrollments in order to have continued funding. Private childcare and preschool programs depend on parent fees. They worry that publicly funded preschools will erode their client base. Likewise, programs that have been in the community for years feel undermined by programs in the public schools that are newly arrived on the scene. All of these circumstances have the potential to promote competitive rather than collaborative attitudes and actions among community programs and between certain community programs and schools. This makes service coordination and the creation of seamless transitions from one program to another more difficult to achieve.

2. A schism remains between education and child care. As mentioned earlier, child care and other forms of early childhood education have developed relatively independent of one another and with different purposes in mind. Knowing what we know today about the importance of early learning and development, it would benefit society for children of working parents to be kept healthy and safe, and to experience high-quality learning environments as well. Unfortunately, public policies for education and child care are poorly integrated and lack a comprehensive vision that encompasses both aims (National Institute for Early Education Research [NIEER], 2002). As a result, there are disparities in the level of funding available to childcare programs and their counterparts in the field. These differences affect teacher qualifications, program standards, and other elements associated with quality, which in turn give rise to tensions among personnel and programs. These conditions detract from mutual understanding and cooperation.

3. Differences in education, compensation, and status between early educators and public school teachers contribute to tensions and hinder collaboration among schools, Head Start, and childcare programs in the community (Jacobson, 1999). Even when schools compensate their preschool teachers at the same rate as teachers in the upper grades, educators funded by other entities may not receive equal compensation. This can lead to informal (but powerful) hierarchies in which some individuals clearly have lower status than others. Such hierarchies get in the way of program personnel establishing respectful professional relationships across program boundaries or seeing one another as colleagues with common purposes.

4. Many people fear that preschools located in the public schools will place too great an emphasis on a narrow range of academic skills, will lose their focus on whole child learning, and will reduce or eliminate time for play. As kindergartens have evolved from a children's garden to a mini first grade, many early childhood educators worry that preschool will follow the same route. Reports of elementary schools tightening schedules, eliminating recess,

removing the blocks and pretend play equipment from K–2 classrooms, dropping learning center time, and exposing children to long periods of whole-group instruction are worrisome in light of core beliefs about high-quality programming for young children. The single biggest concern voiced by early childhood educators is that school-based preprimary programs will move in directions they consider developmentally inappropriate (Elkind, 2007; Wien, 2004).

5. Some people believe that programs for young children do not pay enough attention to literacy and numeracy skills or to learning outcomes and K–12 standards. These worries can be traced to many things: concern about children coming to school ill prepared for academic learning, pressures to ensure children's readiness for the next grade or class level, differences in ideas about what constitutes appropriate learning, as well as the early childhood field's history of custodial care and its not-so-long ago emphasis on maturationism, which some teachers still practice. Moreover, developmentally appropriate practice (DAP), in its earliest iterations, made little mention of outcomes or standards. This gave many people the impression that early childhood teachers should not address subject matter content or specific literacy and numeracy skills in preschool or kindergarten (Kostelnik, 1998). Although such ideas are changing, there is still widespread disagreement about the degree and the manner in which learning standards and outcomes should be incorporated into early childhood curricula or how preschool expectations should be aligned with those in the K–12 system. These differences in perspective exacerbate divisions between school-based preschool programs and child care, between preschool or kindergarten and first or second grade, and between early childhood education (prekindergarten–3) and midprimary (Grades 4–12).

6. The debate over child-initiated learning experiences versus adult-led learning experiences is divisive and volatile. There is a philosophical and emotional divide between people who believe that children's early learning experiences need to be mostly child initiated and those who believe that adult-led instruction is best. The research actually supports a mix of these approaches, but it is not uncommon for people to treat them as mutually exclusive (A. Epstein, 2007). Because young children are so vulnerable and because the early learning stakes are so high, practitioners often attribute adoption of one perspective versus the other as not merely philosophical, but as having moral and ethical ramifications. No matter on which side of the issue they fall, people who think that other people are doing children harm through ineffective practices have a hard time talking to one another and finding common ground.

Looking on the Bright Side

Although formidable issues challenge leaders of early learning communities, there are many positives as well. One such positive is that school principals can position themselves to help bridge the gulf that may exist between early childhood and other education programs in a school or district. With your support, partners on all sides of the issues can begin to create a seamless preschool to Grade 3 continuum of learning that helps children and programs succeed (NAESP, 2005). A way to get this started is to help the various entities involved recognize and appreciate the strengths each brings to the table. Examples of the strengths preprimary education and elementary education have developed over the years are outlined in Box 3.2.

Box 3.2

Preprimary Education

Preprimary education has a long history of

- working with very young children,
- educating the whole child,
- working in teams,
- working with families,
- early identification of children with special needs, and
- integrating children with special needs into classrooms with typically developing children.

Elementary education has a long history of

- providing access to all children regardless of race, income, ability, or language,
- providing auxiliary services to supplement children's educational needs,
- rallying the community to come together on behalf of children,
- aligning curricula from one level to the next,
- addressing issues of accountability, and
- helping children and families make the transition from kindergarten to first grade.

Both preprimary education and elementary education have a long history of experience in

- public service,
- working with multiple funding streams,
- working with community partners,
- drawing on research to shape professional practice, and
- professional organizations that support their members.

As you can see, preprimary and elementary education have complementary strengths. They also have certain assets in common. By combining these assets and making a good faith effort to deal with the concerns represented by the hot button issues described earlier, it is possible that the United States will find new and improved ways to provide high-quality early learning programs to more young children and their families. You could play a significant role in this endeavor.

PRINCIPALS' ROLES

Getting Involved in Early Childhood Education

1. Become an insider, rather than an outsider in early childhood circles. Get to know the early childhood leaders in your area. Participate in local groups and discussions that could lead to enhanced relationships among community organizations and the schools.

2. Promote communication among early childhood programs. Do this by initiating communication yourself or by responding positively to contacts extended to you. Make a special effort to reach out to childcare providers and other state-funded or federally funded preschool programs in the community. Visit their programs and invite them to visit yours to improve communication and to encourage a common vision of appropriate school readiness expectations.

3. Include other school personnel and decision makers in explorations of early childhood education. Invite teachers across grades, specialists, other principals, and school board members to participate in early childhood activities and professional development opportunities.

4. Find someone to serve as a culture broker or early childhood champion for you and others in the school or district. This might be someone who is a member of your staff or otherwise employed in the district. This might also be an outsider, such as a community professional or university consultant. Contact your local chapter of the NAEYC or the NAESP for potential resources.

5. Demonstrate your alignment with early childhood core values. Words will be important, but actions will be critical. School staff, community members, and families will be watching you closely to see if you really get it. Show that you do by the questions you ask, the observations you make, and the opportunities you provide.

6. As you acquire more knowledge about early childhood education, gradually take on some characteristics of the culture broker or early childhood advocate role yourself. Advocate, guide, offer information, interpret, intervene, introduce, mediate, model, network, and translate ideas as necessary.

7. Help subculture group members find common ground around which to develop early learning initiatives. Be prepared for early childhood professionals to vary in their ideas about what is best for children. Listen carefully for values expressed and point out commonalities based on the core values identified in this chapter. Emphasize strengths of the varying perspectives represented around the table (e.g., behavioral versus cognitive developmental, preprimary versus primary, child-led learning versus adult-led learning). Encourage talk about ways in which differing perspectives could be blended effectively without violating the basics tenets of each.

Early Childhood Education

Stakeholders

Stakeholders are key players in an organization. Each school has a specific set of stakeholders. An effective principal knows the stakeholders and identifies the supports and demands they bring to the school enterprise. Stakeholders include the consumers of a program or service. In a school setting, consumers are the students and the students' parents, guardians, and families. The faculty and staff who implement plans and programs and provide the core technology or activity of the school—the teaching—are stakeholders. Principals and superintendents, coordinators, head teachers, directors, and agency heads are stakeholders. Boards and board members, representatives of agencies, and community members are stakeholders. School stakeholders include government, religious, philanthropic, public, private, and business interests. These individuals and groups have a stake in the current school system and in the future of the school system. The degree to which they have "ownership" of the school is key to its success (B. Smith, 2002).

IDENTIFYING THE STAKEHOLDERS

It is the principal's responsibility to identify the school's stakeholders. This role is a familiar aspect of school-community relations. The principal's expertise in identifying stakeholders and establishing positive relationships with them is an asset to the school and the students, community, and society. "Principals must acknowledge the role they play as community leader and promoter of high-quality early childhood education. Principals know they cannot advocate alone for strong early childhood policies, and they value partnership with non-public school educational programs in the community, including health and fitness advocates and others working to create a web of support and learning for young children" (National Association of Elementary School Principals [NAESP], 2005b, p. vii).

Students are the primary stakeholders of a school. They are at the center of the teaching and learning enterprise. In Table 4.1, the numbers of children under the age of five in 2005 in the United States (according to data gathered for the U.S. Census Bureau) are presented. These numbers reflect the children who are the focus of early childhood education.

Table 4.1 Percentage Distribution of Children From Birth Through Age Five, 2005

	Number of Children (thousands)	*No Weekly Nonparental Care Arrangement*	*At Least One Weekly Nonparental Care Arrangement*	*Distribution of Weekly Nonparental Care Arrangement by Type[1]*		
				Relative	**Nonrelative**	**Center Based[2]**
Total	20,665	40	60	35	22	60
Child's age						
<One year	3,519	58	42	48	33	28
One to two years	8,080	47	53	39	30	43
Three to five years	9,066	27	73	29	15	78
Family type						
Two parents	16,294	44	56	31	24	61
One parent	4,036	27	73	46	18	57
Nonparent	335	36	64	42	16	65
Poverty threshold						
At or above	15,900	37	63	33	24	61
Below	4,766	51	49	44	16	57

Source: NCES, 2005.

Notes: Children studied are not yet in kindergarten and are participating in various weekly nonparental care arrangements.

1. Children may have more than one nonparental care arrangement of the same type or more than one nonparental care arrangement of different types.
2. Center-based arrangements include daycare centers, Head Start programs, preschools, prekindergartens, and other early childhood programs.

The changing face of schools is a constant topic in educational circles. Principals need to be alert to the demographic characteristics of the children served by the school. Table 4.2 provides a portrait of the young children in the United States based on 2005 U.S. Department of Education data.

Table 4.2 Noteworthy Characteristics of Children

Of the 20,655,000 (20.7 mil) children five years old (not in kindergarten) and younger,

- 44 percent are minority.

- 21 percent live with only one parent or nonparent guardian(s).

- 28 percent of mothers' highest education is high school/GED.

- 29 percent live in household incomes of $25,000 or less.

- 23 percent live in poverty.

Source: NCES, 2005.

Children come to school from a wide variety of living arrangements. Principals know that they must be attentive to these different living arrangements. As a reminder of these household arrangements, Table 4.3 provides data from the 2006 U.S. Census Bureau.

Table 4.3 Household Relationships and Living Arrangements of Children, Birth to Two Years Old

	Under One Year Old (thousands)	*One to Two Years Old (thousands)*
Total	4,053	8,214
Both parents	2,787	5,628
Mother only	902	1,898
Father only	229	387
Grandparent(s) only	34	145
Other relative	37	59
Foster child	22	30
Other nonrelative	42	66

Source: U.S. Census Bureau, 2006.

Householder. The person or one of the people in whose name the home is owned, being bought, or rented. If there is no such person present, any household member fifteen years old and over can serve as the householder for the purposes of the census.

Two types of householders are distinguished: a family householder and a nonfamily householder. A family householder is a householder living with one or more people related to her by birth, marriage, or adoption. The householder and all people in the household related to him are family members. A nonfamily householder is a householder living alone or only with nonrelatives.

A number of children live in poverty. Figure 4.1, provided by the National Center for Children in Poverty, illustrates the percentages of children living in poverty. The issue of poverty is a serious factor in the lives of young children.

Figure 4.1   Children Living in Low-Income and Poor Families, by Age Group, 2006

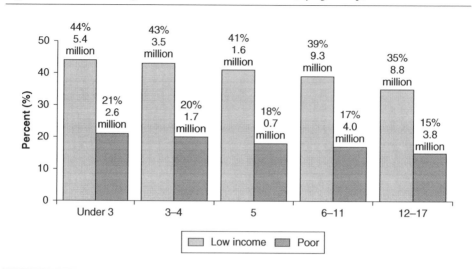

Source: New York. Used with permission. Permission granted by Morris Ardoin on March 17, 2008. Director, Communications and Public Affairs for the National Center for Children in Poverty.

Parents, guardians, and family members are key stakeholders in early childhood education.

> The evidence is consistent, positive and convincing: families have a major influence on children's achievement in school and through life. When schools, families, and community groups work together to support learning, children tend to do better in school, stay in school longer, and like school more. (National Center for Family and Community Connections with School [NCFCCS] 2002, p. 7)

Families bring both supports and demands to the school. When they bring their children to school, they have expectations for the children's success in the early childhood program. They bring specialized information about their children. They assist in the children's education as their first teachers and by their involvement in the children's education. They can be tremendous advocates and spokespersons for the school by their reports of their children's experiences in school. They are key communicators of the school's program and successes.

Early childhood educators are stakeholders. Their commitment is to the education of young children. They bring special knowledge and skills in early childhood education to their work. They have expectations of the principal. They need support, guidance, resources, and assistance in working with children, parents, colleagues, and the community. They seek professional development and renewal opportunities. They are advocates for best practices in early childhood education.

> Principals take the lead by emphasizing professional development that creates learning communities in which teachers meet regularly to discuss common challenges and share effective practice. Principals stimulate teachers' intellectual growth by choosing challenging topics for professional development and making every activity an opportunity to learn. (NAESP, 2005b, p. 52)

Additionally, school board members, superintendents, elementary principals, teachers, school social workers, and interagency coordinating councils are stakeholders in early childhood education.

Federal and state legislators are stakeholders in early childhood education. They represent constituents who are parents, community members, educators, business owners, and members of the work force who demand early childhood education programs. Legislators reflect these interests in policy development and advocacy. They can sponsor legislation that expands and enhances the provision of early childhood education. They can advocate legislation that provides funding to support early childhood education. They can address issues of equity and quality in educational offerings for children. The policymaking role is critical to the provision of early childhood education.

As leaders in education, principals are well-positioned to speak publicly on behalf of children, whether or not the children are enrolled in elementary school. They can carry the message about the need for high-quality pre-K programs as a central focus of their advocacy. (NAESP, 2005b, p. 74)

Publicly funded early childhood programs are stakeholders in schools. For instance, Head Start, a federally funded program, has a long history of providing services to children and families. Historically, a program that runs three hours a day, it cannot single-handedly meet the needs of working parents (Cooper, 2002, p. 6). These programs have an interest in the school's involvement and successes in early childhood education.

Private nursery schools and childcare providers in family homes are stakeholders in early childhood education.

Many children are now being cared for by family, friend, and neighbor (FFN) caregivers in home settings. FFN care is also known as kith and kin care or informal care, as opposed to the care provided in more formal and professional center-based and family child care markets. (National Child Care Information and Technical Assistance Center [NCCIC], 2008, p. 1)

Children from these settings transition to the schools. It is in the best interests of children for private childcare providers and elementary school personnel to work together to facilitate children's learning and transitions. Discussions between the private settings and the school should be frequent so that the children's needs are met. Private childcare providers have valuable special knowledge of the children.

Religious organizations, another category of private providers, often sponsor early childhood programs and are stakeholders in early childhood education. Many of the children in these programs will transition to the public schools. Building linkages with these programs will facilitate the children's transitions. Additionally, these religious groups often have visible outreach initiatives in a community. Examples of these groups include Lutheran Family Services, Catholic Charities, and the Jewish Day Centers. These groups may provide opportunities to strengthen communications between the religious organizations and the public schools about early childhood education and the school's program.

The health care community is an important stakeholder in early childhood education. Physicians' offices and health care centers provide ideal venues for posting information about early childhood programs, events, and opportunities. Physicians and other health care staff members can advocate for early childhood programs. Visiting nurses are an important resource in some communities. The U.S. Department of Health and Human Services is a significant stakeholder as well.

Higher education institutions are stakeholders in early childhood education. Colleges of education in public and private institutions as well as community colleges prepare teachers for early childhood settings. These programs seek student placements for field experiences, practicum experiences, internships, and student teaching. Those who coordinate these placements seek quality experiences for the students who are placed. The colleges also have an interest in the employment of their graduates in early childhood settings.

Higher education faculty members have expertise in early childhood education and are stakeholders in early childhood education. Their knowledge of best practices in early childhood education is a great resource to the schools. These faculty members may be the individuals who "write the books" about early childhood education. In addition to their content knowledge, faculty may seek research sites and laboratories for their scholarly activities. The opportunities for reciprocity between the schools and higher education institutions and faculty members are extensive.

Departments of education at the state and federal level are stakeholders in early childhood education. These departments translate legislative policies into the rules and regulations that guide early childhood education. They may have enforcement and supervisory roles in relation to these educational programs.

> Principals need to be aware of the interface of early childhood data and the broader school district data that is reported, via accountability mandates, by state departments. As an example, in Minnesota, school districts are required to submit program and participant data and program plans to the Minnesota Department of Education (MDE) with respect to the following: Early Childhood Family Education, Early Childhood Screening and School Readiness programs, and Interagency Early Intervention Committees. (G. Zierdt, personal communication, March 17, 2008)

The departments also may be conduits of funding streams to early childhood programs. Personnel in these departments are sources of expertise on best practices in early childhood education. They provide resources, professional development opportunities, and updates on legislation. They can serve as spokespersons and advocates for early childhood education.

Philanthropic organizations are stakeholders in early childhood education. These groups provide funding and advocacy, and sponsor initiatives that enhance the delivery, availability, and prominence of early childhood programs. Among the philanthropic groups with interests in early childhood education are The Pew Charitable Trust and the Annie E. Casey Foundation. "Principals need to be aware of existing philanthropic organizations within their community who are vested in early childhood. One of the nation's largest models of early childhood coalitions is sponsored by United Way" (G. Zierdt, personal communication, March 17, 2008).

United Way's Success By 6 focuses on improving school readiness through community change. Success By 6 (SB6) operates in more than 350 communities or states.

> With support from local United Way organizations, SB6 coalitions are galvanizing business, government and non-profit leaders around early learning. For 16 years, SB6 coalitions have been raising awareness of the importance of early childhood development, improving access to services, advocating for public policies and overhauling systems – budgets, laws and supports – to improve young children's lives. At the national level, United Way Success By 6 provides a strategic framework and support for local innovation. In the last 5 years, more than 500,000 children have benefited from SB6 early learning, child care, parent education, health, literacy and family resource center programs. (http://www.liveunited.org/News/upload/SB6overview.pdf, p. 1)

Public agencies such as the department of health and human services, the police department, fire department, public library, children and family services, social services, public health department, and mental health agencies are important stakeholders in early childhood programs. Each group's contribution enhances the quality of the early childhood program.

Community organizations are participants in the delivery of early childhood programs. The YMCA, YWCA, community education programs, parks and recreation, Hispanic centers, and other organizations may house early childhood programs. These groups are natural partners with the schools in making programs available to children and families.

Business organizations are stakeholders in early childhood education. In order to have a productive workforce, worker parents need reliable and quality child care so that they are able to participate fully in their jobs (Business Roundtable, 2003).

The future workforce and economy rely on well-educated workers. Business leaders recognize the need for early childhood education to meet those future needs. Businesses may provide early childhood programs within the business setting or work in collaboration with schools to provide for employee needs. The condition of the schools and education programs in a community is linked to the attractiveness of a community for new business start-ups. Early childhood programs contribute to the condition of the schools.

Figure 4.2 provides an illustration of the internal and external stakeholders of the early childhood program of the school. The principal must be attentive to the stakeholder groups and work in collaboration with these groups to create the best educational experiences for young children.

Figure 4.2   Internal and External Stakeholders

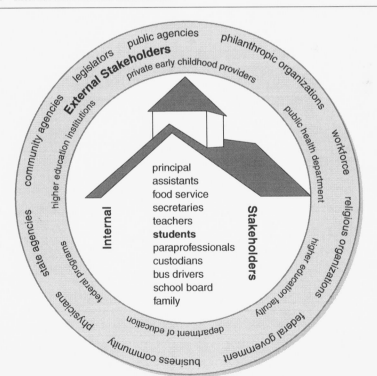

Source: Created by Marilyn L. Grady.

COLLABORATION

Building support for early childhood education requires collaboration, involvement, and a vision of the outcomes. The product of collaboration should be the synergy that occurs when the full complement of stakeholders are involved in the initiative.

> Historically . . . the term collaboration" in government has been pejorative, implying consorting with the enemy. Now it is better understood as a way of improving services to children and their families in the community. Collaborative efforts . . . yield greater results and save money long-term. The whole "is more than the sum of its parts." (Cooper, 2002, p. 7)

For any principal, the prospect of having all the stakeholders at the table is daunting. Collaboration or involvement does not mean having everyone at the table. Instead, there are a number of opportunities for participation. Surveys, interviews, focus groups, committees, and open forums are means of stimulating input, involvement, and ownership of early childhood education. These techniques can be used to provide data, review plans, and elicit comments on plans. The ultimate objective is to give voice to all stakeholders. Figure 4.3 is a principal's illustration of the early childhood programs and components in one school.

Figure 4.3   Early Childhood Program

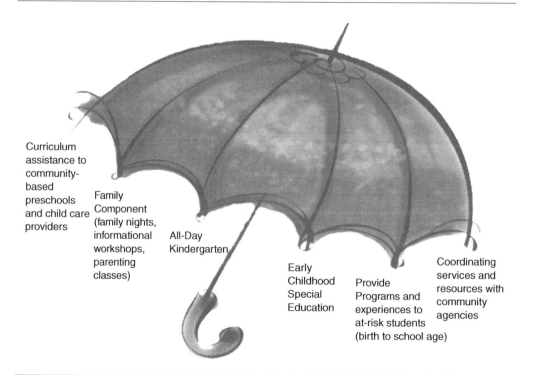

Curriculum assistance to community-based preschools and child care providers

Family Component (family nights, informational workshops, parenting classes)

All-Day Kindergarten

Early Childhood Special Education

Provide Programs and experiences to at-risk students (birth to school age)

Coordinating services and resources with community agencies

Used with permission of York Public Schools, York NE

Principals give voice to stakeholders by

- conducting early childhood education surveys,
- interviewing representative stakeholders,
- holding focus groups,
- inviting committee membership,
- sponsoring open forums on early childhood education, and
- hosting community coffees.

Following are reminders for principals as they consider their leadership and work with stakeholders. Principals will need to work collaboratively with community stakeholders in creating high-quality early childhood programs.

- Planning for involvement of stakeholders is a necessary first step in collaboration. By examining the school community, a principal can determine the natural allies and supports for an initiative. Similarly, a principal should examine the school community for forces that may resist an initiative.
- The principal needs to be alert to the perceived threat public schools pose to care providers' business interests. Consensus building, community dialogues, and trust building are essential parts of the planning process.
- The principal's task is to enlist stakeholders in support of early childhood education. To accomplish this objective, a principal follows the steps similar to those used to introduce other innovations in a school.
- The principal is an information conduit. The principal provides information to the individuals whose support will be necessary for the successful implementation or expansion of early childhood education.
- The benefits of early childhood education must be articulated.
- Principals who speak out about the importance of high-quality early childhood education in their communities take that position based on evidence that children benefit. They are more likely to succeed in school; they develop stronger, more positive relationships with adults and peers; and they are likely to have long-term education, social, and financial gains. Principals are strongest and most credible as advocates when they combine their knowledge of research and advocacy from other groups with examples from their own experience, such as
  - ○ children who made gains in learning and behavior during their preK experience,
  - ○ children who succeeded in kindergarten and beyond as a result of their experience, and
  - ○ declines in behavior problems in the school as a result of succeeding in preK (NAESP, 2005b, p. 75).
- Benefits are specific to each of the stakeholder groups. The principal's task is to emphasize the direct and indirect benefits of involvement in the development of high-quality early childhood programs. The benefits include those that are educational as well as those that are economic (VMAssociates, 2002).
- The principal should develop a handbook or fact sheet of answers to frequently asked questions concerning early childhood education. This resource can be widely disseminated and provides a consistent flow of information. Organizations and individuals who can advocate for early childhood education must be enlisted to garner their support.

- The accessible, comprehensive data in the manual provide powerful information for advocacy conversations. A communication plan to disseminate information about the benefits of early childhood education and the availability of early childhood programs should be developed. All stakeholders should be included in the communication network. Newsletters, newspaper articles, electronic communications, flyer distribution, and postings should be part of the communication plan.
- Posting early childhood information on the school Web site should be part of the plan. Church bulletins and bulletin boards in public spaces like public libraries should be used to disseminate early childhood program information.
- Developing and maintaining a calendar of events is useful to all stakeholders. Principals should network with community education, early childhood family education, and other elementary schools to avoid conflicting dates and events.
- Awareness of the importance of early childhood education will be heightened through these techniques. Recruitment and enrollment of young children will be facilitated by the dissemination of this information.
- The principal must seek stakeholders, partners, or collaborators who reflect a variety of perspectives, experiences, cultures, and levels of authority. Broad and diverse representation can help groups identify new and innovative strategies as well as bring together resources that are flexible and comprehensive (Brown, 2003).
- All stakeholders must be involved. Involvement can be direct or indirect. Those who have the power to effect change as well as representatives of families whose lives will be affected should be included (Brown, 2003).
- Consider three levels of critical stakeholders:
  - Decision makers will need to approve and finance plans. In a school district, the school board must approve and finance plans.
  - Staff members implement plans. In a school, staff members include teachers, teacher assistants, or paraprofessionals, secretaries, administrative assistants, food service personnel, custodians, bus drivers, volunteers, and administrators.
  - Consumers are impacted by plans. The consumers of an early childhood program are students, parents, and guardians (B. Smith, 2002).
- The principal must enlist the willingness of supporters, advocates, and collaborating agencies to learn about and establish trust with each other. This requires the interpersonal skills of the principal as well as the principal's initiative in seeking the involvement of these individuals and agencies. The principal is in the point position and must lead in this process.
- In order to develop a community coalition on early childhood education, a meeting of stakeholders should be convened. The individuals who are invited to a planning meeting need to have a positive attitude toward early childhood education and be willing to work together in a planning process. The objective of the meeting is to build commitment and ownership of a partnership or collaboration (Fullan, 1991). Individuals invited to a planning meeting need to be in administrative roles with decision-making authority. They need to be able to speak on behalf of their organizations.
- The principal must recognize the time and resources that need to be invested in building trust with potential supporters, advocates, and collaborating agencies. Time must be invested in learning about the commitments of each person and organization to early childhood education so that the strengths of each are realized.

- The principal must anticipate resistance to the school's involvement in early childhood. In some cases, the school may be perceived as a competitor with private providers.

  > In meeting with other early care and early education providers, principals should be aware that the school may be seen as a competitor, especially by family child care providers and centers that serve the entire range of young children beginning with infants and toddlers. (NAESP, 2005b, p. 30)

  > These perceptions must be addressed. Public schools serve the needs of a population that typically would not have access to early childhood education in a private setting.

- Some individuals are resistant to change. Others may fear losing power. In all cases, the principal must emphasize the goal of achieving excellence in early childhood education for the benefit of all young children.

- The agenda for meetings should focus on goals, objectives, needs assessment, resource assessment, action steps, participants, desired outcomes, and measures of goal accomplishment (evaluation). A time frame for meetings should be established and followed.

- Principals should develop an evaluation process that will be used to review progress and measure goal accomplishment (VMAssociates, 2002). As data are collected, principals should report the findings, outcomes, and successes to all stakeholders. If possible, principals should enumerate the benefits achieved through early childhood education in the school and school district. The steady flow of information will increase support and awareness of the importance of early childhood education.

- Principals need to identify external resources that will assist the development of early childhood programs. Typically, school funding is not an elementary principal's role. As the defunding of public schools progresses, however, school leaders must become entrepreneurial. Being recognized as an early childhood leader will strengthen a principal's ties to potential opportunity dollars. Being alert to incentive programs, innovation grants, and pilot programs may result in new dollars previously unavailable.

  > More and more monies are tied to collaboratives and partnerships. A savvy principal who is engaged in early childhood education, part of a coalition, or part of the "network" will automatically become far more "in-the-know" about grants . . . and if the public school can partner with county agencies, higher education, or local health care units—they will be in a better position of strength to be awarded monies. (G. Zierdt, personal communication, March 17, 2008)

- One of the goals of collaboration should be to strengthen the linkages between private providers of early childhood education and the public schools. Since children from private settings often transition to the public schools and because the ultimate goal is the best education for all young children, it is essential to nurture the relationships between community settings and school settings. An important source for connecting to private care settings is the Child Care Resource & Referral (CCR&R) Network. This organization works with care providers in regional settings. Sharing curricula, best practices research, events, access to special programming, professional development opportunities, and resources should be considerations in collaborations. Strengthening relationships will help reduce resistance to public school involvement in early childhood education.

Working with stakeholders demands excellent interpersonal skills. The outcome of developing positive, productive relationships with stakeholders is an excellent educational experience for young children!

PRINCIPALS' ROLES

Working With Stakeholders

1. Serve as information conduit.

2. Promote the educational and economic benefits of early childhood education.

3. Invest time in early childhood education.

4. Identify early childhood eucation resources.

5. Anticipate resistance to early childhood education.

6. Seek a variety of perspectives and experiences for early childhood education discussions.

7. Enlist support for early childhood education.

8. Involve all stakeholders in early childhood education.

9. Give voice to stakeholders.

Resources

Council of Chief State School Officers
http://www.ccsso.org/projects/Early_Childhood_and_Family_Education/

ECS StateNote, "Technology and Early Childhood Professional Development"
http://www.ecs.org/clearinghouse/39/15/3915.pdf

KidsCount Snapshot, "Disconnected Kids: Children Without a Phone at Home"
http://www.aecf.org/upload/publicationfiles/disconnected%20kids.pdf

Nebraska Early Childhood Training Center
http://ectc.nde.ne.gov/

The Education Commission of the States, State-Funded PreK Profiles
http://www.ecs.org/clearinghouse/27/24/2724.htm

Education Commission of the States. Pre-kindergarten Quick Facts, 2003
http://www.ecs.org/ecsmain.asp?page=/html/IssuesEL.asp

Trust for Early Education
http://www.trustforearlyed.org/

Developmentally Appropriate Practice

There is a certain look and feel to high-quality early childhood classrooms. One principal summed it up this way:

> When I walk into the preschool or first grade the first thing I look for is children and teachers in action.
>
> **Children in action**: children busy constructing, creating with multimedia, enjoying books, exploring, experimenting, inventing, finding out, building, composing and problem-solving.
>
> **Teachers in action**: teachers busy holding conversations, guiding activities, questioning children, challenging children's thinking, observing, drawing conclusions, and planning and monitoring activities throughout the day.
>
> When I see this kind of action, I am confident children are learning and that teachers are too. (Kostelnik et al., 2007, p. 1)

Action-oriented practices like these are often described as developmentally appropriate. Today, it is nearly impossible to discuss early childhood education without mentioning developmentally appropriate practice, commonly referred to as DAP. In early childhood circles, DAP represents the standard of best practice on which many early childhood teaching strategies and curricula are based (see Box 5.1.) Any teacher with formal training in early childhood education will have encountered DAP and will wonder how knowledgeable and supportive her administrator may be regarding DAP in the classroom. Thus, principals and superintendents charged with supervising early childhood programs and personnel need to be familiar with DAP so they can interact effectively with staff and make informed decisions about programs and practice.

Box 5.1
Examples of Organizations That Corroborate DAP Principles

The most significant effort to define and catalogue practices associated with DAP has been carried out by the National Association for the Education of Young Children (NAEYC). A professional organization numbering more than one hundred thousand members, NAEYC first put forward guidelines for best early childhood practices in 1987. That work has been updated and is now available in *Developmentally Appropriate Practice in Early Childhood Programs Serving Children from Birth through Age 8: Position Statement* (NAEYC, 2009).

Throughout the past decade, the principles associated with DAP have been corroborated by other professional organizations such as

- the National Association of State Boards of Education,
- the National Association of Elementary School Principles,
- the American Association of Colleges of Teacher Education,
- the National Association of Early Childhood Specialists in State Departments of Education,
- the Council for Exceptional Children, Division for Early Childhood,
- the International Reading Association,
- Association for Childhood Education International,
- the National Education Association, and
- the National Academy of Education.

FUNDAMENTAL PRINCIPLES OF DAP

Developmentally appropriate practice involves teaching children what they need to know using strategies that match their developmental needs and abilities (Warner & Sower, 2005). Teachers who utilize DAP make judgments about children and teaching based on their understanding of three interrelated principles:

1. What they know about **how children develop and learn**

2. What they know about the strengths, needs, and interests of **individual children**

3. What they know about the **social and cultural contexts** in which children live

In thinking about the programs they plan and implement, early childhood educators pose these questions: "Is this activity, interaction, or experience age appropriate? Is it individually appropriate? Is it socially and culturally appropriate?" To conform to standards of DAP, the answer to each of these queries must be yes. See Figure 5.1.

Figure 5.1 The Interrelated Dimensions of DAP

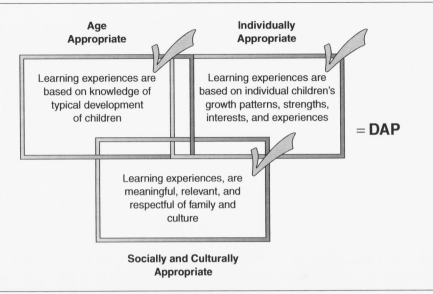

Source: Adapted with permission from T. Udell, P. Deardorff, G. Glasenapp, and D. Norris, 2001, *Developmentally Appropriate Practice,* Teaching Research Institute, Western Oregon University, Monmouth.

DAP Is Age Appropriate

What difference is there in the learning capacity of a 36-year-old versus a 38-year-old? For most of us, this would be a difficult question to answer. In adults, it is hard to predict much about learning based simply on age. Not so with children! During the early years, age tells us a lot. Think about the vast difference between a 1- and a 3-year old, or between a kindergartner and a second grader. Two years or even several months can represent substantial differences in what children know and what they can do (Copple & Bredekamp, 2006)!

Although chronological age is not a guaranteed measure of children's abilities, it does serve a helpful role in gauging children's understandings, capabilities, and characteristics. Consider Jeremy, four years old, and Todd, seven years old. If both children are developing in typical fashion, we can predict the following:

Language   Jeremy has command of more than a one thousand word vocabulary; Todd's range of words could exceed ten thousand words.

Emotions   Jeremy is beginning to recognize common emotions in himself and in others (e.g., happy, mad, sad, afraid). He bases this recognition on overt expressions of emotion, such as laughing or crying. Todd identifies a much wider range of feelings (e.g., pride, satisfaction, disgust) and more subtle variations in how they are expressed.

Social   Jeremy responds to reasons for classroom rules that center around keeping people and property safe. (For instance, we wear a paint smock so we don't get paint on our clothes.) Todd will have expanded his understandings to include people's rights, emotions, and what is fair. (For instance, Sally has been waiting a long time for her turn. It is time for her to have a chance at the computer.)

Cognition   Jeremy can likely count to twenty by rote and grasp concepts like biggest, same, and more. He can create sets of objects based on a single common property (such as color or texture or size). Todd can count from memory far beyond twenty (by ones, twos, and fives) and understands ideas that are more complex, such as small, smaller, and smallest and first, second, and last. He can create sets of objects according to multiple properties (color and size), and he can create subsets and supersets.

These distinctions between Jeremy and Todd result from more than simple accumulated experience. They come about due to actual changes in the children's cognitive structures and physical abilities. As children mature, they undergo both qualitative and quantitative changes in how they conceptualize the world, how they take in information, how they organize their experiences and in how they act on the environments in which they live. This clearly affects how they learn and what is meaningful to them.

Effective early childhood teachers understand the nuances and benchmarks of child development and use that information to create age-appropriate learning environments. Knowledge of child development helps them establish reasonable expectations of what might be interesting, safe, achievable, and challenging for children to do at different points in time (NAEYC, 2009). Such age-related understandings provide a strong foundation for developing curricula; planning, designing, sequencing, and pacing activities; diagnosing student learning needs; assessing student progress; organizing the classroom; and teaching process and content skills (Horowitz, Darling-Hammond, & Bransford, 2005).

For instance, children throughout the early childhood period benefit from opportunities to interact with books every day. Jeremy's kindergarten teacher thinks about age appropriateness as she selects picture books that range from no words to a few words per page for the library area of her classroom. The young age of her students further influences her decision to read often to the children in small groups and to include a whole-group book reading time as part of the daily routine. After reading a book aloud to the class, Jeremy's teacher places it in a prominent place for students to "reread" individually during their free-choice time. Todd's teacher also makes age-related choices when she picks books for her second graders. Her classroom library includes books varying from five to fifteen sentences per page, with some short books, some long books, and some chapter books. Children may choose books that have been "leveled" according to difficulty, by gradually working their way through a series of increasingly complex narratives. While the schedule involves a story time each morning and children reading with the teacher individually and in small groups, the older children are independent enough to engage in silent reading or reading with a partner. Thus, these activities are incorporated into the daily routine as well. Both teachers base their choice of materials and routines on their knowledge of child development and their observations of what five-year-olds and of what seven- and eight-year-olds find doable and challenging.

DAP Is Individually Appropriate

The principle of individual-appropriateness helps us remember that although children within a common age group tend to share similar developmental abilities and characteristics, no two children are exactly alike. Every child is a unique being, the result of a combination of tens of thousands of genes inherited from his parents. Consequently, each has an individual pattern and timing of growth, as well as a unique personality and learning style (Kostelnik, Whiren, Soderman, & Gregory, 2009). Certain children are more physical than others; some prefer time alone while others crave company; some children are skillful readers at five years of age and others achieve reading proficiency two to three years later. In addition, each child brings a different combination of prior experience to the classroom that further differentiates one child from another. All these variations must be considered in the design, application, and evaluation of program activities. Interactions and expectations must also be tailored to address the needs of specific children in the classroom.

Individual differences you might observe in five- and six-year-olds' knowledge of the natural world were evident during a recent visit by a wildlife specialist to the Buffalo County (Wisconsin) After School Program. The specialist came to show students some varieties of turtles that lived in their state—mud turtles, painted turtles, and wood turtles. The children were fascinated.

Alan: Those are some funny animals. Can I touch one?

The specialist nodded yes, and guided the child's hand to gently touch a wood turtle.

Beth: I can see his eyes and his tail. Where are his ears?

Specialist: Turtle ears are inside their heads. Their ears don't have any outside parts. Nothing sticks out, that helps them swim faster.

CJ: We have turtles in our pond. That one is just like ours at home. That one is different. I never saw one of those before.

Susan: Do they bite? Do they eat people?

Denise: No, they just eat fruit and stuff—you know stuff falls off the trees and bushes and they eat it. (Kostelnik, et al., 2007, p. 47)

The children spent the next several minutes watching the turtles, asking questions and talking about what they saw and knew. Listening carefully, their teacher noted that each child brought some prior knowledge to the experience, but that knowledge was not the same for everyone. Alan had a concept of animals. Beth recognized some of the turtles' body parts. CJ had prior experience with turtles and could distinguish one kind of turtle from another. Susan knew animals needed to eat. Denise was aware that turtles didn't eat people, but ate things available in nature. Thus, within this small group children's understandings ranged from very little to considerable, and from less accurate to more accurate.

Based on the DAP principle of individual appropriateness, Ms. Morris, the children's teacher, responds to these differences rather than ignoring them. She observes the children carefully and makes specific plans and modifications to accommodate children's varying degrees of interest and understanding. She plans some lessons to expand children's awareness of the basic characteristics and needs of turtles; she also plans activities to challenge children who already know a lot about turtles and who stand to benefit from more in-depth study of their habits and habitats. In carrying out these plans, the teacher takes into account what the students are ready for and what they need to learn. She chooses tasks that are challenging but achievable, and she organizes the classroom so each student has a chance to understand and apply new information and skills. Finally, she monitors the children's progress to gain insights into what the children are learning, how they are learning, and what reasonable next steps might be (Horowitz et al., 2005). In this way, the principle of individual appropriateness helps Ms. Morris support children's success and continued engagement in the learning process.

DAP Is Socially and Culturally Appropriate

Culture provides a framework for our lives. It is the paradigm humans use to guide their behavior, find meaning in events, interpret the past, and set aspirations. (Robles de Melendez, 2007, p. 44)

Nothing escapes the influence of culture. The foods people enjoy, the words they use, how they spend their waking hours, the customs they keep, what they find funny or offensive, how people behave, and what they believe is authentic, right, or wrong all come about as the result of social and cultural influences. Culture is defined by values, traditions, and beliefs that are shared and passed down from one generation to the next.

Growing up as members of a family and community, children learn the rules of their culture—explicitly through direct teaching and implicitly through the behavior of those around them. Among the rules they learn are how to show respect, how to interact with people they know well as compared to those they just met, how to organize time and personal space, how to dress, what and when to eat, how to respond to major life transitions and celebrations, how to worship, and countless other behaviors that humans perform with little apparent thought everyday. (NAEYC, Bredekamp & Copple, 1996b, p. 42)

Because culture is such an integral part of the human experience, to create meaningful and supportive early childhood programs, we must continually consider children within the context of their family, their community, and their culture. The third principle of DAP, therefore, is social and cultural appropriateness. Consider this principle in the following classroom interactions.

Interaction 1

Ms. Wallace notices two four-year-olds disagreeing over a magnifying glass at the science table. Their voices are becoming shrill, and some minor grabbing ensues. She approaches the children, carefully separates them, and begins to talk with them about their argument. Chico stands quietly, eyes downcast. Ms. Wallace says, "Chico, I want you to listen carefully. Look at me when I'm talking to you." Chico keeps his head down. Ms. Wallace gently lifts Chico's chin and insists that the child look her in the eye to show that he is attentive. In a few minutes, the children agree to look for a second magnifier so both can have one to use.

Interaction 2

Ms. Johnson overhears two four-year-olds disagreeing over who will get to paint at the easel next. Their voices are becoming shrill and some minor grabbing ensues. The teacher approaches the children, carefully separates them, and begins to talk with them about their argument. Amalia stands quietly, eyes downcast. Ms. Johnson keeps talking with the children. In a few minutes they agree to share the easel with each child taking a side for herself.

In both episodes, the teachers reacted calmly and made a genuine effort to help children work through typical classroom problems. Each adult relied on reasoning rather than harsh words to guide the interaction. All of these behaviors fit professional standards of practice for early childhood educators. However, there was a difference between the adults. Ms. Wallace insisted that Chico look her full in the face to signal his attention. Ms. Johnson did not require the same of

Amalia. Amalia's teacher was operating according to the principle of socially and culturally appropriate practice; Chico's was not.

Ms. Johnson understood that in many Latin American and Asian families, children show respect for adults by avoiding their gaze, especially when being corrected (Trawick-Smith, 2009). She realized Amalia was listening, even though she wasn't looking directly at the teacher. Ms. Wallace misinterpreted Chico's behavior as inattentive or disrespectful. She mistakenly assumed that because her own cultural upbringing made eye contact synonymous with respect, the same was true for Chico and all children in the class. That assumption was faulty. Requiring Chico to "look her in the eye" ran counter to important family and cultural teachings that were integral to Chico's understanding of the world. Even if she didn't mean to, Ms. Wallace communicated that Chico's family code was inappropriate and that Chico was less valuable than other children who were more familiar with the behavioral customs she understood to be correct (Chipman, 1997). Although a workable solution for sharing was reached in both classrooms, there was an unnecessary social cost attached to Ms. Wallace's interaction with Chico that could have been avoided. Had the teacher been more aware of her own cultural perspectives and had she been more cognizant as well as respectful of cultural contexts that differed from her own, her interaction with Chico could have been more effective.

Educators committed to DAP work hard to learn about the cultural beliefs that children bring from home. They understand that the more congruent expectations are between family and school, the more productively children learn. When they are unsure about culture, they make an effort to find out. As they seek to understand and apply what might be meaningful to and respectful of children and their families, educators are acting in accordance with the principle of social and cultural appropriateness.

The Interrelated Nature of DAP

The principles of age appropriateness, individual appropriateness, and social and cultural appropriateness are intertwined. Considered as a whole, they form a comprehensive framework for thinking about, planning, implementing, and evaluating high-quality programs for young children. Most important, DAP requires everyone responsible for educating young children to recognize that children are not miniature adults. Early childhood is a distinct time of life both qualitatively and quantitatively unlike later childhood or adolescence. Having said this, we also must remember that children are individuals whose needs and abilities vary even among peers. Consequently, DAP tells us to think of children as distinct persons, each of whom is like no one else. Finally, DAP underscores the powerful influence family, culture, and community have on young children's learning. Decisions about how children are taught and what they are taught cannot be properly made without considering the social and cultural worlds in which children are being brought up. All of these understandings need to be reflected in the content and strategies that characterize early childhood programs as well as in the training of early childhood personnel. As you read the next section of this chapter, consider how the three interrelated principles of DAP are evident in the practices described.

A Dozen Practices Typically Associated with DAP

The current NAEYC document, *Developmentally Appropriate Practice in Early Childhood Programs*, gives examples of appropriate and inappropriate practices for infants and toddlers, children ages three to five years, children ages five to six years, and children ages six through eight years. Refer to Table 5.1 for an example of how such practices are described in relation to assessment.

Table 5.1   Examples of Appropriate Practices and Inappropriate Practices Related to Assessing Children's Learning and Development—Integrating Assessment with Teaching and Curriculum

	Appropriate Practices	*In Contrast*
Three-to five-year-olds	• Teachers use assessment to refine how they plan and implement activities. • Teachers develop short- and long-range plans for each child and the group based on children's knowledge, skills, interests and other factors.	• There is no accountability for what children are doing and little focus on supporting their learning and development.
Five- to six-year-olds	• Teachers assess children on an ongoing basis (i.e., observe, ask, listen in, check). They collect and later reflect on documentation of children's learning and development, including written notes, photographs, recordings and work samples. They use this information in shaping their teaching moment by moment and in planning learning experiences	• Teachers don't determine where each child is in learning a new skill or concept, so they give every child the same learning experiences as every other child. • Assessment results go straight into a folder and are filed away. They are not reflected on to inform teachers how to help or challenge individual children.
Six-to eight-year-olds	• Assessment is consistent with the developmental and learning goals identified for children and expressed in the primary curriculum.	• Assessments look at goals not in the curriculum—or content not taught to the children—and often include skills or methods not used in the classroom • Assessments narrow and/or distort the curriculum when teachers "teach to the test."

As you can see from Table 5.1, inappropriate practice sometimes reflects errors of omission (ignoring assessment altogether) as well as errors of commission (teaching to the test). Appropriate practices are often defined between these extremes (carrying out systematic assessment based on observations of child performance and student work samples). There are twelve overarching practices that capture the essence of DAP in programs:

1.   Adults build warm, caring relationships with children. Teachers and principals get to know children as individuals. They take time to talk with children and to interact with them in ways that provide opportunities for development of positive self-identity, social competence, and intellectual growth.

2. Child guidance is directed toward helping children achieve self-regulation. Teachers engage children in the rule-making process and patiently remind children of classroom rules as well as the rationales behind them. When rules are broken, adults reason with children. If necessary, they enact logical consequences to help children learn more appropriate conduct from the act of being corrected. Teachers model for children the skills they need to solve problems on their own and support children in resolving conflicts that arise. Teachers also recognize that acknowledging children's positive behavior is critical in helping children learn to behave more successfully.

3. Curricula are comprehensive. Aesthetic, affective, cognitive, language, social, and physical development and learning are dealt with regularly, as are critical subject matter areas. Typical curriculum areas include

- social and emotional development,
- language development,
- literacy development,
- mathematics,
- technology,
- scientific inquiry and knowledge,
- understanding ourselves and our communities,
- creative expression and appreciation for the arts, and
- physical health and development (NAESP, 2005; NAEYC 2005).

4. Curricula address the learning needs of all children. Activities are planned for a wide developmental range. Program planning, implementation, and evaluation are adjusted to accommodate variations in children's learning needs, abilities, levels of functioning, and interests. All children, including children with disabilities, are included as full participants in the classroom community. The environment, activities, and staff interactions reflect understanding and respect for the diverse backgrounds and cultures children and families bring to the program.

5. Curricula are integrated. Children have opportunities to make connections across disciplines through integrative projects and activities that combine subject areas such as math and science, or reading and technology.

Mr. Bergstrom Knows his Kids

Jerry Bergstrom, principal of Pershing Elementary School in Lexington, Nebraska, was recently named his state's principal of the year. During the recognition ceremony, several of the youngest students shared their thoughts about their principal's best qualities. Most (though not all) of their comments focused on his relationship with them:

○ He is nice to me.
○ He knows my name.
○ He says hi to me every day.
○ He smiles a lot.
○ He's fun.
○ He has a shiny, bald head.
○ He is friendly.
○ He listens when I talk to him.
○ He knows about kid stuff.
○ He knows how to listen.
○ He likes me.
○ He never yells.

Principals like Mr. Bergstrom as well as classroom teachers have a big role to play in creating early childhood environments in which young children feel valued and safe. Strong supportive relationships are key.

6. **Children have many opportunities to learn through firsthand experiences.** The early childhood classroom is filled with hands-on materials for children to directly manipulate, listen to, smell, touch, taste, and observe. The activities in which they participate are relevant and meaningful to them. New concepts are introduced by giving children chances to work with the real thing (e.g., real leaves) before asking children to learn via more abstract means such as looking at pictures or listening to verbal descriptions.

7. **Children initiate many activities and make choices about how they will learn.** Children are treated as active contributors to the learning process. Each day is planned to give children a variety of activities, learning formats (e.g., small-group, large-group, or independent work), and materials from which to choose and pursue educational goals. The same goal is addressed in multiple ways, which allow children to learn content and skills via means that best suit their learning styles and interests.

8. **Classroom environments are safe and stimulating and routines are well suited to the needs of young children.** Classrooms are designed to be safe, while enabling children to develop appropriate levels of independence. Children have access to a wide array of worthwhile learning experiences, involving interesting materials as well as opportunities to work alone, with peers, and with adults. Objects and routines enhance children's abilities to explore, discuss, investigate, solve problems, practice, encounter new knowledge, learn from errors, and apply what they know in meaningful ways. Routines enable children to move freely, to become absorbed in their learning, and to avoid long periods of inactivity or waiting.

9. **Teachers assume a variety of roles and use a wide array of strategies to support children's development and learning.** Depending on the situation, teachers function as observers, planners, diagnosticians, designers, instructors, and evaluators (Kostelnik et al., 2007). They develop routines that include individual, small-group, and whole-group instruction. The learning activities in which children participate range from exploratory child-initiated experiences to direct instruction by the adult. Teachers address subject-matter content and learning standards while framing instructional choices around the needs of the children— taking into account age, individual rates of development, and social and cultural contexts. This large amalgamation of teacher roles and strategies is not always understood. See Box 5.2 for some misperceptions of DAP.

10. **Children have many opportunities to learn through play.** Play is an integral part of the early childhood classroom. It is recognized as an important means through which young children actively construct meaning and expand their knowledge and skills. Play is not viewed merely as a reward or a time for children to "let off steam."

11. **Assessment is continuous, multidimensional, and observation based.** Teachers gather information about what children know and can do through observations, by making written records, and by collecting children's work samples. Assessment happens in the classroom, on the playground, in the halls, and at meal times. It covers all curricular domains. Assessment is an ongoing process, not an isolated event. Results are used to inform teachers of children's progress, their needs, and what modifications or follow-up plans might best support their learning.

Box 5.2

Some Misperceptions About DAP

Misperception A

DAP compatible curriculum is derived solely from child interests. Adults cannot introduce subject-matter content or material derived from curriculum standards that children have not expressed curiosity about first.

Reality

Curriculum for young children is based on a combination of child-interests and curriculum-related topics (these are not always different or incompatible). Many activities in DAP classrooms come about through child exploration and initiation; others are introduced by the teacher to spark children's interest in something new.

Misperception B

Teachers in DAP classrooms do not engage in explicit instruction. Teachers support children's explorations, but never teach children information or skills directly.

Reality

Developmentally appropriate practices encompass a continuum of instructional techniques from open-ended experiences to outcomes-focused lessons; from child-directed to adult-directed approaches; from pervasive to targeted strategies; from purposeful plans to taking advantage of teachable moments.

See Chapters 7, 8, 11, and 13 for detailed information about DAP-related curricula and teacher practices.

---

12. Education involves reciprocal relationships with families. Families are valued as partners and decision makers in childhood learning. Classroom activities incorporate ideas and languages from children's homes and cultures into the early childhood environment. Family members are welcome to observe, discuss, recommend policies, and participate in the program's activities. Reciprocal relationships are established. These are characterized by mutual respect, cooperation, shared responsibility, and a willingness to seek common ground when differences arise (Copple & Bredekamp, 2006; NAESP, 2005).

These twelve Overarching Principles of DAP are summarized in Box 5.3.

Take a moment to consider the classroom depicted in Box 5.4. Which of the twelve principles of DAP are illustrated in this example?

Box 5.3

The Essence of DAP

- Adults build warm, caring relationships with children.
- Child guidance is directed toward helping children achieve self-regulation.
- Curricula address the whole child.
- Curricula address the learning needs of all children.
- Multiple curricula are integrated.
- Children have many opportunities to learn through firsthand experiences.
- Children initiate activities and make choices about how they will learn.
- Classroom environments are safe and stimulating and routines are well suited to the needs of young children.
- Teachers assume a variety of roles and use a wide array of strategies to support children's development and learning.
- Children have many opportunities to learn through play.
- Assessment is continuous, multidimensional, and observation based.
- Education involves reciprocal relationships with families.

Box 5.4

Sam Cooper's K–1 Classroom

Sam Cooper teaches in a class that includes five- through seven-year-olds in a public elementary school. During the few minutes we observe his large, attractive classroom, we see a number of groups containing three to five children busy in several areas of the classroom. Three children are talking to each other as they puzzle over a computer game. Four boys are sitting at a round table, busy with notebooks, crayons, pencils and markers. One boy explains to us that they are writing in their journals. Sam arrives at that point, and responds to one child's comment about his work with a specific and enthusiastic response that indicates his familiarity with the child's story. He encourages another child to share his idea with a peer, and suggests to a third child that his friend help him figure out his spelling for the word he asked about.

Sam surveys the room, and moves over to two girls who are in a heated discussion about balancing objects on a scale. Sam does not interrupt, listening seriously to each child's point of view, nodding thoughtfully, and then asking a question. As the girls try the scales again, Sam looks around at other busy children. He notices a child standing by the bookshelf, moves over to discuss his selection, and speaks with him quietly, finally leaving him after a pat and a smile. A child and adult enter the classroom. Sam moves over to greet them both, and engages in relaxed conversation with the parent, who seems equally relaxed with Sam. Sam gives the children a prearranged signal to gather at the meeting carpet; the parent has been invited in advance to conduct a mini-lesson about American sign language, since children are so interested right now in different methods of communication.

Source: Reprinted from *The Essentials of Early Education,* by C. Gestwicki, 1997, p. 60. Copyright 1997 by Thomson/Delmar Learning, Clifton Park, NY. Used with permission of the publisher.

DEVELOPMENTALLY INAPPROPRIATE PRACTICE

Procedures that are contrary to or undermine the twelve DAP practices just described are characterized as developmentally inappropriate practices (DIP). Teachers demonstrate DIP when they do one or more of the following:

- Fail to establish and maintain supportive relationships with children
- Engage in behavior management practices that focus on punishments and children's mistakes
- Fail to address problem behaviors that violate safety, damage property, or disrespect the rights of others
- Create environments that impede self-regulation
- Focus on only one or two developmental domains (e.g., cognitive or social), while ignoring the rest
- Expect all children to learn the same thing at the same time in the same way
- Create programs in which children have few opportunities to pursue challenging but achievable educational goals: teacher-directed activities dominate, children are passive receivers of information rather than active problem solvers and constructors of meaning, adults miss opportunities to extend children's higher-order thinking
- Maintain curricula in which one lesson has little relation to another and in which children have few opportunities to integrate learning across subject areas
- Give children few opportunities to make real choices or practice decision making
- Create lessons that involve limited firsthand experience and hands-on learning, relying mostly on paper and pencil activities
- Develop routines that are too hurried, too rigid, or are otherwise unresponsive to children's need to move about freely and interact with peers
- Fail to plan adequately
- Treat play as frivolous and something apart from learning
- Ignore assessment, assess children's learning through a single high-stakes test, or fail to link assessment and planning
- Ignore family members or treat them as adversaries

For examples of DIP and DAP in action see Box 5.5.

Kindergarten A with its rigid schedule, narrow focus, and requirement that teachers stick with the prescribed lesson plan so strictly that all other learning opportunities are ignored illustrates developmentally inappropriate practices with young children. Kindergarten B, in which teachers pursue curricular goals while having the freedom to respond to children's interests outside the "tested" curricula, is illustrating DAP. Most likely these differences were obvious to you. Sometimes, the distinctions between DAP and DIP are more subtle.

Box 5.5

DIP and DAP in the Kindergarten

A reporter for *Education Week* visited two kindergartens in the same city and came away with two very different impressions.

Kindergarten A

I walked into the kindergarten classroom with the school superintendent and the principal. The well-behaved children were discussing butterflies with their teacher. Then, as we left the room . . . the teacher rushed after us with a panicked look on her face and apologized: "I'm sorry. We had finished our lesson early, and one of the children asked if he could bring his caterpillar to school, which led us to a discussion of how caterpillars turn into butterflies."

   At first I couldn't figure out why the teacher was apologizing and why her supervisors looked displeased. And then I understood: This young teacher was worried because she had committed what is considered taboo at this particular school. She had gone off script. In seizing what she thought was a teachable moment . . . [she had deviated from the prescribed curriculum which was closely aligned to year end tests] . . . this teacher felt she was in danger of receiving a negative evaluation and perhaps even of losing her job. (Gill, 2007, p. 33)

Kindergarten B

The next week, I visited a very different kind of school. In this kindergarten class, the teacher was relaxed and energetic. As the admissions director took me into the classroom, I saw that many of the children were building structures in the sandbox. The teacher smiled and explained to us that the children had acted out the story of the Three Billy Goats Gruff the day before, and that one child had wondered how bridges are built so they don't fall down before they are completed. That night, the teacher phoned one of the fathers, a structural engineer, to invite him to come to the class to explain how bridges are built. He was coming the following day and bringing some models with him; in preparation for his visit the 5- and 6-year-olds were using their own structures to guess what they would learn.

   As we left the room, the admissions director beamed as he explained, "We have a school full of teachers like her—people who constantly think of new ways to get our students excited about the world around them." Obviously bridge building was not specifically identified as part of the kindergarten curriculum, and it would not appear on any high-stakes test. But when the subject came up, the teacher knew she was free to allow her students to use class time to explore a mystery that interested them, and she had the freedom to invite someone in who could answer her students' questions. (Gill, 2007, p. 33)

APPLYING DAP REQUIRES JUDGMENT

Having just read two lists, one outlining developmentally appropriate practices and one depicting potentially inappropriate ones, you might wonder if all it takes to enact DAP is to memorize the items on each list and apply them. While such inventories provide useful reference points, the reality is more complex than that. Every practice must be considered in the context of the children, the physical environment, and the circumstances at hand. Consider the following classroom situations. Try to determine if they represent DAP or DIP.

> The three-year-olds are studying winter weather. The teacher has planned a variety of activities for children to examine how snow is formed and how animals adapt to the cold. DAP or DIP?

> The children have been working in learning centers and soon it will be time for cleanup. The teacher gives a five-minute warning to help children prepare for the upcoming transition. DAP or DIP?

> The teacher has ordered low shelves for her classroom to enable children to independently choose and help themselves to certain classroom materials. DAP or DIP?

Your first impression may be that all of these practices reflect DAP. Certainly, weather is of interest to children, giving children a warning prior to a change in routine is a generally accepted early childhood practice, as is giving children opportunities to make choices. However, closer examination of each situation might prompt you to reconsider.

For instance, the three-year-olds studying winter weather are in southern Mississippi where snow is rare. None of the children has ever seen snow, and there is no snow available for them to examine firsthand. They are learning about snow mainly through pictures and written descriptions. For this age group in this place the topic is not particularly relevant or meaningful. Their time would be better spent studying something more easily accessible in their immediate environment such as local plants and animals.

The transition from learning centers to cleanup will be smoother because of the five-minute warning. However, the children have only had access to the learning centers for fifteen minutes. This is not enough time for them to become absorbed in learning or to carry out meaningful tasks from start to finish. With such limited time, children are likely to feel frustrated and rushed.

Low shelves that enable children to select some materials on their own are common in early childhood settings. However, in this classroom, the shelves are in disarray. Materials are heaped together. Nothing is in a particular place. It is hard to tell what is available and many items are broken or incomplete as a result.

In each of these examples, deciding whether a practice was DAP or DIP required more than memorizing a list of strategies. A practice that might be DAP under one set of circumstances might be DIP under another. To avoid confusing the two, teachers and principals need to look at the context of each situation and ask themselves these three questions:

1. Is this practice in keeping with what we know about child development and learning?

2. Does this practice take into account children's individual strengths and needs?

3. Does this practice demonstrate respect for children's social and cultural lives?

How you respond will depend on your interpretation of what is age-appropriate, what is individually appropriate, and what is socially and culturally appropriate? Conversations about such issues should be common in early childhood programs among all staff members, including principals and superintendents. Your knowledge of child development and learning, your understanding of curriculum development and implementation, your awareness of family and community relationships, your knowledge of assessment and evaluation, and your interpretation of your professional role will all influence your interpretation of DAP and guide the decisions you make relative to the early childhood programs and practices in your school or district (NAEYC, 1996b).

Until now, we have discussed what to "look" for in DAP classrooms. Before we move on, take a moment to consider what to "listen" for as well.

THE SOUNDS OF DAP!

DAP classrooms are seldom silent. Instead, they are filled with the pleasant hum of language: children talking to one another, children talking with adults about their experiences and things that matter to them, adults using language to extend children's understandings and skills. In these rich verbal environments, young children make significant gains in vocabulary development and oral language. Such skills are strong predictors of children's future success as readers and writers, and enhance children's cognitive and social abilities (Justice & Vukelich, 2008).

To create stimulating verbal environments, adults must listen carefully to young children and respond to them in meaningful ways. Unfortunately, careful listening does not come naturally to adults. In fact, unless trained to do otherwise, adults are accurate listeners only about 25 percent of the time. This happens because they are often preoccupied, distracted, or in a hurry to get their ideas across when talking to young children (Kostelnik et al., 2009). Likewise, language has many purposes:

- To express wants and needs
- To regulate or manage others' behavior
- To make contact with others and form relationships
- To promote imagination
- To solve problems
- To express feelings or opinions
- To convey knowledge and facts
- To gain knowledge from others (Halliday, 2006)

Analysis of adult–child interactions reveals that in group settings the majority of adult language (more than 70 percent) is used to regulate children's behavior (e.g., telling children what to do—"Come here," "Sit down," "Turn to page 12"). The other functions, which are more expressive and vocabulary rich, are employed much less often (Kostelnik et al., 2009).

Lack of skillful listening and a predominance of regulatory language detracts from children's overall development and learning. For this reason, teachers with special training in early childhood education learn to listen more effectively and spend less time merely telling children what to do. They converse with children individually and in small groups every day about a whole host of subjects. They also recognize that language is learned not only through listening, but also through talking, and so give children many chances to express themselves. Most important, adults in DAP classrooms encourage children to explore the multiple purposes of language, creating opportunities for relationship building, problem solving, and investigating. Finally, teachers extend children's language skills by the following:

- Posing open-ended questions ("What do you think will happen next?" "How do you think this story will end?")
- Using information talk to describe children's actions and use of materials ("You're building with square blocks." "You found a way to make the pieces fit.")
- Introducing new vocabulary and grammatical structures through paraphrasing (Child: "We are having a snack." Adult: "You and your friend are eating together.")
- Encouraging children to expand on what they are saying ("Tell me more." "And then what happened?")
- Offering children scripts ("Tell him, 'You can have it next.'")
- Scaffolding children's use of language (Adult to children in a pretend restaurant, "Ask Jonathan what this restaurant has for lunch." "That noodle is the longest. It is longer than any of the others.")

These are the sounds you as an administrator need to listen for as you observe early childhood classrooms. The more you hear language used in these ways, the more confident you can be that teachers are engaged in DAP and that young children are learning critical skills. This link between DAP and children's skill development is becoming increasingly clear.

EMPIRICAL SUPPORT FOR DAP

In today's accountability-focused climate the talk is all about evidence-based practice. A natural question for anyone to ask is, "To what extent does research support DAP?" There is good news in this regard. Evidence is mounting that early childhood programs that implement DAP lead to positive learning outcomes for children. When contrasted with programs that ignore DAP principles, DAP-based curricula are more likely to produce long-term gains in children's cognitive development, social and emotional skills, and life-coping capabilities (Dunn & Kontos, 1997; Huffman & Speer, 2000; Marcon, 1999; Montie, Xiang, & Schweinhart, 2006; Wiltz & Klein, 2001). Although there is more to be learned, we have a growing body of data showing that DAP has both immediate and long-lasting benefits for children. See Box 5.6 for a brief summary of what current findings suggest based on studies conducted in the United States. In Box 5.7, important international results are reported.

Box 5.6
Research Findings Associated With DAP

Social Outcomes

Children whose teachers use DAP tend to exhibit

Better social problem-solving skills
More cooperation
More favorable attitudes toward school and teachers
More positive attitudes about themselves as learners
Fewer negative social behaviors
Fewer stress-related behaviors

Cognitive Outcomes

Children whose teachers use DAP tend to exhibit better

Creative thinking skills
Memory skills
Mathematical problem solving skills
Grasp of mathematical concepts
Scientific knowledge and inquiry skills
Reading comprehension
Listening skills

Source: From Marjorie J. Kostelnik, Anne K. Soderman & Alice Phipps Whiren *Developmentally Appropriate Curriculum: Best Practices in Early Childhood Education*, 4/e. Published by Allyn and Bacon/Merrill Education, Boston, MA. Copyright © 2007 by Pearson Education. Reprinted by permission of the publisher.

Box 5.7
International Support for DAP

The largest long-term (1986–2003), multinational (seventeen countries) study ever conducted provides evidence from around the world that programs enhance young children's learning when they

- emphasize child-initiated activities,
- limit the use of whole-group instruction, and
- provide abundant materials in the classroom.

One phase of the study

- followed children from age four through age seven,
- involved five thousand children in two thousand preschool settings,
- controlled for family and cultural influences,
- used data derived from direct observations of children's and teachers' classroom behaviors, and
- involved ten countries, both developed and developing, in Asia, Europe, and North America.

Researchers found that when children participated in preschool at age four, the following results were evident by age seven.

- Language performance was higher if free-choice activities made up most of the preschool day.
- The activities that promoted language development best, in order of influence, were gross motor and fine motor; dramatic play; arts, crafts, and music; preacademic activities involving hands-on materials (reading, writing, numbers, mathematics, physical science, and social science); and personal care.
- Cognitive performance was higher if they experienced more free-choice activities (child chose what, how, and how long to be involved) than whole-group activities (child had little choice of what to do, how to do it, or how long to spend in an activity).
- Cognitive performance was higher when they participated in preschools that had a wide array and abundance of equipment and materials.

These findings, which emphasize child-initiated activities in a variety of domains and which de-emphasize whole-group instruction in a limited set of domains, are consistent with the principles of DAP described in this chapter (International Association for the Evaluation of Educational Achievement, 2008; Montie, Xiang, & Schweinhart, 2006).

COMMON QUESTIONS ABOUT DAP

Our school has all kinds of children—some are well off and others live in poverty. Children are of different races and demonstrate different abilities; some children have special needs. Is DAP suitable for all of these children?

The positive learning outcomes associated with DAP (summarized in Box 5.3) have been recorded for boys and girls, for children from higher-income and lower-income families, for typically developing children and for children with disabilities, as well as for African American and European American students (Hart, Burts, & Charlesworth, 1997; Odom, Wolery, Lieber, & Horn, 2002). At the preschool level, the most powerful results have been recorded for children living in poverty (Bowman et al., 2001; Karoly et al., 2005). The same is not true in classrooms characterized by DIP. In those programs, all children tend to experience poorer outcomes. However, males, children of lower socioeconomic status, and African American children perform least well and report the highest levels of stress (Missouri Department of Elementary and Secondary Education, 2001).

Our district has several programs for children ages three to-8 years—Head Start, a state-funded four-year-old program, a childcare center, kindergarten, first and second-grade classrooms, and a Grades 1 and 2 multiage unit. Can DAP be applied in all these settings?

Strategies associated with DAP can be implemented in all kinds of education settings—formal and nonformal education programs; part time or full day; home-based, center-based, and school-based; private or public; and, not-for-profit and for-profit. DAP has been embraced internationally and is in use in large and small programs as well as in urban, suburban, and rural locations worldwide.

What elements of the early childhood program will DAP influence?

Considering DAP will affect the following:

- Staff qualifications and staffing patterns
- The physical setup of the environment
- The kinds of materials made available to children
- The routines that define the schedule of the day
- The manner in which adults interact with children, including the teacher's role and the social climate she strives to create
- The kinds of activities and lessons teachers provide
- The instructional strategies teachers use in certain situations and in relation to individual children
- The curricula programs adopt
- The goals and standards programs address
- The time teachers spend on formal curricular goals and time spent accommodating children's interests and abilities
- The assessment strategies teachers choose
- The relationship between home and school
- Resource allocations
- The role of classroom practitioners, specialists, and principals

Chapters 6 through 14 provide details regarding what such impacts look like across all these dimensions.

Is DAP only for preschoolers?

DAP is applicable for programs that serve infants, toddlers, preschoolers, and school-aged children. The principles of age appropriateness, individual appropriateness, and social and cultural appropriateness are relevant across the age span. They can be applied effectively from children's earliest education experiences throughout their schooling. In support of this premise, a commission sponsored by the National Academy of Education identified educating teachers for DAP as one of the key elements representing state-of-the-art standards for teacher education at all grade levels (Horowitz et al., 2005).

Where do academics fit in to DAP?

Some people have the impression that academics and DAP do not mix. That is not true. Academics are a natural facet of young children's learning. Children do not wait for grade school to become interested in reading, writing, and mathematics. They manifest literacy-related interests as infants when they mouth a book and again as toddlers when they beg, "Read it again." Young children make lists, write stories, create signs, and otherwise use their own versions of print to communicate messages to others. Likewise, preschoolers count one cookie, two shoes, and three candles on the birthday cake. They compare, "Which has more?" "Who still needs some?" "Is your piece bigger or smaller than mine?" High-quality early childhood programs, therefore, build on children's interests and include relevant academic learning as part of the whole-child profile.

Although academic content is developmentally appropriate, some approaches to academic instruction are poorly suited to how young children learn best. Early learning settings that focus primarily on isolated skill development and those that rely on long periods of whole-group instruction or abstract paper-pencil activities are relying on DIP. Such practices may produce short-term gains, but are not strongly associated with lasting achievement, and may actually yield less-desirable results in the long run (Karoly et al., 2005; Montie et al., 2006; Neuman & Roskos, 2005). Programs that address academic concepts and skills through small-group instruction, active manipulation of relevant or concrete materials, and interactive learning are in line with DAP and the benefits described earlier in this chapter.

With so much concern about literacy, what are some early reading strategies that principals should expect to see in DAP classrooms?

According to the National Early Literacy Panel, there are five elements of language and literacy development that are most predictive of children's later success in reading and writing:

1. Oral language development

2. Phonological/phonemic awareness

3. Alphabetic knowledge

4. Print awareness

5. Invented spelling (Strickland & Shanahan, 2004)

Some language and literacy learning comes about through children's everyday experiences and activities they initiate themselves. Other learning depends on explicit instruction initiated by adults (Armbruster & Osborn, 2001; A. Epstein, 2007). Children's vocabulary acquisition illustrates this combination. Young children learn many new words through day-to-day conversations with adults and peers. Talk that centers around child-initiated topics are particularly rich vocabulary builders. In addition, children absorb new words through book reading with adults and through play-based activities such as storytelling, singing songs, and pretending with others. Concurrently, children develop important vocabulary skills when they are deliberately taught individual words and word-learning strategies, such as listening for certain letter sounds or using particular vocabulary words in a written message. Neither day-to-day child-initiated activities nor explicit adult-initiated instruction is sufficient on its own. Children need both kinds of experiences.

DAP classrooms address all five literacy elements purposefully and in ways that correspond to how young children develop and learn. Researchers have found that experiences with storybook reading, discussions about books, listening for comprehension, and writing are essential for all young learners, but especially for children who have few such experiences at home. Consequently, the International Reading Association (IRA) recommends that the preschool curriculum "emphasize a wide range of language and literacy experiences including, but not limited to, story reading, dramatic play, storytelling and retelling" (IRA, 2005, p. 2). Teachers are further encouraged to model reading and writing for many purposes, to regularly employ language extension strategies with children, and to include reading and writing routines as part of the daily schedule. It is especially effective for teachers to introduce language and literacy lessons in small-group or circle-time activities, and then follow up with children during free-choice and other learning-center times (Justice & Vukelich, 2008; Neuman, 2007).

The Abecedarian Project, an early learning program targeting at-risk children that we highlighted in Chapter 1, illustrates this purposeful integration of strategies. That program zeroed in on children's language development intensely every day. Teachers carried out extended conversations with each child, provided children with daily reading experiences, created literacy-infused learning centers, offered children a rich array of play-based activities in multiple domains, and explicitly taught prephonics concepts and skills to children individually twice a week. All of these strategies align with principles of DAP and are key elements of effective literacy instruction in early childhood.

What about scripted reading instruction in early childhood. Is it DAP or DIP?

Knowing that children benefit from direct instruction in certain early literacy skills such as phonological awareness and alphabet knowledge, some early learning settings are choosing scripted curricula to help teachers deliver instruction. The upside to scripted teaching is that it can help teachers who are not reading experts carry out a sequenced series of lessons around important reading-related content. Such scripts may provide initial scaffolding for staff learning new strategies or help teachers better grasp how to target their instruction more effectively for some struggling readers (Christie, 2008; G. Trainin, personal communication, February 22, 2008). The downside to scripted instruction is that teachers may not pay adequate attention to individual children's needs (some children may already know the material, for example; some children may answer in chorus without really grasping key concepts). Some teachers adopt a "drill and kill" style that can dim children's enthusiasm for reading over their lifetime (Katz, 2008; Wilson, 2008). Some scripted programs require so much classroom time that children have inadequate opportunities to experience other facets of literacy such as story telling and retelling, or to engage in self-selected activities, or to participate in other areas of the curriculum, such as science, art, or music. Some programs are really designed for older children, which makes them unsuitable for preschoolers or kindergartners. How all these issues are addressed influences whether particular applications of scripted instruction are DAP or DIP. Here are some questions to ask and factors to consider when making those judgments.

Questions to Ask Yourself	What the Research Tells Us	Practices That Tip Toward DIP
How long will the instruction last?	With young children, a little direct instruction (including scripted instruction) can go a long way. Short lessons are best. Effective direct instruction lessons for preschoolers and kindergartners range from five to twenty minutes at a time (Christie, 2008). Lessons may be a few times a week or daily (Karoly et al., 2005; Neuman, 2007).	Children spend extended periods (thirty minutes at a time per half-day session) in scripted instruction activities. Multiple teacher-directed instructional periods are carried out in a day, leaving less than one-third of the daily schedule devoted to child-selected activities.
Is scripted instruction the best choice for what is being taught?	A variety of teaching methods contributes to children's success in learning to read (Armbruster & Osborn, 2002; Christie, 2008). Scripted instruction is a supplemental curriculum to other early literacy strategies (R. R. Nelson, Cooper, & Gonzalez, 2007). Direct instruction is best suited for teaching children discrete facts, skills, and routines (A. Epstein, 2007)	Direct instruction dominates classroom early reading routines. Children have few opportunities to explore literacy and print prior to participating in scripted reading instruction. There is little follow-up to scripted instruction in learning centers or in other ongoing classroom activities.
What literacy-related knowledge and skills does the scripted program address? What literacy-related knowledge and skills does the program omit? How will the early learning program address this gap?	Most scripted reading programs address print awareness, alphabet knowledge, and phonological awareness. Children need opportunities to develop additional literacy strategies and skills for reading comprehension, writing, reading for pleasure, and reading for information (Justice & Vukelich, 2008).	Teachers ignore aspects of literacy not covered by the scripted program. Children have limited or no access to high-quality narrative picture books, expository texts, and writing materials. Teachers do not read aloud to children one or more times every day. Children have few opportunities to talk with one another or with their teachers informally. Children have few opportunities to engage in hands-on activities in which literacy and emergent writing are incorporated.
How does the scripted program relate to other parts of the curriculum?	Young children need rich learning experiences in every domain to experience optimal brain growth and long-term school success (Bowman et al., 2001).	Children have limited opportunities to engage in literacy-infused learning centers that span the curriculum.

How does DAP relate to childcare licensing and early childhood accreditation?

Standards of professional practice require that programs serving preschool-aged children be licensed by their state. Licensing may be monitored through a department of education or a department of social services, depending on the locale. In either case, practices regulated through early childhood licensing represent critical but minimum standards that are mostly related to health and safety. Preprimary programs that choose to become accredited are the most likely to demonstrate the DAP principles advocated in this volume. The national accrediting body for early childhood programs in centers and schools is the NAEYC Academy for Early Childhood Program Accreditation. To achieve NAEYC accreditation, early learning programs volunteer to be measured against rigorous national standards on education, health, and safety. Today, more than eleven thousand NAEYC-accredited early childhood education programs serve children and families throughout the United States.

How has DAP changed over the years?

It has been more than twenty years since DAP was formally introduced. Here are some ways DAP looks different today from how it looked in 1987.

Then . . .	*Now . . .*
DAP was founded on principles of age-appropriate and individually appropriate practices.	Socially and culturally appropriate practice has been incorporated as a third guiding principle for DAP.
DAP focused primarily on classroom practices.	DAP includes more discussion of learning outcomes and curriculum standards.
People interpreted DAP as only involving child-initiated learning and responsive teaching.	DAP is now understood to include adult-initiated learning and explicit teaching.
Although DAP was defined as birth to age eight, most of the focus was on children from birth through age five.	DAP more clearly addresses the needs of children from five through eight years of age.
DAP was most often described in relation to childcare and preschool settings.	DAP addresses the needs of early elementary school children more clearly.
DAP relied mostly on theory to make its case.	DAP is more evidence based.
DAP relied on research support for individual practices.	DAP has been studied more holistically; results demonstrate the overall impact of DAP practices for various populations.
DAP research was primarily cross-sectional and short term.	DAP research now includes longitudinal work.
DAP research was based on work in the United States, for the most part.	DAP has been studied more fully worldwide.
DAP was supported by early childhood practitioner-based organizations.	Formal support for DAP now includes principals, subject-matter experts, economists, neuroscientists, and K–12 professional groups.

PRINCIPALS' ROLES

Supporting DAP

Supervisors and school principals play a vital part in the extent to which teachers and programs implement DAP principles (McCaslin, 2004). In recent research, administrator modeling and active support were identified as two of the top four factors associated with practitioners' adoption of DAP in schools (along with teachers' exposure to concrete learning about DAP and opportunities to practice DAP in the classroom). Administrative behaviors associated with active support of DAP include the following strategies:

1. Know what DAP is and refer to DAP when talking about early childhood programs with staff.

2. Encourage all of the preprimary programs under your supervision, including kindergarten, to achieve NAEYC accreditation.

3. Periodically arrange staff meetings and provide inservice sessions that include all early childhood personnel in your building or district, regardless of each program's funding stream. Invite principals of the various programs as well.

4. Initiate conversations in which teachers and principals together explore notions of age appropriateness, individual appropriateness, and social and cultural appropriateness.

5. Observe early childhood programs with the mutually agreed-on goal of focusing on DAP. Encourage peer observations focused on DAP. Engage in conversations with teachers privately and in small groups regarding classroom observations.

6. Recognize that teachers who are moving toward adoption of DAP will demonstrate both DAP- and DIP-related behaviors as they make the transition to new teaching practices. (See Box 5.8 for an example of mixed practices in the classroom of a teacher whose ultimate goal is to increase her use of DAP.)

7. Help teachers recognize their progress in DAP-related knowledge and skills.

8. Engage in goal setting with staff related to DAP. Model the adoption of personal goals relative to DAP.

Box 5.8

One Principal's Observation of the PreK Program at His School

The following observations were made during the first forty minutes of a typical day in a preprimary program for four-year-olds. The principal made a running record of his observations and later categorized them as DAP or DIP. (We added the principles of DAP or DIP associated with each one for further clarification.)
Observations of DAP in the classroom for four-year-olds:

Several pictures around room were at children's eye level depicting men and women, boys and girls, of differing ethnic groups. (Inclusive of all children)

(Continued)

(Continued)

Bulletin board near door included a plan for the week, a newsletter for parents, and a "home recipe" from a parent that would be used for lunch later that week. (Reciprocal family relations)

Teacher encouraged children to choose from three activities during the early morning arrival period: read a book, write in their journals, or put together puzzles at the small table. (Child choice)

Teacher and aide greeted each child at morning circle. (Caring relationships)

Teacher invited children to read each other's names from nametags at morning circle time. (Stimulating environment, attention to emerging literacy)

Children chose song to sing in morning circle time by voting, and the teacher recorded the votes on a large sheet of chart paper for all the children to see. (Child choice, attention to social domain)

Children sang songs while aide used hand to point to words written in large colorful letters on chart paper. (Stimulating environment, attention to literacy)

Teacher used morning circle time to review new materials that had been added to centers and discussed with the children their appropriate and inappropriate uses. (Child choice, self-regulation)

Growing plants were located in clear containers at windowsill near library corner; teacher pointed out the growing roots that were just appearing, suggested children look for themselves at center time. (Attention to science and cognitive domain, first-hand experience)

Centers available included water table, library corner, math center, magnet activity, block area, pretend play (post office), art table, and open snack area. (Child choice, whole child, hands-on learning, play)

Aide alerted the children ahead of time of impending transitions: snack, cleanup, storytime. (Appropriate routines)

Teacher conducted on-the-spot discussion between two children of alternatives to "hitting to let people know what you want" and offered children potential scripts to consider: "It's my turn next" (Caring relationships, self-regulation)

Teacher stopped by magnet activity twice and stayed about five minutes each time, wrote an anecdotal record, and asked one open-ended question (e.g., "What could you do to find out?") (Assessment, varied teaching strategies)

Observations of DIP in the classroom for four-year-olds:

Teacher and aide ignored a child who was flitting from one activity area to another without becoming involved in any for more than a few minutes. Chile never became involved in an activity long enough to complete any task. (Failure to address problem behavior)

Teacher had no prior plan for group time, pulled book from shelf, stumbled over words, and later said she was unfamiliar with the book's contents. (Poor planning)

Group lessons included too much waiting for turn taking. Children became restless, and teacher failed to adapt circle time lesson when children lost interest. (Routine was unresponsive to children's needs and abilities)

Teacher and aide did not intervene during group time when children got up from the circle or sat on their knees blocking the views of other children. (Failure to address problem behavior)

Learning centers did not include enough materials for more than one or two children at a time, not enough spots from which children could choose, and not enough materials for children to remain engaged for very long in any one center. (Poor planning, failure to extend children's learning, environment that impedes self-regulation)

Aide raised her voice and implemented time-out during learning center time when two children did not instantly comply with the rule to "walk" in the classroom. She did not remind children of rule or use a logical consequence (e.g., go back and walk more slowly) and had children stay in time-out for twenty minutes. (Poor behavior management)

The teacher asked many yes/no questions, failed to follow-up on children's observations about the magnets, and answered her own questions rather than giving children a chance to answer. (Missed opportunities to extend children's higher-order thinking)

Teacher used same praise statement more than eleven times ("nice work") and did not specify what children were doing well (Lack of emphasis on self regulation)

What Principals Need to Know About How Young Children Develop and Learn

Effective principals engage the school community in understanding children's early development and use that combined knowledge to strengthen learning throughout the school. (NAESP, 2005, p. 12)

Although effective education programs for young children share many things in common with those designed for older students, they are not identical. What works well for a nine-year-old cannot simply be down-sized for a three-year-old child. Physical space, materials, lessons, routines and expectations need to match the unique ways in which young children develop and learn. The better the match, the more likely it is that participating children will ultimately succeed in school.

High-quality early learning programs are not identical. They may vary along several dimensions—location, size, population served, funding source, schedules, physical plant, and staff composition. However, one thing they all have in common is being designed around accurate understandings of early childhood development and learning (Horowitz et al., 2005: Shonkoff & Phillips, 2000). These understandings determine how educators interact with children, the kinds of environments they create for them, and the kinds of learning outcomes they expect. Such understandings are necessary not only for staff members who work directly with children in the classroom, but also for the principals and superintendents responsible for program administration. Young children benefit when principals

- demonstrate thorough knowledge of early child development and learning,
- take action to ensure that young children's development and ways of learning are supported by program practices and policies,
- communicate to others the importance of young children's development and learning needs, and
- resist pressure to create or maintain programs that ignore or run counter to what we know about how young children develop and learn (NAESP, 2005).

In today's high-pressure academic environments, young children need principals to assume these roles with vigor. To help you in this task, we start small—focused on small children, that is. We will think about what they are really like and what their unique qualities mean for the early learning programs you supervise.

THE ESSENTIAL NATURE OF YOUNG CHILDREN

You walk into the kindergarten just as the children are about to act out *Jack and the Beanstalk*. You notice that Wally and Eddie disagree about the relative size of the room's two rugs.

Wally: The big rug is the giant's castle. The small one is Jack's house.

Eddie: Both rugs are the same.

Wally: They can't be the same. Watch me. I'll walk around the rug. Now watch—walk, walk, walk, walk, walk, walk, walk, walk, walk—count all these walks. Okay. Now count the other rug. Walk, walk, walk, walk, and walk. See? That one has more walks.

Eddie: No fair. You cheated. You walked faster.

Wally: I don't have to walk. I can just look.

Eddie: I can look too. But you have to measure it. You need a ruler. About six hundred inches or feet.

Wally: We have a ruler. (He holds up a twelve-inch wooden ruler.)

Eddie: Not that one. Not the short kind. You have to use the long kind that gets curled up in a box.

Wally: Use people. People's bodies. Lying down in a row.

Eddie: That's a great idea. I never even thought of that.

Wally announces a try out for "rug measurers." He adds one child at a time until both rugs are covered–four children end to end on one rug and three on the other. Everyone is satisfied and the play continues with Wally as the giant on the rug henceforth known as the four-person rug. (Paley, 1981, pp. 13–14)

There are many words that could describe these children:

- Active
- Curious

- Capable
- Resourceful
- Collaborative
- Absorbed
- Knowledgeable
- Inventive

Most important, Wally and his peers, like young children everywhere, are natural learners. From birth, they strive to make sense of their experiences and to increase their competence and understandings. This is an intrinsic outgrowth of child development.

HOW YOUNG CHILDREN DEVELOP

Young Children Develop Holistically

> **One Principal's Words of Advice**
>
> I don't care what else you do . . . if you want effective programs for young kids, you have to start where they are—you have to understand child development. Don't rely on your memory of when your own kids were little— don't figure that course in child psych from freshman year will tide you over—a lot has happened since then—educate yourself about young children and then use that knowledge to educate others. (Elementary school principal)

If you have ever watched children dance the Hokey Pokey you know that the last verse is always their favorite.

> *You put your whole self in,*
> *You put your whole self out,*
> *You put your whole self in,*
> *And you shake it all about!*

Just like in the song, when young children come to school, they put their whole selves in. They do not come as disembodied brains or as physical entities one minute and social entities the next. They come as whole human beings whose aesthetic, cognitive, emotional, language, physical, and social development are all in gear and are all interrelated. Consider the following example of children interacting in a pretend grocery store set up in their preschool classroom. As the youngsters "play store," their actions illustrate multiple facets of child development.

Aesthetic Children make "beautiful" signs to advertise their wares, create pleasing arrangements of fruits and vegetables, and sing as they work.

Cognition Children decide how to categorize the items on the shelves, remember who has had a chance to be the cashier and who is still waiting, count food items as they take inventory, and add up the prices of customers' purchases.

Emotional Children cope with the disappointment of not being the "cashier" first, gain confidence in their ability to negotiate disputes, use age-appropriate tools such as hammers and nails to create props for the store, and make choices about what will go where and how to make the area look like a "real grocery store."

Language	Children determine what words to use as the cashier and what scripts to use as a customer, describe items for sale, consult a book to find out what kinds of exotic fruits to add to their produce section, and make lists of what to shop for at the store.
Physical	Children print inventory sheets by hand, move shelves and boxes, bag the groceries, and maneuver the shopping cart along the aisles.
Social	Children negotiate who will take what role, figure out how to enter and exit the scene, wait for a turn to be in charge of stocking the shelves, collaborate with peers to create signs to advertise a sale, and use words to resolve a dispute about how much to charge for the lemons.

The holistic nature of these preschoolers' interactions in their grocery store is typical of every activity in which young children participate. Cognitive processes shape social ones, emotional processes affect language development, physical processes influence cognition, and so on (Kostelnik et al., 2007). No area of development stands independent of the others, and all areas interact to influence childhood learning. As an outgrowth of their holistic nature, young children take in the global aspects of an experience prior to recognizing or attending to its component parts. This will be discussed in detail later in the chapter. For now, readers are reminded that the importance of the "whole child" was identified in Chapter 2 as a core value of the early education field. That value has its basis in the research on child development and is a key factor in what distinguishes early childhood from later developmental periods.

There Is an Orderly Sequence to Early Childhood Development

Researchers throughout the world have identified typical sequences of development in every domain (Berk, 2009). Their findings confirm that development is a stepwise process in which understandings, knowledge, and skills build on each other in succession. We see this illustrated through the emergence of the developmental milestones associated with children's writing.

Writing Awareness

Children as young as two write messages. They have seen others write and mimic this behavior for their own purposes. Children's earliest forms of writing are mostly scribbles. However, as the receiver of any such message can tell you, these scribbles are meaningful to the child, even though the recipient is unable to decipher them without the child's assistance.

Emergent Writing

Children use more letterlike forms in their writing. They write strings of letters that run together and use single letters (usually an initial consonant) to represent entire words. There are often no spaces between their words and no punctuation. (See Figure 6.1.)

Figure 6.1   Emergent Writing: Four-Year-Old

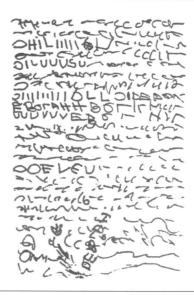

Early Writing

Children come to know the letter names and letter sounds and use this understanding to increase the number of letters in each word. Proper spacing, increasingly accurate spelling, and punctuation are more evident. Children begin to use capital letters in the correct places as well. (Refer to Figure 6.2.)

Figure 6.2   Early Writing, La Tosha, 5.8 Years Old

Fluent Writing

Children develop greater literacy skills such as using blends, suffixes, and prefixes correctly. They write in a variety of forms—letters, stories, essays, factual reports, poems, and lists. Fluent writers sequence their ideas, correctly divide narratives into paragraphs, and edit their writing to make it more interesting or accurate. (This is depicted in Figure 6.3.)

Figure 6.3   Fluent Writing: Celia, Seven Years Old

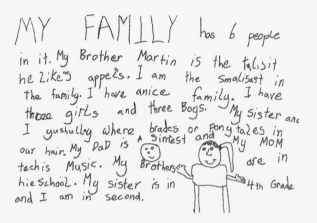

Source: From Anne K. Soderman & Paatricia Farrell, *Creating Literacy-rich Preschools and Kindergartens, 1/e.* Published by Allyn and Bacon/Merrill Education, Boston, MA. Copyright 2008 by Pearson Education. Reprinted by permission of the publisher.

Developmental milestones like these are generally but not rigidly defined by age. There is a broad "normal" range for their acquisition, with individual children spending more or less time on each one. Progress from one benchmark to the next happens in fits and starts, rather than in a smooth or lockstep fashion. Even so, development remains fairly predictable and emerges in roughly the same order for most children. Initial skills and abilities form the foundation for those yet to be acquired.

Children Develop at Varying Rates

Although all children progress through the same developmental sequences, each one does so according to his personal timetable that is influenced by maturation as well as experience. This leads to variations in development

- within the same child (different threads of development are at different levels of maturity at any one time), and

- from one child to another (peers vary in their size, their language skills, their cognitive abilities, and their social awareness).

While variations in rates occur throughout childhood and adolescence, developmental differences are most pronounced in young children (Copple & Bredekamp, 2006; Slentz & Krogh, 2001). This means that within any group of preschoolers, kindergartners, first graders, and second graders, you see children demonstrating a wide range of "normal" behaviors.

Early Childhood Is a Sensitive Period for Future Learning

You want to say it is never too late. But there seems to be something very special about early childhood . . . there are windows of opportunity that nature flings open, then closes again, one by one, with every additional candle on the birthday cake. (Begley, 1996, p. 56)

As human beings mature, there are opportune times for certain types of learning to become established. If strong foundations are created during these sensitive periods, individuals are developmentally primed to acquire new understandings and skills. If those foundations are missing, it is harder for children to develop more sophisticated functioning later in life (Bailey, 2002; Shonkoff & Phillips, 2000). This blend of potential opportunity and vulnerability is most evident in early childhood (Horowitz et al., 2005). The range of developmental tasks with which individuals are involved and their potential influence on future functioning are greater from birth to age eight than at any other time in the life span.

Examples of developmental tasks for which early childhood sets the stage include the following:

- Aesthetic awareness
- Attitudes toward authority and rules
- Attitudes toward physical activity
- Attitudes toward self as a learner and toward school
- Attitudes toward work
- Coping strategies
- Emotional awareness
- Fundamental motor skills
- Interpersonal communication
- Listening skills
- Logical mathematical thought
- Musicality
- Oral language and vocabulary
- Problem-solving strategies
- Second language development
- Self-awareness
- Self-efficacy
- Self-regulation
- Sense of independence, initiative, and industry
- Social awareness
- Social skill development
- Trust

All of these facets of child development are important. None can be ignored without negative consequences. The breadth of developmental tasks children are working on during early childhood underscores the importance of providing children with learning opportunities that enhance their capacities in every domain. This explains why high-quality early childhood programs are broad in scope, providing children with a rich array of varied learning experiences. It also explains why efforts by schools and public officials to narrow the early childhood curriculum to focus on only a few of these tasks are viewed by early childhood educators with great concern.

Development Has Cumulative Effects

On one hand, few single events in children's lives have the power to "make or break" their developmental progress. On the other hand, development is strongly influenced by the cumulative impact of individual minor events. Such influences may be either positive or negative (e.g., a child who experiences numerous opportunities to make small choices and initiate activities grows in self-confidence and autonomy; a child who is subjected to a steady stream of fault-finding develops long-term feelings of inferiority and pessimism). These cumulative effects result from acts of commission (e.g., children subjected to long periods of sitting and listening gradually become passive rather than active learners) or acts of omission (e.g., children who are regularly deprived of opportunities to engage in active physical play and exercise are more likely to become obese as they grow older).

By the end of the early childhood period, positive developmental trends seem to be fairly well fixed, making it easier for children to tackle new challenges as they mature. Negative cumulative effects tend to be fairly stable, as well, making it harder for children to catch up, and ultimately to succeed. These cumulative impacts are why there is such a strong call for early, deliberate intervention for children potentially at risk of school failure. They are also why early childhood educators pay attention to the potential long-term impacts of program practices in addition to short-term goals. For instance, having children fill out an occasional worksheet or participate in short periods of whole group instruction are not likely to do much harm. However, if these methods become the norm for significant portions of the school day, children's enthusiasm for formal learning tends to decline (Justice & Vukelich, 2008; Katz, 2008). Similarly, teachers take the time to reason with children to build up children's self-regulatory skills even though it might be easier in the short term to enforce rules without a rationale.

Linking Child Development
Principles to Effective Educational Practices

The origins of developmentally appropriate practice (DAP) can be traced to the principles of child development just described. Linking those principles to classroom procedures is associated with the long-term benefits attributed to high-quality early childhood programs. Examples demonstrating the links between theory and practice are depicted in Table 6.1.

In addition to understanding child development and its implications for program design, early childhood educators must create programs that accommodate the distinct ways in which young children learn.

Table 6.1 Linking Developmental Principles With Educational Practice

Because children develop holistically . . .	early childhood educators create early childhood programs that address all developmental domains: aesthetic, cognitive, emotional, language, physical, and social . . .	and do not focus on one or two domains to the exclusion of the rest.
	early childhood educators design educational activities to encompass multiple domains . . .	and do not focus on content or skills in isolation.
	early childhood educators devote classroom time and space to pretend play and construction activities because these experiences draw on all domains simultaneously . . .	
Because child development is relatively predictable and sequential . . .	early childhood educators use knowledge of developmental sequences to gauge whether or not children are developing as expected . . .	and do not try to hurry children through developmental sequences.
	early childhood educators determine reasonable expectations and goals for children based on knowledge of development . . .	and do not simply wait and see.
	early childhood educators select appropriate strategies to scaffold children's progression to higher levels of development and learning . . .	and do not avoid challenging children to strive for increasingly higher levels of performance.
Because children develop at varying rates . . .	early childhood educators observe children carefully to recognize individual patterns of development . . .	and do not treat all children the same.
	early childhood educators provide opportunities for children to regulate their own pace of learning, by spending more or less time with certain topics, materials, or tasks . . .	and do not require children to follow strict timetables to complete tasks.
	early childhood educators repeat activities throughout the year so children benefit from participating according to their changing needs and abilities . . .	and do not address content or skill development only once.
	early childhood educators design lessons with multiple objectives so children of varying abilities can participate successfully and make progress . . .	and do not teach to a single objective.
Because early childhood is a sensitive period for future learning . . .	early childhood educators know the developmental tasks of early childhood and provide activities to help children master those tasks . . .	and do not concentrate on only a few "sensitive" areas or skills.
	early childhood educators provide a rich array of experiences to support children's development of critical attitudes, dispositions, knowledge and skills in every domain . . .	and do not ignore important areas of development (e.g., social, emotional, physical, language).
Because child development has cumulative effects . . .	early childhood educators avoid short-term strategies that may have long-term ill effects . . . early childhood educators work patiently to achieve goals that may be harder to address in the short-term, but which could have long-term payoffs.	and do not focus on immediate objectives only.

HOW YOUNG CHILDREN LEARN

Young children learn in a different manner from that of older children and adults, yet we can teach them many things if we adapt our materials and mode of instruction to their level of ability. We miseducate young children when we assume that their learning abilities are comparable to those of older children and that they can be taught with materials and with the same instructional procedures appropriate to older school-age children. (Elkind, 2006)

Children's Learning Is Influenced by How Safe and Secure They Feel

Children who feel psychologically safe and secure learn more easily than children who are worried, angry, or afraid. (See Box 6.1.) For young children, security comes from being in the company of warm responsive adults with whom they develop close personal relationships (Children's Defense Fund [CDF], 2004; National Association for the Education of Young Children [NAEYC], 2009). Such adults demonstrate their liking for children, tolerate childish mistakes, guide children socially as well as cognitively, and create environments where routines and expectations are predictable and well matched to children's capabilities. Teachers who set reasonable limits on children's antisocial behavior, promote problem solving in the classroom, and address bullying behavior effectively also create conditions children interpret as safe.

Box 6.1

Emotions Are Gatekeepers to Learning

While helping children feel secure makes common sense, it makes neurological sense, too. Emotions signal the brain whether all is right with the world or whether the world is an unjust or dangerous place. Positive emotions such as love, excitement, enthusiasm, and joy enhance the ability of the cerebral cortex to process information (Kovalik and Olsen, 2001; Sylwester, 1996). Feelings of threat, loss, or injustice interfere with this higher-order brain activity. When humans feel fear or fury, those emotions trigger reactions in the brain stem leading to rudimentary responses such as fight or flight, or shutting down sensory intake as a way to cope. None of these reactions contributes to advanced cognitive processes. In addition, when children experience extended periods of stress their bodies produce elevated levels of the hormone cortisol. Prolonged exposure to cortisol weakens neural connections, particularly in those parts of the brain responsible for memory and learning (Shonkoff & Phillips, 2000). Neuroscience suggests that strong, positive, emotional attachments with adult caregivers actually reduce the production of cortisol. This promotes and protects neural connections.

Children Are Active Learners

There is an indivisible bond between the body and the brain, particularly in young children. More than 2,500 years ago, the Chinese philosopher Confucius observed

I hear, and I forget,

I see, and I remember,

I do, and I understand.

Confucius knew then what we know now: Children are doers. They are not passive creatures waiting for learning to happen; rather, children are stimulation seekers. Their active bodies and active minds work in partnership to make sense of the world in which they find themselves. Observe any high-quality early childhood setting and you will see children on the move— exploring one material and then another, moving from one spot to the next, and seldom sitting perfectly still. To the untrained eye, this high level of activity may be misinterpreted as unproductive. In actuality, the opposite is true. Children moving about a DAP classroom are using their entire bodies to learn. Recent studies underscore the connection between children's physical activity and subsequent cognitive functioning (Bjorklund, 2005). Through active engagement with the world around them, children continually connect thought with action—exploring, discovering, and acquiring new knowledge and skills. See Box 6.2 for a Children's Active Learning Checklist that will be useful for classroom observations.

Box 6.2

Active Learning Checklist

☐ Children move about the room purposefully.

☐ Children initiate activities based on their personal interests.

☐ Children choose materials and decide what to do with them.

☐ Children explore materials using all their senses.

☐ Children discover relationships through direct experience with objects.

☐ Children transform and combine materials.

☐ Children use age-appropriate tools and equipment.

☐ Children utilize their large muscles to learn.

☐ Children talk about their experiences (Hohmann & Weikart, 2002).

Children Learn Through a Combination of Physical Experience and Social Interaction

The four-year-olds are learning about leaves.

- They go on a leaf hunt outdoors to see what kinds of leaves they can find in the play yard.
- They examine a variety of leaves gathered from many sources. With their teacher, they create a graph depicting differences in the color, size, texture, and shape of the leaves.

- The teacher asks the children to predict what will happen to two leafy plants when one is placed in the dark and the other is left in the sunshine. A lively discussion ensues. The teacher records the group's predictions. After the experiments are carried out, the children compare their predictions with the results.

The children's study of leaves illustrates how physical experience and social interaction combine to support active learning. Such learning "depends on the use of materials–natural and found materials, household objects, toys, equipment and tools" (Hohmann & Weikart, 2002, p. 17). From the beginning, young children learn about the world by acting on it directly. Taking in data through all their senses, they manipulate, taste, touch, hear, look at, and smell things in order to find out more about them. As children act on objects (e.g., examining real leaves with a magnifying glass, cutting open fruits to reveal the seeds, pouring water through rubber tubing in the water table), they discover the properties of those objects, how they function, and how they relate to one another. They also gain practice in observing, comparing, counting, hypothesizing, predicting, remembering, testing out ideas, interpreting, and drawing conclusions. There is no substitute for this kind of direct interaction with objects and materials. If we want children to learn about leaves, the most effective lessons involve real leaves for them to handle and examine. Pictures and drawings of leaves are poor substitutes if children have had little prior experience with the real thing. In addition, the more senses children tap in the investigative process, the better (Marzano, 2003). Maximum sensory engagement makes learning more vivid and increases the likelihood that children will take away new understandings from their activities.

Children's physical experiences with objects are enriched by their interactions with people. When children observe, talk, and interact with others, they

- exchange and compare interpretations, ideas, and information;
- devise hypotheses;
- ask questions;
- generate answers;
- experience contradictions; and
- formulate new understandings.

In addition, people are purveyors of factual knowledge children cannot discover entirely on their own (Bransford, Brown, & Cocking, 2000). Only through social interactions do children become aware of social conventions and expectations (e.g., "Say, 'Excuse me,' if you interrupt someone," "People in our family go to synagogue on Saturday," "Step on a crack, break your mother's back") as well as certain facts and skills (e.g., "That bird is a cardinal," "Here's how to dribble a basketball," "This is the letter 'R'"). In all these ways, peers and adults serve as models, sounding boards, sources of information and the counterpoints children need to hone and deepen their understandings.

Children Vary in Their Approaches to Learning

Although children use all their available senses to learn, there are many different ways in which they combine these to perceive, act on, and take in information. Consider the following examples:

- Kyle responds best to what he sees and envisions things in his mind as a way to recall them. In problem situations, he prefers working out solutions in collaboration with others.

- Molly has a way with words. She relies on hearing and talking as her primary means of processing stimuli. For her, sound is the message, and she sometimes moves her lips or talks herself through tasks to make them easier. When a problem arises, she likes to figure it out on her own.
- Leon is very tactile in how he approaches objects and situations. He moves and constantly touches things in order to grasp concepts. It is not unusual for him also to have to touch himself in some way to remember or process information. He is very tuned in to the natural world and finds the company of animals particularly satisfying.

Kyle, Molly, and Leon are demonstrating different combinations of knowing and learning or different "intelligences." Based on more than twenty years of study, Howard Gardner postulates that intelligence is not a single construct. Instead, different intelligences develop independently in the brain and individuals may be above average in some areas, while being average or below average in others (Gardner, 1993). Thus, people have many ways of being smart and each person's blend of intelligences produces a unique learning profile. Gardner currently theorizes that everyone possesses at least eight intelligences: linguistic, logical-mathematical, musical, bodily-kinesthetic, visual-spatial, interpersonal, intrapersonal, and naturalist. These are described in Table 6.2.

Table 6.2   Eight Intelligences That Contribute to Children's Learning

Intelligence	*Children Learn Through . . .*
Linguistic	Writing, talking, and reading
Logical-mathematical	Exploring patterns and causal relationships, working with numbers, and carrying out experiments
Musical	Hearing, recognizing, and manipulating sound patterns; listening to and making music
Bodily-kinesthetic	Touching, moving, using their whole body to solve problems
Visual-spatial	Representing the physical world in the mind's eye, drawing, building, designing, and creating tangible things they have envisioned
Interpersonal	Relating to others, sharing, cooperating, comparing
Intrapersonal	Reflecting to themselves, being aware of inner moods, seeking opportunities for solitude
Naturalist	Observing nature, interacting with plants and animals, recognizing relationships among living things

Children's approaches to learning also may vary due to temperament or other cultural factors (Kostelnik et al., 2007). For example, some children think rapidly and impulsively, and others are deliberate and reflective. Some children focus on the big picture, and some think more about the details. Some children constantly look for connections among ideas, while others take a single thought and follow it in multiple directions. Some children organize their thoughts in a linear fashion, and some think in a more circular way.

When children's strengths and optimal ways of learning are accommodated, their comprehension and skills increase. However, if children's learning styles are ignored, they are likely to become frustrated or disengaged (Baum, Viens, Slatin, 2005). Thus, one of the challenges for early childhood educators is to meet the needs of individual children whose learning profiles vary greatly.

Children's Learning Advances in Predictable Directions

Just as child development progresses from rudimentary to more sophisticated levels, so does learning. Initially, children's learning is informal, concrete, and exploratory. Over time, it becomes more formal, more abstract, and more outcome oriented.

Following a rainstorm, children in the preschool notice several worms on the sidewalk and become curious about them. With the help of their teacher, they bring some worms in to the classroom to examine them more closely. They watch the worms move in soil in a bucket and handle the worms carefully to see if the two "ends" are the same or different. Others compare the live worms to pictures of worms in a book. As the children talk about the worms and what they notice, the teacher records their ideas on large sheets of easel paper. Throughout the activity the teacher verbally summarizes children's observations and asks questions to extend their thinking.

Children in the second grade are learning about worms as part of the K–2 science curriculum. Together, the teacher and the children generate a list of what children think they already know about worms and what they want to find out. Small groups of children work collaboratively to discover the answers. They conduct experiments and look up information in books and on the computer. They invite a "worm expert" to class and generate interview questions to ask him when he arrives. The class also creates a compost pile outside that is rich with worms and that they examine every day, making note of what they observe about the worm's activities.

These teachers have created stimulating and developmentally appropriate lessons for the children in their classes. They based those lessons on the understanding that children's learning progresses from

- known to unknown,
- self to other,
- whole to part,
- concrete to abstract,
- enactive to symbolic,
- exploratory to goal directed,
- less accurate to more accurate, and
- simple to complex.

Definitions and examples of the learning sequences listed above are provided in Table 6.3.

Table 6.3   Common Learning Sequences

Learning Sequence	Definition	Example
Known to unknown	Children base new learning on what is familiar. Concepts that are more sophisticated grow out of those they already know.	The teacher introduces the topic of "plants," by beginning with common plants in the children's immediate environment. Over time, children apply what they learn to plants that are less familiar.
Self to other	Children focus on their own needs, perspectives, and experiences prior to being able to focus on the needs, views, and experiences of others.	Two children are in an argument over who will get to use the yardstick next. The teacher begins mediating the conflict by acknowledging each child's personal desires prior to asking them to consider each other's point of view.
Whole to part	Children take in experiences as a whole first. After they grasp the overall nature of a concept or experience, they begin to concentrate on the details.	Children comprehend the general idea that writing is a way to communicate ideas to others prior to getting all the mechanics right.
Concrete to abstract	Children learn from tangible experiences with real objects by using multiple senses. The further removed an experience is from this material state and the fewer senses children can use, the more abstract the learning becomes. Concrete experiences must precede more abstract ones for children to acquire deep, lasting knowledge.	Teachers who want children to learn about shells start with the real thing. Giving children real shells to handle is more concrete than showing them pictures of shells or simply talking about them.
Enactive to symbolic	This sequence refers to how children represent the world. At first, children represent or enact experiences using their whole body. In time, children make iconic representations such as pictures or three-dimensional constructions from blocks or art materials to depict something they have experienced or imagined. Eventually, children engage in symbolic representation using written words, numerals, or signs to represent their ideas.	Following a field trip to a post office, the children do the following: • They enact the post office through pretend play, taking on the roles of postmaster, mail carrier, and customer developing scripts and creating ideas for how the play should proceed. • They engage in iconic representation by drawing pictures of what they saw at the post office and by constructing a post office in the block area. • Children participate in symbolic representation by dictating a thank you letter to the people at the post office. Their teacher writes the children's words on poster paper in front of them. She goes back over their message pointing out certain words and punctuation.

Learning Sequence	Definition	Example
Exploratory to goal directed	Children need opportunities to explore objects and procedures before using them in prescribed ways.	The teacher has new math objects for the children to count and put into sets. Prior to asking them to carry out the math activity, the teacher gives the children time to handle the objects, to examine them closely, and to make observations about them.
Less accurate to more accurate	Children's early learning is characterized by inaccurate ideas and mistaken notions. As children explore, experiment, predict, test, and reflect on their interactions with people and objects, they develop more accurate notions of how the world works.	At the water table, some children hypothesize that only blue things float. Rather than simply telling children they are wrong, the teacher encourages them to test out their ideas. As children add more objects to the water table they note that some blue objects float, but some red things float too, and that some blue items sink. Through such experiences over time, children eliminate color as a property that determines whether or not objects sink or float.
Simple to complex	Learning is simpler when it is • more closely tied to what children know than what they don't know, • more focused on self than on others, • more focused on the whole than on the parts, more concrete than abstract, • more enactive than symbolic, • more exploratory than goal directed, and • more accepting of inaccuracies. Learning is more complex when the inverse of the above is true. Complexity increases as the number of variables goes up and as differentiations among variables are more subtle.	It is usually more challenging to put together a two hundred–piece puzzle than one that has fifty pieces. It is usually more complex to put together a puzzle in which all the pieces are the same color or shape than one in which each piece is different.

Children's Learning Must Be Meaningful to Be Lasting

"Donnie, come show Miss Nita how good you are at numbers!" Donnie's parents smiled broadly in expectation as their four-year-old son took a deep breath and began an addition recitation in a sing-song voice, "One plus one is two. Two plus two is four. Three plus three is six. Four plus four is eight. . . . " Young Donnie continued the addition fact recitation with very little error until he ended triumphantly with "Ten plus ten is funny!" The listening adults all laughed appreciatively; however, their perceptions of Donnie's

Don't Mistake Children's Eagerness to Please as a Sign That Instruction Is Meaningful

In some preschool classrooms, young children can be found busily filling out worksheets and counting by rote. At first, "young children remain remarkably willing to undertake any number of decontextualized, abstract or even frivolous and superficial tasks. Their eagerness to please the teacher, their general good will toward her, and their desire to participate in the ongoing life of the class typically last through the first few years of school" (Katz & Chard, 2000, p. 46). However, if children are subjected to a steady diet of such tasks, it is not long before they find little pleasure in learning and teachers find it difficult to motivate them. This is a precursor to the fourth-grade slump we have all heard about.

mathematical learning were very different. Donnie's parents had taught their son to recite the basic facts after listening and memorizing a song. Miss Nita (his child care provider) on the other hand, wondered how much Donnie understood about the words he had memorized and later, while playing store, discovered that his concept of numbers was quite incomplete. (Copley, 2003, p. 47)

Donnie is an example of a child whose number fact learning is still superficial, as is generally the case for children his age. Although he is beginning to understand the concepts of "oneness" and "counting," he has little grasp that ten plus ten equals twenty. Simply memorizing the combinations was not meaningful learning. That will come with more practice with real objects and opportunities to solve mathematical problems in relevant situations.

Learning is most meaningful for young children when new knowledge and skills

- build on what is important to them,
- begin with what they already know, and
- are readily observable in their immediate environments.

The things children ask about, show curiosity in, enact in their play, or discuss with others offer useful insights into what might be most meaningful to them. Upcoming and common events in children's lives provide further clues. As a result, lessons on "family," "local plants," "backyard animals," and "the foods we eat" are pertinent to nearly all preprimary and early elementary–aged students because they help children better understand their daily lives and immediate surroundings (Kostelnik et al., 2007). In contrast, elaborate lessons on "electricity" or "penguins" are too abstract or too far removed from most children's day-to-day experiences to be very meaningful in the early years. Locale as well as family, community resources, and traditions further influence what content is relevant to a particular group of students. For children in rural Wyoming, meadowlarks, downy woodpeckers, and wild turkeys are common "backyard animals," which makes them easy and meaningful for children to investigate. These would not be the most relevant birds for a group in New York City to study, where pigeons, sparrows, and robins are more common. In any case, meaningful learning has significance to the children, by representing things that intrigue them and prompting them to want to learn more.

Children Need to Experience Both Mastery and Challenge to Remain Motivated to Learn

David likes to work with clay. He often spends time at the art table rolling and patting the clay or using cookie cutters to make shapes. Now, however, he is trying to make a dog. He has rolled a sausage-shaped body and is trying to attach four stubby legs to make it complete. However, the legs keep falling off. David is showing signs of frustration.

The paraeducator comes over to the table and, using a separate ball of clay, demonstrates how to "score" two pieces of clay and then push them together to make the pieces adhere better. David keeps working at the table until finally he holds up his creation (four legs—wobbly, but attached) and announces, "Look. It's a dog!" For the next several days, David tries the "scoring" technique on a variety of clay creations, each one more elaborate than the one before.

Young children learn best when they are stimulated and successful in acquiring new knowledge and skills. They enjoy the challenge of learning what they nearly understand but do not quite grasp, and of trying to do what they can almost but not quite achieve immediately. This excitement prompts children to pursue concepts and skills just slightly beyond their current levels of proficiency. It also encourages them to keep striving until they achieve greater competence (Bodrova & Leong, 1996). Children who frequently master new learning tasks remain motivated to learn. They perceive themselves as up to the task, even when it is not easy or instantly attainable. Conversely, youngsters who are overwhelmed by the demands of a task tend to fail. Those who lack stimulation tend to fail as well. In either case, children who fail repeatedly will stop trying (NAEYC, 2009). Children who stop trying also stop learning. Adults play a major role in managing the environment and offering learning tasks in ways that stimulate children rather than frustrate them. More about these strategies are presented in Chapter 7.

Children Learn Through Play

Play is the highest form of research.

—Albert Einstein

Children do not learn everything through play, but they learn many things that way. All the facets of development and learning described in this chapter are enhanced through children's play. Play is the natural medium through which children gather and process information, learn new skills, and practice the ones they are trying to master (Fromberg, 2002). Within the context of play, children act on objects and figure out more about how the world works—hypothesizing, predicting, and testing their ideas. Play gives children opportunities to understand, create, and manipulate symbols as they take on roles and transform objects into something else ("Let's pretend this chair is the pilot's seat in our plane"). Children explore social relationships, too. They experiment with various roles such as leader and follower, or novice and expert. As children play with peers, they are confronted with points of view unlike their own, with working out compromises, and with negotiating differences. Play enables children to expand their physical skills, their language capabilities, and their creativity. Play also provides a safe means for children to release tensions, express their emotions, and explore anxiety-producing situations such as the arrival of a new sibling at home, the uncertainties of moving, or the loss of a family member through divorce or death. In all these ways, play is of great value to young children; most researchers agree that play is critical to children's learning (NAEYC, 2009). Even with research in its favor, adults are sometimes uneasy about having children play in the classroom. This is often because of the myths that surround play. To carry out their roles effectively, early childhood educators and principals need to be aware of these myths and the realities associated with each. A brief summary is provided in Box 6.3.

Box 6.3
Confronting Myths About Play

Myth: Play is like dessert: enjoyable, but nonessential.

Reality: If play were food, many adults would equate it with candy—tasty, but not very nutritious; a treat, not a dietary staple. In reality, if play were food, it would be the staff of life—tasty, packed with nutrients to build healthy bodies and healthy minds; a dietary staple to be consumed every single day.

Myth: Children play when they have nothing else to do.

Reality: Play is not a random activity. Children are biologically compelled to play in order to make sense of their experiences, to build their knowledge and skills, to satisfy their curiosity, and to increase their competence in every developmental domain. Play is the primary means through which young children discover, adapt, and create new concepts and skills. It is not an extraneous activity.

Myth: Play and learning are two separate activities.

Reality: Play and learning are all the same to young children; they do not differentiate between the two. Here is what we know about play.

Play is intrinsically motivated.	(No one forces children to play; children play to satisfy their curiosity and their desire for mastery.)
Play is active.	(Children are mentally and physically engaged when they play.)
Play is stimulating.	(Children are interested and challenged by play.)
Play is meaningful.	(Children find play significant and relevant.)
Play is pleasurable.	(Children enjoy play.)

Now substitute the word "learning" for each mention of "play" above. The words that describe play are the same as those educators use to describe learning. From preschool through the early elementary grades, **play and learning are synonymous.** Moreover, the same conditions that support play also enhance learning. These include providing children with adequate materials, space, time, background experiences, and adult guidance.

Myth: If children are playing, adults aren't teaching.

Reality: Adults have important educational roles to carry out as children play. They act as

Observers:	Adults observe children's interactions with objects, peers, and adults; children's play themes; skills children exhibit; gaps in children's knowledge and skills; and who plays with whom.
Elaborators:	Adults support children as they play—adding or taking away props, posing questions, and providing information.
Models:	Adults demonstrate how to enter play, how to extend play themes, how to exit play, how to carry out various play skills, and how to resolve differences.
Evaluators:	Adults evaluate what children are learning, what individual children need, how materials and activities support curriculum goals, and to what extent activities need to be simplified, maintained, or extended to promote learning.
Planners:	Adults plan new experiences that build on children's knowledge, skills, and interests.

Myth: There is not enough time for children to play—we have to get them ready for school, the next program level, the next grade, the world of work.

Reality: Play is how all mammals acquire the basic skills they need to survive in the adult world. Human beings play with language, movement, ideas, objects, symbols, events, and people. In doing so, children practice motor skills, language skills, reasoning, social behavior, and coping with emotionally challenging problems. When we deprive children of play opportunities we actually undermine their preparation for the future. Unfortunately, there are many barriers to play in early childhood: lack of safe, appropriate play space; an overemphasis on adult-centered activity; and the erosion of time and chances to play. For instance, in the United States, 40 percent of the elementary schools in the country have eliminated recess or are in the process of considering this to allow more time for "formal learning" (Fronczek, 2004). In some programs, children as young as two spend long hours seated at tables or desks, reciting the alphabet and counting to one hundred. Such attempts to "get children ready" take away time from the more sophisticated and essential learning that occurs as children play. This is not merely a theoretical claim. There is growing evidence that children who have rich play opportunities early in life are more developmentally advanced later on than children who have few opportunities to play. This ultimately influences children's academic success. Recent studies show that children who have early access to active, play-based early learning experiences earn better grades and experience fewer referrals for special services in the upper elementary grades than children whose early education is characterized by few play-centered activities and routines (Marcon, 2002, 2003; Mills, Dale, Cole, & Jenkins, 1995; Montie et al., 2006).

Practical Implications

Understanding principles of childhood learning is a prerequisite for meeting children's educational needs. However, understanding alone does not ensure that children's learning needs will be met. For that to happen, teachers and principals must link knowledge with action. Some specific early education practices associated with the learning principles just described are presented in Table 6.4.

Table 6.4   Linking Learning Principles with Educational Practice

Because children learn best when they feel safe and secure . . .	early childhood educators develop close, nurturing relationships with children . . .	and do not ignore children's emotional needs.
	early childhood educators provide children with consistent adult supervision so children can easily identify a specific adult from whom to seek help, attention, comfort, and guidance . . .	
	early childhood educators address children's biological needs (e.g., snacks, meals, rest, going to the bathroom as needed rather than on schedule) . . .	and do not deprive children of rest, recess, or opportunities to go outdoors each day.
	early childhood educators create environments that are physically safe . . .	
	early childhood educators establish predictable and stable classroom routines . . . early childhood educators explain changes in routines to children in advance so they know what to anticipate and how to adjust . . .	and do not rush children through the day.
	early childhood educators use positive discipline strategies to enhance children's self-awareness and self-regulation as well as their abilities to get along with others . . .	and do not shame children or use harsh disciplinary methods.
	early childhood educators teach children social skills and conflict mediation strategies so children can resolve some problems for themselves when adults are not around . . .	
	early childhood educators address issues of bullying and aggression calmly, firmly, and proactively . . .	
Because children are active learners . . .	early childhood educators devote large portions of the day to times when children can move about the classroom freely . . .	and do not expect children to sit still or remain inactive for long periods.

	early childhood educators make sure children have opportunities to engage in active, gross-motor activities daily . . .	
	early childhood educators develop daily schedules in which inactive times are kept short and are interspersed with longer more active periods . . .	
Because children learn through physical experience and social interaction . . .	early childhood educators provide children with daily hands-on experiences involving a variety of materials . . .	and do not make children mostly sit and listen or engage in mostly paper-pencil activities.
	early childhood educators provide a mix of child-initiated and adult-directed activities . . .	and do not engage in teacher-directed activities the majority of the time.
	early childhood educators become actively involved with children—listening, making observations, posing questions, responding to the children's lead, offering information, exchanging ideas and prompting children to reflect on their experiences . . .	and do not engage in learning activities that are far removed from children's day to day experiences.
	early childhood educators offer peers many opportunities to interact both formally and informally . . .	and do not work in isolation.
	early childhood educators support peer interaction through all parts of the day to help children develop relationships and learn from one another . . .	
Because children's learning is shaped by multiple intelligences . . .	early childhood educators implement educational activities that are multisensory . . .	and do not focus most learning experiences on a single intelligence.
	early childhood educators create activities so children can work on their own and in collaboration with others; with natural and human generated materials; indoors and outdoors . . .	
	early childhood educators present the same skills and information in a variety of modalities . . .	
	early childhood educators give children choices about how to engage in the learning process . . .	
Because children's learning advances in predictable directions . . .	early childhood educators design learning experiences that support children's progress toward more elaborate concepts and skills . . .	and do not teach to a single objective.

(Continued)

Table 6.4 (Continued)

	early childhood educators provide enough different materials and experiences that children can explore, practice or advance in their learning no matter where they are on the learning continuum . . .	and do not avoid repetition.
	early childhood educators simplify, maintain, or extend activities in response to children's demonstrated levels of functioning and comprehension . . .	
	early childhood educators sequence educational plans over the year to support children's increasingly advanced levels of comprehension and skills . . .	
Because learning experiences must be meaningful to be lasting . . .	early childhood educators observe and interact with children to discover what they are interested in learning . . .	and do not teach content and skills that have no connection to children's lives.
	early childhood educators interact with relevant people in children's lives (e.g., family or community members) to discover what might add meaning to children's experiences in the program . . .	
	early childhood educators relate new knowledge and skills to what children already know . . .	
	early childhood educators relate new knowledge and skills to children's immediate environments . . .	
	early childhood educators provide children with access to objects, images and activities in the early childhood program that reflect their home experiences . . .	
Because children need to experience both mastery and challenge to remain motivated to learn . . .	early childhood educators monitor learning activities to make sure they are manageable for children . . .	and do not understimulate children.
	early childhood educators challenge children to stretch their understandings . . .	
	early childhood educators support children as they attempt new skills . . .	
	early childhood educators help children figure out alternative approaches when the task at hand is beyond their current capabilities . . .	
	early childhood educators prompt children to reflect on what they know and how they know . . .	
	early childhood educators help children document their learning . . .	

Because children learn through play . . .	early childhood educators integrate play throughout the entire day and within all aspects of the early childhood program . . .	and do not attempt to isolate play from other forms of learning.
	early childhood educators provide a variety of props and materials with which children may play . . .	and do not treat play as frivolous or as a reward.
	early childhood educators support and enhance children's play—sometimes as observers and sometimes as participants . . .	and do not ban play from the classroom.

Besides knowing how children develop and learn, it is useful to consider what children are learning during the all-important years from birth to age eight.

WHAT YOUNG CHILDREN ARE LEARNING

Today, in Jessie Brooks's four-year-old class, you observe the following:

• Two pairs of children are "reading and writing the room." One child, acting as the reader, finds examples of print in the room (including labels, charts, sight words, posters, signs, and messages) and then reads them aloud. The other child, acting as the writer, records what the reader is reading by writing on a notepad attached to a clipboard. The children take turns being the reader and the writer. Later in the morning during circle time, all four children report on the information they gathered.

• Trev and Sam are arguing over who will get the next turn with the magnifying glass. When it becomes apparent that they can't settle the dispute themselves, the assistant teacher steps in to meditate. She begins by asking each child to state what he wants and by asking each one to listen to what the other has to say.

• The children are discussing whether or not a cactus that Jessie has brought to class is a plant or something else. After several ideas are mentioned, Tonya jumps up and says, "I know, I know. We saw one like that in that book." She eagerly runs over to the science table to retrieve the book she has in mind and begins looking through the pages.

In this brief visit, you have observed children engaged in activities representing four essential types of learning most relevant to the education of young children—knowledge, skills, feelings, and dispositions (Katz & Chard, 2000).

Knowledge

For young learners, knowledge consists of vocabulary, facts, procedures, rules, concepts, constructs, stories, and ideas. Some knowledge comes to children through external sources—someone explains something, answers a child's question, offers instruction, or provides descriptions and accounts of events past, present, and future. Other knowledge emerges through more internal processes, as when children stretch their current thinking or construct entirely new ideas in order to make sense of their observations and interactions with people and objects. As noted earlier in this chapter, children's acquisition of knowledge tends to be global at first (rather than detail oriented) and includes accurate understandings as well as misunderstandings. Through countless incidents, such as those noted in Jessie Brooks's classroom, children gather new data, reflect on their experiences, and adjust their thinking in new ways (not always consciously). In this manner, they gradually refine, improve, and deepen their understandings. Thus, knowledge both accumulates and changes as children mature. Refer to Figure 6.4 for a brief summary of five different types of knowledge children are incorporating into their knowledge base during early childhood. These include physical knowledge, logical-mathematical knowledge, representational knowledge, social-conventional knowledge, and metacognitive knowledge.

Figure 6.4   Five Categories of Knowledge

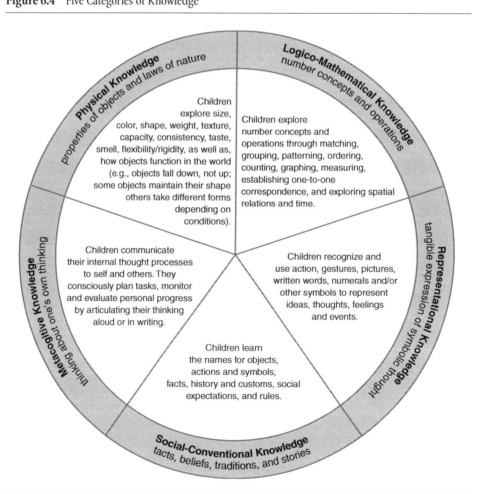

Skills

Skills consist of observable actions that can be used singly or in combination to master a task. Children learn skills through modeling and direct instruction. Opportunities to practice skills and apply them in meaningful circumstances further support skill development. In your observations of Jessie Brooks's kindergartners, children are displaying and practicing many skills—sharing materials, taking turns, identifying print, forming letters and words, verbally communicating ideas, drawing on memory skills, listening to one another, compromising, developing conclusions, seeking out relevant resources, and looking up information. These are just some of the hundreds of skills young children develop in early childhood.

Feelings

Some feelings are biologically programmed at birth (e.g., joy, anger, sadness, and fear), others are learned. "Among the feelings that are learned are ones of competence, confidence, belonging and trust. Feelings about school, teachers, learning and other children are also learned in the early years" (Katz, 2008, p. 55). Young children learn about feelings in several ways: experiencing them firsthand, seeing them modeled, hearing people discuss feelings, hearing talk about the circumstances that prompt them, and experiencing people's reactions to the emotions they themselves express. The lessons young children learn in situ are the most relevant and powerful of any lessons they learn. They are less able than older children to derive meaning from hypothetical discussions or activities that are decontextualized from their direct experience. The kindergartners you just observed are expressing a range of feelings from confidence and satisfaction to anger and distress. Their teachers will make a significant difference in how well (or how poorly) they learn to cope with those feelings in themselves and in others.

Dispositions

Sometimes described as "habits of mind," dispositions are relatively predictable tendencies toward particular patterns of thinking, behaving, and perceiving the world (Katz & Chard, 2000). In line with her dispositions, a person may be more inclined to be curious or to be disinterested, friendly or unfriendly, bossy or acquiescent, generous or stingy, a problem solver or a problem avoider.

> Dispositions are not learned through formal instruction or exhortation. . . . Many dispositions that most adults want children to acquire or to strengthen—for example, curiosity, creativity, cooperation, openness, friendliness—are learned primarily from being around people who exhibit them (Katz, 2008, p. 54)

Children are also more likely to adopt dispositions when they have opportunities to express those dispositions in their behavior and to gain satisfaction from them (e.g., the curious child has opportunities to explore and experiment, the friendly child has opportunities to interact with others). Of course, positive dispositions like these can be discouraged if they are ignored or rebuffed. For instance, curiosity is squelched when only one answer will do, when opportunities to explore are limited, and when children's interests are repeatedly put off in order to attend to adult agendas. In Jessie's classroom, you are seeing routines, activities, and adults that support children's development of dispositions such as cooperation, friendliness, and the ability to solve problems.

Implications for Early Learning Programs

How well children develop the fundamental knowledge, skills, feelings, and dispositions associated with early childhood makes a difference in the degree to which they become contributing competent members of society. Detailed information about the precise ways in which each facet of learning develops is beyond the scope of this book, but the principles of development and learning outlined in this chapter hold true for each learning type. As a result, the strategies we identified earlier that support how children learn also support what children are learning at this age. In addition to the actions already mentioned, in high-quality early childhood programs adults do the following:

- Address knowledge, skills, feelings, and dispositions in their planning and in program implementation.
- Pay attention to all five critical areas of knowledge every day.
- Create programs and policies that enhance dispositions such as curiosity, cooperation, flexibility, problem solving, and friendliness (e.g., through small-group work, projects, learning centers, adults modeling curiosity).
- Avoid routines and strategies that detract from children gaining a wide array of knowledge and skills or that undermine desirable dispositions.

Now that you have had a chance to think about how children develop and learn as well as about the content of their learning, here are some ideas on how to apply this knowledge in your school or district.

PRINCIPALS' ROLES

Supporting Development and Learning

1. Hire teachers and direct supervisors of early childhood programs who have formal training in child development and specialized knowledge of childhood learning from birth to age eight.

2. Attend at least one professional development activity annually that focuses on early childhood education or early development and learning.

3. Read the NAEYC journal *Young Children* to keep up with emerging trends in child development and learning.

4. When making program decisions, use the principles of development and learning outlined in this chapter as benchmarks against which to determine if policies and practices are appropriate for young children. If a practice runs counter to these principles, discard it or change it.

5. Watch young children in action in classrooms and outdoors; identify behaviors indicative of child development and learning in a variety of domains. Refer to these examples when talking with program staff, parents, stakeholders, and the public.

6. Work with staff members, parents, and others to identify the dispositions you would like young children to develop in your program. Examine different aspects of the program (e.g., staffing, routines, activities, and adult behavior) to determine the extent to which these elements support or detract from your goals.

7. Create opportunities for early childhood teachers to examine how well their daily plans and practices support child development and learning.

8. Create mechanisms whereby early childhood education plans and programs are examined to determine how well they

- address all developmental domains and sensitive areas of development;
- support challenge and mastery as part of the learning process;
- enhance children's forward movement through the learning sequences;
- accommodate multiple intelligences; and
- address knowledge, skills, feelings, and dispositions.

9. Adjust staffing schedules to ensure that each child has one or more consistent adults with whom he interacts every day.

10. Monitor programs to ensure that children have materials and opportunities to engage in hands-on activities, space to move about safely and freely, and time to freely interact with peers and adults.

11. Provide inservice training for staff regarding child development and learning by providing opportunities for continuing education in child development. Pay particular attention to new findings in brain growth development.

12. Sponsor family education events centering around child development and learning topics.

13. Create opportunities for parents and family members to discuss with program staff how their child has developed and how she learns best.

14. Take the initiative to talk about the importance of child development and learning with members of school boards, community groups such as Rotary, and parents.

15. Take corrective action to bring program policies into greater alignment with child development and learning principles as necessary.

Early Childhood Curriculum

Effective principals ensure high quality curriculum and instructional practices that foster young children's learning and development. (NAESP, 2005, p. 49)

In developmentally appropriate classrooms, the curriculum is designed to help young children become lifelong learners, think critically and imaginatively, ask meaningful questions, formulate alternative solutions, appreciate diversity, form constructive relationships with others, and work collaboratively (NAESP, 2005, 49). The role of the principal in seeing that this happens is crucial. Teachers and support staff cannot do it alone, no matter how skilled they are. In fact, early childhood practitioners identify the supportive attitudes and behaviors of principals as critical to their ability to create developmentally appropriate programs for young children. Conversely, lack of knowledge and support from principals—and even worse, actions that run counter to principles of developmentally appropriate practice (DAP)—frustrate teachers and sometimes prompt then to leave the field (Click & Karkos, 2008; Wien, 2004).

The essential functions of school principals in terms of curriculum include the following (NAESP, 1998, 2005; Ricken, 2007):

- Knowing enough about early childhood curriculum content and design to recognize signs of quality as well as indicators of concern
- Advancing a schoolwide curriculum that carefully balances children's intellectual learning with other developmental domains

- Providing ongoing professional development for the school community that fosters holistic, integrative approaches to curriculum and instruction
- Creating opportunities for school personnel at all levels to engage in open discussion about developmentally appropriate curriculum for young children
- Developing procedures, policies, schedules, and methods to meet the unique learning needs of young children
- Interpreting internal groups to one another
- Helping to bridge learning expectations and curriculum implementation from preschool through the upper elementary grades
- Interpreting the early childhood curriculum to outsiders: parents, school board members, middle school personnel, and high school personnel
- Partnering with community-based prekindergarten (preK) programs (preschools, child care, Head Start) to provide seamless transitions for children and families from home to school and from one program level to the next

This is a tall order. However, school principals who strive to address these functions are much appreciated by early childhood staff and create conditions that lead to increased academic achievement among their youngest students (Armstrong, 2006).

Our principal brought two parents to observe my classroom prior to enrolling their son for the fall. We were doing learning centers when I overheard the dad say, "Should we come back another day, during the real learning time?" The principal said, "There is real learning going on right now. Take a look over there in the block area—see those children building that road—listen to the 'para'—they are working with math concepts—sizes, shapes, fractions. They are even exploring some physics as they work out how to get all those odd shapes to balance."

I could have hugged him! It's great when you have a principal who "gets it" and can help others get it too. It makes you feel like your work is important and that there's someone who knows enough to back you up when you need it. (Kindergarten teacher)

WHAT IS THE EARLY CHILDHOOD CURRICULUM?

For young children, learning occurs across developmental domains simultaneously. For instance, while painting at the easel, Samantha practices both small- and large-muscle coordination (physical), learns the names of the colors and what happens when they are mixed (cognitive), shares the paints (social), uses her imagination (aesthetic), and chooses words (language) to describe events and feelings (emotional) as a result of creating something new (NAESP, 2005). Because young children's learning is holistic and integrative, the early childhood curriculum must be that way too.

Early childhood curriculum involves all the organized experiences, activities, and events, both direct or indirect, that occur in settings designed to foster young children's learning and development. It includes

a. the content and skills children are to learn;
b. activities, strategies, and materials teachers use to address curricular goals;
c. interactions among children and adults, and among and between peers; and
d. the context in which teaching and learning occur (Kostelnik et al., 2007).

During the early years, curriculum integrates care and education and includes both planned experiences and interactions that arise spontaneously (New Zealand Ministry of Education, 2003). In the United States, we assume that the curriculum at all levels, including early childhood, is shaped by our desire for children to become happy, contributing members of a democracy (Darling-Hammond et al., 2005). As mentioned in Chapter 2, there was a time when early childhood educators believed that such learning happened best in environments that were warm, safe, and well supplied, but in which the curriculum was relatively informal and teachers played a passive role in the learning process. That view has changed. Today, the field recognizes that early childhood curricula must be robust and that teaching must be intentional. Thus, policy makers, principals, and teachers have a shared responsibility to implement early childhood curricula that are thoughtfully planned, challenging, engaging, developmentally appropriate, culturally and linguistically responsive, comprehensive, and likely to help learners acquire the knowledge, skills, and values that society deems most important for its members to possess (National Association for the Education of Young Children and the National Association of Early Childhood Specialists in State Departments of Education [NAEYC/NAECS/SDE], 2003; Trister Dodge, 2004).

Dimensions of Effective Curriculum

Throughout the United States, programs that receive federal or state funding are required to identify a curriculum they will use. Currently, there is no one curriculum under which every early childhood program operates. Some programs adopt models that have been developed by others and for which commercially available resources exist (e.g., High/Scope, Creative Curriculum, Montessori, Project Approach). Many others rely on teachers and principals to fashion a localized curriculum that evolves over time and that is especially suited to the needs of their particular groups of children. In either case, the most effective early childhood curricula share the following characteristics:

- The curriculum is designed so that children of all ages and abilities are active and engaged.
- Curriculum goals are clearly defined, shared, and understood by program administrators, teachers, and families.
- The curriculum is evidence based and organized around principles of child development and learning.
- Valued content is learned through investigation, play, and focused intentional teaching.
- The curriculum builds on children's prior learning and experiences and are inclusive of children with disabilities as well as children whose home language is not English.

- The curriculum is comprehensive, encompassing all areas of development and all subjects.
- Professional standards validate the curriculum's subject-matter content.
- The curriculum is likely to benefit children (NAEYC/NAECS/SDE, 2003, p. 2).

Most important, the curriculum is organized and intentional in its implementation. It has clear objectives, outcomes, and means for assessment that relate to its goals. Programs that lack these elements and have no fixed curriculum are generally ineffective and are associated with fewer positive outcomes for children (Fukkink & Lont, 2007).

To enhance curriculum development, thirty-seven U.S. states have created comprehensive early learning guidelines for children ages three to five. Twenty-two states have guidelines that begin at birth (U.S. Department of Health and Human Services [DHHS], 2007). Although these guidelines do not take the place of curriculum, they provide resources teachers and principals can use to select or create appropriate curriculum and measure how well it is being implemented.

State Guidelines in Early Childhood Curriculum Adoption or Development

When states first became formally involved in early childhood education (in the 1980s and 1990s), they pulled together people from across the early childhood spectrum to create state documents defining the enterprise. Those early documents mostly focused on the teaching strategies one might expect to see in developmentally appropriate early childhood programs as well as definitions of meaningful learning experiences for young children. These were important first steps in defining expectations for program development and teacher behavior in the classroom. However, most state documents did not talk much about the content of early childhood lessons or typical expectations for children's learning in the preschool years. This omission made it difficult for child care, preschool, and elementary personnel to link early learning with K–12 standards.

More recently, the notion of learner outcomes that is playing such an important role in elementary and secondary education is also being considered in relation to preK programs. As a result, most state documents have been updated to include expected learner outcomes and benchmarks related to young children's conceptual learning and basic skill acquisition in various developmental domains. Although the wording varies from state to state, most states have identified learning expectations for the whole child. For instance, the state of Nebraska (Nebraska Department of Education, 2005) has identified widely held expectations for young children's learning in the following areas:

- Social and emotional development
- Approaches to learning
- Health and physical development
- Language and literacy development
- Mathematics
- Science
- Creative arts

Similarly, Connecticut (Connecticut State Board of Education, 2006) has used the following domains around which to organize content standards and performance expectations:

- Personal and social development
- Physical development
- Cognitive development
- Creative expression and aesthetic development

The inclusion of benchmarks for early childhood learning has greatly expanded the influence of state guidelines on early childhood programs nationwide. Such guidelines provide useful tools teachers and principals can use to better understand the "why," the "how," and the "what" of early childhood education. They also provide a basis on which preschool curriculum and K–12 standards can be aligned.

An example of outcomes or indicators of progress in the area of mathematics prior to kindergarten is presented in Table 7.1. As you read, consider how such expectations link to what children are learning in kindergarten, first grade, and second grade.

Table 7.1   Expectations for Four-Year-Old Children's Concepts of Mathematics (Kentucky Early Learning Guidelines)

Numbers and Counting

Children demonstrate an understanding of numbers and counting when they

- imitate rote counting using the names of numbers,
- count in sequence to five and beyond,
- arrange sets of objects in one-to one correspondence,
- count concrete objects to five and beyond,
- use math language to express quantity in everyday experiences,
- compare concrete quantities to determine which has more,
- recognize that a set of objects remains the same amount if physically rearranged,
- realize that the last number counted is the total amount of objects,
- recognize some numerals and associates number concepts with print materials in a meaningful way, and
- name and write some numerals.

Shapes and Spatial Relationships

Children recognize and describe shapes and spatial relationships when they

- recognize some basic shapes,
- create and duplicate shapes,
- identify shapes,
- recognize parts of a whole,
- recognize the position of objects, and
- use words that indicate directionality, order, and position of objects.

(Continued)

Table 7.1 (Continued)

Comparisons and Patterning

Children use the attributes of objects for comparison and patterning when they

- match objects,
- sort objects by one or more attributes,
- describe objects by one or more attributes,
- recognize, duplicate, and extend simple patterns, and
- create original patterns.

Measuring

Children measure and describe using nonstandard and standard units when they

- compare and order by size,
- use tools to explore measuring,
- explore, compare, and describe length, weight, or volume using nonstandard units,
- show awareness of time concepts, and
- categorize and sequence time intervals and use language associated with time in everyday situations (Kentucky Department of Education, 2006).

To support children's pursuit of benchmarks like those presented in Table 7.1, most state early learning documents outline

- rationales for providing high-quality early childhood programs for young children,
- ideas for involving families in children's learning,
- goals for children in a variety of developmental domains and academic arenas,
- learning benchmarks,
- guidelines for planning appropriate learning experiences for children in programs,
- sample assessment strategies and recommended assessment or evaluation tools,
- frameworks for program evaluation,
- ideas for staff training and development, and
- a context for assessing the impact of public policies on young children and their families.

Such guides enjoy widespread distribution in each state and provide an excellent resource for creating early childhood programs within individual schools and school districts. Some early childhood programs go a step further and adopt a nationally validated curriculum model that has a proven record of effectiveness with children from urban, suburban, and rural settings. Examples of three such curriculum models are presented in Table 7.2. Although these are not the only models, they are among the most commonly used and best documented at this time (Trister Dodge, 2004). The models are listed in the order in which they first came on the scene.

Table 7.2 Examples of Three National Preschool to Grade 2 Curriculum Models

Criteria for inclusion follow:

- The curriculum spans preschool through second grade (and beyond).
- The curriculum addresses **all** subject areas and developmental domains.
- The curriculum incorporates elements associated with developmentally appropriate practice (DAP).
- The program provides appropriate tools for assessing children's progress and program effectiveness.
- Resources for teachers and principals are available, including Web site, teaching materials, books, and videos.
- Professional staff development opportunities are available, including workshops, consultants, and site visitors.
- There is a solid body of independent research–based evidence that the curriculum enhances child development and learning, including increased academic achievement.

The High Scope Curriculum (Introduced in 1964)
High/Scope Educational Research Foundation
600 North River Street
Ypsilanti, MI 48198-2898
(734) 485-2000
http://www.highscope.org

The Responsive Classroom (Introduced in 1981)
Northeast Foundation for Children
85 Avenue A, Suite 204, PO Box 718
Turners Falls, MA 01376-0718
(800) 360-6332
http://www.responsiveclassroom.org

The Creative Curriculum (Introduced in 1988)
Teaching Strategies
5151 Wisconsin Avenue, NW, Suite 300
Washington, DC 20016-4119
(202) 362-7543
http://www.teachingstrategies.com

Whether an individual school or entire school district adopts a national curriculum model or creates its own program, certain questions will facilitate the adoption and development process (Trister Dodge, 2004).

- Does this curriculum fit our beliefs and goals for children, families, and early education?
- Does this curriculum address program mandates?
- Is this curriculum based on research?
- Is there evidence that the curriculum is effective when it is implemented well?
- Is this curriculum comprehensive?

- Are resources available to support curriculum implementation?
- Are resources available to support staff development?

Questions like these need to be revisited frequently. Conversations that address such queries promote greater understanding among staff and stakeholders (e.g., families, policy makers, and upper elementary teachers) about what constitutes an effective, developmentally appropriate curriculum for young children, and about how to carry it out.

"GOODNESS OF FIT" BETWEEN EARLY LEARNING AND LATER SCHOOLING

Although early childhood education is officially defined as addressing the learning needs of children from birth to age eight, the reality is that there is often a chasm between the people and settings in which younger children are served and formal school programs for older children. This chasm is deepened by real and perceived differences in philosophy, training, funding, and demands for accountability. Nevertheless, research shows that children benefit when they can move from one educational level or program to another with maximum continuity (Darling-Hammond et al., 2005; O'Connell, 2005). In other words, children need to experience stronger connections among all the early childhood programs they encounter. Connections are strengthened when preschool to Grade 3 (P–3) program personnel

- know and respect the role each one plays in children's early learning;
- share common routines and practices uniquely suited to younger learners;
- create seamless transitions from home to school, from preschool to kindergarten, to first and second grades; and
- align learning expectations for children from the preK period through the elementary years.

Familiarity and Respect

It is difficult for people to work toward common goals if they do not know one another and if they are unfamiliar with each other's work. One way to address this is for teachers and principals in preschool and elementary programs to come together to discuss mutual needs and interests, exchange information, and visit one another's programs while the children are in session. Another strategy is for teachers and principals to join professional organizations that span the entire range of early childhood education (such as the National Association for the Education of Young Children [NAEYC], the Association for Childhood Education International [ACEI], and the Association for Supervision and Curriculum Development [ASCD]).

Shared Practices

Children benefit whenever preschool and early elementary programs are more similar than dissimilar in the ways they look and feel. Routines and practices that are relatively the same from one program level to the next enhance children's self-confidence and prompt children to be more accepting of new experiences. Such continuity also helps children attain important skills, such as self-direction and familiarity with materials, which in turn enable them to build on what they already know to pursue new knowledge and competencies.

Seamless Transitions

The transition from home to external early childhood setting is a significant milestone for young children and their families. Likewise, even children who have spent most of their lives in care outside the home see the transition to kindergarten and from kindergarten to first grade as major life events. How early education programs handle these transitions can have long-term influences on children's academic achievement. Unfortunately, national surveys indicate that only a few schools and communities currently have comprehensive transition plans in place that allow preschool teachers, elementary personnel, and family members to exchange important information about child development and curricular expectations (R. F. Nelson, 2004). This situation is beginning to change. Communities all over the country are now seeking ways to create smoother transitions for children from home to school and from one early childhood setting or level to another.

> PreK teachers at McFerran Elementary School in Louisville, Kentucky, get a first-hand view of what their students will experience in kindergarten: They spend the first week of every school year helping teach kindergarten. This leads to great discussions between teachers and increased continuity between preschool classrooms and the kindergartens (NAESP, 2005).

A significant amount of research is being conducted around the transition issue. So far, four elements have been identified as key to successful early childhood transitions (DHHS, 2003). Early childhood transitions are smoother when the following elements are in place:

1. Children experience developmentally appropriate curricula in preK, kindergarten, first grade, and second grade.

2. There is ongoing communication and cooperation among preK, kindergarten, and elementary personnel.

3. Children are prepared for transitions in advance.

4. Families are actively involved in the transition process.

A few examples of specific strategies that illustrate these elements are offered in Table 7.3 (DHHS, 2003; O'Connell, 2005).

Table 7.3   Examples of Effective Transition Strategies Involving Educators, Young Children, and Their Families

---

- Schools work closely with families, community organizations, and feeder early childhood programs prior to children formally enrolling at the school.
- In communities with multiple preschools and kindergartens, community transition committees are established and create a step-by-step plan and materials to support multiple programs (e.g., joint kindergarten registration, community workshops for parents, school visits).
- Schools invite preK personnel to take part in the kindergarten intake process.
- Early childhood programs transfer records to one another (parents are given information about their rights to privacy regarding the records of their children).
- Teachers make home visits to families after children are enrolled at both the preK and kindergarten levels.
- Programs work together to provide special information and assistance to non-English-speaking families.
- Programs share joint training across traditional boundaries.
- Programs collaborate on curriculum and assessment across programs serving children from birth to age eight.

Aligning Learning Expectations

Many states are in the process of aligning their expectations for young children's learning with Head Start Performance Standards, with curriculum standards identified by learned societies in each discipline, and with the K–12 core curriculum standards for their state. A useful follow-up is for early childhood programs in a community to study these expectations together and to discuss how such expectations will be addressed in each program.

Kindergarten Readiness: A "Goodness of Fit" Challenge

An important "goodness of fit" issue principals face during early childhood is how ready entering kindergarteners are for more formal schooling and to what extent their school is ready to accommodate young learners in kindergarten.

Currently, there is no one profile of what a child who is "ready" for kindergarten should know and be able to do. When polled, kindergarten teachers maintain that physical well-being, social development, and curiosity are critical contributors to early school success. Additional skills teachers like to see in incoming kindergartners are

- being able to communicate basic needs and thoughts,
- showing enthusiasm for learning,
- following simple directions,
- cooperating in class,
- demonstrating sensitivity to other children's feelings, and
- showing interest in print. (Bowman et al., 2001)

These are skills teachers hope children will bring to kindergarten in a rudimentary form. They are also skills teachers expect to work on during the kindergarten year. At the same time, it must be remembered that the only legal requirement for kindergarten entry in most states is for children to turn age five by a certain cutoff date. This makes kindergarten a "come as you are" proposition; it is to be expected that kindergarteners will exhibit wide variations in development and prior experience. Schools must be prepared to deal with these variations constructively. Thus the best kindergarten readiness questions are, "What can we do so every entering kindergartner learns and thrives?" and "How can we best meet the needs of each child who walks through our doors?" These questions put the "goodness of fit" responsibility on families, preK programs, schools, and communities to create conditions to make school success more likely for each child.

Effective Strategies

We have already discussed how familiarity and respect among P–3 educators, shared practices, seamless transitions, and aligned curricula contribute to "goodness of fit," but there are other effective strategies, too (Ackerman & Barnett, 2005; Pianta, Cox & Snow, 2007):

Intervening Early

Starting appropriate programs with children as young as infants and toddlers

Being Inclusive

Including families as partners in the education process

Using Appropriate Kindergarten Curricula

Implementing kindergarten curricula that match young children's learning styles

Offering Full-Day Kindergarten

Offering full-day kindergarten programs that provide inexperienced and less-advantaged children more time and opportunities to learn that are less pressured

Ineffective Strategies

Certain strategies detract from promoting readiness in children and schools and need to be avoided (Ackerman & Barnett, 2005; Pianta, Cox, & Snow, 2007).

Holding Children Out

Keeping age-eligible children out of kindergarten with no educational intervention does not help them become more ready for school and, in fact, can put them further behind.

Holding Children Back

As a general policy, requiring children to repeat another year of preschool or kindergarten does not give most children enough of an academic boost to warrant the practice. Children who move on to the more challenging curricula of the next early learning level tend to improve at the same rate (with fewer problem behaviors) than do children who remain behind.

Creating Special Programs That Segregate Younger,
Less-Experienced Children from Older, More-Experienced Children

Developmental kindergarten and curricula for young fives are often designed to accommodate children who are age eligible for school, but who are less mature than their peers. When such programs are put in place it is common for regular kindergarten and first-grade curricula to be ratcheted up to meet the needs of the more-experienced students, leaving the others even further behind. Most young children learn best in environments in which ability levels vary. Segregating children appears to establish patterns of lowered expectations for younger children that negatively influence their school experiences over the long run.

Narrowing the PreK Curriculum

Some preschool and kindergarten programs focus on a narrow set of academic skills to get children ready. Such approaches fail to encompass the wide range of skills children ultimately need to be successful in school and are not well suited to young learners.

IMPLEMENTING THE
EARLY CHILDHOOD CURRICULUM

Visit any high-quality early childhood setting and you will see children moving about, talking, observing, working on their own, interacting with peers or working with a teacher. At first glance, it may seem that the children are randomly engaged or that there is little formal learning going on. But take a closer look and you will find children

- examining objects,
- talking about their experiences,
- asking questions,
- collecting information,
- relating current experiences to prior learning,
- making discoveries,
- proposing explanations,
- testing out ideas,
- comparing their thinking with the thinking of others, and
- constructing new understandings.

Their teachers will be actively engaged, as well—observing, listening, instructing, guiding, supporting, and encouraging them. Consider the learning going on as three children and their teacher interact around a math game in the kindergarten.

> Three 5-year-olds have just finished a game of "Memory," making pairs among face down cards on the table. "I won," one player announces.
>
> Their teacher approaches and asks, "How did you figure out that you won the most cards?"
>
> "Well, because," exclaimed the child, holding a mass of cards in one hand and placing them next to a classmate's pile in comparison. "See? I've got more!"
>
> "Does everyone agree?" the teacher asks.
>
> "Wait a minute!," another child protests. "Let me look at something." He spreads his cards end to end in a line on the floor. His line contains so many cards that it extends from the math area out into the center of the classroom. He makes similar lines next to his of each of his classmates' cards.
>
> The teacher, observing this, asks, "What do you think?
>
> "Look. See?" He answers. "My line is longer. I won. I have the most."
>
> "Does everyone agree with that?" the teacher asks the group. "Are there any other ways to figure out who won?"
>
> With the teacher's guidance and encouragement, the children continue to try solutions to the problem until clean-up time (Frost, Worthman, & Reifel, 2004, p. 321).

By the end of the session, they have generated several more solutions including counting and measuring with string.

ACTIVITIES YOU SHOULD EXPECT TO SEE IN EARLY CHILDHOOD CLASSROOMS

The children in the activity described above are discovering important math concepts such as "more" and "most." They are also finding out that number is a function of the amount of objects, not simply how much space the objects fill. A stack of cards may seem like more in one instance and a line of cards like more in another. In this activity, both children and teacher are actively involved in the learning process. This form of guided discovery is just one example of several different kinds of educational activities you should see regularly in early childhood classrooms. Six of the most common types are

- explorations,
- guided-discovery activities,
- problem-solving activities,
- discussions,
- demonstrations, and
- direct instruction.

Explorations

Exploration is where all learning begins. Since the world is very new to young children, there is much to explore. Exploration is open ended and self-initiated. Children cannot progress to more advanced steps in the learning process until they have had plenty of time and many opportunities to investigate materials and objects in their own ways, motivated by their own interests (Slentz & Krogh, 2001b). In exploratory activities, the following are true:

Children
- Choose what to explore
- Explore things firsthand
- Discover things for themselves
- Take activities in whatever direction suits their interests
- Proceed at their own pace
- Make most of the decisions about what to do and how to do it

Teachers
- Make available a wide range of age-appropriate materials for children to explore firsthand
- Pay attention to issues of health and safety so children can explore freely
- Verbally acknowledge children's actions and discoveries
- Observe children and add new materials to extend children's explorations over time
- Provide opportunities for children to explore materials before asking them to use items in some particular way
- Avoid requiring children to come to one particular outcome or conclusion

Example The teacher puts out a variety of green-colored objects for children to examine on their own. The teacher observes the children, listens to their observations, and acknowledges the discoveries they make. "You're excited to find seeds inside that fruit." "You noticed the lime squirted out juice when you squished it." "You got some of the peel under your fingernails." "That tasted sour."

Guided-Discovery Activities

Guided-discovery activities proceed primarily along the lines of the children's interest with strategic teacher support (Epstein, 2007). As children interact with people and objects, they build concepts and make connections from one experience to another (Maxim, 2003; NAEYC, 2009). In guided-discovery activities, the following are true:

Children
- Construct knowledge about the world and how it works
- Observe and recall
- Make choices and decisions
- Experiment
- Interpret, compare, and contrast
- Order, group, and identify patterns
- Raise questions
- Pursue answers of their own making

Teachers
- Structure the parameters in which learning occurs
- Serve as a resource
- Model how to find answers
- Provide information and tools
- Offer opportunities for practice (rehearsals, repetitions, and elaborations)
- Use scaffolding to support children's progress
- Ask questions
- Challenge children's thinking
- Acknowledge children's ideas and discoveries

Example The previous description of the three children and their teacher who are figuring out who "won" the memory game are engaged in a guided-discovery activity.

Problem-Solving Activities

Problem solving is a specialized form of guided discovery. These lessons focus on helping children work through the steps necessary to address a problem or investigate something new. Adult strategies are designed to help children develop potential solutions as well as gain experience with problem-solving processes. Teachers do not try to lead children toward a single, correct answer. Instead, solutions are of the children's own making, and more than one conclusion may be derived for each situation (Freiberg & Driscoll, 2005; Kostelnik et al., 2007).

It is possible to investigate many kinds of problems—movement problems ("How many different ways can you throw the beanbag?"), strategy problems ("What strategies will you use to play this game?"), skill problems ("How many different ways can this set of objects be sequenced?"), social problems ("How will we decide who gets the next turn?"), and physical science problems ("What do you think will happen if we heat this up?"). An individual problem (e.g., naming the new guinea pig) may be resolved in a single sitting, while other problems are revisited over and over again (e.g., what sinks and what floats, magnetic properties of materials). In problem-solving activities, the following are true:

Children
- Notice, observe, question, and identify a problem
- Hypothesize about why something happens
- Gather information, make predictions, construct explanations, brainstorm, and generate solutions
- Experiment, take action, and test ideas
- Draw conclusions, observe results, reflect on outcomes, explore patterns, make comparisons, develop alternative explanations, and translate knowledge into new context
- Evaluate results and plans, and make plans for new experiments or approaches
- Communicate results

Teachers
- Plan simple investigations to enhance children's thinking, analyzing, interpreting, understanding, and reasoning
- Plan activities that engage children in a variety of ways
- Choose problems that are concrete and observable
- Put forward problems that have more than one solution
- Take advantage of naturally occurring situations to enhance children's problem-solving skills
- Address both physical and social problems
- Are more concerned with how children derive their answers than the accuracy of those answers
- Avoid solving children's problems for them

Example Taking advantage of a problem-solving opportunity in the classroom:

Teacher: (Kneeling between two boys with an arm around each.) You look angry, Lyle, and Hank, you seem really upset. (The boys nod in agreement.) What's the problem?

Lyle: I want to be the dad. I said so first.

Hank: You're always the dad. I want to be big.

Lyle: I'm the biggest, so huh! You can't be the dad. You're too little.

Teacher: So the problem is, Lyle, you want to be the dad, and, Hank, you want to be the dad too. (Both boys shake their head yes.) What can we do to solve this problem?

Lyle: I could be the dad today, then you can be the dad the next day.

Hank: Well, I could be the dad today.

Teacher: It sounds like you both want to be the dad today.

Lyle: We don't need two dads. Hank, you could be the ladder guy and wear the tool belt!

Hank: And the gloves?

Lyle: OK, the gloves (Both boys smile.)

Teacher: So, Lyle, you're going to be the dad, and Hank, you're going to be the ladder guy who wears the tool belt and the gloves.

Both boys nod yes and go off to the pretend play area. When the teacher checks on them later, the dad and the ladder guy have built a "swamp boat" and are giving rides to the other children. (Epstein, 2007, p. 19)

Discussions

Young children and their teachers have many things to talk about.

- *What is happening in the program?* "Who will feed the fish?" "Why are some people upset about what is happening on the playground?" "Today we will begin a new lunch routine."

- *What is happening to children away from the program?* "Logan has a new kitten at his house." "Laura's grandma is visiting." "Denise will be moving to another part of town."
- *What is happening in the community?* "There was a big storm last night." "A new park is being built across the street from our school." "There will be a parade on Saturday."

Discussion activities involve joint conversations between teachers and children. Such conversations often take place in small groups, but children as young as three years of age can successfully participate in short discussions involving a whole group of children at once (Warden, 2008). Discussions might be impromptu, but often are planned, taking the form of a class meeting, a brainstorming session, conversations that involve planning, and discussions in which children reflect on what they did during the day. During discussions, the following are true:

Children   Talk, listen, comment, pose ideas, come to agreements, summarize, build concepts, and adjust their thinking to accommodate new information that doesn't fit their old notions

Teachers   Talk, listen, comment, pose ideas, come to agreements, summarize, gain insights into children's thinking, provide information, and sometimes keep records for children to refer back to at another time

Example   A Dinosaur Discussion with the four-year-olds (Kostelnik, 2006)

> The children were sitting with their teacher in a circle. They had been studying dinosaurs and were now deeply involved in a discussion about paleontology.
>
> Teacher: How did those dinosaur bones get under the ground?
>
> Eze: They died in the ground. The dinosaurs, uh, laid down in the mud, and then they just, uh, died in the ground.
>
> Chris: Quicksand—it was quicksand that got 'em.
>
> Carlos: Somebody put the bones there; I think it was the sand man.
>
> Sara: There was a big hole and the dinosaurs fell in and they got all buried up.
>
> Nathan: After the dinosaurs died, then the people came and buried up the bones.
>
> Teacher: It sounds like you know a lot about dinosaurs and how they became fossils. Remember, there were no people alive when the dinosaurs were on earth.
>
> Nathan: Oh yeah. That's right. That's right. I know! It was a front-end loader. That's it! A front-end loader buried 'em, but it didn't have no driver.

In this example, the teacher's social and language goals included having children carry out a discussion involving multiple participants, for them to generate verbal ideas, and for children to engage in conversational turn taking. Her focus was not on having the children pose correct scientific answers. The children's responses, gave her insights into their thinking and provided useful information for future planning.

Demonstrations

Basically, demonstrations involve one person showing others how to do something or how something works. Most often adults demonstrate and children watch. However, there are times when roles reverse and children lead the interaction with peers or with their teachers. During demonstrations, the following are true:

Observers	• Watch
	• Summarize
	• Practice
	• Imitate
	• Apply what they have learned to new situations
Demonstrators	• Use demonstrations to stimulate interest or curiosity
	• Show a phenomenon
	• Illustrate instructions
	• Offer a preview of something that will happen later
Example	Before adding "Feed the Guinea Pig" to the job chart, the teacher walks the children through the process of opening the food canister, measuring out the correct amount, putting the food in the dish, and then closing the canister and putting it away. The children then talk her through the steps as practice. The next day, Jonathan becomes the first child to carry out the new job on the Job Chart.

Direct Instruction

Direct instruction follows closely along the lines of the teacher's goals, but is also shaped by the children's responses (Epstein, 2007). It is used to teach children factual information or routines they could not discover easily or safely on their own (e.g., phonetic information such as how to pronounce words that end in "*e*," how to behave during a fire drill, how to answer the telephone politely, certain spelling rules such as "*I* before *e*, except after *c*"). In this type of activity, adults carry out a series of prescribed steps that lead children toward a single correct response. It is this focus on working toward a single known answer that distinguishes direct instruction from all the other activity types described so far. However, direct instruction involves more than simply telling children things. Teachers use "gestures, intentional mistakes, surprises, pauses, and enthusiasm to enhance children's interest and understanding. The advantages of direct instruction is that it is efficient, produces immediate results, teaches children to follow directions, and lends itself to on-the-spot evaluation" (Kostelnik et al., 2007, p. 80). During direct instruction activities, the following are true:

Children	• Observe and pay attention
	• Show or tell something
	• Differentiate examples and nonexamples of the information or action
	• Apply what they have learned
Teachers	• Gain children's attention
	• Show or say something
	• Prompt children to respond
	• Reinforce correct responses
	• Correct or ignore inaccurate responses
	• Give children opportunities to practice
Example	The teacher in the preschool class is using direct instruction in this short lesson on animal sounds with a group of four children sitting on a rug with the flannel board. The adult's goal is to teach children to associate a picture with a sound as a prereading skill.
	Teacher: Look up here. I have some pictures of farm animals we saw on our field trip.

(Continued)

(Continued)

The children look at the flannel board and individual photographs of a cow, a sheep, a horse, and a chicken.

Teacher: I'm going to make some animal sounds. Listen. When I make a sound you point to the animal that makes that sound.

The teacher makes one sound at a time.

The children point to an animal in response to the sound.

If a child points to the correct animal, the teacher responds by saying, "That's right, the cow makes the Moo sound." If a child points to an incorrect picture, the teacher ignores the response until the child gets it right. Or, the teacher says, "You think the sheep says Moo. It says Baa. Let's try again."

Later in the day the children have a chance to play with the pictures and flannel board on their own. The teacher is pleased to hear the children using the animal sounds (mostly correctly) in association with the pictures.

How Early Learning Activities Relate to One Another

All six of the learning activities described above are typical for children from preschool through the second grade. Refer to Figure 7.1 for a summary of these activity types and the relationship among them.

Figure 7.1 Activity Pyramid

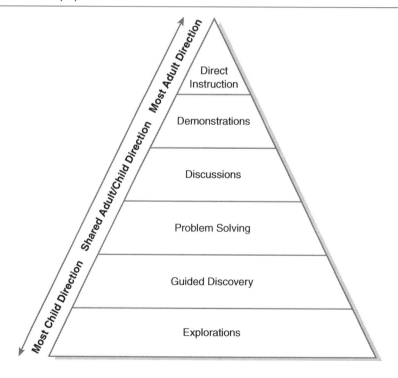

As you can see, the direction some activities take are mostly child determined. These form the foundation of the activity pyramid and are the most prevalent in high-quality early childhood settings. The younger the child, the more this is so. Other lessons involve shared adult–child outcomes and play a significant role in the early childhood curriculum. Activities that are mostly adult directed play a valuable but smaller role in children's early learning. Such lessons are most effective when they are short and when they are supplemented by activities lower on the activity pyramid. All six activity types are adaptable to any area of the curriculum and can be used in any of the learning centers we discuss in the next chapter.

PRINCIPALS' ROLES

Curriculum Development

1. Become familiar with your state's preK learning standards.

2. Get to know the early childhood personnel in your state department of education who can serve as resources to you and personnel in your programs.

3. Observe accredited early childhood programs in the community to better understand how they are approaching the curriculum. Develop strategies to bridge learning expectations from those programs to the entry-level programs in your school or district.

4. Arrange opportunities for P–3 personnel to visit one another's programs, exchange relevant information, and plan joint activities.

5. Observe the early childhood programs in your school or district regularly. (Do more than simply "breeze" in: stop and watch for at least twenty minutes to get a better idea of how the program really works.) Make sure curriculum content reflects a balance of all areas of development and learning as well as all six activity types depicted in Figure 7.1, the Activity Pyramid.

6. Meet periodically with early childhood staff to discuss curriculum issues. Convey high expectations for children's learning while advocating developmentally appropriate practices. Review the early childhood curriculum annually. Include the early childhood program in the school's or district's school improvement plans.

7. Periodically review the written curriculum plans for the early childhood classrooms in your school. Discuss how the plans encompass holistic learning as well as how they address preK learning standards.

8. Work with community professionals, in-house early childhood personnel, district-level administrators, teachers, and families to create formal transition programs that ensure close contact among Head Start programs, preschools, childcare programs, and the public schools.

9. Develop committees and task forces to align learning expectations from preschool through the third grade. Sit in on these yourself as a signal of their importance. Include early childhood curriculum topics in inservice presentations to school personnel at all levels to familiarize them with what constitutes appropriate curriculum and instruction for young children. Provide curriculum-based professional development opportunities to early childhood staff.

10.   Encourage the use of a bottom-up approach to curriculum development and reform, rather than a top-down approach, in which the highest grades drive the entire curriculum development process.

11.   Share information with families and community members about the holistic, seamless nature of young children's learning from preschool through the later grades. Discuss what this could look like in your community.

12.   Become an advocate for developmentally appropriate curricula preK through Grade 3 with community decision makers.

Learning Centers and Classroom Routines

Early childhood classrooms are not physically arranged with desks in rows. They are typically centered around the use of learning centers. Learning centers are well-defined interest areas that provide children with a wide range of materials and opportunities to engage in hands-on learning across the curriculum (Stuber, 2007). Each center is carefully constructed to address specific educational goals. Usually children have multiple centers from which to choose at a given time: blocks, art, pretend play, books, science, and math are common examples of centers. Because children self-select the activity, the pace, the order and the specific means through which they will approach different learning tasks, learning centers are well suited to their educational needs. Learning centers give children chances to

- make choices,
- move about as needed,
- build on previous experience in meaningful ways,
- progress at their own rates within and among activity areas,
- choose activities that fit their particular learning styles and needs at the time,
- sustain self-directed activity,
- integrate knowledge and skills from one activity to another,
- develop concepts and consolidate their learning across the curriculum, and
- develop skills in working on their own, with peers, and with adults.

Teachers value learning centers too, because they make it easier to

- address children's need for hands-on experiences, mobility and physical activity, social interaction, and independence;
- accommodate children's varying attention spans and abilities;
- build activities around children's individual interests;

- move about the room asking probing questions, offering information, and otherwise scaffolding children's learning when most appropriate to do so; and
- regularly assess student understanding and skills through observation and other developmentally appropriate assessment practices.

Disciplinary problems, which can come about if children are disinterested in an activity or if children's skills are out of sync with whole group instruction, are minimized when learning centers are included as part of the early childhood day (Kostelnik et al., 2007). In fact, learning centers are so crucial to early childhood education that national accreditation standards and state licensing requirements in all fifty states require their use at the preprimary level, by recommending approximately sixty minutes of center-based instruction in half-day programs and two sixty-minute periods if children attend the program all day. Early childhood organizations including the National Association of Elementary School Principals (NAESP) advocate incorporating learning centers as part of the daily routine for children through age eight (NAESP, 1998; Stuber, 2007; Warner & Sower, 2005). See Table 8.1. for an example of how children in second grade could learn more about the algebraic concept of patterns through a variety of learning centers in their classroom.

Table 8.1   Centers and Activities Supporting the Algebraic Concept of Patterns in Grade 2

Center	*Activity*
Standard	The child uses algebraic concepts and procedures in a variety of situations (Kansas State Department of Education, 2003).
Second-grade knowledge indicator	The child uses concrete objects, drawings, and other representations to work with types of patterns (for example, repeating and growing)
Science	The child builds a pattern using different kinds of rocks. This can be a pattern students create, or a model shown on a worksheet that they follow. Children then record the pattern in a journal using pictures, words, or drawings.
Art	The child creates an abstract artwork with multiple patterns, using self-selected materials (pieces of tissue paper, crayons, markers, pencils, and so on).
Literacy (writing, reading)	The child writes a paragraph or two describing the abstract artwork and attaches it to the picture.
Mathematics	The child builds patterns with Unifix cubes, small blocks, or other manipulatives, then reproduces the patterns on paper in a math journal. The child can represent the pattern using written numbers or letters (for example, ABB).
Blocks (house building)	The child copies a picture of a building and shows patterns of windows and doors using colored blocks. The child can create a neighborhood of houses and buildings that show a pattern.
Dramatic play (store)	The child makes a list of items needed to set up a store, using written words and symbols to represent the items (fruit, drink, food). The list will form a pattern: fruit, fruit drink, fruit pie.

Source: Stuber, G. M. 2007. Of Primary Interest. Centering Your Classroom: Setting the Stage for Engaged Learners. *Young Children* 62(4): 58–59. Reprinted with permission from the National Association for the Education of Young Children.

TYPICAL LEARNING CENTERS FOR YOUNG CHILDREN

There is no single array of learning centers that is universal. However, some of the most common are

- art,
- blocks,
- language arts,
- math/manipulatives,
- music,
- physical,
- pretend play,
- sand/water,
- science/collections, and
- woodworking.

The content and skills most typically associated with each of these centers is depicted in Box 8.1.

Box 8.1

Sample Early Childhood Learning Centers

Art Center

In the art center, children

- think and act as artists and people who enjoy art;
- recognize and respond to elements of art (color, line, composition, shape, texture, and pattern);
- express themselves through art;
- use art tools;
- practice independence;
- practice cooperation;
- develop fine motor skills; and
- contribute to the aesthetic environment.

Block Center

In the block center, children

- think and act as builders;
- reconstruct "images in their mind" in tangible ways (this contributes to cognition and abstract thinking);
- encounter math and science concepts (size, shape, height, balance, patterns, and proportion);
- gain vocabulary, oral language, and writing skills;
- practice social skills;
- develop good work habits (planning, implementing, and evaluating); and
- acquire problem-solving skills.

Language Arts Center

In the language arts center, children

- think and act as writers, readers, and communicators;
- increase vocabulary;

(Continued)

(Continued)

- connect print with meaning;
- develop foundations of reading and writing;
- use writing tools;
- explore books;
- develop listening skills;
- express selves to others;
- develop sense of plot, character, and setting; and
- use books as resources.

Math/Manipulatives Center

In the math/manipulatives center, children

- think and act as doers and thinkers;
- develop math skills (counting, sequencing, patterning, grouping, matching, estimating, and measuring);
- use math vocabulary;
- use math tools;
- gain experience with number, numerals, shapes, attributes of objects, and sets;
- participate in problem solving;
- use logic skills; and
- practice metacognition (how you know what you know).

Music Center

In the music center, children

- think and act as musicians and people who enjoy music;
- recognize and respond to elements of music and dance (tempo, rhythm, beat, tone, melody, mood, and dynamics);
- express themselves;
- use musical objects;
- participate with others to create music and dance;
- develop preferences; and
- connect music and dance to other curriculum centers.

Physical Center

In the physical center, children

- think and act as active people who enjoy moving their bodies;
- develop fundamental motor skills (throwing, catching, kicking, running, hopping, jumping, galloping, and skipping);
- develop perceptual motor skills (balance, spatial awareness, figure-ground perception, and body and spatial awareness);
- develop fine motor skills; and
- combine skills in simple games.

Pretend Play Center

In the pretend play center, children

- think and act as anything they wish;
- mimic things they have seen or experienced;

- use actions and words to represent/interpret experiences;
- assign symbolic meaning to objects and actions;
- experiment with language and roles;
- develop social skills; and
- engage in problem solving.

Sand/Water Center

In the sand/water center, children

- think and act as experimenters;
- gain sensory experience;
- encounter math and science concepts (gravity, motion, liquids, solids, measurement, quantity, mass, volume, weight, and comparisons);
- use a variety of tools;
- engage in pretend play;
- learn to share space, time, and materials; and
- develop verbal scripts for expressing wants and needs and responding to others.

Science/Collections Center

In the science/collections center, children

- think and act as scientists;
- acquire science vocabulary;
- use scientific tools;
- gain factual knowledge;
- gain experience in science processes (observing, predicting, hypothesizing, experimenting, testing ideas, collecting data, looking for patterns, evaluating, and reflecting);
- build natural and physical science concepts;
- develop reporting skills;
- participate in problem solving; and
- practice metacognition (how you know what you know).

Woodworking Center

In the woodworking center, children

- think and act as builders and craftspeople;
- develop fine motor skills and perceptual awareness;
- express themselves;
- follow directions;
- apply math concepts (shape, measurement, size, texture, weight, consistency, angles, and geometry); and
- develop safety habits and independence using tools.

In reality, any learning center can be used to address knowledge and skills in every area of the curriculum. For instance, while children are building in the block area, the teacher might emphasize vocabulary development one day (long, short, tall, thick, or thin) and math concepts the next (half, quarter, whole, measuring, and so on). On another day, he might focus on a social goal such as cooperation and sharing. On yet another day, the emphasis might be on the scientific process as children build ramps and predict how changes in the angle of the ramps will affect how far their small cars and trucks will roll. In this way, learning centers can be used to support many facets of the curriculum based on educational goals, how the children use materials, and how teachers choose to respond and scaffold children's learning.

How Learning Centers Work

Learning centers are usually introduced to children from the beginning of the year. Initially, each center contains simple open-ended materials that are generally self-directing and self-explanatory. Teachers gradually introduce materials that are more complex and lessons that are more specific as children's skills and interests develop. New items are introduced, and old favorites are given a periodic rest to keep the areas appealing.

Certain learning centers are available to children every day (e.g., blocks, pretend play, and science center); others are offered a little less frequently (e.g., sand/water and woodworking). Teachers develop new centers and revise current ones based on their observations of children in center-time activities and their assessment of how well children are progressing in relation to the educational goals they have established.

Some teachers treat center-based activity times as wholly child initiated. Children may move from one activity to another at will. Other teachers designate some "have-to" centers that children are expected to complete within the day or week. Once the required center activities are finished, children may move into other centers of their own choosing. In either case, children do not rotate through centers as a group on a timed schedule. That kind of routine would undermine many of the benefits described above.

Adults supervise the centers by moving about the room, checking in with children, and offering instruction as appropriate. In team teaching situations, one or more adults may be stationed in a particular center or group of centers, carrying out given lessons for some or all of the session. In such circumstances, another adult serves as the "center manager" moving from center to center as needed. In each case, both teachers and children interact with and learn from one another. This learning involves a constant exchange of thoughts and ideas. Teachers observe, listen, instruct, guide, support, and encourage their students. Likewise, children ask questions, suggest alternatives, express interests, and develop plans. These interactions move the instruction forward, and sometimes lead it in new directions. In this way, teachers keep their long-range objectives in mind and at the same time keep their moment-to-moment decisions flexible in order to capitalize on input from the children and to meet children's educational needs more effectively.

Well-constructed learning centers share the characteristics listed in Box 8.2 (Kostelnik et al., 2007).

Box 8.2

Characteristics of Well-Designed Learning Centers

Learning centers have the greatest educational benefits when the following are present:

• Center activities are designed to address specific educational goals. Goals are aligned with state early learning standards, the program curriculum, and the needs and interests of individual children

• Centers include both planned activities and materials children can use on their own to support development and learning in various domains (e.g., "Today the math center includes a specific measuring activity as well as several other math materials children can use to explore math concepts that intrigue them").

• Center activities are flexible enough to accommodate children's varying abilities and interests. Teachers simplify or extend activities in accordance with children's learning needs.

• Teachers plan a variety of center-based activities over time to address all areas of development—aesthetic, cognitive, emotional, language, social, and physical—and the core disciplines (literacy, mathematics, science, and social studies).

• Specific center-based activities are repeated periodically so children have more than one chance to try them and to expand their skills.

• Teachers use each learning center to address different areas of the curriculum over time and to integrate instruction across disciplines (e.g., combining reading and writing, or integrating science and math).

• Centers are designed so children can use them with minimal adult guidance.

• Teachers use learning center time as instructional time—engaging children in conversation, interacting with children to enhance their learning, and working with children individually and in small groups.

• Learning centers encompass a range of activity types—explorations, guided discovery, problem solving, discussions, demonstrations, and direct instruction, with explorations, and guided-discovery and problem-solving activities predominating.

• Teachers use learning center time to observe, document, and assess children's learning.

See **Tool A: Learning Center Checklist**, at the back of this book for an instrument teachers and principals can use to assess how well these principles are implemented in the classroom.

SKILLS TEACHERS NEED TO RUN EFFECTIVE CENTERS

To operate a smooth running center-based program, teachers need appropriate background and training. Based on reading and actual experience in the field, early childhood educators need to learn how to

- set up age appropriate learning centers,
- equip each center properly,
- plan for center-based learning,
- monitor centers daily,
- simplify and extend center-based activities to accommodate children's varying rates of learning,
- create self-sustaining centers,
- work with children in centers, individually and in small groups,
- integrate center work with other kinds of instruction and routines, and
- assess children's learning as they use centers.

Teachers also need the support of their school principals. What that support entails is described in Box 8.3.

Box 8.3
What Teachers Need from Principals Regarding Center-Based Instruction

Teachers need principals to

- value center-based instruction,
- understand how and what children are learning in centers,
- believe that center time is learning time,
- support learning center–based instruction through the purchase of appropriate furnishings and materials,
- support center-based instruction through appropriate scheduling, and
- articulate to others the value and content of center-based instruction.

The simple act of creating learning centers does not guarantee effective instruction. There are certain warning signs that tell teachers and principals that adjustments in planning or supervision are necessary. These telltale signals are delineated in Box 8.4.

Box 8.4

Signs That Learning Center Time Needs Attention

- Children rotate through centers according to a fixed timetable.
- Learning center time is too short or space is too limited to enable children to engage in meaningful activity.
- Too few centers are offered (not enough for children to be able to move freely from one center to another without undue waiting).
- Too many centers are offered (teacher can't monitor them all and children are too dispersed to interact much with peers or adults).
- Centers lack substance (no clear tie to educational goals).
- Centers are too rigid (e.g., only one way to carry out activity, or no way to simplify or extend activity to accommodate children's varying levels of learning).
- Centers do not address learning across the curriculum (and instead consistently focus on one or two curricular areas).
- Children do not have enough support or direction to participate in centers effectively.
- Seat work is seen as "real" learning time, and centers are viewed as play time, and different from "real" learning.
- Children are required to whisper or be silent during center time.
- During center time teachers mostly to do things other than interacting with children (e.g., planning, getting ready for the next part of the day, preparing materials, calling families).

HOW CLASSROOM ROUTINES SUPPORT CURRICULAR GOALS

Although adults may find doing the same thing over and over again monotonous, young children thrive on repetition and routine. From birth, children rely on simple routines to provide structure in their lives. This continues when they come to the early childhood setting. Knowing what to expect and what comes next brings order and organization to children's time away from home. Once children become familiar with the rhythm of the program day, they feel comfortable and secure moving about the room and about spending hours apart from family. Routines also contribute to children's increasing ability to do more things independently and to sustain activities for longer periods of time. Typical routines in early childhood programs are briefly described in Box 8.5.

Box 8.5

Typical Early Childhood Routines

During arrival time, children

- are individually welcomed to the program, and
- remove and store coats, backpacks, and things from home.

In some programs, this is also a time when family members drop off children directly, making it an ideal time for teacher and families to communicate.

(Continued)

(Continued)

During greeting time, children

- are welcomed to the program as a group,
- participate in opening routines (hello song, movement activity, morning message, job chart),
- learn about what to expect during the day, and
- plan how they will spend their day.

During learning center time, children

- carry out plans for the day;
- participate in activities designed by the teacher to enhance aesthetic, cognitive, emotional, language, social, and physical development, and learning;
- work alone or with peers;
- work with the teacher individually or in small groups to practice or learn new skills; and
- have the choice of participating in a wide array of centers that address several domains or a limited array of centers that encompass more than one activity within a single domain, such as language arts.

During snack time and meal time, children

- experience new foods and balanced nutrition,
- engage in relaxed conversation,
- practice self-help skills, and
- practice language, math, and social skills.

Snack may take place with everyone sitting down to eat at the same time or it can be treated as a learning center within Center Time. Breakfast or lunch are usually group sit-down meals served family or cafeteria style. Hand washing, moving to the meal area, eating, and clean up after the meal are all included in this time.

During cleanup time, children

- practice self-help skills and following directions,
- work cooperatively to get a job done, and
- evaluate the quality of the group effort.

During nap time or rest time, children

- sleep as necessary, and
- lie down or sit quietly and listen to soft music.

During transition times, children

- move from one activity or routine to another, and
- practice following directions.

During toileting, children

- develop self-help skills and greater autonomy: they use the toilet, wash hands, and sometimes brush teeth.

The particulars of this routine are determined by children's ages and location of bathrooms. Some programs have toileting facilities inside the classroom enabling children to use the toilet at will; others have facilities down the hall, which requires children to visit the bathrooms in groups. These variations make significant differences in the role of the adults and the time that is allotted to toileting in the day.

During large-group time, children

- gather with teachers and peers as a whole group;
- sing, dance, and experience music;
- act out stories or hear them read aloud;
- play games and participate in movement activities;
- receive instructions or observe a demonstration;
- engage in group discussions or class meetings; and
- reflect on plans and what they have done.

During small-group time, children

- work with teachers and a few classmates to practice specific skills (e.g., targeted language and literacy skills based on student assessments).

During physical activity time, children

- move freely and use their whole bodies indoors or outside, and
- practice gross motor skills (throwing, catching, jumping, hopping, and so on).

During read-aloud time, children

- listen to stories read to them,
- engage in shared book reading and other small group reading activities,
- read with a partner, and
- share stories they have written with other members of the group.

During Drop Everything And Read (DEAR) time, children and adults

- look at books and engage in individual silent reading or reading with a partner.

During evaluation and reporting time, children

- describe to teachers and peers what they have done or learned,
- show things they have made, and
- document their activities.

During dismissal, children

- gather things to leave for the day, and
- depart.

Departures can be challenging for young children who may be leaving one early childhood setting for another before going home. As a result, many young children need extra support during this routine. In some programs, dismissal is also a time when family members pick up children directly, which makes it an ideal time for teacher and family communications.

Each of the routines listed in Box 8.5 has an educational purpose. For instance, during arrival time, adults help children develop social skills and increased language abilities as they greet teachers and peers. During mealtime, teachers encourage children to pour their own juice (self-help and physical skills), take turns (social skills), talk about the day's events (language skills), and reflect on what they might do next (cognitive skills). Any routine can be adapted to any area of the curriculum and is most effective when planned carefully with specific curricular goals in mind.

The best routines are simple, easy for children to follow, and relatively predictable day after day. Most have a beginning, a middle, and an end. For example, large-group times start with an opening (teacher signals that the activity is beginning and captures the children's attention). Next, there is the body of the activity (the main event—story, discussion, and demonstration). Finally, group time ends with a closing (teacher signals that the activity is over and helps children transition to the next routine). These miniroutines within routines help children learn how to follow along and adapt their behavior accordingly.

The transitions from one routine to the next are usually the most challenging times of the day for children and teachers to manage. During transitions, people are on the move and small groups of individuals are often doing more than one thing at a time. These are unsettling conditions for many young children and may lead to problem behaviors. To reduce confusion, teachers warn children a few minutes in advance of changes in routine (through words or visual signals). This allows children to prepare to end their current activity and to move smoothly to the next part of the day. Adults also provide explicit instructions and other cues (such as a cleanup song) to help children navigate these portions of the day more easily.

A TYPICAL DAY FOR CHILDREN

One of the building blocks of effective curriculum is the daily schedule. Every portion of the children's time in the program provides opportunities for learning. Which routines teachers choose and how time is allocated from arrival to dismissal influence what and how well curricular goals are addressed (Epstein, 2007; NAESP, 1998). Well-designed schedules

- remain fairly fixed from one day to the next;
- give children enough time to become absorbed in learning activities without constant interruptions or admonishments to hurry;
- are flexible enough that teachers can make decisions to allow children more time as needed and take advantage of spontaneous or unexpected learning opportunities;
- alternate quiet more sedentary activity times with ones during which children may be more boisterous and active;
- balance the times during which children engage in individual, small-group, and whole-group instruction;
- balance the times during which children engage in teacher-directed activities with ones in which children are more self-directed;
- devote at least one-third of the day to child-initiated instruction, usually in the form of learning center activities;
- address all curricular domains each day;
- utilize all six activity types each week (explorations, guided discovery, problem solving, discussions, demonstrations, and direct instruction);
- treat transitions, meals, cleanup, rest, and toileting as educational opportunities, not downtime;

- remember to include enough time for children to make the transition from one routine to the next on the daily schedule; and
- minimize the number of transitions children make each day.

Sample schedules for half-day and full-day early childhood programs are provided in Table 8.2. An example of a two-hour block of activities with a special emphasis on early literacy development is presented in Table 8.3. This block could be incorporated into a half-day or full-day schedule for children in preschool, kindergarten, or first grade.

Table 8.2 Sample Schedules for Prekindergarten and Kindergarten

Half-Day Program	*Full-Day Program (morning)*	*Full-Day Program (afternoon)*
Arrival	Arrival	Rest Time 20 minutes
Greeting Time 15 minutes	Greeting Time 15 minutes	Read-Aloud Time 20 minutes
Center Time (includes open snack and teachers working with children in small groups) 60 minutes	Center Time (includes open snack and teachers working with children in small groups) 60 minutes	Small-Group Instruction 20–25 minutes
Small-Group Instruction 15 minutes	Small-Group Instruction 15 minutes	Transition to Outdoors/ Physical Activity & Nature Study 5–10 minutes
Clean Up 5 minutes	Clean Up 5 minutes	Outdoors/Physical Activity & Nature Study 40 minutes
Group Time 20 minutes	Group Time 20 minutes	Transition Indoors 5–10 minutes
Transition to Outdoors/Physical Activity Time 5–10 minutes	Transition to Outdoors/Physical Activity Time 5–10 minutes	Center Time (may continue outside with no transition indoors; if so, transition takes place after clean up) 60 minutes
Physical Activity Time 30 minutes	Physical Activity Time 30 minutes	
Transition Indoors 5–10 minutes	Transition Indoors 5–10 minutes	
Read-Aloud Time 15 minutes	Read-Aloud Time 15 minutes	Clean Up 5 minutes
Evaluation Time 10 minutes	Transition to Lunch 5 minutes	Evaluation Time 10 minutes
Departure	Lunch 20 minutes	Departure

Table 8.3 Literacy-Rich Early Childhood Morning Schedule

Time and Activity	Language and Literacy Skills Addressed	Grouping Pattern	Materials	Procedure
9:00–9:15 Morning movement and song	Phonological awareness	Whole group, teacher led	Poetry chart Finger-play chart	Teacher and students recite a familiar nursery rhyme or poem while acting it out.
9:15–9:30 Shared-Book reading and conversation (questioning)	Oral language, print awareness, vocabulary, concept knowledge	Whole group, teacher led	Selected book	Teacher shares book with children (prereading, during reading, after reading activity).
9:30–10:30 Centers and independent practice	Alphabet knowledge, print awareness, concept development, oral language, and collaboration	Independent center exploration, child-centered	Center activities that correspond to a wide range of student needs and interests	Children move to several centers throughout the classroom.
9:30–10:00 Small-group instruction	Targeted language and literacy skills based on student assessments	Small group, guided instruction	Small-group materials that support instructional focus	Teacher works with several small groups of children to address specific literacy needs.
10:30–11:00 Recall and sharing	Print awareness and concept of word	Small group	Chart paper and markers	Language Experience Approach (LEA)— students recall activities they enjoyed as teacher writes them down

Source: Purcell, T. & Rosemary, C. A. (2008). *Differentiating Instruction in the Preschool Classroom,* in L. M. Justice & C. Vukelich (Eds.). *Achieving Excellence in Preschool Literacy Instruction.* New York, NY: Guilford Press, 238.

PRINCIPALS' ROLES

Centers and Routines

1. Observe teachers and staff implementing learning centers, using **Tool A: Learning Center Checklist,** found at the back of this book. Refer to Box 8.2, Characteristics of Well-Designed Centers, and Box 8.4, Signs that Learning Center Time Needs Attention, to further guide your observations and feedback.

2. Discuss with teachers what materials, furnishings, and further knowledge or skills they need to carry out learning centers effectively.

3. Talk with teachers and staff about how they are using daily routines to address curricular goals.

4. Observe to what extent routines and the daily schedule support curricular goals and expectations.

5. Determine scheduling and equipment needs for the early childhood programs in your school. Make sure these programs have an equal opportunity to gain access to the materials and scheduling considerations they need to function well.

Assessing Young Children's Learning

Jessica Caine is a "kid-watcher." Each day as children enter her classroom, she has particular activities set out for them and spends the first portion of the session moving among the busy children, interacting with them, and gathering data on how they are responding to the materials, interacting with one another, using previous learning, and making learning choices. At times, she asks children to explain and describe their work and their thinking processes. She systematically targets four to five children each day, making sure that every child is formally observed during the week. Her purpose is twofold: to gather information about each child's development and to improve the instruction and support she provides for each of them.

Six-year old Simon has been diagnosed with Asperger's syndrome. It has been determined that a critical need as he moves through first grade this year will be to improve his social skills in working and playing with his classmates. To keep track of his progress in this regard, his teacher makes weekly notations about his peer interactions and reviews them regularly to inform her planning. Because she is also concerned about his overall development, she is documenting strengths and limitations she sees in six developmental areas, by using the Child Observation Record (COR). She has made three observations using the COR so far. The information from these multiple assessments has proven helpful both to Simon's parents and to the others attending his individualized education plan conferences (IEPC).

In March, Belleair Elementary School will be hosting its annual learning celebration for children, parents, and teachers. Everyone is getting ready for the student-led conferencing that is scheduled, preschool through elementary. With the help of their teachers, children are choosing dated samples of their best work during the year and reflecting on why they prefer those pieces. They are excited to share their accomplishments and are practicing by showing their portfolios to one another and to children in another class. A preschooler has chosen three digital pictures of his block buildings taken at different times within the past few months. He tells something about each one. Eight-year-old Kevin says to his portfolio partner, "Look. This is my best one yet!" referring to a piece of work he had just produced.

The children, teachers, and family members described above are actively involved in activities focused on assessing young children's learning. Such assessments play an essential role in early childhood education.

THE NEED FOR EARLY CHILDHOOD ASSESSMENT

One of the most critical elements in structuring effective early childhood programs is to make sure they are providing documented benefits to the children who are enrolled. Today, parents, teachers, administrators, policy makers, and those who are funding early learning programs all want to know that children are spending time in meaningful activities that promote concept and skill building, and later school success. Thus, assessment needs to begin as early as possible in the community, since research affirms that academic success in school is strongly influenced by a combination of child, family, and education factors that are evident long before children enter "big school" (Dickinson & Tabors, 2001; Ramey & Ramey, 2006, p. 445; Zigler & Styfco, 2004). At every educational level (including early education), communities must have high-quality programs and well-trained professionals who are skilled in constructing the learning climate and delivering engaging activities and experiences for children. There must be an efficient way to document whether each child is moving forward in skill and concept development in each of the following areas:

- Emotional and social development
- Language development
- Literacy
- Numeracy
- Concept development and problem solving
- Understanding and appreciating one's own culture and people from other cultures
- Large- and small-motor abilities
- Self-care in health and safety
- Appreciating and participating in the creative arts

This is where carefully planned assessment and methodologies matter.

KEY CONSIDERATIONS

Whether one is assessing the learning of a three-year-old or a thirty-year-old, certain things must be true if the assessment is to yield trustworthy results. Every assessment tool and method must strive to be **reliable** (accurate and consistent), **valid** (measuring what it is supposed to measure and not something else), **sensitive to language and culture**, and as **bias free** and **fair** as possible (McAfee, Leong, & Bodrova, 2004).

In addition, the purpose of the assessment must be clear, for that determines the choice of assessment tool and method for collecting information. Legitimate purposes for educational assessment include the following (Egertson, 2008; Shepard, Kagan, & Wurtz, 1998):

Purpose 1: To guide children's learning and to inform instruction

Instruction cannot support children's development and learning unless teachers know what children know and can do. Educators use their interactions with children to gather data about how to add to or modify learning opportunities for individual children and for the group.

Purpose 2: To identify children's special needs

Young children need to be screened for health needs, including hearing and vision checks, as well as language development as soon as possible. Children with possible developmental delays need to be referred for in-depth follow-up assessment.

Purpose 3: To assess the strengths and needs of programs and to judge the worth of the effort

Program evaluation includes assessment of quality of the setting and information about child outcomes in the aggregate. Analysis of the data helps teachers and program leaders make adjustments in order to strengthen child outcomes overall.

Purpose 4: To hold programs accountable for academic achievement

Accountability assessments involve external examinations mandated by an authority outside the school to gauge academic achievement. These assessments often include group-administered paper-pencil academic achievement tests. The latter accountability measures are not suitable for children eight years of age and younger. Therefore, in early childhood education, it is best to think about accountability in terms of responsible behavior on the part of adults. "Program staff members demonstrate accountability when they engage in regular observation-based classroom assessment and use what they learn on a continuous basis to improve their practice. Program leaders are accountable when they make sure teachers have the tools they need to be their best. Policy leaders are accountable when they enact informed and reasonable policies and provide the resources for practitioners to be successful" (Egertson, 2008, p. 33).

These four purposes are depicted in Figure 9.1 proportionate to their emphasis in early education. Although a comprehensive assessment system will eventually encompass all four components, when it comes to young children, the bulk of attention focuses on teachers finding out more about children's developing strengths and limitations in order to plan instruction. Screening and program evaluation are also critical pieces of the early childhood assessment picture. Paper-pencil assessments of academic achievement and other group-administered accountability measures do not play a role in credible early childhood assessment (Council of Chief State School Officers [CCSSO], 2003; National Association of Elementary School Principals [NAESP], 2005; National Association for the Education of Young Children and the National Association of Early Childhood Specialists in State Departments of Education (NAEYC/NAECS/SDE), 2003).

Figure 9.1 Reasons for Early Childhood Assessment

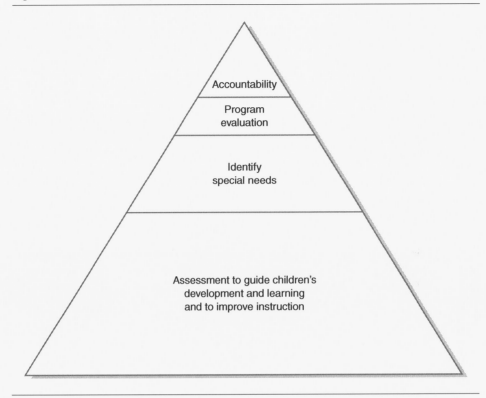

Based on the four purposes outlined in Figure 9.1, different assessment questions might be raised by community leaders, principals, or early childhood educators. A few examples are offered here:

Guiding children's development and learning and improving instruction

- Is this child learning age-appropriate skills and concepts as outlined in the curriculum?
- Do other children identify this child as a "friend"?
- What is this child interested in?
- What is this child ready to learn next?

Identifying children's special needs

- Does this child have developmental needs that require further attention?
- Are there special services that would benefit this child?

Program evaluation

- What changes have been made in the school's or district's approach to early education based on collected data?
- To what extent is there a seamless approach to early childhood assessment that connects preschools in the community with kindergarten and the elementary grades?

- How effectively are teachers implementing developmentally appropriate practices (DAP) in their classrooms?

Accountability

- To what extent does the school meet performance standards (for Grade 4 and above) established by the state?
- Are federal requirements being met sufficiently for children with special needs?

These and other questions about the quality and state of children's learning are answered best when comprehensive child assessment strategies are an integral part of the early childhood program.

Dan Coram, a P–6 [preschool to Grade 6] principal in Wheeling, West Virginia, says that while the mission and goals of Steenrod Elementary School serve to drive and weave curriculum, instruction and assessment, it is assessment that begins, rather than ends, the process. It is assessment that helps them fine tune the curriculum to meet the identified needs of the students, from those who need more time to learn to those who need extensive enrichment (Harris, 2005, p. 88).

Special Considerations Regarding Young Children

In thinking about appropriate early childhood assessment, teachers and principals in high-quality programs recognize that young children differ significantly from older students in how they learn and in how they demonstrate learning. Those differences must be considered when it comes to developing reliable, valid, bias-free, language-sensitive, and culturally sensitive assessment tools and methods. Some of these considerations are listed here:

- Child development is uneven across developmental domains and changes dramatically over a year. What is true today may be out of date tomorrow. This makes single assessments unreliable.
- Children have immature language skills. This limits their ability to follow oral directions, read printed instructions, or express themselves adequately in words.
- Children are sensitive to the setting, the timing, and the people involved in the assessment process. The less natural and less familiar the context, the less likely that assessment outcomes will be accurate.
- Young children have little competence with paper-pencil tasks and such tasks do not capture some skills that are essential to school success (such as social competence, positive approaches to learning, or motivation).
- Children tire quickly and are easily distracted.
- Children have no concept of the importance of assessment and may have little understanding or interest in doing well.

As you can see, young children, by their very nature are not good test takers. Consequently, it is imperative that the need for information about progress on either an individual or group basis not take precedence over safeguards that should be put in place to protect children against inappropriate expectations or mistaken judgments. These safeguards are best described within the framework of authentic assessment.

AUTHENTIC ASSESSMENT

When educators collect a variety of data over time, assess all developmental domains rather than just academic growth, and assess children in the natural learning context, they are using authentic assessment. Authentic assessment calls for having children exhibit learning by doing what they normally do and relies on data gathered through teacher observations, children's work samples, and child demonstrations. Sometimes such opportunities happen spontaneously, and sometimes teachers arrange for appropriate occasions to occur. Most important, authentic assessment is incorporated naturally into children's daily activities so children are comfortable and so valuable learning time is not sacrificed. Here are some additional characteristics of authentic assessment:

- Data collection is purposeful and systematic.
- Data are collected carefully and thoughtfully, using valid and reliable measures.
- Data collection is continuous—progress is gauged at multiple checkpoints.
- Assessments are conducted by persons familiar to the child.
- Assessment is based on discovering children's best performance rather than on documenting what they do not know or cannot do well.
- Assessment is a shared responsibility among teachers, children, parents, and other professionals involved in the child's overall development, and effective communication is ongoing among these partners (Kostelnik et al., 2007, p. 170).

Finally, "assessment practices in programs serving children in prekindergarten through third grade must be carried out in ways that bring benefits to children" (Egertson, 2008, p. 28). Authentic assessment **does not** rely on a single test or assessment process. It should never be used to rank, exclude, or label children, or to sanction teachers.

Strategies That Teachers Use for Authentic Assessment

In developmentally appropriate early childhood classrooms, authentic assessment can take a number of forms (Brown, Scott-Little, Amvake, & Wynn, 2007):

- Naturalistic observation when the teacher or designated observer records children's involvement in the regular classroom setting
- Direct assessment when children are asked to perform specific tasks
- Checklists and rating systems when teachers or family members indicate how well a child does on specific tasks or knows certain content

- Standardized assessments when children are assessed for diagnostic or research purposes
- Record reviews where the services children have received are evaluated

There are many different methodologies that classroom teachers use to find out what young children know or how well they can do something. Teachers who carry out authentic assessment

- incorporate different assessment modalities in their weekly routines with children,
- teach children ways to measure their own progress, and
- teach children to take pride in their achievements (Fleck, 2005).

Although an exhaustive listing of these strategies is beyond the scope of this chapter, we provide several examples to demonstrate that there are many ways to assess learning that are interesting and valuable to teachers and children. Principals who administer P–3 programs should see a variety of these being used.

STRATEGIES TO GUIDE LEARNING AND IMPROVE INSTRUCTION

Assessments built around teacher's observations and analysis of student's work can help create a true continuum of early childhood learning that allows children to steadily build new skills from pre-K through the start of fourth grade. (NAESP, 2005, p. 63)

Observation and Notation in Early Childhood Classrooms

When early childhood teachers have solid knowledge about child development and learning to serve as a basis for evaluating what is typical and nontypical behavior, focused observation is a powerful assessment tool. It is nonintrusive for the child; it yields instant, credible information that has on-the-spot utility for improving interaction and instructional practices; it has important value for formulating hypotheses to evaluate at a later date; it can be used wherever people are behaving; and it allows professionals to capture, in natural settings, important data that could not be obtained by other methods. (Kostelnik et al., 2007, p. 172)

Observations can be recorded in the form of anecdotal records; running records; frequency counts or tallies of specified behaviors as they occur; rating scales; and participation charts.

Simple notations for individual children over the course of a day are another common form of observational record keeping. In this case, teachers schedule observations of a small number of children each day, pay specific attention during the day to those children, and make brief notes on the spot and before going home about what they have observed. These notes can easily be made on sticky notes and then inserted into the child's individual folder for later reference and use (see Figure 9.2).

Until teachers have actually implemented a notation process, they often think they do not have time to actively observe children at the same time they are teaching an entire group of children. However, when they try it, they learn that it does not detract from their ability to be

Figure 9.2   Teacher Observation of Simon on Friday, March 21, 2008

March 21, 2008

9:32 — Simon notices that Chris is having a lot of trouble with the tape dispenser; shows him how to use it

11:30   Large group debriefing; simon comments about how fish have a swim bladder like a balloon, only not round long! that them keep up in the water.

2:17   playground, soccer: especially good eye\foot coordination, flexibility, quickness, shows leadership

2:42   washes hands after using toilet and uses soap without a reminder!

---

attentive to all children; it just enhances their attention to a small group of children or an individual child's overall development. As can be seen in Figure 9.2, the teacher noted examples of Simon's empathy for a fellow classmate and willingness to be helpful; proficiency in explaining a life science concept; documentation of large motor skills; and evidence of good hygiene practice—a lot of information for a small investment of time.

Teachers who have about twenty children may observe four to five students each day during the week, taking care to observe children on different days of each time. If they teach for thirty-six weeks (180 days), they have the capacity to make thirty-six observations of each child and the opportunity to pick up a great deal of documented, factual information about each one. It takes less than five minutes per child to enter such notes at the end of the day. These records become enormously helpful in preparing for conferences with parents, for follow-up miniconferences with children, and for conversations with individual children. Most of all, teachers come to know each of the children in their classrooms in a way they could not without active observation and notation.

Early Childhood Teachers Have Many Opportunities for Focused Observation

Because children are learning everywhere, early childhood teachers have the benefit of being able to observe children's learning inside and outside, all day long! For instance, a teacher looking for young children's understanding of mathematics might observe and make notes when

Children constructing in the block center model their understanding of the attributes of geometric shapes. Children gathering enough materials for an art project demonstrate their concept of number and one-to-one

(Continued)

(Continued)

correspondence. Children acting out a restaurant scenario and calculating the bill represent numerals and their understanding of numbers and operations. Children deciding on a fair way to share materials during outside play demonstrate their ability to divide numbers or time into equal groups or intervals. Children participating in the daily class routines, counting the number of students in the group, or the number of days until a big event are modeling counting strategies. All of these examples are common occurrences in early childhood settings and, for the focused observer, provide an opportunity for the assessment of mathematical learning. (Copley, 2003, p. 48)

Checklists and Inventories

Teacher-developed checklists and inventories of desired curricular outcomes help teachers keep track of the skills they want children to develop over the course of a year and how many children at any particular time are proficient in each skill. Many teachers use checklists to document developing concepts of print, social-emotional competence, or children's mathematics skills, and then mark these periodically, making a check mark if the child has demonstrated the skill and leaving it blank for the next marking if the child has not. For example, Ms. Shartrow's checklist indicates that a Grade 1 standard is "for children to identify upper and lower case letters." At the first marking in early October, only seven of the first graders can do so. This knowledge helps the teacher shape future instruction. For instance, the next day, during small-group time, she writes the upper-case letter of each child's first and last name and invites each child to write the corresponding lower-case letter alone or with help from the teacher or someone in the group. The teacher has the child draw a circle around the completed pair of letters and repeat, "Upper case __ and lower case __!)." After all children have had a turn, the teacher then summarizes, inviting the children to say with her, "upper case *J*, lower case *J*. . . . upper case *r*, lower case *r*," by designating particular groups of letters. With other focused and engaging activities that she creates to bring letter meaning to these children, youngsters will soon be able to add this literacy capability to other skills they are learning.

KWL Assessments

K = What do we KNOW?

W = What do we WANT to know?

L = What did we LEARN?

These are questions early childhood teachers often ask children in conjunction with themes and projects conducted in the classroom. Before beginning a project or series of thematic-based activities, teachers use KWL to model writing in the classroom and to determine what children are interested in learning or have learned about some sort of phenomenon. This preassessment highlights both factual knowledge and misunderstandings that children may have about a particular topic.

The second phase of the process assesses what children are truly interested in learning (perhaps something the teacher did not think about), by giving the children direction for resources or experts she can bring into the classroom or possible field trips to plan.

The last phase serves as a good review for the children and a reiteration of specific facts or concepts developed during the study. Children may do this through group discussions or through 3-D graphic representations using objects, written records, drawings, and photographs to depict their learning. Teachers can also use miniconferences with individual children to debrief with the "What did we learn" phase or ask children to enter some facts or concepts learned in their journals for the day, combining literacy and other areas of the curriculum. See Box 9.1 for an example of a KWL record one preschool teacher kept for the three- and four-year-olds in her class.

Box 9.1
A KWL Assessment Chart: Spiders

What do we already KNOW about spiders?

- Spiders have a lot of legs. (Marvin)
- Spiders are creepy. (Megan)
- Spiders eat bugs. (Kelvin)
- Spiders make webs. (Sophie)
- Spiders have eight legs but flies have just six. (Dan)

What do we WANT to know about spiders?

- What kind of bugs do they eat? (Lina)
- Why don't they stick to their web? (Tom)
- Where do they go in the winter? (Stan)

What did we LEARN about spiders?)

- Some parts of the web are sticky and some parts aren't, so that's why they don't stick. (Andy)
- Spiders eat flies and mosquitoes. (Kara)
- Spiders can't bite or chew, but they can suck stuff. (Tammy)

Sociograms

Because learning depends so much on our connection with others and because emotional intelligence is so important to later success in all areas of life, we need to keep track of children's social relationships and then provide coaching or other supports as necessary. Sociograms are a good way to do this; they need not be complicated. Periodically, the teacher meets with each individual child for a moment, asking this question: "Who is your favorite person to play with in this room? If _____ is absent, who would be your *next* favorite?" In this way, children nominate others they like to work and play with. The teacher can actually assign scores, assigning two points each time a child is nominated as a first choice and one point for each second nomination. Scores are totaled. What needs to be observed is whether there are children who were not nominated by anyone for either choice. This is not meant to be a popularity contest; it is a strategy to determine which children need more support in building friendships and to observe how children's peer relations change during the course of the year.

When certain children remain in a non-nominated category, teachers can begin to observe more closely the social behaviors of the child and try to give the child support to develop stronger social skills. Teachers might offer scripts that will be useful for entering play, discuss friendship building strategies with the child, pair the child with another child for collaborative work, suggest afterschool play dates to parents, or enact other strategies to enhance the child's ability to interact with peers. Sociograms can play an important part in documenting who needs support, when that support is needed and whether changes in the social dynamics of the classroom occur over the year. An example of a sociogram is presented in Table 9.1.

Table 9.1   Sociogram

Child's Name	# of First Nominations	# of Second Nominations	Child's Favorite Person To Play with Is . . .	Child's Next Favorite Person to Play With Is . . .
Alvin	1	2	Stanley	Christopher
Anky	0	1	Sacha	Marc
Christopher	2	2	Stanley	Alvin
Connors	0	1	Richard	Kevin
Emma	2	2	Vanessa	Sophie
Jackson	0	1	Joel	Connors
Joel	2	1	Emma	Stanley
Juanita	0	0	Emma	Sophie
Kenna	0	0	Sophie	Vanessa
Kevin	0	1	Christopher	Joel
Marc	1	1	Sacha	Jackson
Nicolas	0	0	Joel	Stanley
Richard	1	0	Stanley	Christopher
Sacha	2	0	Marc	Anky
Sophie	2	2	Vanessa	Emma
Stanley	3	3	Christopher	Alvin
Vanessa	2	1	Sophie	Emma
Zi Xin	0	0	Alvin	Stanley

In interpreting and applying the data from Table 9.1, Zi Xin, a relatively new child entering the classroom from Taiwan, has been nominated by none of the children. In addition, he hesitated when asked to nominate a favorite classmate, though it was clear that he understood the question and knew the names of the children in the classroom. The teacher acknowledges that she will have to structure class activity so that Zi Xin has more opportunities and support to develop a friendship. Similarly, Nicholas, Kenna, and Juanita received no nominations, though they have been in the classroom since the beginning of the year. While some children have clearly formed strong friendships and preferences for friends (e.g., Stanley, Alvin, and Christopher), other children need additional help in forming and maintaining friendships.

Child Miniconferences

One-on-one miniconferences are extremely useful in meeting with individual children or small groups to see directly what they know about something that has been studied. These conferences can take less than a minute or as long as needed to perform a more formal assessment, such as completing a sociogram or a simple demonstration to evaluate progress in an area of development (e.g., cutting with scissors). Children enjoy the individual attention, which helps to build rapport, and teachers can document particular skills or understanding in very little time. Such conferences often take place during small-group time or during center time as part of the daily routine.

Dated Work Samples

The work that a child produces at any particular time can be compared with past and future work. Children should be in the habit of dating all of their work and writing their name on it before putting it away. When making comparisons, the teacher and child can look for details related to what was being communicated in terms of increased refinement, neatness, accuracy, abstractness, depth, length, and other details of interest. As long as children have done their best in creating a particular piece, it is important that the latest work become the new standard, not the object of criticism. What needs to be centered on is that particular improvements have been made since the last production, by reflecting new learning and achievement on the child's part. These pieces become an excellent documentation of how a teacher has scaffolded a child's skill toward greater levels of achievement.

Repeated Performances

What can a child actually do in terms of performance from one point in time to another? Teachers can find out by asking children to repeat certain tasks throughout the year and then documenting the results. This could include documenting children's growing sophistication of block construction or their use of art construction tools at the preschool level, challenging kindergarten children in the block area to create individual buildings for a village, asking children to create self-portraits or pictures of their families, having children paint their names on the easel, inviting children to do a "whiteboard write" where they write all of the words they can think of that start with B, asking children to draw Humpty Dumpty and then write the nursery rhyme from memory, or observing children playing a game with others. The stimulus or challenge from the teacher to perform the activity should be exactly the same for each performance. At least three repetitions offer good comparisons. To document the results, there are a number of options: the teacher might make notes about the outcome for a particular child, take a digital picture of what is created each time and date it, enter the pictures into the child's folder, or save the actual products if possible. Teachers then note children's progress in a summary or by using an appropriate rubric. An example of a nursery rhyme repetition for Kayla at age four and seven months and age four and ten months can be seen in Figure 9.3.

Figure 9.3   Kayla's Humpty Dumpty Writing Repetition

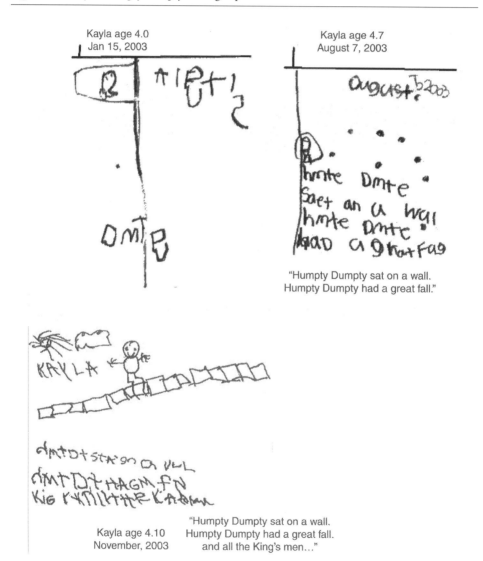

Kayla age 4.0
Jan 15, 2003

Kayla age 4.7
August 7, 2003

"Humpty Dumpty sat on a wall.
Humpty Dumpty had a great fall."

Kayla age 4.10
November, 2003

"Humpty Dumpty sat on a wall.
Humpty Dumpty had a great fall.
and all the King's men…"

Source: From Anne K. Soderman, Kara M. Gregory, & Louise T. O'Neill *Scaffolding emergent literacy, A Child-centered Approach For Preschool Through Grade 5,* 2 /e , Published by Allyn and Bacon, Boston, MA. Copyright 2005 by Pearson Education, reprinted with permission of the publisher.

Reading Accuracy Assessments

Once children have moved on to first grade, it is important to make sure that they are growing in their ability to decode text and get information from what they are reading. Reading accuracy can be tested quickly by having a child read one on one with an adult from an unfamiliar narrative picture book. The recorder notes the number of words read and the number of errors made each time the child substitutes a word, leaves out a word, or needs assistance with a word. At the end of one hundred to two hundred words, the adult calculates the percentage of correct words read. Multiple readings over several months should indicate increased percentages. Alternatively, the percentage may be compared to a standard, such as 95 percent accuracy.

Teachers assess reading comprehension by asking children to retell the story, assigning a "4" for full and complete understanding, a "3" for fairly complete understanding, a "2" for partial understanding, and a "1" for fragmentary understanding. These scores may be kept in the child's folder for reference prior to the next assessment and to keep track of progress in developing skills in decoding and understanding text. Again, this process takes very little time and requires nothing unique in terms of materials or formal testing. Early childhood educators who are interested in expanding their understanding of this process are referred to *Scaffolding Emergent Literacy* (Soderman et al., 2006) or other sources delineating procedures for running records. An example is offered in Table 9.2.

Table 9.2   Reading Accuracy Assessment

February 27, 2008	
Child:	Winny S.
Text:	L. Lionni, Fish Is Fish
Words read:	125
Errors	18
Correct	107
Accuracy rate:	107/125 = 86 percent (Goal 95 percent)
Comprehension:	2
Recommendation:	Move Winny to less difficult texts for practice. Needs to improve comprehension, fluidity, decoding. Reassess end of March.

Getting Children Involved in Self-Appraisal

There is great value in involving the learner in self-evaluation. Children begin to better understand the results of their own effort in learning a new skill and demonstrate pride in work they have accomplished. Following are several methods teachers may use to bring the learner into the assessment arena.

Self-Check Lists

Teachers (and sometimes children and teachers together) may develop a checklist of six to ten skills in any of the curricular areas to have children work on (see example in Figure 9.4). These may be skills that all children are working on or individual lists of skills for particular children. Periodically, the teacher sits with the child and goes over the list, having the child color in the square indicating achievement or place a check mark indicating that the task was accomplished. At first, the teacher should always include one or two skills in the list that the child can do so that the child understands the process. The skills listed should be observable. "I enjoy listening to the story in large group" would not be a good item to list because it is subjective. "I can write five of my friends' names" would be a good item for a beginning first grader. It advances writing skills, is objective, and can be demonstrated by the child.

Figure 9.4   Child Self-Appraisal Checklist

Child's Name: Kassie

Things I Can Do Now That I Couldn't Do Before Preschool

Skill	Oct.	Nov.	Dec.	Jan.	Feb.	Mar.	Apr.	May
I can write my first name.	X							
I can count 10 objects.	X							
I can tie my shoes.			X					
I know my teacher's name.			X					
I can recognize a friend's name.					X			
I can name 15 uppercase letters.					X			
I can.	X							

Source: Adapted from Anne K. Soderman, Kara M. Gregory, & Louise T. O'Neill. *Scaffolding Emergent Literacy: A Child-Centered Approach for Preschool Through Grade 5,* 2/e. Published by Allyn & Bacon, Boston, MA. Copyright 2005 by Pearson Education. Reprinted with permission of the publisher.

Each time the teacher and child meet to update achievement of items on the list, the session should end with the teacher asking the child, "Which one of these that are left will you be really working on?" Once all of the skills have been accomplished, the list is placed in the child's folder for future reference and a new list of desired outcomes that can be accomplished with reasonable work on the child's part should be developed. The use of these checklists puts some of the onus for learning on the child and develops pride in a child relative to her achievements in the classroom. It also keeps both the teacher and child focusing on goals to be reached and serves as a basis of activities the teacher designs to help children move toward more purposeful learning.

Portfolios

Nothing is more useful than portfolio collections in terms of children organizing evidence of their own learning and sharing it with others. While the idea of portfolios has been around for a while, there are entire programs and schools where children have no concept of systematically storing and reflecting on the products they produce. Portfolios can be used with children as young as three and can evolve into creative and sophisticated schemes: upper elementary children may organize their work electronically, including digital pictures of products or PowerPoint presentations. A preschooler may simply select a broad array of favorite work samples (e.g., from scribbles to stories) to include. Children in first through third grades may classify the contents by curricular area, and include a reflective introduction to the body of work or narratives about particular pieces.

Early childhood teachers have very young children begin by keeping individual portfolios or folders of their work, telling children periodically, "Today, this piece that we are working on should be dated and put into your portfolio. We will not be taking this home today." At least once during the year, children can go through their individual portfolios with the teacher, and select a number of pieces to go into a "Showcase Portfolio" that can then be shared with others in student-led conferences (see Documentation and Documentation Boards below). Children may share their "Showcase Portfolio" in a dyad with another child, in small groups of four, or with children in other classrooms. The teacher may choose to keep particular copies of work from the individual portfolios to place in the student's class portfolio before individual portfolios are sent home to the child's family.

Portfolios are especially beneficial when staff determine schoolwide what samples of a child's work should be kept at each grade level and then pass an institutional portfolio on from year to year to each child's new teacher. These samples can be kept by each teacher in an individual child's folder for the year and cleaned out at the end of the year, leaving only the samples agreed on by the faculty. They are returned to the office in the spring and redistributed in the fall to the children's new teachers. This provides the receiving teacher with immediate information about the child to begin building rapport, as well as a solid basis of understanding where the child left off the previous year in terms of particular skills documented in the folder. For example, there can be dated self-portraits, a sample of the child's best writing at the end of the year, some math work, a copy of a social-emotional checklist, and reading accuracy and comprehension scores and notes. A picture of the child and a best friend that year may be included, as well as a photo of a completed project.

Documentation and Documentation Boards

One of the most exciting contributions from Italy's popular Reggio Emilia approach for preschool is the increasing use of documentation and documentation boards in U.S. preschools and primary grades. Documentation is the process of

- gathering evidence and artifacts that represent the learning that goes on in the everyday classroom;
- reflecting on and analyzing that collection or part of the collection to think about the learning both retrospectively (what has happened) and prospectively (about what should happen next); and
- displaying the evidence, artifacts, documentation panels, videos, posters, booklets, portfolios, newsletters, Web pages, and other products produced in a way that makes learning visible to the children, to the teachers, and to other adults, including parents and visitors (Rinaldi, 1994).

Documentation boards are a collection of photos and brief narratives placed on posters or panel boards. Included are direct quotes, images, sample products, and interpretations by children and adults about the work conducted. They tell an educational story and are meant to reveal growth in children's competence. Rather than comprising randomly chosen pictures or pieces, there is a cohesive theme that creates a relationship with the viewer, drawing the viewer into the problem studied by the children and adults in the setting (Edwards et al., 2007). Boards are put on display for children to refer to in the classroom and for families to see, as well. See Figure 9.5 for a very simple example of vocabulary and concept development in the play yard, where Lucas (age four) and Palmer (age two and eight months) debated what kind of fruit was on a tree (Miller & Wang, 2008). Examples like these give teachers insights into children's thinking and provide a foundation for planning experiences that might come next. Documentation boards can also be more elaborate, sometimes taking up entire walls of the classroom to represent children's thinking and reflections on their learning over the course of several days/weeks or in relation to a particular line of inquiry. Frequently, family members are invited to "documentation celebrations," which gives children opportunities to share what they have learned with others. Whether focused on a single learning episode or several, documentation boards give children a chance to revisit their learning as the year goes on. This can prompt new discoveries and metacognitive awareness. That was evident last spring when Ian reviewed a documentation board he helped create in October, and then said to his kindergarten teacher, "Teacher, can we change that? I don't think that anymore."

"Apple or Cherry"

Documented by Jenny Leeper Miller and Cixin Wang

Ruth Staples Child Development Lab School

Figure 9.5A

Figure 9.5B

Figure 9.5C

Palmer, age two, was playing on the playground with his big friend, Lucas. Palmer looked up and saw the fruit, small, red, and round, on the tree.

"Apple, apple!" cried Palmer with excitement, reaching toward the tree.

"No, Palmer, it is not an apple tree," said Lucas. "It is a cherry tree."

Palmer was confused, looking at the fruit on the tree. (Why not apple?)

Lucas held the branch to show Palmer, "See, it's a cherry."

Palmer looked at the crabapple carefully.

This didn't clear it up for Palmer. "Apple?" he said.

Lucas wondered what to do. He thought for a moment, then pulled the branch down so Palmer could touch and feel it.

Finally, Palmer stopped saying, "Apple," which made Lucas smile.

Interpretation: When children learn language, they are mastering concepts along with vocabulary. Both Lucas and Palmer are in the process of learning to make discriminations among fruits and brought some useful previous knowledge to the interaction. They enjoyed their discussion

Follow up: Our next step will be to explore: How are these various fruits the same? How are they different? We will give children chances to examine apples, crabapples and cherries side by side, and compare them in terms of shape, size, color, texture, and other characteristics.

Child Satisfaction Surveys

Important data to gather are the opinions of children and their families about what goes on at school; children from preschool through third grade can complete surveys about teachers and classrooms. Rarely, however, are they asked their opinion. Such assessment is useful in research related to intervention programs or diverse approaches to teaching, as well as by teachers in presenting evidence to a principal or school district that quality teaching and learning are going on in their classrooms.

At the preschool level, small booklets with about five items that are read by an independent person can be completed with a three-point scale (*Yes, Sometimes, No*) with smiley, neutral, and frowning faces corresponding to these descriptors. Examples of poor items in a survey for primary children would include asking if the teacher is "fair" or if the teacher makes the child want to do his best work (Peterson & Peterson, 2006, pp. 50–53). Examples of appropriate items may be seen in Figures 9.6 and 9.7.

Figure 9.6 Example of Potential Items on Preschool Children's Survey Form

Preschool Children's Survey Form

	No	Sometimes	Yes

I like to play and work at this school.

I am learning new things at this school.

I am making friends at this school.

We have lots of books and things to play with in this room.

Our teacher reads to us.

I like the center activities the teacher has for us.

I like the large-group time.

I like the snacks at this school.

Source: K. D. Peterson & C. A. Peterson (2006) *Effective teacher evaluation: A guide for principals* (p. 53). Thousand Oaks, CA: Corwin. Adapted with permission of the publisher.

Figure 9.7 Example of Potential Items on Student Survey Form

Elementary Student Survey Form

	Agree	Not Sure	Disagree
I know what I'm supposed to do in class.	3	2	1
The teacher shows us how to do new things.	3	2	1
There is enough time to finish class work.	3	2	1
This class is not too noisy or rowdy for learning.	3	2	1
I learn new things I can tell you about.	3	2	1
I know how well I am doing in class.	3	2	1
The rules in class help us to learn.	3	2	1
We have enough materials and supplies to learn.	3	2	1

Source: K. D. Peterson & C. A. Peterson. (2006). *Effective teacher evaluation: A guide for principals* (p. 53). Thousand Oaks, CA: Corwin. Adapted with permission of the publisher.

Involving Parents in Authentic Assessment

The concept of DAP includes the importance of having parents genuinely and continuously involved in all aspects of what goes on in their schools, including the assessment process. Some opportunities to do that are listed below. More examples of garnering family input are provided in Chapter 10: Family Involvement.

An ecomap is a graphic illustration (see Figure 9.8) of the child's world outside the school setting. It is an excellent activity to conduct at the beginning of the year on a home visit or the first parent/teacher conference in order to learn more about who is in the household, extracurricular activities in which the child is involved, how often the child sees grandparents, favorite neighborhood friends, animals in the family, and other information that can help the teacher understand how the child spends time away from school. After a timeline of events since the child's birth is created, information about hospitalization, family transitions, developmental milestones such as when the child learned to walk, talk, or ride a two-wheel bike can be discussed. Teachers and parents build rapport as they build these pictures of the child together, and the teacher can use the information to build rapport with the child by referring to the information. Parents should be encouraged to let the teacher know when there are any significant changes in the child's ecosystem, just as the teacher will let a parent know of important events in the child's life at school. This creates a team approach toward supporting that particular child throughout the school year.

Student-Led Conferencing

Portfolios that the children develop eventually contain a wealth of information over time that should be shared with others. Instead of the ordinary parent/teacher conference in which the learner is often omitted altogether, more and more schools are scheduling student-led conferences where children take the lead in showing family members their achievements in the school setting. These can be carried out successfully by children as young as three years of age. Teachers who have implemented student-led conferences report that they would not have it any other way. Parents who have participated in student-led conferences are often quite amazed at their child's ability to organize the portfolio and then lead them through a series of activities in the classroom.

Usually four to six families are scheduled at one time in a classroom for approximately half an hour. Activities in addition to viewing the portfolios are planned with the children. For example, children may construct a large floor puzzle with parents, play a math game, write a secret message that parents have to solve, read a favorite book together, read the word wall, and serve their parents refreshments, using a menu they have written and illustrated. Great numbers of pictures showing the children at work and play in the classroom are posted on the walls for the children and parents to enjoy, and sometimes an ongoing video of recorded events during the year is set up. Children work with the teacher ahead of time to arrange the learning celebration by choosing music that can be played in the background, cleaning and organizing the room, and making refreshments. They practice introducing their parents to the teacher. The excitement builds as the evening grows closer, and children are quite serious about their responsibilities in pulling off the conferences.

Debriefing following the conferences is important. Parents are asked to fill out a survey to evaluate the conference approach and to indicate whether or not they still want to meet with the

Figure 9.8 Ecomap

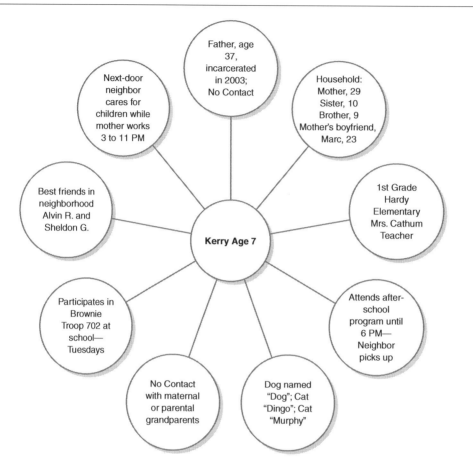

Critical events in Kerry's life, obtained in conference with Mom, November 12, 2007

February 24, 2000	Kerry born in Detroit, MI; Normal birth weight; No complications Parents unmarried; Mother 17, drops out of high school; Father Gary P is 8 years older
April 2002	Sister Kayla born. Normal birth weight. No complications. Father is Gary P.
October 2003	Gary P incarcerated for auto theft and drug possession
June 2004	Brother Kevin born (Father is Marc T); Low birth weight. Hospitalized for 2 months
September 2004	Kerry enrolled in Detroit Head Start
February 2005	Mother and children move to Ohio to live with Kerry's maternal Grandmother Marc T stays in Detroit; Kerry does not attend Head Start in Ohio. Mother takes part-time job at Walmart
August 2005	Children removed to foster care for 6 months (due to lack of adequate adult supervision)
September 2005	Kerry enrolled in kindergarten in Ohio while living with foster family
January 2006	Children and mother reunited. Kerry transferred to kindergarten at school in maternal grandmother's district
June 2006	Children and mother return to Detroit, reunited with Marc T; Mother takes job as custodian at Dental Service (3 to 11 PM)
September 2006	Kerry repeats kindergarten
September 2007	Kerry enters first grade

teacher without the child present. Few parents ever make this request. Children debrief with their teacher the following day, discussing what they enjoyed most and what they might do differently the next year. Often, teachers have the children draw a picture of something they remember about the evening and have them write about the experience in their journals. Teachers debrief with one another and the administrator to talk about what went well and what might be changed for the following year. All in all, student-led conferences are one of the most enjoyable events during the school year. Many schools have them in January and again in May. Others hold them only once, in the spring. They put the learner squarely on the stage, reflective about, responsible for, and proud of the achievements over the course of the school year—a truly meaningful growing experience.

STRATEGIES FOR IDENTIFYING CHILDREN'S SPECIAL NEEDS

Assessing children as they enter Kindergarten is particularly important to help determine the child's areas of strength and needs so the teacher can adapt the learning environment and activities to the needs of all children in the classroom. (Pennsylvania Early Learning Standards Report on Assessment, 2007, p. 6)

We screen children in, not out, so we can serve them better in our program. (P–5 principal)

All children entering prekindergarten and kindergarten programs should be screened for vision and hearing and other health needs. Children with possible developmental needs should be referred for further assessment. Screening should be used for the purpose of determining whether children may require diagnostic services, not to sort children for program placement or to exclude them from services. However, in the 1980s and 1990s, many elementary schools used a variety of screening instruments to determine if children were "ready" for school. Hundreds of dollars were spent on standardized instruments, and school districts sent teachers to be trained in assessment to determine whether children could fit comfortably into existing programs, should be sent home to wait for another year, or were candidates for the Young Five programs. It is now recognized that all of this was highly inappropriate.

Young children differ dramatically in any number of ways before and after they come to school, and will always do so. No matter what is done to control age of entry, there will always be a youngest and oldest child. Some children have extensive experiences that help them with academic foci, and some have few; some have rich vocabularies in English, while others are learning English as a second language. Boys and girls differ significantly in the early years in terms of school readiness, and there are extreme differences in children's experiences inside and outside the family system. We now know that all children can benefit more from daily attendance in a good program than by being sent home to wait for another year. As a result, early childhood teachers expect to handle a wide range of skills in the young children who will be working and playing together in their classrooms. Universities are strengthening preservice teacher training programs to include coursework in understanding and supporting special needs, and many school districts are providing inservice training for staff who may not have had such training or need updated information.

Observational Screening

In early childhood programs where teachers want to learn more about the children's strengths and needs before program entry, observational screening has grown in popularity. In structuring this experience for children, early childhood classrooms are reserved in the springtime for a visit by children who will be enrolling for the following year. Usually, no more than ten children at one time are invited into the classroom for a one-hour session, while their parents take part in an information session elsewhere in the building. This allows teachers and staff to observe the separation behaviors of parents and children.

Children get a nametag and have their picture taken for later discussion of each child's participation. Several engaging activity centers are provided and overseen by experienced adults, but the classroom teachers become observers rather than serving in the teaching role, and are free to simply observe the comfort and participation level of the children. They gather a language sample from each child by having a very brief conversation at some time during the session. They note the child's behavior during transition from activity to activity, and watch the child's ability to interact with others socially. Activities are carefully considered to elicit observation of particular skill levels in children. For example, clay and scissors may be at one table, drawing materials or puzzles at another. Blocks and small vehicles are available, as well as a dramatic play center with stuffed animals and dolls, and a book area where children may choose to participate in lap reading.

The schedule includes the following:

- A welcome and farewell to parents
- Provision of a nametag
- Picture taking for later reference
- Free-choice activities for thirty minutes
- Large-group activities for ten minutes (song, finger play, story)
- Toileting, washing hands, and snack
- A brief good-bye session during which children are provided with a copy of the book that was read during large group and parents are welcomed back

During this time, teachers make notes about children's reactions to the planned activities, language facility, the choices they make during the time for free play, skill in handling materials, ability to interact with peers and adults, how well they are able to attend to and participate in the large-group activities, and any difficulty in the transition to snack.

Once children have left, teachers meet to talk about placement of children into the available programs for the following year. This type of assessment allows a school to better distribute high-needs children if several classrooms are available. It also introduces children and families to the physical facility, a sample of routine, and school personnel. A connection has been made that can be maintained over the summer with a follow-up newsletter or by having teachers send a postcard with her picture on it to each child, once placements have been made, and a welcoming message. A picture book is sent home for reading, along with a brief listing of additional suggested activities and experiences that can enhance children's development over the summer. The observational screening experience is different in every school, depending on the goals and creativity of principals and teachers in setting it up, but it is usually considered highly beneficial by everyone who participates. It is frequently used for prekindergarten programs, but can be extended into and modified for the lower elementary grades as well.

ASSESSING EARLY CHILDHOOD PROGRAMS AND LEARNING CONTEXTS

For principals who would like a tool to assess the quality of program implementation or learning contexts, three well-developed instruments are suggested here:

Preschool and Child Care

Early Childhood Environment Rating Scale—Revised (ECERS-R) (Harms et al., 1998). Instrument measures the quality of the early learning environment, including spatial, programmatic, and interpersonal features that directly affect children and adults in the setting. Seven subscales are included: (1) space and furnishings, (2) personal care routines, (3) language and reasoning, (4) activities, (5) interaction, (6) program structure, and (7) parents and staff. Item scores range from one point (*inadequate*) through seven points (*excellent*), and NA (not applicable). A profile can be constructed and used to compare areas of strengths and weaknesses.

Kindergarten through Grade 3

Assessment of Practices in Early Elementary Classrooms (APEEC). This tool was developed to measure three broad K–3 domains: (1) physical environment, (2) curriculum and instruction, and (3) social context. As in the ECERS-R, items are formatted along a seven-point continuum with descriptors ranging from one to seven points (*inadequate* to *excellent,* respectively). Higher scores reflect higher quality classrooms and are correlated with positive child outcomes.

Preschool through Grade 3

Early Language and Literacy Classroom Observation (ELLCO). Environmental factors related to early literacy and language development are the focus of this tool. It is useful for baseline assessment and subsequent progress. Of interest is whether learning environments are age appropriate and whether they support children's evolving interests, intentional direction of the teacher, and ability of the teacher to engage children in exploring beyond their current knowledge and skills (Soderman & Farrell, 2008).

PROS AND CONS OF STANDARDIZED TESTS IN EARLY CHILDHOOD

One way to achieve more valid and reliable results is to standardize certain aspects of the assessment process. Standardization is a useful way to ensure that methods and tools are consistent over repeated applications and for assessing the same skill in different children (McAffee et al., 2004). However, it is not an all or nothing proposition. There is a progression in how assessment may be standardized, which makes certain formats more or less suitable for young children. (See Table 9.3.)

Table 9.3 Variations in Standardization

Standardized Approach	Standardized Assessment	Standardized Tests
Least Structured	More Structured	Most Structured
Suitable for children birth to eight	Suitable for young children as specified	• Suitable to identify special needs • Not suitable to assess academic achievement in children below Grade 3
Used to assess children's progress and to improve instruction	Used to assess children's progress, to improve instruction, and to evaluate program effectiveness	Used for diagnostic or accountability purposes
Teachers give the same instructions, provide the same materials, record the same behaviors, follow the same steps, and use the same format and rubric each time the assessment is done.	• Specified procedures and instruments • Teachers specially training to implement and interpret findings	• Specially constructed (according to testing standards) instruments and methods • Trained examiners are required • Scoring conducted by people other than the children's classroom teacher
Examples Notations, anecdotal records, running records, rating scales, checklists, KWL assessments, sociograms, dated work samples, repeated performances, reading accuracy assessments, self-check lists, portfolios, documentation boards, child satisfaction surveys, ecomaps	Examples • Work sampling system • Developing skills checklist • See Tool B for more examples	Examples • Teacher-Child Rating Scale (T-CRS) • See Tool B for more screening examples • Metropolitan Achievement Test • Statewide tests created to assess reading, writing, mathematics, science, and social studies

This chapter has concentrated on the first two categories of standardization outlined in Table 9.3 because those methods are the most universally suitable for young children. We now turn our attention to standardized testing and how early childhood educators, state department of education officials, and academic researchers view it.

Standardized testing has grown exponentially in the United States. As educators move out of the realm of assessment primarily to determine children's progress or to inform instruction and toward program evaluation, research, and accountability, they need to appreciate the value of standardized testing when used appropriately. They also need to be knowledgeable about where it can be destructive with young children. Paying careful attention to such issues is an important leadership role for principals.

Standardized tests can be very helpful

- in diagnosing children's special needs when good tools are selected,
- when conducting research to look at the effects of educational approaches on the development of children,

- in responding to evaluation requirements of federal funders of early childhood programs, and
- to demonstrate overall effects and directions of programs relative to accountability concerns in the community.

The negative aspects of using standardized tests have more to do with poor judgment on the part of those who use them than on the tests themselves. NAESP noted recently that standards being developed for prekindergarten education can clarify expectations for school readiness, but when they are extended to standardized testing, "principals need to provide a leading voice in explaining that skilled teachers are the best judges of pre-K growth and performance" (NAESP, 2007, p. 63). See Box 9.2 for an example of the unhappy consequences that can occur when principals fail to speak up about the inappropriate use of standardized testing in the form of group-administered, paper-pencil, multiple-choice achievement tests, for example.

Box 9.2
Kindergarten Takes a Test!

One school in a Midwestern state recently agreed to have all of its kindergartners involved in the "renorming" of a well-known standardized measure in which the children had to be tested in a large group format and "bubble in" their answers on paper. Such conditions do not match how young children best demonstrate learning. Despite several adults in the room helping, pictures that served as place markers for the children, and lots of assurances from the adults, the children lost it! As 5-year-olds will do when confronted with inappropriate demands from adults, some cried, others just didn't pay attention, and some filled in anything in order to comply and get the job done. When the principal was asked why she had agreed to participate in the norming process when it was clearly against best practices with young children and the school's stated philosophy, she indicated that the district had agreed to be a "test site" and was being rewarded with funds they needed for use in the schools. She was told that her school had been selected to participate and felt that "she didn't have an option to say no." Unfortunately, neither did the children.

As a result of these circumstances, integrity and ethical delivery of services to young children in this school were compromised. Teachers were unhappy about being involved, particularly when they saw the children's reactions. What the school lost in terms of administrative rapport with teachers and parents, instructional time, and children's trust that school was a good place to be could hardly compare to what the school received from the funding source (Soderman, 2004).

When looking historically at early childhood education, standardized testing to assess academic achievement has been largely reserved for Grades 3 and above. However, federally funded programs like Head Start or legislated programs such as the 2002 No Child Left Behind Act (NCLB) have generated a burst in nationwide standardized testing. As of 2008, NCLB assessment has not been formally mandated below Grade 3; however, some states are beginning to implement statewide assessment in literacy and math at Grade 2 to prepare children for what is coming. In addition, those school systems that have accepted funding for federal programs for kindergarten to Grade 3 are currently mandated to collect specific kinds of data and a three-tiered assessment system (Salinger, 2006, p. 427).

While these programs could be short-lived, once particular assessment procedures and practices find their way into schools they usually have a long shelf life. They should be judiciously considered before they are adopted. Some schools have taken precious time away from classroom instruction in order to have time to prepare children for test taking. It is ironic that the very thing that could best improve a child's performance, that is, classroom instruction and related activity, is being usurped.

Also, principals worry about fairly assessing students with limited English skills when required to use instruments developed by their state and what will happen to their accountability ratings when English language learners have to take the test (Lewis-Moreno, 2007, p. 772). Certain schools across the country are mandated to participate in the Grade 4 National Assessment of Educational Progress (NAEP) assessments. NCLB requires that all public schools, charter schools, and districts be accountable. For rural districts with small enrollments and where the highest grade level is Grade 2, a school would be required to submit children's scores on a nationally normed achievement test. All of this adds to the drive to adopt standardized achievement tests for younger and younger children.

Timed tests such as DIBELS (Good & Kaminski, 2002) to assess letter recognition, phonetic awareness, and reading accuracy were used in more than 1 million K–3 classrooms during the 2003–04 school year (Hiebert & Mesmer, 2006). While it is good to know whether or not children are developing such skills, it is unwise and unnecessary in the early years to overtly time children during the assessment. Concepts of print assessment, designed originally for entering first graders, is now commonly administered **prior** to first grade. Such practices violate principles of authentic assessment.

Still, carefully designed and administered standardized assessments and tests are legitimate tools to consider if valid and reliable and if they match young children's ways of learning. They can provide greater understanding of a child's strengths and weaknesses when compared to an established standard. They can also be used to document pre- and postintervention status of groups of children who may be considered at risk because of socioeconomic or other factors (Kostelnik et al., 2007, p. 169).

The U.S. Department of Education's 2007 Regional Educational Laboratory at the University of North Carolina, Greensboro, recently conducted a comprehensive review of methods and instruments used in state and local school early childhood evaluation. The report provides detailed information about key instruments, important considerations in selecting instruments, and the following recommendations for those who are considering the use of a standardized measure for assessment or diagnostic purposes (Brown et al., 2007):

1. Carefully select outcomes for assessment that match the goal of the program and addres components of children's learning and development that are linked with later success in school.

2. Clearly define the purpose for which the assessment data will be collected and select instruments that have been designed and validated for that purpose.

3. Select instruments that have a proven track record with children who have characteristics of those who will be assessed (instruments that have adequate reliability and validity) and that have been tested with children similar to those served by the program.

4. Select instruments that are culturally and linguistically appropriate for the children who will be assessed.

5. Consider whether outside observers or people who work directly with the children are the best collectors of data.

6. Plan carefully for how the assessments will be administered, provide adequate training for data collectors, and carry out reliability studies to determine whether the data are being collected reliably and accurately.

7. Collect data on the children's home context and the nature of the school program in which the children are enrolled.

In addition, the report identified instruments that were selected most often nationally for program evaluation purposes. A summary of these is provided as **Tool B** in the Resources section at the back of this book.

PRINCIPALS' ROLES

Promoting Authentic Assessment

1. Encourage teachers to use child observation as a primary assessment strategy. Help teachers figure out how to incorporate systematic child observations into their daily routines.

2. Coordinate prekindergarten assessment goals with the early learning standards for your state. Identify a variety of age-appropriate assessments to gauge children's progress in each domain.

3. Provide opportunities for staff development in early childhood assessment. Identify the best assessment tools and methods currently available to measure developmentally appropriate and meaningful learning goals. Help staff learn more about the various types of child assessments as well as the purpose and techniques associated with each type. Train and involve classroom teachers in high-quality data gathering. Encourage teachers to use multiple measures over time and to use the data for instructional purposes.

4. Involve students in monitoring their own learning in age-appropriate ways. Encourage even very young children to think about what they know and can do as well as set goals for further learning and skill building. Provide opportunities for children to share their achievements with others.

5. Support teachers in using assessment data to benefit each child through curriculum adjustments or more individualized instruction. Encourage staff to identify learning barriers, design strategies to overcome them, and to plan new experiences for children.

6. Facilitate conversations about assessment across grade levels. Encourage P–3 teachers and staff to work together to develop common goals and share practices within the group. Strive to create a seamless continuum of developmentally appropriate assessment from prekindergarten through third grade.

7. Make your assessment practices and policies, and the rationale for them, known to parents and other stakeholders within the community. Discuss assessment as a natural component of the learning and teaching cycle.

8. Include parents in the assessment process. Report to them about their children's development and learning using a variety of modes (e.g., conferencing, notes home, portfolio and documentation celebrations). Gather information from them to round out your understanding of children's learning and development and to elicit family support for children's learning at home.

9. Share demographic characteristics of your learning population and general outcomes publicly. Highlight children's overall achievements while protecting confidentiality of individual learners. Put forward plans for enhancing any significant gaps in learning.

10. Protect children from inappropriate testing methods and errors in judgment that can result when unreliable or nonvalid tools are used. Help others recognize that paper-pencil multiple-choice tests, group-administered assessments, and assessments administered out of context are not appropriate for young learners. Speak out against using a single test to make summative inferences about children or to exclude them from entrance to school or placement in a special program.

Early Childhood Education

Family Involvement

T he message to principals and teachers is clear: focus on family involvement. One of the National Association of Elementary School Principals' (NAESP's) standards is Engage Families and Communities: "Effective principals work with families and community organizations to support children at home, in the community and in pre-K and kindergarten programs" (NAESP, 2006c, p. 23).

"Substantial research supports family involvement, and a growing body of intervention evaluations demonstrates that family involvement can be strengthened with positive results for young children and their school readiness" (Harvard Family Research Project, 2006a, p. 1).

Bronfenbrenner's statement is an enduring message to principals.

> The family seems to be the most effective and economical system for fostering and sustaining the child's development. Without family involvement, intervention is likely to be unsuccessful, and what few effects are achieved are likely to disappear once the intervention is discontinued. (Bronfenbrenner, 1974, p. 300)

The No Child Left Behind (NCLB) Act (2002), widely familiar to principals, provides direction and a specific definition that answers the question, "What is parent involvement?" According to NCLB, parent involvement is "the participation of parents in regular, two-way, and meaningful communication involving student academic learning and other school activities" (Sec. 9101[32]). Parents, the law suggests, should be full partners in their child's education, play a key role in assisting in their child's learning, and be encouraged to be actively involved at school (U.S.

Department of Education, 2004 p. 1; Center for Comprehensive School Reform and Improvement [The Center], 2006).

Successful family involvement is the active, ongoing participation of a family member in the education of the child (The Center, 2005, p. 1). J. Epstein (1988) reports six types of school, family, and community involvement:

1. Parenting

2. Communicating

3. Volunteering

4. Learning at home

5. Decision making

6. Collaborating with the community

Following is a summary of Lunenberg and Irby's (2006) application of Epstein's types of involvement to the principal's role. In parenting involvement, principals provide training and information to help families understand their children's development and how to support the changes they undergo. In communicating, principals are conduits of information to families about school programs and student progress. To increase volunteering involvement, principals create flexible schedules and match talents and interests of parents with needs of students, teachers, and administrators. To encourage learning at home, principals encourage teachers to train family members to assist children at home. To facilitate decision-making involvement, principals arrange training opportunities and information so families can participate. To encourage collaborating with the community, principals help families gain access to support services such as health care, cultural events, and tutoring.

Five important points about involvement are

1. parent involvement makes a difference for students.

2. parents don't have to come to school to be involved.

3. informed parents are a school's best customer.

4. working together creates a better school.

5. it's about children (The Center, 2006, pp. 1–2).

The emphasis on family involvement in a child's education is all about the child. Family involvement makes a difference for the students.

Regardless of income and background, students with parents who are involved in their academic careers are more likely to earn high grades and test scores, enroll in higher level programs, and be promoted. These students attend school regularly, show improved behavior, adapt well to school, and have better social skills. (Mapp, 2002, p. 1)

Parents demonstrate involvement at home by reading with their children, helping with homework, and discussing school events. They demonstrate their involvement at school by attending functions or volunteering in classrooms. Schools with involved parents engage those parents, communicate with them regularly, and incorporate them into the learning process.

Families do not have to come to school to be involved in a child's education. Parents can have a positive effect on school achievement by promoting learning at home and by reinforcing what is taught in school (Henderson & Berla, 1994).

THROUGH THE EYES OF THE FAMILIES

Consider what families feel, see, and remember as they walk through the front door of the school. Add to this the young child they bring to you for the first time—their child—their precious child.

Keep these points in mind as you meet the families:

- Each of them is a significant person in a young child's life,
- Each has an emotional investment in that child,
- All have ideas and opinions about raising and educating young children, and
- Each family member has the potential to become more actively involved in the early childhood program in which his child participates. (Kostelnik et al., 2007, p. 188).

Educators—principals and teachers—typically have fond and happy memories of school. This is part of the reason these individuals have never left school. They have been successful at academics, activities, or sports. They have made friends easily. They were accepted and fit in.

This lens, or frame of reference, may make it difficult for a principal to see the school through the eyes of the families. The tendency is to expect families to see the school as the principal does.

Many families may have had wonderful school experiences. However, some families bringing young children to school may not have had an experience of success during their school days. For a number of individuals, school was difficult. School may have been a lonely or a demeaning experience. Many did not remain in school or reach high school graduation. School may have been a daily misery of feeling like an outsider. Some may have struggled with schoolwork. Some may have been bullied or discriminated against. For instance, Chavkin and Gonzalez (1995) report, "often parents view the school as a bureaucracy controlled by non-Hispanics. The school often reminds Mexican American parents of their own educational experiences including discrimination and humiliation for speaking Spanish" (p. 1).

These school experiences influence families' willingness to come to the school or to enter the school doors. Imagine the feelings families broadcast nonverbally to young children. Principals often remark about the separation anxiety families experience when they must leave their young children at school. Consider their past experiences that may be influencing those feelings. Past experiences may shape the messages families deliver about school and may be invisible barriers to families' participation with the schools. The principal's efforts to engage families in the school for the benefit of their children may be more challenging when families bring these past experiences with them.

Language issues are potential barriers to participation in the school. Immigrants, new to a community, may not speak English. Individuals from other cultures may have different experiences and expectations of the school. Families living in poverty may have challenges that are barriers to participation in school activities and initiatives. Some families have no time to come to school because of their work schedules and home responsibilities. Families bring these differences and many others to their involvement with the schools. The principal's challenge is to anticipate and plan for these differences so that all families are fully engaged in their children's learning.

Families may feel uneasy because of their limited formal education. Some families may be hesitant to visit with teachers or the principal about their children or their education. Some families may feel isolated from other families who are actively involved with the school. Family issues may limit school involvement (Peña, 2000).

Each family in the school community is unique. It is the principal's task to get to know the families.

As experts in what schools expect and the goals the education system is working to reach, elementary school principals are in a unique position to take the lead in creating connections between families, educators and providers of community services. (NAESP, 2006c, p. 26)

Every principal should have the experience of being an unannounced visitor in ten different elementary schools. The opportunity to record the sights, sounds, smells, and impressions of those experiences would be a powerful reminder of the experiences of families who may be strangers in a new school building. See Table 10.1.

Table 10.1   Welcoming Environment Checklist

When you enter the school, do you encounter . . .	Yes (√)	No (√)
a welcoming entryway?		
a bright and cheery building?		
a clean environment?		
picture signs to guide the school visitor?		
signage in languages of the community?		
the prominent display of the works of young children?		
welcoming greetings from school personnel?		

As families walk toward the doors of the school, is the environment welcoming? When families enter the school, do they feel welcome? Is the school a warm, inviting, happy place for the families?

It is the principal's role to ensure that the school is a welcoming place for everyone—children, families, teachers, visitors, and staff members. To create this culture, the principal has to establish the vision of what the school's welcoming environment will be. The principal must work with children, families, teachers, and staff to establish the standards that will be maintained to achieve the climate that signals, "**You** are welcome here!"

- The welcome begins at the front door of the school. Is the entry bright, cheery, and decorated in a manner that says, "We're open for business and our business is kids and learning?"
- The personal welcome follows. Is each person (secretary, teacher, staff member, principal) prepared to greet and spread the welcome message?
- The children in the school are the best conveyors of the message and possibly the most authentic. Do the children mirror, by their behaviors and words, that they feel welcome in the school?
- Children may ride buses to school. Are the bus drivers prepared to share the welcome message with the bus riders?
- The food service personnel have contact with the children. Do the food service workers share the welcoming message with the children and staff members they encounter?
- Teachers work with children and with families. Are the teachers prepared to welcome children and families?

Each of these individuals or groups is both inside and outside the school. They are boundary spanners. When they leave the school, what message do they share outside the school? Does the welcome message extend beyond the school grounds? Consider the number of conversations that occur outside the school and consider the impact of spreading the school's welcome message throughout the community. The potential impact is enormous.

Strategies principals use to accommodate families vary from school to school and community to community. However, principals should nurture the following relationships identified by the National Association for the Education of Young Children (NAEYC).

Establishing Reciprocal Relationships With Families

- Reciprocal relationships between teachers and families require mutual respect, cooperation, shared responsibility, and negotiation of conflicts toward achievement of shared goals.
- Early childhood teachers work in collaborative partnerships with families, establishing and maintaining regular, frequent, two-way communication with children's parents.
- Parents are welcome in the program and participate in decisions about their children's care and education. Parents observe, participate, and serve in decision-making roles in the program.
- Teachers acknowledge parents' choices and goals for children and respond with sensitivity and respect to parents' preferences and concerns without abdicating professional responsibility for children.
- Teachers and parents share their knowledge of the child and understanding of children's development and learning as part of day-to-day communication and planned conferences. Teachers support families in ways that maximally promote family decision-making capabilities and competence.
- To ensure more accurate and complete information, the program involves families in assessing and planning for individual children.

- The program links families with a range of services, based on identified resources, priorities, and concerns.
- Teachers, parents, programs, social service agencies, health agencies, and consultants who may have educational responsibility for the child at different times should share developmental information about children as they pass from one level or program to another" with family participation (NAEYC, 1997, pp. 14–15).

LOOKING INSIDE AND LOOKING OUTSIDE

Perhaps there was a time when the work of the principal was contained within the walls of the school or the boundaries of the playground. The contemporary school leader, however, must look beyond the boundaries of the school to provide connections children need to strengthen their learning.

Communities experience constant change. Principals need to be alert to demographic shifts that impact the number of children coming to school and the children's needs. One significant demographic factor is contained in the following statement:

> Nearly one of every five children in the United States is a child of immigrants. Helping these children and their families in the settlement process is an enormous challenge that poses special difficulties for communities and schools. This demands much greater outreach by the schools to other institutions in the community, including the integration of health, employment and other services. (NAESP, 2006c, p. 23)

Principals find that they must connect children and their families with community resources so that their adjustment to school and success in school is possible. For many principals, the role of liaison to community resources is a new or significantly enlarged administrative role.

Box 10.1

Community Resources

In the family resource room, provide pamphlets or flyers on community resources, such as the following:

- Food assistance
- Housing assistance
- Clothing assistance
- Utility assistance
- Temporary employment agencies
- Job services
- Drivers license examination center
- Bus or other mass transportation routes and schedules
- Health department
- Immunization requirements
- Mental health services
- Immigration and Naturalization Office
- Library programs
- YMCA programs
- YWCA programs
- Parks and recreation programs
- Literacy programs

Many families may benefit from coordinated community resources. The school that provides a family meeting or resource room can provide information about health and medical resources, nutrition, fitness, and child development. Many schools have pamphlet racks installed for displaying small information sheets on topics pertinent to families. These are offered in the languages of the school community. Box 10.1 is a list of possible community resources.

Maslow's hierarchy of needs (Maslow, 1943) is an important reminder in working with families. Children's basic needs must be met. If children are to have the full advantage of the learning environment, principals and teachers must assist in connecting families with community resources.

SUGGESTIONS FOR FAMILIES

Principals and teachers are frequently approached by families who want to do what's best to enhance their children's learning experiences. These are excellent opportunities to help the children and families.

Use the opportunity to provide concrete and practical suggestions. The NAEYC (2002) provides the following suggestions:

Read with, to, and in the presence of children . . .

Reinforce the value of a family routine. The routine should involve homework, meals, and a regular bedtime. Children thrive on structure. Conversation during dinner helps improve children's language skills—both their understanding of what they hear and their ability to express themselves.

Monitor the use of television. Help children choose what to watch, watch TV with them, and talk to them about what they have seen.

Offer praise and encouragement. Kind words and constructive criticism play an important role in influencing children to become successful learners. (NAEYC, 2002; The Center, 2006, p. 2)

Maryland's plan provides a clear, succinct message to families. "Dedicate at least 15 minutes each day to reading [to] and talking with your child" (Maryland State Department of Education, 2004, p. 27; emphasis in original). Keep in mind that

[t]he continuity of family involvement at home appears to have a protective effect on children as they progress through our complex education system. The more families support their children's learning and educational progress, the more their children tend to do well in school and continue their education. (National Center for Family and Community Connections with Schools (NCFCCS), 2002, p. 30)

THROUGH THE EYES OF TEACHERS

Teachers rely on principals for leadership in working with families. Teachers may not have had extensive experience in creating positive working relationships with families. It is the principal's role to work with the teachers to build their strengths in this area. One initial task is to dispel misperceptions teachers may bring to working with families.

One misperception is contained in the following statement: "[T]eachers perceive that families don't want to be involved when, in fact, families don't know how to be involved," says Karen Salinas, communications director for the Center on School, Family, and Community Partnerships at Johns Hopkins University (The Center, 2005, p. 1).

Teachers who have had a difficult experience with a family may be hesitant in future work with families. Teachers may not have clear goals for working with families. The principal can assist teachers and families by working collaboratively to establish expectations for family involvement in the school.

North Carolina is a leader in the integration of family support into education, early intervention, and health and human services for families with young children. Family Support America has identified principles that guide the use of a family support approach (Thegen & Weber, 2002).

Principles of Family Support

Of specific importance to principals' work with families are the principles that encourage

- building relationships based on equality and mutual respect;
- viewing families as resources—to their families, other families, and the community;
- recognizing the school as part of and contributing to the community; and
- affirming and strengthening families' cultural, racial, and linguistic identities.

Building a trusting relationship with parents requires effective communication between the principal, teacher, and families.

They want communication that is frequent, reliable, and two-way.

They want opportunities to share information and opinions.

They want to hear about their child's progress . . . .

They want information about the school policies, programs, and schedules.

They want information about classroom activities (Brock & Grady, 2004, p. 51).

The NAEYC offers the following statement of appropriate practices:

Educators and parents share decisions about children's education. Teachers listen to parents and seek to understand their goals for their children. Teachers work with parents to resolve problems or differences of opinion as they arise and are respectful of cultural and family differences. (NAEYC, 2002, p. 177)

PARENTS WANT COMMUNICATION WITH THE SCHOOL

The communication should be two way with the possibility of feedback throughout the process (Brock & Grady, 1995). Traditional school communications are one way:

- Newsletters
- Newspaper articles
- Handbooks
- School calendars
- Flyers
- Information on topics related to early childhood education
- Notes
- Letters

Two-way communications include these:

- Home visits
- Open houses
- Family-teacher meetings
- Telephone calls
- E-mails
- Web sites

A number of schools and school districts use communication tools such as ParentLink (2008) to increase communication with families. Typical features of these communication systems include the possibility of

- reporting attendance concerns;
- providing access to homework assignments and grades;
- providing emergency alerts;
- distributing notification about school activities, events, holidays, and vacation days; and
- increasing communications between teachers and families (ParentLink, 2008; The Center, 2005).

Communication systems need to be tailored to the family population served. What works in one school may not work in another. If families do not have computers or e-mail access in their homes, e-mail is not an appropriate communication tool.

- Communications have to be prepared and sent in the language of the intended recipient.
- If families cannot read, written communication will be ineffective.

Face-to-face communications may be more satisfying to all participants. However, care must be taken so that face-to-face conversations are not stressful for the families. Location is an important consideration. Home visits provide valuable information for teachers and families. The goal in initial home visits should be to build trust (Brock & Grady, 2004). Keep in mind that families are the most important partners in a child's education.

Meetings and workshops can be held at neighborhood centers near where families live. Translators may be required for these events, depending on the families' needs. Holding neighborhood meetings reduces the families' transportation needs (The Center, 2005; J. Epstein & Salinas, 2004). Meeting in community centers may be more familiar and comfortable for families.

Encouraging teachers to provide families with a weekly, personal update on their child's progress is important in the young child's education. The face-to-face interaction provides families with the opportunity to receive positive information about the child's development and accomplishments and the families have an opportunity to provide positive information about the teacher's work and classroom activities, and to ask questions. Both the teacher and the families can share concerns and ask questions during these weekly updates. The conversations can be "stand up" visits; over time, teacher–family familiarity increases and the conversations tend to become routine and cordial peer exchanges.

Teachers should be encouraged to send home weekly folders of children's work. Teachers can help families learn to recognize what to look for in students' work so that families can comment on and encourage the child's efforts (The Center, 2005; J. Epstein & Salinas, 2004).

FAMILY ROLES

Family involvement in the community can support the work of the school. Family members can serve as liaisons with other families. Their connections can provide the school with an additional communication link (The Center, 2006, p. 2). Family buddies can be assigned for families new to the school. These relationships can build on the positive welcoming message of the school.

The traditional model of family involvement in the school was that the family member was a helper. This approach led to a parade of family members at the school to help with an array of activities such as

- school carnivals,
- classroom helper,
- chaperones for field trips,
- fundraising activities, and
- classroom parties.

The new model of family involvement calls for families to be partners in their children's education. This approach places the emphasis on involvement that facilitates and enhances children's learning.

The NAEYC provides the following description of appropriate practices.

Members of each child's family are encouraged to participate in the classroom in ways that they feel comfortable. For example, family members may take part in classroom activities (sharing a cultural event or language, telling or reading a story, tutoring, making learning materials, or playing games), contribute to activities related to but not occurring within the classroom (designing or sewing costumes, working in the school library), or participate in decision making. (Bredekamp & Copple, 1997, p. 177)

Boileau (2003) reported on a program that encourages family involvement called Family Night Out. Each classroom of kindergarten families met with the teacher, counselor, and principal. A family meal and child care for siblings was provided at no charge to the families. The families met with the teacher, counselor, and principal after the meal to learn about and share information on ways to build on assets with the children at home and in school. Kindergarten students met with an instructor and had activities similar to the family activities so they could discuss them at home. Six sessions were held for each class. The topics were rules and consequences, safety, positive and negative influences, gifts that do not cost money, and a family celebration.

Family Nights Out were held after school, during dinner hours. The time was convenient for families and attendance was 50 to 80 percent per meeting. Lasting relationships developed greater family participation at school, resulting in improved academic performance (Boileau, 2003).

The possibilities for expanding and strengthening family involvement are extensive. The opportunities for enhancing young children's learning make the tasks worthwhile and the principal's role essential.

PRINCIPALS' ROLES

Family Involvement

- Assess the welcoming aspects of the school.
- Consider the experiences and feelings families bring to school.
- Consider the experiences and feelings teachers bring to working with families.
- Identify the potential barriers to family involvement in the child's education.
- Reduce barriers to family involvement in the child's education.
- Establish a family resource room in the school.
- Provide information about community resources in the family resource room.
- Provide opportunities for family involvement in the school that are linked to the child's learning experiences.
- Encourage continuous, two-way communication with families.
- Provide strategies families can use to increase their involvement with their child's learning.
- Encourage and facilitate two-way communication between families and teachers.
- Greet the families whenever possible.
- Remember: Hospitality calls for coffee and treats!

11

Early Childhood Teachers

"Mommy, listen," three-year-old Shelley commands, warding off the coat her mom is trying to put on her at the child care center. With her hands on her hips, Shelley sings, "I'm a little tea pot, short and stout." She works her arms to be the handle and the spout.

"You know what else my teacher teached me?" she asks. Without waiting for an answer, she swings into "A, B, C, D, F, E, M, O," and stops. "I forgot what's next," she tells her mom. "I didn't learn it all today. But I will tomorrow." (Steiner & Whelan, 1995, p. 7)

Shelley is excited about what she learned at "school" today and confident that she will learn more tomorrow. With this kind of daily experience, she is well on her way to developing the attitudes and skills associated with academic and social success. Shelley is lucky: her eagerness to learn is being nurtured by a good teacher.

Good teachers can and do make a significant difference in children's lives. In fact, research shows that the top three predictors of early childhood program quality involve teachers and staffing (Phillips, Mekos, Scarr, McCartney, & Abbott-Shimm, 2000). To achieve a high quality, programs must have

- well-educated teachers,
- low staff turnover, and
- low child-to-staff ratios.

Quality is further enhanced when teachers receive ongoing, informed supervision (Howes, James, & Ritchie, 2003). These essential elements are the subject of this chapter.

TEACHERS MATTER

Early childhood teachers start children along the path to formal learning. They help children make the transition from "home" child to "school" child, and they introduce them to the fundamentals of mathematics, language, science, social studies, and living and of learning beyond the family. They also influence children's overriding sense of efficacy and potential as learners. In doing so, they lay a foundation for future learning that either enhances or undermines children's sense of themselves as learners and doers in school. This is true regardless of how formal or informal the early childhood setting may appear to others. Most young children think of going to the childcare center, Head Start, or preschool as "going to school." In addition, children don't wait until the late elementary grades or middle school to determine whether being a good student is part of their self-definition or if school is a good place to be. Those judgments are made early. In fact, by six or seven years of age, most children have come to one of the following conclusions:

> *School is stimulating/worthwhile/fun. I am a good learner.*

or

> *School is dull/worthless/painful. I am not a good learner.* (Kostelnik, et al., 2007, p. 2)

Regardless of what form the early childhood program takes, who has jurisdiction over it, or where it is housed, teacher effectiveness is the single most important program-related variable affecting young children's learning and adjustment (Peske & Haycock, 2006; Stipek, 2004). More than the curriculum, more than the physical space, more than equipment and materials, **teachers matter**.

Early Childhood Teacher Responsibilities

Early childhood teachers matter in a whole host of ways (Krogh & Morehouse, 2008):

- They establish the socioemotional environment that pervades the classroom.
- They plan activities for solitary children, for small groups of children, and for the entire class to participate in together.
- They organize the educational environment to foster children's learning across and within developmental and subject-matter related areas.
- They serve as models of behavior—toward self, toward others, and toward learning.
- They provide stimulating learning opportunities for children.
- They function as observers, facilitators, instructors, and supervisors.
- They reflect on their teaching and evaluate their performance as well as that of the children.
- They engage parents and other family members as partners in the educational enterprise.

As you can see, the roles early childhood teachers assume mirror those of teachers at other grade levels. This has implications for how practitioners think about themselves and for how they should be regarded in the education community. Due to the important and comprehensive nature of their work, it is critical that early childhood teachers see themselves as **genuine teachers** and that their K–12 colleagues share this perspective. Principals play a significant role in the extent to which this happens.

THE CRITICAL FUNCTION OF PRINCIPALS

It is difficult to achieve program excellence without knowledgeable leadership. Thus program quality is highly influenced by supervisors and other principals responsible for early childhood operations (Morgan & Fraser, 2007). Programs left to function virtually on their own and those that are thwarted in their attempts to enact developmentally appropriate practices (DAP) are programs in which children and teachers do not thrive as they should. Such programs are less likely to attract highly qualified teachers or to retain them over time (Horowitz et al., 2005; Wien, 2004). The opposite occurs when principals take an active role in the following tasks:

- Assembling a highly qualified staff;
- Supporting teachers in their implementation of the program by
  - demonstrating a thorough understanding of the early childhood period,
  - taking the lead in articulating a developmentally appropriate program philosophy,
  - assuring the availability of appropriate curriculum and assessment materials and strategies, and
  - recognizing and rewarding effective teaching; and
- Providing appropriate professional development opportunities to teachers and other staff members

Principals find it easier to fulfill these responsibilities when they have a clear sense of what constitutes a "good" (highly qualified) teacher and what to expect from such teachers in the classroom.

CHARACTERISTICS OF "GOOD" TEACHERS

The teacher characteristics that have the most long-lasting positive effects on young children are well substantiated (Morgan & Fraser, 2007, p. 167). Based on longitudinal studies going back more than forty years, we know that children learn best when their teachers

- demonstrate warmth,
- are responsive to children (their needs, ideas, and emotions),
- develop positive relationships with individual children and families,
- primarily interact with children one-to-one or in small groups,
- create intellectually stimulating experiences and environments,
- value emotional and social development as essential readiness factors,
- allow children to express their feelings,
- permit and encourage children to talk and extend children's conversations,
- work in partnership with parents, and
- display intercultural competence.

These characteristics are not simply a function of personality. They are tied to standards of performance (competencies) identified for the preparation of early childhood professionals. Those standards are presented in Box 11.1. To meet them requires formal education and continuing professional development.

Box 11.1

What Early Childhood Teachers Should Know and Be Able to Do

Competent early childhood educators

Standard 1. Promote child development and learning

- Understand what young children are like
- Know what influences children's development and learning
- Use their understanding to create learning environments in which all children can thrive

Standard 2. Build family and community relationships

- Are familiar with and value children's families and communities
- Create respectful, reciprocal relationships
- Involve all families in their children's development and learning

Standard 3. Observe, document, and assess

- Understand the purposes of assessment
- Use effective assessment strategies
- Use assessment responsibly, to positively influence children's development and learning

Standard 4. Use their knowledge of teaching and learning to connect with children and carry out meaningful curricula

- Build close relationships with children and families
- Use developmentally effective teaching and learning strategies
- Demonstrate sound knowledge of academic disciplines and content areas
- Combine all of these variables to provide children with intentional experiences that promote development and learning

Standard 5. Conduct themselves as professionals

- Identify with the early childhood profession
- Be guided by ethical and other professional standards
- Be continuous, collaborative learners
- Think reflectively and critically
- Advocate for children, families, and the profession

Source: National Association for the Education of Young Children (NAEYC), 2003, p. 6; American Association of Colleges of Teacher Education (AACTE), 2004, p. 5.

FORMAL TEACHER QUALIFICATIONS

A principal was describing the qualifications of the pre-kindergarten teachers in his building. The Head Start teacher had a Child Development Associate (CDA) credential, the two state-funded preschool teachers had BA degrees in early childhood education and the teacher in charge of child care had an Associates degree. Although their levels of education differed, all of them had similar responsibilities and all of them met state requirements.

The Credentialing Dilemma

There is growing support for improving early childhood teacher qualifications. However, not everyone agrees to what extent this should be done. Some researchers call into question the link between teacher training and child outcomes (Early et al., 2007). Others point out that degrees are not quality guarantees. Many people fear that requiring a bachelor's degree for preprimary teachers will make program costs soar, making early childhood education unaffordable for anyone other than wealthy families, or families that receive public assistance. Still more people worry that if public schools require four-year college degrees of head teachers and other public and private preschool programs do not, "we will create a two caste system—one consuming major public funds operated by school systems serving four and five year olds, and one operating with limited funding by private, non profit, and for profit early childhood organizations" (Neugebauer, 2007, p. 1).

Among the proposed solutions to these concerns are (1) developing a comprehensive (not necessarily federal) funding system of early education that operates on a sliding scale basis and (2) using the bachelor's degree in early childhood as a starting point for a universal prekindergarten–3 certification that would link preprimary and early grade experiences for teachers and children throughout the United States (Bogard, Traylor, & Takanishi, 2007; Neugebauer, 2007). As noted in Chapter 8, people are working on solutions like these, but much more needs to be done before they become reality.

The current level of education required of preprimary teachers involves a patchwork of standards. In most states, teachers may be legally hired to teach children prior to kindergarten with anything from a high school diploma to a bachelor's degree. Currently, fourteen states require no special training beyond high school to teach preschool children; thirty-six states require some special training in prekindergarten education for teachers in state-funded programs, but do not have those same requirements for teachers in privately funded programs. Recent figures show that 87 percent of the preschool programs administered through public schools are taught by a teacher with a bachelor's degree; the same is true for only 39 percent of the teachers in for-profit programs and 30 percent of the teachers in Head Start (AACTE, 2004; National Institute for Early Education Research [NIEER], 2007).

In spite of their differing levels of preparation, early childhood teachers everywhere are being asked to apply increasingly sophisticated principles of learning, pedagogy, subject-matter content, assessment, and parental involvement to their daily work. Most experts in early childhood education agree that such knowledge "is best achieved through a four-year college degree, which includes . . . specialized content in early childhood education or child development" (Whitebook, 2003, p. 3). They base their assertions on studies that show that higher levels of formal education in child development/early education are associated with more positive child outcomes (NIEER, 2007). There is also evidence that, unless they receive specialized training in early childhood, teachers and principals tend to treat young children as miniature versions of older students, rather than by creating age-appropriate environments that accommodate younger children's unique ways of learning. Alternatively, without the proper background, practitioners may underestimate children's abilities, by creating programs that fail to stimulate or challenge children appropriately. Neither circumstance yields the benefits we hope children will gain from early education. This is especially true for young children living in poverty, children with disabilities, children whose program attendance is sporadic due to family mobility, and children whose home language is not English (Christensen, 2007; Fleer & Raban, 2005; Hinkle, 2000).

As the result of such findings, professional organizations such as the National Association for the Education of Young Children (NAEYC), the National Association of Elementary School Principals (NAESP), the Council for Exceptional Children, and the American Association of Colleges of Teacher Education (AACTE) have taken the position that lead teachers in all early childhood programs should be required to have a bachelor's degree with special training in child development and early childhood education.

Now that you have the big picture regarding standards of effective teacher performance, we consider what some of these standards look like in the classroom. The examples that follow are all directly related to instruction (Standards 1 and 4). Additional examples regarding assessment, families, and professionalism are addressed in other chapters.

TRANSLATING TEACHER STANDARDS INTO PRACTICE

Effective Teachers Know Child Development and Learning

Effective early childhood educators use their understanding of young children's characteristics and needs, and of multiple influences on children's development and learning, to create environments that are healthy and respectful, supportive and challenging for all children. (NAEYC, 2003, p. 30)

Teachers who have a thorough understanding of child development and learning are more likely to be effective in the classroom . . . new teachers who have had coursework in learning and development are more likely to stay in the field. (Horowitz et al., 2005, p. 89)

Early childhood education, like all education, demands well-prepared personnel who appreciate the unique characteristics of the students they teach. An understanding of the nature of young children, as described in Chapter 6 of this book, contributes to this appreciation. Combining that knowledge with a strong grasp of how to support children as they engage in all phases of the *cycle of learning* is an important way teachers promote children's academic achievement and social adjustment. When principals recognize and appreciate the teacher's role in this cycle, they are better able to assist the early childhood educators with whom they work (NAESP, 2005).

The Cycle of Learning

Figure 11.1   The Cycle of Learning

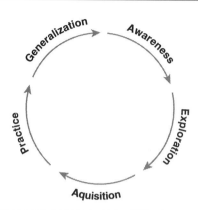

Source: From Marjorie J. Kostelnik, Anne K. Soderman & Alice Phipps Whiren, *Developmentally Appropriate Curriculum, Best Practices in Early Childhood Education,* 4/e. Published by Allyn and Bacon/Merrill Education, Boston, MA. Copyright 2007 by Pearson Education. Reprinted by permission of the publisher.

The cycle of learning represents the process children go through from when they first become aware of a new idea or skill to when they independently apply that knowledge in new situations. It consists of five phases (Figure 11.1).

1. *Awareness.* This phase begins when children first realize that they are encountering something new.

2. *Exploration.* Exploration is a time of self-discovery. Children use all their senses to develop new concepts—mentally organizing and reorganizing the information they gain from their experiences.

3. *Acquisition.* Children move toward acquisition when they ask, "How does this work? Can I play? Where do butterflies go at night?" The outcome of this phase is when children take some action (count, circle something, write a word, draw a map, compare two objects, sequence a series of items, etc.).

4. *Practice.* During the practice phase, children use their new learning repeatedly to improve mastery.

5. *Generalization.* Children apply what they have learned in many ways, adjusting and adapting as necessary to fit new situations.

Effective Teachers Match Instruction to the Cycle of Learning

Generally, children do not move through all five phases of the cycle of learning in a single lesson. Progress from awareness to generalization occurs over days, weeks, and sometimes even years, depending on the concept or skill. As with all other aspects of development, children advance at varying rates. As a consequence, although all children in a group may experience the same lesson at the same time, each child will be in a different phase of the learning cycle for that lesson depending on her backlog of experience and current understandings (Kostelnik et al., 2007). For instance, among a group of children learning about worms, you might observe children at the following awareness levels:

- Some children at the awareness level because they have never encountered worms before up close and personal
- Some children who have a general awareness of worms, but who still need a great deal of time to explore and examine them
- Some children who may have accumulated enough past experience to be interested in acquiring facts about worms and detailed information about worm behavior
- Some children who are worm aficionados and who already know a lot about red worms and night crawlers. They are into the practice phase of finding worms in different places outdoors as well as identifying different kinds of worms from pictures in books.
- One or more children who know so much about worms that they can generalize what they know to better understand other small animals, such as garter snakes or salamanders

To accommodate these differences among children, teachers' planning and teaching must be flexible enough to address all five phases of the learning cycle at once.

Principals are seeing a match between teaching and learning when early childhood teachers

- design open-ended activities that allow individual children to engage in the phase of the learning cycle that suites them best;
- work with children in small groups so as to better observe individual children's progress;
- invite children to explore new objects and experiences without requiring them to carry out prescribed tasks too quickly;
- provide a wide variety of materials for children to explore;
- offer feedback, provide information, and ask relevant questions as children show interest in acquiring new knowledge and skills;
- make practice opportunities available to children throughout the year; and
- provide children with many occasions to generalize what they have learned to new situations.

To determine what knowledge and skills each child brings to the activity as well as what phase of the learning cycle particular children are experiencing, early childhood teachers carefully observe individual children. Based on their observations, teachers provide supports to help children extend their abilities and conceptual understandings beyond their current levels of functioning. This is called teaching in the *zone of proximal development*.

Teaching in the Zone of Proximal Development

Although all children learn, they often learn better with the support of others. (Fleer & Raban, 2005, p. 3)

There is a quantitative and qualitative difference between the tasks children can perform entirely on their own and the ones they are able to carry out while working collaboratively with others or with assistance from peers or adults (Chaiklin, 2003; Copple & Bredekamp, 2006). For instance, three-year-old Shelley, described in the opening to this chapter, could recite some of the Alphabet Song independently, but not all of it. However, with prompting from other children and the teacher, Shelley may make it the whole way through with only a few errors. Gradually, with practice and further cues from others, Shelley will be able to sing the ABCs with little help from anyone else and may even become a mentor to another child who is just learning the song himself. This is illustrated in Figure 11.2.

FIgure 11.2   Teaching in the Zone of Proximal Development (ZPD)

What Shelley can do with assistance	The whole alphabet in order	"A,B,C,D,E,F,G, . . ."
Z P D	Adult provides support for higher-order thinking (more letters in sequence), by using verbal and visual prompts	**Z P D**
What Shelley can do independently	Initial letters of the alphabet in order; some letters out of order	"A,B,C,D,F,E,M,O, . . ."

Teaching in the zone of proximal development is the single most important way teachers individualize the curriculum to meet children's learning needs. Consequently, this strategy is critical to achieving high-quality early education. Working within the zone of proximal development helps teachers keep learning tasks manageable and enables them to provide appropriate stimulation when children show signs they are ready for "more." Both are necessary if children are to progress in their learning. A child who is overwhelmed by a task may be unable to absorb the lesson no matter how important it is. Conversely, children who experience little challenge become bored and stagnate in their learning (Marzano, 2007). Teaching within the zone of proximal development reduces such problems.

In addition to knowing **when** to step in to support children as they progress to more advanced and more independent learning, teachers need a large repertoire of teaching strategies to determine **how** to intervene appropriately.

Effective Teachers Use Varied Teaching Strategies

Early childhood professionals know, understand, and use a wide array of effective approaches, strategies, and tools to positively influence young children's development and learning. (NAEYC, 2003, p. 36)

Because young children develop and learn in many ways, the teaching strategies that support their learning must be quite **diverse**. Likewise, since early childhood curricula address the whole child, teachers need a **comprehensive** array of teaching tools. Some of these strategies are depicted in Table 11.1, The Teacher's Tool Box.

A teacher has planned an activity in which the children are examining seeds. This lesson is linked to the math/science curriculum, with a particular emphasis on observation skills and learning about objects from nature. The children have access to a wide variety of seeds, magnifiers, paper, and markers to use in their work. Table 11.1 presents some instructional techniques the teacher could use to expand children's learning as they carry out the activity.

Table 11.1   The Teacher's Tool Box

Strategy	*Description*	*Example*
Invitations	Creating an opening for child to begin or enter an activity	Teacher says, "Come and check out all the seeds we have in this tray."
Information talk	Orally describing children's actions	A child is sorting seeds and seedpods into piles. Teacher says, "I see that you put the big seeds in one pile and the smaller seeds in another."
Paraphrase reflections	Restating or expanding on something a child has said	Child says, "Look! This one has little seeds inside." Teacher says, "You discovered that there are tiny seeds inside that big seed pod."
Modeling	Demonstrating a way of behaving in order for child to imitate that behavior	Teacher looks closely at a seed with a magnifier and says, "When I looked through here, I saw little yellow specks I couldn't see before."
Effective praise	Using specific comments to acknowledge children's behavior or compare their progress with their past performance. Effective praise links children's success to the effort they are making and is individualized to fit the child and the situation.	Teacher says, "Great! You are being very careful not to mix all the seeds together. That makes them easier to see."
Telling and explaining	Providing information that builds on children's first-hand experiences and that takes place within a meaningful context. Information is often given as children demonstrate a need to know.	Teacher says, "This is a seed pod. The seeds are inside. This outer part keeps the tiny seeds safe until the seeds are ready to grow."
Chaining	Introducing the steps of a task one at a time.	Teacher says, 1. "Pick a seed to look at." 2. "Show me your seed." 3. "Tell me what colors you see. What kind of shape does it have? Describe the texture of your seed." 4. "Draw your seed on your paper to help you remember what you saw."

(Continued)

Table 11.1 (Continued)

Strategy	Description	Example
Successive approximation	Rewarding children for gradually approximating desired goals (e.g., getting more and more accurate)	The teacher has been having the children observe and examine a variety of natural objects since the beginning of the year. As children gain experience, the teacher notes increasingly more specific details about their observations and drawings.
Scaffolding	Providing and then gradually removing external support until children can carry out a task on their own that they initially needed assistance to pursue	Children are counting their seeds. The teacher notices that Jeff can say the numbers in order, but counts some seeds multiple times and skips others altogether. The teacher takes Jeff's hand and points with the child to each seed saying the number aloud. With repetition, the teacher eventually stops counting aloud, but continues to help Jeff point to the seeds one at a time. Eventually, Jeff will be able to do this task without the physical or verbal assistance of his teacher.
Guided practice	Giving children opportunities to learn through repetition. Practice may take the form of rehearsals, repeating an activity with variations, or extending an established skill in a new direction.	The teacher provides numerous chances for children to practice counting—seeds, leaves, shoes, crackers at snack, and so forth.
Do-it signals	Directions or statements that lead children to a specific action	Teacher says, "Look up here. Find a seed that looks like this one."
Challenges	Open-ended variations of do-it signals that motivate children to create their own solutions to teacher-suggested tasks and that prompt children to think about something in a new or different way	Teacher says, "Find as many different colors of seeds as you can. How many did you discover?"
Redirection	Shifting children's attention to more salient or more constructive elements of a task or situation.	Teacher says, "You think the color will tell us what kind of seed this is. We have many black seeds at the table. What else did you notice about the size or shape of your seed that could add to what you already know?"
Addressing misconceptions	Challenging children's perceptions Offering information that is more accurate	Teacher says, "You thought this was a pear because it is green. Not all green fruits are pears. This is an apple. Sometimes apples are green, and sometimes they are red or yellow."

Strategy	Description	Example
Questions	Queries that are purposeful (tied to specific learning objectives), thought provoking (stimulate higher levels of thinking), clear (understandable), and brief (to the point)	Teacher says, "What do you see?" "What happened when you looked inside the seed?" "How did you decide these seeds go together?" "What can we do to find out what kind of seed that is?" "What do you think we should do now that we know_____?"
Silence	Remaining quiet, while attentively observing children and the context in which they are operating	Two girls are engaged in a graphing activity in which they are cataloguing all the characteristics of the seeds they have been examining. They are deeply absorbed in their discussion. The teacher listens attentively for a few moments and then moves to another pair of children. The girls continue their work.

Effective Early Childhood Teachers Know Content

Well prepared early childhood educators understand the importance of each content area in young children's learning. They know the essential concepts, inquiry tools, and structure of content areas including academic subjects and can identify resources to deepen their understanding. (NAEYC, 2003, p. 39)

Researchers note that quality, as reflected in rich, stimulating learning environments, is compromised when staff have inadequate or incorrect content knowledge ... practitioners with inadequate knowledge miss opportunities to scaffold learning and extend children's thinking and problem solving. (Mellor, 2007, p. 30)

Effective early childhood teachers have a good grasp of the following content:

- Language and literacy,
- The arts,
- Mathematics,
- Health and fitness,
- Science,
- Social studies,
- Security and self-regulation,
- Problem-solving and thinking skills, and
- Academic and social competence.

Teachers use content knowledge to build on the interests children bring with them to the classroom and to introduce children to concepts, skills, and knowledge encompassed by formally established early learning guidelines and curriculum standards.

Effective Teachers Pay Special Attention to Literacy and Numeracy . . .

. . . but they do not do so to the exclusion of all other curricular areas. For most adults, the measure of children's academic progress is how quickly they begin to read, write, and do their numbers. We are delighted when a toddler can hold up two fingers to show her age and are charmed when a young child begins singing the "Alphabet Song". We surround children with numerals and geometric shapes from the moment they are born and encourage parents to begin reading to their children from the very first days of life. This desire to promote children's interest in number and print is compatible with a large body of research indicating that literacy and numeracy concepts begin early. Of course, the same can be said for other important things such as the development of scientific curiosity, social competence, and enjoyment of the arts. Based on the premise that we want children to become fully functioning human beings, early childhood programs need to address multiple curricular domains (aesthetics, affective, cognitive, language, social, and physical) and provide children with daily experiences in all of them. However, because young children have a strong interest in reading, writing, and mathematics, and because early childhood is when essential literacy and numeracy concepts either are or are not well established, these areas deserve special attention in early childhood classrooms (Bowman et al. 2001; Makin, 2003).

Recent studies on pedagogical knowledge among preprimary and early-grade teachers indicate that teachers' abilities to create stimulating learning environments are significantly influenced by how well they understand three things:

1. The fundamental components of early literacy and numeracy,

2. The experiences that contribute to children's literacy and mathematical learning, and

3. The strategies that support young children's growth in literacy and numeracy across the curriculum and throughout the day.

Conversely, inadequate knowledge of these components significantly detracts from teachers' abilities to create developmentally appropriate programs for young children in which literacy and numeracy skills are effectively addressed (Fleer & Raban, 2005). Principals who understand these components, too, are better able to support and guide their early childhood staff.

The Fundamental Components of Early Literacy and Numeracy

Literacy in early childhood education encompasses

- listening,
- viewing,

- speaking,
- writing, and
- reading (phonemic awareness, phonics, fluency, vocabulary, and comprehension). (Soderman & Farrell, 2008)

As we look toward the future, it is likely that skills associated with the use of information technology also will be considered essential to literacy development (Arthur & Makin, 2001).

Numeracy in early childhood involves

- understanding number, ways of representing number, relations among numbers, and number systems;
- understanding meanings of operations and how operations relate to one another;
- computing and making reasonable estimates;
- recognizing, describing, and extending patterns;
- sorting, classifying, and ordering objects by size, number, and other properties;
- representing and analyzing mathematical structures;
- adding and subtracting whole numbers using objects, pictures, and symbols;
- analyzing and describing shapes and the spatial relations among objects;
- measuring;
- using mathematical tools;
- working with data; and
- developing inferences and predictions. (Jung, Kloosterman & McMullen, 2007; Kostelnik et al., 2007; Willis, 2002)

Experiences That Contribute to Children's Growth in Literacy and Numeracy

Take a moment to consider the literacy and numeracy skills these four-year-olds are exhibiting during learning center time in their preschool.

The pretend play area has been transformed into a hairdressing shop. The children have created the following signs:

Hr cataz [haircuts] 2$ 99c
Shampoo
Karlazz [curlers] 2$ and 99c
Prmz [perms] 2$

Both boys and girls move into and out of this area and take turns as customers, receptionists, haircutters, and cashiers. They enact cutting hair, giving permanents, having manicures, making appointments, writing down appointments, writing out receipts, using the play cash register, and making change.

At the same time, four children are working with a balance scale trying to balance a series of objects against wooden cubes; pairs of children write down their predictions and compare their results. Two other children are playing checkers and two are playing Kalah. Players of this African game plan ahead to empty pebbles in each of their pots.

Six children who are building with blocks roll small trucks down an incline and discuss how to build together. One child writes a sign, Dajs HL (Dangerous Hill), and attaches it to the ramp with tape. Three children write in their journals; two mark the water level on a measuring tape attached to a jar under a leaky faucet. A few children sit in the library corner looking at books. Some are finding words they recognize, others are "telling" the story from memory. (Fromberg, 2002, p. 17)

All the while, the teacher and an aide move in and out of the play, while observing, asking probing questions now and again, modeling problem solving skills, and helping children to record their findings. The adults are careful not to interrupt or take over. At the same time, they provide cues and support to help children advance in their understandings as demonstrated through their actions and words.

Chances are you noticed children engaged in the basics of literacy—listening, speaking, reading, and writing. Measuring, predicting, comparing, strategizing, weighing, and counting are some of the mathematical concepts children are exploring. Embedded in play, these concepts are taking place in a context that is meaningful and intellectually stimulating to the children involved. These are just the kind of self-initiated experiences that research tells us lead to significant gains in children's language and cognition development as they move from preschool to the elementary grades (Montie et al., 2006).

As you can see, much literacy and numeracy learning flows out of children's natural interests and pursuits. While children interact in the classroom they scribble, draw, engage in oral language or "read" a story to the "baby." Children solve mathematical problems: "How can I make this more?" "How can I figure out how big this is?" "There are three cookies and five kids. What can we do so everyone gets a snack?" In all of these instances children are investigating literacy and numeracy through everyday experiences and naturally occurring interactions. At other times, children's learning is more closely guided by adults in lessons designed with targeted literacy and numeracy content, skills, and standards (e.g., phoneme manipulation or patterning) in mind. Examples might include book reading, letter identification practice, or creating and performing songs and poems using alliteration and rhyming (A. Epstein, 2007). Such lessons may take place during different times in the day—circle time, small-group time, free-choice time, or outdoor time.

Whether the lessons are child led or adult initiated, children's productive engagement in literacy and numeracy learning does not happen simply by chance. Early childhood teachers create plans and then provide time, materials, and guidance to help children become engaged in varied literacy and numeracy experiences throughout the day, every day. During these activities, teachers carefully scaffold children's progress through the cycle of learning, by using strategies described earlier in this chapter.

Unfortunately, when teachers are less deliberate about literacy and numeracy or when they focus on only limited skill development, children are less likely to thrive as readers, communicators, and problem solvers (Mellor, 2007). Thus, to be most effective, early childhood teachers need to employ purposeful plans and strategies to

- stimulate and support children's interest in literacy and numeracy,
- structure literacy and numeracy "rich" classroom environments,

- design activities to promote a wide range of literacy and numeracy-related thinking and concepts,
- take advantage of incidental opportunities to enhance literacy and numeracy, and
- help children associate literacy and numeracy with enjoyment, usefulness and personal competence.

More-specific ways teachers accomplish these goals are outlined in two checklists found in the "Tools" section of this book: **Tool C: Daily Literacy Checklist** and **Tool D: Daily Numeracy Checklist.** These can be duplicated for use together by teachers and principals. They provide comprehensive descriptions of the daily routines and strategies highly qualified early childhood teachers use every day to enhance children's literacy and numeracy skills.

Based on your knowledge of early childhood teachers, there are several things you can do support teachers in their work.

PRINCIPALS' ROLES

Supporting Early Childhood Teachers

1. Keep early childhood teachers (regardless of funding stream) involved in school conversations and part of school planning. Create clear channels of communication between principals and teachers, between teachers and staff, and among teachers across programs and grade levels. Involve early childhood staff in relevant program decision making (such as goal setting, distribution of work, individual responsibilities, and program directions); strive for group consensus on important philosophical issues.

2. Treat all early childhood teachers as you would teachers at other grade levels (eligible for school awards, allocated planning time, invitations to inservice events and school celebrations).

3. Become actively involved in recruiting and choosing early childhood personnel; establish specific goals and strategies aimed at choosing high-quality early childhood staff as part of school improvement plans.

4. Adapt personnel policies to take into account the special circumstances involved in early childhood education that may not be typical of the later elementary grades (e.g., additional time and pay for lesson planning or making home visits).

5. Take the lead in talking about and advocating for DAP; provide appropriate curricula, classroom equipment, and assessment materials to teachers and staff.

6. Encourage teachers to use a variety of teaching strategies, from exploration to direct instruction.

7. Look for the following signs that teachers are addressing the cycle of learning and teaching in the Zone of Proximal Development:

- Offering children open-ended activities
- Working with small groups of children
- Encouraging exploration

- Offering children a wide range of materials
- Offering feedback, providing information, and asking relevant questions to enhance inquiry
- Making practice opportunities available
- Giving children chances to generalize

Make comments to the teachers that show you understand and value these early childhood practices.

8. Provide administrative support to improve early childhood practices (e.g., visit classrooms, carry out classroom observations, arrange regular feedback from peers and supervisors, conduct regular evaluations).

9. Use **Tool C: Daily Literacy Checklist** and **Tool D: Daily Numeracy Checklist** to guide classroom observations and conversations with teachers about literacy and numeracy.

10. Recognize and reward effective teaching.

Finding and Keeping Good Teachers

Finding qualified early childhood teachers and staff is key to creating high-quality programs for young children. In some schools and districts this task is delegated to someone other than the principal (e.g., an early childhood coordinator, central office staff, community agency personnel, or committee). Even when this is the case, it is useful for principals to find some way to participate in the hiring process (Lockwood, 2008). Such participation signals the importance of the position and makes clear the principal's personal interest in the program. It is not necessary for principals to be involved every step of the way or to be experts in early childhood in order to help determine who should be hired. The competencies identified in Chapter 11 provide a convenient list of qualities to consider.

Most of the usual policies and procedures that govern district hiring will apply to early childhood hiring, too. However, on-site observations of candidates with children and position-specific interviews with each candidate are two practices that can serve school-level hiring committees and principals well.

OBSERVING TEACHER CANDIDATES WITH CHILDREN

Asking the Right Questions

I knew we were in trouble the moment the candidate walked in the door. We had asked her to be prepared to carry out a simple activity with three- and four-year-olds in our preschool classroom. She came dressed in a white dress suit and heels. The moment a child came close with "jelly" hands, she flinched. She never got down to the children's level to talk. She remained standing the whole 20 minutes. It was clear she had not come with real interaction in mind. Even though she looked great on paper, we knew she wasn't the kind of teacher who would fit with our philosophy. (Principal, early childhood center, preschool to second grade)

Watching Della in the art area was very reassuring. She responded to each child individually, even as she kept her eye on everything happening in the area. She was particularly good at extending the children's language—paraphrasing now and again— asking open-ended questions. I also noticed she apologized when she interrupted a child— that said a lot to me about her respect for children. (Parent observer and search committee member, preschool lead teacher search)

On-site observations of head teacher candidates with children provide valuable information that goes beyond written applications, résumés, references, and student teacher evaluations (Click & Karkos, 2008). Some schools check out potential hires by inviting them to serve as paid substitutes for the day; others invite candidates to come into an ongoing classroom as part of the interview schedule. Some school districts include a prehiring observation at every grade level, while others concentrate this practice in the preschool and early grades. In any case, there is good evidence that prehiring observations of teachers lead to fewer hiring mistakes and less remedial action later (Neugebauer & Neugebauer, 2005). See **Tool E: Guidelines for Structuring Informative On-Site Observations** at the back of this text for more specific guidelines about how to use on-site observations to get the best information possible.

In addition to on-site observations, principals and other members of the selection committee need to utilize early childhood specific questions as part of the interview process. The more specific the interview, the more likely interviewers and candidates will be able to engage in meaningful conversations. Questions should address early childhood philosophy, curricula, child guidance, assessment, working with families, and working as part of a team. Forty potential interview questions are provided as **Tool F: Sample Interview Questions for Teacher Candidates** in the tools section of this book. The list could be duplicated for use by a search committee or interview team.

ADDRESSING THE SHORTAGE OF QUALIFIED EARLY CHILDHOOD TEACHERS

As more communities expand their early childhood education programs, the need for qualified teachers is growing. Unfortunately, supply has not kept up with demand (U.S. Department of Labor, 2007). In a recent national survey, directors of early learning programs identified shortages of qualified teachers as the largest challenge facing the field (Exchange, 2008). In light of this dilemma, institutions of higher education worldwide are gearing up to produce larger numbers of early childhood educators. At the same time, advocates are working hard to make the field more viable and appealing to potential teacher candidates.

In the meantime, early childhood education has a sizeable paraprofessional workforce. One way to address immediate teaching needs is to help current staff members, who are not yet fully qualified, pursue higher levels of education. Such efforts can be supported by financial assistance offered through a variety of sources. Some of these are described in Box 12.1.

Box 12.1

Sources of Financial Assistance to Help Early Childhood
Teachers and Principals Upgrade Their Formal Qualifications

There are several sources for financial aid for early childhood teachers and principals working on their degrees. Here are some examples:

- Child Care Resource and Referral (CCR&R) agencies. Local licensing agencies also may have information on scholarships in the state and community.
- T.E.A.C.H. (Teacher Education and Compensation Helps) Early Childhood Project. Scholarships are available in many states. There are also a variety of federal grants and loans available for early childhood educators:
  - o Pell Grant. Typically awarded to undergraduate students, but in some limited cases, a student can receive this grant if enrolled in a post-bachelor's teacher certificate program.
  - o Federal Supplemental Educational Opportunity Grant. Grant for under-graduates with exceptional financial need—students with the lowest Expected Family Contribution (EFC). Priority is given to students who receive federal Pell Grants.
  - o Federal Perkins Loan. Low-interest (5 percent) loan for both under-graduate and graduate students with financial need. This loan can be forgiven (up to 100 percent) for full-time teachers in designated ele-mentary or secondary schools serving students from families with low incomes, for Head Start education component staff, and for those in some other categories.
  - o Stafford Loan. A variable interest rate loan for both undergraduate and graduate students. Students must be attending school at least halftime to be eligible for a Stafford Loan. Half-time enrollment is not a requirement for the other federal grant and loan programs.

For more information on financial assistance for early childhood educators, visit the National Child Care Information and Technical Assistance Center (NCCIC) Web site at http://nccic.acf.hhs.gov/poptopics/financialassist.html.

Source: Stuber (2007b).

In line with the idea of schools developing their own fully qualified teachers, in Table 12.1, we offer a potential timeline that programs can use to ease into securing enough fully qualified teachers.

Table 12.1   Sample Timelines for Meeting Teacher Qualifications, 2006–2020

Year	One Class, One Teacher	Two Classes, Two Teachers
2006	• Teacher must have a Child Development Associate (CDA) or equivalent certificate. • Teacher must be working toward a higher degree (associate's, bachelor's, or an equivalent). • Annual reports must show continuous progress.	• Both teachers must have a CDA or equivalent. • Both teachers must be working toward a higher degree (associate's, bachelor's, or an equivalent). • Annual reports must show continuous progress.
2010	• Teacher must have an associate's degree or its equivalent.	• Both teachers must have an associate's degree or equivalent. • At least one teacher must be enrolled in a bachelor's degree program or equivalent. • Annual reports must show continuous progress.
2015	• Teacher must have an associate's degree or its equivalent. • Teacher must be working toward a bachelor's degree or its equivalent. • Annual reports must show continuous progress.	• At least one teacher must have an associate's degree or its equivalent. • At least one teacher must have a bachelor's degree or its equivalent. • Annual reports must show continuous progress.
2020	• Teacher must have an associate's degree or its equivalent and be working toward a bachelor's degree or its equivalent. • To achieve National Association for the Education of Young Children (NAEYC) accreditation, the teacher must obtain the bachelor's degree by the next accreditation cycle.	• At least one teacher must have a bachelor's degree or its equivalent. • The second teacher must have an associate's degree or its equivalent and be working toward a bachelor's degree or its equivalent. • Annual reports must show continuous progress.

Source: NAEYC 2005, 2006 Additional examples for programs with three or four classrooms are available at the NAEYC accreditation site (http://www.naeyc.org/accreditation/).

SEEKING TEACHERS TO WORK EFFECTIVELY WITH DIVERSE CHILDREN AND FAMILIES

All children benefit when they have opportunities to interact with a diverse cadre of teachers. In addition, children need access to adult role models who look and speak as they do and whose background experiences mirror some of their own. The majority of U.S. teachers today, including those at the prekindergarten level, are European American females from middle-class backgrounds who speak only English (Banks et al., 2005). Yet, their classes include

- boys and girls,
- growing numbers of children of color,
- many children who live in poverty, and
- many children who speak a home language other than English.

Two ways we can address this demographic "disconnect" between teachers and children are to

1. make sure that current teachers develop the cultural competence they need to effectively teach children of diverse backgrounds, and

2. strive to diversify the array of adults to whom young children have access in the program.

Both strategies need the support of many people to succeed—public policy makers, business leaders, teacher educators, career counselors, early childhood personnel, K–12 teachers, principals, and superintendents.

> ### Early Childhood Education Needs More Teachers of Color
>
> According to the Bureau of Labor Statistics, 31.5 percent of the preschool-kindergarten workforce is African American, Hispanic, and Asian American. This is about twice as many minority teachers as are employed in elementary school through high school in the United States. However, to have the early childhood workforce more closely resemble the overall preschool child and family minority population (about 41 percent), it is important to keep working to attract teachers of color into the field.

Developing Cultural Competence

Sensitivity to children's cultural contexts is one of the three principles of developmentally appropriate practice (DAP) discussed in Chapter 5. All teachers must implement culturally responsive teaching practices to work effectively with young children.

To develop culturally responsive practices, teachers need to

- examine their own cultural assumptions to understand how these shape their starting points for practice,
- know how to inquire into the backgrounds of their students so they can connect what they learn to their instructional decision making,
- interpret cultural symbols from one frame of reference to another,
- mediate cultural incompatibilities, and
- build bridges or establish linkages across cultures to facilitate the instructional process. (Banks et al., 2005, p. 243)

Cultural competence must be introduced in initial teacher preparation programs at all levels and then honed continuously on the job. As an administrator, you can support this by offering teachers opportunities to reflect on their practices, by emphasizing the importance of meeting the needs of all children, and by providing teachers with professional development opportunities targeted at culturally responsive teaching.

Attracting Underrepresented Groups to Early Learning Programs

The current supply of male teachers, teachers of color, and multilingual teachers is small. Attracting more such teachers to the profession will require comprehensive, long-term strategies at the policy level. However, there are some things you can do in the short run to make it more likely that diverse candidates will apply to your program. Since males are the least-represented demographic group in the early childhood workforce, we take a moment to consider how to attract more men to early childhood classrooms.

Few Male Teachers Work With Young Children

A young boy could go through his entire education without ever having a [male] teacher like me. This is not a reflection of our world or our communities, and it is certainly not a reflection of how we want kids to see the world. (Reg Weaver, NEA president, 2003)

Young boys and girls need to interact with caring men and women to get a balanced view of life's possibilities. Yet, according to the latest statistics, the percentage of male teachers is barely 9% at the elementary level. In kindergarten and preschool, fewer than 2% of the teachers are men (B. Nelson, 2006).

Barriers to Getting Men Into Classrooms

There are several reasons why men have a limited presence in early childhood classrooms:

- Economics
  - Many men do not see teaching as a lucrative (or viable) way to make a living.

- Gender stereotypes
  - Many people believe that teaching young children is "women's work."

- Public mistrust
  - Parents sometimes express concerns about male teachers touching their children (while comforting children, helping them get dressed, or snuggling at group time).

- Isolation in the field
  - Male teachers-in-training have few males to talk to or refer to as role models.

- Lack of career information
  - Young men get little information about teaching young children as a potential career option.
  - Male youth have few opportunities to discover that they might enjoy working with young children. (Neugebauer & Neugebauer, 2005; Rolfe, 2005; Scelfo, 2007)

Recruiting Male Teachers

Male teachers are more likely to consider early childhood education as a career choice when principals

- include specific goals about recruiting men in school improvement plans;
- are up-front with parents about the intention to hire more male teachers, address any concerns objectively, and focus on the assets men bring to the early childhood setting;
- include the statement, "Men encouraged to apply" or "Men welcome," on hiring notices;
- advertise strategically: in publications read by men such as the newsletter for various men's groups, in locations frequented by men (sports clubs, recreation centers, health clubs, sports activities);
- use words like leadership, professional development opportunities, and advancement in describing the position;
- interview the qualified men who apply (data indicate males who apply frequently fail to get an interview);
- hire men for entry-level positions such as teacher assistants and then help them progress to higher positions through continuing education;
- work with middle school and high school programs to give all students, including males, an opportunity to volunteer or engage in work study or service learning in an early childhood program to foster their interest in the field;
- make clear to teacher education programs that the program has practices in place to support male student teachers (e.g., a male teacher is available to check in with the student periodically—even if he is not the cooperating teacher); and
- actively seek male student teachers for the program. (Neugebauer & Neugebauer, 2005; Rolfe, 2005)

Retaining Male Teachers

Retention of male teachers goes up when principals

- make staff assignments that allow all staff to engage in a full range of practices. Female assignments should go beyond so-called female tasks (preparing food or comforting children who are sick) and men should not be solely responsible for traditional male tasks (disciplinarian, playground manager, handyman).
- create program policies that encompass both genders. Avoid special policies for men (such as, "Males cannot be left alone in the classroom with children"). While the intentions behind these policies may be well meaning, they reinforce the notion that "men are not to be trusted." A better policy would be, "No staff member may be left alone in the classroom with children."

(Continued)

(Continued)

- make buildings male friendly—include art depicting male caregivers, teachers, and parents; make special efforts to communicate with and include fathers as well as mothers in program activities and communications; use DAP-related practices to address the needs of boys as well as girls; consider school policies (e.g., rules on the playground and policies governing learning centers or recess) keeping male as well as female needs in mind.
- make cluster hires of more than one male teacher at a time to reduce isolation.
- create opportunities for male teachers to meet one another and share their experiences (across program, school, or district boundaries, as needed). (B. Cunningham & Watson, 2002; NEA, 2004; Rolfe, 2005)

Not only is it important to assemble a highly qualified diverse teaching staff, but it is also important to figure out how to keep them. Early childhood education has the highest annual rate of staff turnover (annual rates range between 20 to 40 percent) of any profession (Shellenbarger, 2006). This rate is both disruptive and costly to school programs.

REDUCING STAFF TURNOVER

I remember when Leon first came to us. Kids didn't want to be around him. He was aggressive and had a hard time making friends. Now, he has buddies and can tell people what he needs instead of poking or hitting them. It makes me feel great to see him doing so much better. (Preprimary teacher)

Early childhood teachers often feel personally responsible for the development of the children in their charge. They report that the achievements children make confirm their value as teachers (Click & Karkos, 2008). Surveys show that early childhood teachers gain the most job satisfaction from

- observing children's progress,
- forming relationships with children,
- experiencing challenge in their work,
- establishing relationships with parents and other family members, and
- gaining recognition for their work from colleagues.

In addition, they take pride in performing a valuable service for the community (Neugebauer & Neugeauer, 2005).

From these findings, we can see that early childhood teachers derive satisfaction from the intrinsic nature of their work (as opposed to extrinsic factors such as a lovely office or opportunities to travel) and from the relationships they develop with children and families. Other things such as perceived congruence between personal beliefs and program philosophy, self-efficacy in the classroom, positive relationships with supervisors and peers, and adequate material support also factor into job satisfaction (J. Johnson, 2007; Jorde-Bloom, 1997; Wien, 2004). All of these variables are summarized in Box 12.2.

Box 12.2

What Makes Teachers Want to Stay on the Job?

Nature of the Work

- Teachers can see that children are making gains and that their work is making a difference.
- Teachers have opportunities to develop close personal relationships with children and families.
- The work remains interesting and challenging; teachers recognize that they are becoming more skilled.
- Teachers perceive that they can make decisions and exercise judgment in their own classrooms and in their professional interactions with children and families.
- Teachers have genuine input into program operations and policies.

Pay and Opportunities for Advancement

- Rewards are related to performance.
- There are opportunities to advance and be recognized.
- There are opportunities for professional development.
- The value of the work and the teacher's preparation to do the work are acknowledged through adequate pay.

Coworkers

- Fellow staff members are perceived as knowledgeable, caring, and committed to children and families.
- The staff holds high expectations for the children and themselves; they do their best and believe that all children can learn.

Relations With Principals

- Principals are perceived as valuing the staff and the work they do.
- Principals are knowledgeable about early childhood education.
- Principals are good at setting goals, assigning reasonable workloads, and avoiding crisis management as their typical management style.
- Teachers receive regular feedback on the results of their efforts.

General Working Conditions

- Teachers perceive that their beliefs and the program's philosophy are compatible.
- Teachers have access to appropriate tools and materials to do the job.
- Teachers periodically have time, resources, and space to plan, reflect on their work, and take a break from the children.

Why Early Childhood Teachers Leave the Field

Resentment festers when teachers lack control over the basic elements of their jobs and when they feel undervalued or unappreciated.

> *I came in one morning to find I had two new children in my group. Nobody told me ahead of time. I had no chance to get ready for them in advance. That's so typical. People act like it shouldn't matter, but it matters a lot to me.* (Head Start teacher)

> *We're in the same building and I've had some of these kids for two years. Yet, when the kids move on, no one asks me for suggestions about what to do when they cry or what they've learned so far. It's like we're not even here.* (Prekindergarten teacher)

Every year, an estimated 20 to 40 percent of the early childhood workforce leaves the field, most often due to burnout arising from some combination of long hours with children, isolation, low pay, and perceived lack of respect for what they do (Shellenbarger, 2006; J. Johnson, 2007). Additional factors that contribute to frustration among early childhood staff include

- poor physical work environments,
- poor prospects for advancement,
- lack of support from supervisors,
- inflexible personnel policies,
- being subjected to a negative management style,
- time pressures in the classroom, or,
- unhappiness over being required to engage in practices with children that teachers interpret as inappropriate. (Click & Karkos, 2008; Neugebauer & Neugebauer, 2005; Wien, 2004)

Some factors associated with burnout such as poor pay and lack of respect for early education require long-range solutions that should involve principals, but cannot be solved by them alone. However, several variables related to worker dissatisfaction are things principals can do something about. Teachers know this. When asked what factor is most likely to encourage them to remain in the field in spite of difficult conditions, teachers put a caring, supportive administrator, committed to student learning and knowledgeable about what makes a good program, at the top of their list (Amrein-Beardsley, 2007).

Creating a Positive Environment for Early Childhood Staff

Principals who want to retain good early childhood educators need to consciously

1. enhance conditions that promote job satisfaction, and

2. reduce sources of frustration.

Attention to only one or the other of these is less effective than attention to both simultaneously. See Table 12.2 for examples.

Table 12.2 What Principals Can Do to Enhance Satisfaction and Reduce Frustration Among Early Childhood Personnel

Because Early Childhood Teachers Gain Satisfaction From . . .	*Principals Enhance Satisfaction When They . . .*
Seeing children make progress	• Help teachers develop their observation skills • Promote the use of observation tools in the classroom such as anecdotal records and observation checklists • Structure staffing so teachers have opportunities to stand back and make formal observations of children in the classroom • Set aside time in the daily or weekly schedule for teachers to reflect on children's progress and adapt their plans accordingly • Elicit feedback from families regarding children's progress, and share these anecdotes with teachers • Set aside time in staff meetings for teachers to talk about the progress they are observing in the children
Developing relationships with children	• Make sure the classroom schedule and setup allows time and places for teachers to interact with children individually and in small groups • Keep adult–child ratios low enough that teachers get to know a small number of children well • Keep teachers and children together long enough for strong personal relationships to develop
Developing relationships with families	• Make it possible for teachers to conduct home visits to establish rapport with families • Provide time in the daily or weekly schedule for teachers to communicate with families (via newsletters or "happy notes," periodic phone calls, journals that pass back and forth between teachers and parents, and so on) • Recruit volunteers for the beginning or end of the day so teachers can have a chance to chat with parents or family members as they drop children off or pick them up • Support opportunities for parent or teacher interactions such as potlucks and parent volunteers in the program
Developing relationships with colleagues	• Work on team building • Plan professional development opportunities for staff members to learn to work more effectively with other adults in the classroom, including how to work with volunteers • Plan professional development opportunities for lead teachers to learn effective adult supervision techniques—including how to direct staff effort, how to delegate, and how to provide constructive feedback • Provide opportunities for teachers and staff to get to know and communicate with other adults who provide support services such as custodians, librarians, specialists, and food service personnel
Feeling a sense of efficacy in their classrooms	• Encourage teachers to personalize their classrooms rather than requiring all classrooms to look the same • Provide some petty cash for teachers to use to supplement the materials in their classrooms without having to go through elaborate permissions and accounting procedures

(Continued)

Table 12.2 (Continued)

Because Early Childhood Teachers Gain Satisfaction From . . .	Principals Enhance Satisfaction When They . . .
	• Allow teachers to create their own classroom schedules in which times are relatively stable, but also as flexible as necessary to meet the needs of children and teachers • Allow teachers to create some of their own plans, rather than requiring them to use only lesson plans developed by others; give teachers the flexibility to adapt plans to meet the individual or cultural needs of children
Feeling isolated	• Support team teaching, keeping teams together long enough for members to get to know one another well • Pull staff together across program or grade-level boundaries to discuss common issues or children's progress from one program level to the next • Create schedules that allow time for teachers to plan together
Poor physical work environments	• Provide adult-sized furniture • Provide functional space and tools for planning and writing • Make available tools to create classroom materials • Offer adults access to the outdoors and natural world
Long hours	• Work with teachers and staff to create schedules and staffing patterns that allow for some time away from the children each day, time to adequately set up the classroom each day, time to observe children in action, and time to make home visits
Inferior status in the field	• Bring early childhood educators to the table (and do not always deal with them separately) • Include early childhood teachers in programwide staff training; choose some training topics that focus on early childhood to help other staff members better understand the nature of early childhood work • Incorporate early childhood programs in schoolwide improvement plans • Use the same titles to address early childhood staff as are used with other teachers (if teachers in school are called Mrs. Jones or Mr. Smith, then early childhood teachers should be addressed this way too, not Miss Betty or Mr. Sam)
Low pay	• Whenever possible, apply similar pay scales and benefits across grade levels including prekindergarten • Provide extra pay for planning time or home visits since many early childhood teachers spend longer hours with children than is true for teachers at other grade levels • Become an advocate for higher pay for early childhood educators

At the beginning of this chapter, we noted that well-trained teachers and low staff turnover characterize high-quality early childhood programs. Those topics have dominated our discussion so far. The third teacher-related variable associated with high quality is stable staffing combined with low child-to-staff ratios.

STABLE STAFFING AND ADULT-TO-CHILD RATIOS

Young children learn best in predictable, responsive, environments in which they are treated as valued individuals. Such environments are characterized by close personal relationships between children and the same adults over time. Children who experience a revolving door of caregivers early on are less likely to thrive and are more susceptible to developmental risks. For these reasons, it is important to establish stable staffing patterns that allow children and teachers to spend significant amounts of time with one another, each day and throughout their years in the program.

In addition, adults need to be responsible for small numbers of young children so they are able to get to know individual children well and so they can respond to young children's needs. NAEYC has established the following adult-to-child ratios and class-size guidelines with these principles in mind. (See Table 12.3.)

Table 12.3 Adult to Child Ratios Within Group Size

Age Group	Group Size 12 Adult–child ratio	Group Size 14 Adult–child ratio	Group Size 16 Adult–child ratio	Group Size 18 Adult–child ratio	Group Size 20 Adult–child ratio	Group Size 22 Adult–child ratio	Group Size 24 Adult–child ratio
Three-year-olds	1:6	1:7	1:8	1:9			
Four-year-olds			1:8	1:9	1:10		
Five-year-olds			1:8	1:9	1:10		
Kindergarten			1:8	1:9	1:10	1:11	1:12

Note: Adults include teachers, assistant teachers, and teachers' aides, but do not include volunteers or preprofessional students-in-training.

Stable staffing is good for children and good for adults. Recognizing that there is someone in the program who knows and cares about them gives children a sense of security about the school setting. This makes it easier for children to engage in the full variety of experiences they need to enhance their development and learning. On the adult side, as mentioned earlier, developing relationships with children is a major job satisfier that enhances teacher effectiveness and reduces staff turnover. Programs that keep children with the same teacher for significant portions of the day and those that allow teachers to follow children for multiple years exemplify this concept.

Keeping at least two adults with young children at all times is an important guiding principle for prekindergarten classrooms. Usually this includes a lead teacher and an assistant or paraprofessional. Both adults need to be available to the children throughout the session. It is not appropriate to include the food service personnel, the bus driver, or other supplementary personnel in adult-to-child ratios. Such individuals are out of contact with children too much to provide the instruction and guidance young children need. Additionally, in emergencies, it takes at least two adults to handle most situations (one in the front of the fire exit line, one at the back; or one to stay with a convulsing child, one to make emergency contacts). Volunteers are usually thought of as a bonus. In most states, they cannot be included in the ratios necessary for licensing and they do not count for national accreditation.

PRINCIPALS' ROLES

Hiring and Retaining Good Teachers

1. Play an active role in selecting early childhood teachers and staff.

2. Encourage interview teams to observe teacher candidates work with young children. Use **Tool E: Guidelines for Structuring Informative On-Site Observations**, provided at the back of this book, to guide this practice.

3. Refer to **Tool F: Sample Interview Questions for Teacher Candidates**, for ideas of what to cover in the interview phase of the selection process.

4. Provide ongoing opportunities for teachers to engage in professional development and continued growth and challenge in the job; help staff connect to training programs and the fiscal support they need for advancing their education.

5. Take advantage of teachers' intrinsic motivators (children's progress, relationships with children and families, respect of coworkers, efficacy in their work). Refer to Table 12.2 and identify strategies you can use to enhance teacher satisfaction. Select one or two of these to put in place.

6. Recognize factors that prompt teacher frustration (isolation, poor work environments, long hours, inferior status, and low pay). Identify strategies such as those listed in Table 12.2 to address one or two of these at a time. Follow through in using them.

7. Help early childhood staff navigate the school bureaucracy in order to achieve their goals for children and families (e.g., elicit cooperation from custodians, make it easier for children to go on field trips, allow the youngest children to eat their lunch in their room rather than the large loud lunchroom if teachers think that is best, give young children a chance to be on the playground without the older children)

8. Advocate for stable staffing, class sizes, and the child to staff ratios as recommended in Table 12.3.

13

Physical Environments That Support Early Learning

S chool-based early childhood programs are found in elementary school buildings, in portables, in high schools and in facilities devoted to the youngest children in a district. There is no conclusive evidence that any of these locales is automatically better than any other. However, no matter where they are found, the physical features of the early childhood classroom will influence children's lives.

Early childhood classrooms are unique places. There is no confusing a classroom designed for young children with a room set up for fifth graders, a middle school classroom, or a high school chemistry class. Everything is scaled down in size, there are special furnishings not found elsewhere in the school, and rooms are arranged differently than they are in the upper grades. Figuring out what space to allocate to the program, what to put inside that space, and how to arrange it all are among the first and most important decisions principals make in the early childhood program.

THE IMPORTANCE OF THE PHYSICAL ENVIRONMENT TO YOUNG CHILDREN

The physical environment is a powerful force. It affects how we feel, influences what we do, determines how we interact with others, and impacts how successful we are at reaching our goals (Dodge, 2003; Weinstein & Mignano, 2007). This is true for people of all ages. However, the impact of the physical environment is even greater on children than it is on adults. This is because children learn everything through their senses. They touch, taste, smell, observe, and act on the world in order to comprehend it. As a result, the physical environment plays a major role in how children learn and what they come to know. The younger the child, the truer this is.

Because young children do not get to choose the environments in which they live and learn, the kinds of experiences they have are determined by the physical settings we create for them. Consequently, early childhood educators and principals are obliged to know all they can about indoor and outdoor environments—how to design them, how to manage them, and how to use them to enhance child development and learning. This requires developing environmental competence.

> School districts are increasingly investing in preschool and early education initiatives . . . however, much more will need to be done . . . to develop appropriate learning places in schools for this cohort of children. Our nation's schools must become committed to improving the quality, attractiveness, and health of the learning spaces and communal spaces [for young children] in our schools. Over the past several decades, research and experience have demonstrated the significance of spatial configurations, color, lighting, ventilation, acoustics, and other design elements on student achievement. Far from luxuries, these design decisions affect children's ability to focus, process information, and learn. (Bogle & Wick, 2005, p. 5)

ENVIRONMENTAL COMPETENCE

Environmentally competent educators and principals treat the physical environment as an integral part of the early childhood program (Lackney & Jacobs, 2002; Steele, 1980). They know how to use physical elements to foster children's comfort and competence and to stimulate children's interest in learning. Teachers and principals who are environmentally competent plan spatial arrangements that support instructional plans. They are sensitive to the messages communicated by the physical setting. They know how to evaluate the effectiveness of the environment. They are alert to instances when physical factors contribute to behavior problems, and modify the (physical setting) when the need arises (Weinstein & Mignano, 2007, p. 27).

To achieve environmental competence, teachers and principals must incorporate three areas of knowledge into their understanding of early childhood education:

1. Basic propositions about how physical environments operate

2. Ways physical environments and child development and learning are related

3. Fundamentals of environmental planning

ENVIRONMENTAL PROPOSITIONS

Creating early learning environments is exciting and fun. Teachers love looking through catalogues and dreaming about how they will put their classrooms together or what the new playground will look like. However, before everyone starts talking about wall coverings, room arrangements, lighting, or outdoor equipment, they must consider five propositions about how physical environments function indoors and outside.

Proposition 1. Physical environments influence children directly.

Where space is located, how it is designed, and the materials made available to children either inhibit certain learner outcomes or make it more likely that those outcomes will happen (A. Epstein, 2007).

- The outdoor space for young children at Glencairn Elementary centers around a large open grassy area where children play group games and have access to large portable building materials to create pretend structures. Children in the preschool at Washburn Elementary have access to a play yard in which the focal structures are swings and a slide. Based on their designs, these outdoor environments offer very different learning opportunities for the children.

Proposition 2. Physical environments have symbolic impacts on children.

The symbolic influence of the physical environment is subtle, but potent. How space is set up, to what degree children have access to materials, and the extent to which the physical surroundings are attractive or unattractive convey a variety of messages to children (Clayton, Forton, Doolittle, & Lord, 2001; Kahn & Kellert, 2002).

- The physical environment speaks to children. Children recognize symbolic messages quite clearly. One principal described his first time visiting a four-year-old class in the basement of the Rec center. In spite of the teacher's best efforts to humanize the windowless setting with pillows and pictures, when the principal asked the children about their classroom, one child said it was "a gunky place." Others quickly agreed— it smelled of disinfectant, the walls were made of concrete blocks, and it was isolated from other people in the building. Contrast this with a kindergartner at a different school on her first day last fall. Surveying the sunny room and rich array of materials available, she sighed contently and said, "Ma, look at the party they made for me." This setting told her she was important: it was clean, it was pretty, and it was an integral part of the school (Kostelnik et al., 2007).

Proposition 3. Physical environments reflect the philosophy of those who create them.

Classroom environments reflect adult beliefs about children and childhood learning. They also reflect ideas about curriculum—what goals and content are important and how people are expected to relate to one another (Gestwicki, 2007; Tarr, 2001). Consider the philosophical differences demonstrated by the way space and materials are used in the block areas in Classroom A and in Classroom B.

- Classroom A—Block Area. This classroom is divided into several small-group activity areas. In the block area thirty-two wooden unit blocks are randomly mixed together on a shelf; a sign at the entrance to the block area indicates that only two children are permitted to play here at a time. A sign on the wall states, "Blocks are for building, not throwing. Take turns. No crashing blocks." The area measures three feet by three feet. A masking tape square on the linoleum helps define the space where children can build.
- Classroom B—Block Area. This classroom is divided into several small-group activity areas. The block area is inviting: More than two hundred wooden unit blocks are arranged by shape on two open sets of shelves. Each shelf has a picture of the shapes that belong on that shelf. Block accessories such as traffic signs, wooden figures, and

small plastic vehicles are available in individual bins. Picture books showing roads and buildings are displayed on top of the shelves and are easily reached by the children. There are paper, markers, and tape for children to use to make their own props. A sign at the entrance to the block area indicates that six children are permitted to play here at a time. The space measures six feet by nine feet. A carpet flat enough and smooth enough to support children's block structures covers the space.

What did the environment convey to you about the importance of the block area in each of these classrooms? What expectations do teachers have for peer interactions in the block area? Chances are, whatever you answered, you noted differences in the two classrooms based on how each teacher designed his block area. The same would be true for all other spaces in both the indoor and outdoor environments.

Proposition 4. Children have opinions and preferences regarding the early learning environments in which they participate.

Children are quite aware of their physical surroundings and have definite ideas about what should and should not be included in the classroom (ACNielsen, 2004; Kostelnik et al., 2007; Weinstein & Mignano, 2007).

- When preschoolers were asked to complete the sentence, "I wish my classroom had . . . " here is what they said:

  - I wish my classroom had a pig. I can't have one at home.
  - I wish my classroom smelled good.
  - I wish my classroom had bouncy tires we could climb on inside.
  - I wish my classroom had more books that I could read myself.

- Kindergartners and first graders answered like this:

  - I wish my classroom had goldfish and snakes and plants and worms we could touch.
  - I wish my classroom had blocks. I miss my old room with the blocks.
  - I wish my classroom had a place I could be alone sometimes.
  - I wish we didn't have to sit in chairs all the time. I wish my classroom had beanies where kids could lie down to read books or just rest for a minute (maybe five minutes would be good).

Developing a Child's Eye View of the Classroom

Jim Greenman, an expert on children's indoor environments made this observation:

Children and adults inhabit different sensory worlds. What we (as adults) often don't notice are the elements a child will zoom right in on: the right place with the right shape . . . the right feel. Our cold utilitarian eyes assess [only] for order and function, cleanliness and safety. (Greenman, 2005, pp. 21–22)

Of course, order, safety and health are essential to environmental design, however, they must be tempered with an eye for what appeals to children. A way to develop this eye is to observe children as they interact in the environment and with one another. What do you see? Are certain areas of the room utilized more heavily than others? Are certain spots avoided altogether? Do particular spaces seem to provoke conflict? Where do you see children laughing and interacting with peers? What captures children's attention? A second strategy is to get down on your hands and knees and explore early childhood classrooms through children's eyes. What do you see, hear, smell? What is there to touch? Watch the children from this perspective and reassess how they are using the space. Keep these impressions in mind as you plan and observe learning spaces for young children.

Proposition 5. Effective learning environments take into account adults' needs as well as those of children.

Early childhood professionals spend approximately two thousand hours a year on the job with children. The quality of their work is strongly influenced by the work environment itself (Groark, Mehaffie, McCall, & Greenberg, 2007). Supportive work environments lead to higher-quality interactions among children and staff and result in more stimulating programs for children. Early childhood settings that fail to take into account what adults need to do their jobs more easily and well are ones in which staff morale suffers, contributing to poorer quality programming (Feine, et al., 2002; Whitebook et al., 1997).

- The physical design of the classroom makes a difference in how teachers spend their time and how comfortable they feel on the job. For instance, visual barriers (e.g., pillars, tall room dividers, large pieces of furniture) can make it hard to see from one area of the classroom to another, which keeps teachers from having a global view of the whole. This often prompts them to remain on the move in order to monitor children's behavior. In such environments, teachers feel uncomfortable taking time to interact with individuals or small groups of children for more than a minute or two. An opposite result occurs when physical spaces are designed so children are easily observable from any location in the room. Under these conditions, teachers can visually scan the room to keep track of what children are doing even as they take time to work with an individual child or groups of children. This condition contributes to more interaction time between the adults and the children in their charge. It also helps teachers feel more at ease in their supervisory roles.

One Teacher's Ideal Classroom

Bright and light. Warm. A good sized space. Plenty of it. A water area. Plugs everywhere—I want to use the phone and the PC in class. Kids may want to call the zoo. A place where we can make a mess and not raise the wrath of the custodian. Flexibility of setup. (First-grade teacher)

- In addition to the ideal classroom, teachers asked to complete the sentence "I wish my building had . . . " answered:
  - Private space for me to think quietly, write, plan, keep records, store personal belongings, and where I could take a break from the children for a few minutes without noise or interruption
  - Adult-sized rest rooms, not used by children
  - Comfortable adult-sized furniture
  - Laundry facilities
  - A workroom with well-organized resources (tape, paper, markers, and so on) and space to lay out big projects in preparation, as well as technology such as a phone, a computer with e-mail, and a copier
  - Professional resources such as journals, newsletters, instructional manuals, curriculum guides, regulatory guidelines, professionals books, audiovisual materials, and equipment catalogues
  - An isolation space for ill children
  - Staff access to the natural world
  - Communal staff space where teachers and principals can talk with one another and learn what is happening with coworkers and children's activities taking place in other parts of the building
  - A comfortable private space for meeting with families
  - Designated waiting and observing spaces for parents and other family members
  - A design that facilitates the socialization of new staff, substitutes, and volunteers into the program (Abbott, 1995; ACNiel, 2004; Curtis & Carter, 2003; Taylor, 2002).
- Unfortunately, recent studies of early childhood settings in the United States indicate that fewer than half have the kinds of convenient, flexible functional physical environments adults need and dream of working in (Curtis & Carter, 2003; Dunn & Kontos, 1997; Whitebook et al., 1997).

The propositions outlined above provide a foundation for thinking about the physical context of early childhood programs. Next, consider how physical environments influence childhood learning and behavior.

HOW PHYSICAL ENVIRONMENTS INFLUENCE CHILD DEVELOPMENT AND LEARNING

An environment needs to be designed for learning. It should enhance the students' ability to learn and the teachers' ability to provide a range of learning opportunities. (Elementary school principal)

During the past fifty years, we have become increasingly aware that human-built environments significantly impact every area of early development and learning (Evans, 2006; NAEYC, 2005). Let's examine a few of these associations and their implications for environmental design.

SOCIAL-EMOTIONAL DEVELOPMENT

Social Behavior and Self-Regulation

Children's social behavior is affected by design elements such as density, materials, color, sound, and light. Well-planned early childhood settings help children to behave in socially acceptable ways as well as to practice skills associated with self-regulation (Kostelnik et al., 2008). When children misbehave, the first thing to consider is to what extent the problem is a result of the physical setting (Weinstein & Mignano, 2007).

Density

High-density situations (many people in a small area) are associated with increased aggression among children and less cooperation (Evans, 2006). A low-density classroom (few people in a very large area) can also lead to problems. When classrooms have very low density, children tend to wander the room, adult supervision is often poorer, and accidents are more likely to occur. Current NAEYC (2005) recommendations indicate that thirty-five square feet per preschool or kindergarten child (excluding hallways, bathrooms, sinks, built-in cabinets, and closets) represents a reasonable amount of space for preschoolers; a minimum of fifty square feet per child is appropriate for infants and toddlers.

Materials

The extent to which materials are available affects how well children get along and the extent to which they interact with one another. Fewer materials lead to fewer playful interactions and more conflicts among children. More materials prompt greater amounts of cooperative play and sharing. This is particularly true during the preschool years when instrumental aggression in the form of arguments over objects, territory, and rights reaches its peak (Bell & Quinn, 2004; Garbarino, 2006). For these reasons, having enough materials is essential to a smooth running classroom (Evans, 2006). "Enough" means not only a large quantity, but also several of the same item so more than one child can use a particular material at the same time.

Color

There is evidence that color has a bearing on children's attitudes, behaviors, and learning (Jago & Tanner, 1999). Bright, vibrant colors (red, orange, or yellow) stimulate children and are most appropriate in areas where activity and interaction are expected and encouraged. Cool, pastel colors (green, blue, purple) tend to calm children and are best in quiet areas such as those for reading, concentrating, or resting (Taylor, 2002). Today's professional designers suggest that the color scheme for walls, window coverings, and carpets tend toward warm, soft, neutral colors (Gonzalez-Mena & Widmeyer-Eyer, 2006). This is especially true for prekindergarten and kindergarten classrooms where there is a lot going on and a lot for children to take in.

Sound

Soothing, jarring, invigorating, confusing, frightening—sound can be all of these things. When it comes to early childhood classrooms, those in which children are expected to be quiet much of the day interfere with children's natural ways of learning—talking, exploring, and moving about. On the other hand, too much noise and constantly noisy environments detract from children's overall social development, cognitive learning, and academic achievement (Maxwell, 2000). This makes sound management a critical element of architectural design in early education programs. Acoustical tile, upholstered furniture, fabric pillows, wall hangings, carpets, and other sound-absorbing features are necessary to diminish the auditory impact of children talking and moving about an enclosed space. Similarly, it is desirable to separate spaces that require quiet concentration from those in which children are interacting in small or larger groups as well as from ones in which children are more vigorously engaged.

Light

Lighting has psychological, aesthetic, and physical impacts on children (Evans, 2006). Children perceive dimly lit rooms as uninviting. Rooms in which the light is harsh are also unappealing. Both conditions are associated with disruptive behavior (Jago & Tanner, 1999). Since children spend large amounts of time engaged in visual tasks, appropriate and varied lighting is critical (e.g., ambient lighting, task lighting, and accent lighting). In addition, designers suggest natural light over artificial sources whenever possible. Natural light is important both for its health benefits and because it gives children access to seasonal and daily changes that keep them in touch with the surrounding natural environment (Dinos, 2004). Consider that some children spend up to ten hours a day at the center or school. These youngsters may come in the dark and go home in the dark. For such children, being in rooms without windows or ones in which the blinds are drawn most of the day literally means they lose sight of the natural world.

Peer Interactions

Young children experience more-frequent and more-positive interactions with peers in small, well-defined areas than at individual desks or in large open rooms (Hohmann & Weikart, 2002). The greatest amount of peer interaction occurs in the pretend play area, the block area and on apparatuses such as climbers on which several children can play at once (Kostelnik et al., 2007; Weinstein, 1987). The more these areas are enriched with props, the more likely it is that children will experience positive peer interactions.

Self-Esteem

Self-esteem has three dimensions: worth, competence, and control (Marion, 2007). The extent to which children feel valued is a measure of their worth. Competence involves children's belief that they have the knowledge and skills to accomplish tasks and achieve goals. Control refers to the degree to which children feel they can influence outcomes and events. All three dimensions are influenced by the physical environment.

Worth

"Too often classrooms resemble motel rooms—anonymous, impersonal spaces designed to serve everyone and to belong to no one" (Weinstein, 1987, p. 162). Such conditions do little to promote self-esteem. Conversely, classrooms that are personalized to reflect the individual children in the class contribute to children's feelings of worth. This is exemplified by classrooms filled with children's products instead of teacher-made or commercially created bulletin boards. Examples include

> children's artwork and emergent writing, products of their science experiments and discoveries such as models or simple charts, rules they create for games and activities in the room, family and class photographs, mementos of field trips, turn-taking lists for distributing snacks or choosing a song, and so on. (A. Epstein, 2007, p. 12)

Products like these convey the symbolic message—"Who you are and what you do, think, and say matters."

Competence

In response to the age-related needs of young children, developmentally appropriate early childhood programs strive to support children's independence, foster decision making, and encourage discovery and problem solving. Maria Montessori was among the first to experiment with how the physical environment could serve a significant role in promoting these competencies (Montessori, 1912/2002). Her work was the impetus for creating child-size furnishings. Current experts in physical design maintain that competence is further enhanced when children have access to drinking fountains, sinks, toilets, doorknobs, and light switches that are accessible and convenient to use. Shelving that is low, open, well organized, and labeled enables children to get things and return them with minimal assistance. Tables, chairs, climbers, slides, and swings that are child scaled allow children to use them without adults having to lift youngsters into place (Gonzalez-Mena & Widmeyer-Eyer, 2006). In a recent visit to a prekindergarten classroom, one of the authors noticed that other visiting adults were charmed by the setting, but stood back from it. When they went into the space, they mostly looked at things much like a tourist might survey an unfamiliar site. It was clearly not designed as a world for adults. Preprimary guests, though, moved right in, making functional use of the space and the materials in it. They recognized a setting created just for them and felt competent using it.

Control

A well-ordered setting makes the environment predictable and gives children cues about how to be successful (Colbert, 1997; Hohmann & Weikert, 2002). This increases children's sense of control. Such control is best achieved through the establishment of well-defined activity areas using obvious spatial boundaries. In the most functional early childhood classrooms, activity areas are set off from one another using physical cues such as furniture, partitions, and floor space (e.g., the pretend play area is bounded by a small stove and refrigerator; the large group area is defined by a rug; within the art area are clustered the easel, art table, and sink). Symbolic cues are also used to define space—signs at the entrance to an area (showing how many children can participate at any one time) or mobiles hanging above certain parts of the room provide cues about area content such as books or math.

COGNITIVE DEVELOPMENT

Problem-Solving Skills

Children demonstrate better problem-solving skills when classrooms have a large variety of age-appropriate materials from which to choose and adequate space in which to use them (Evans, 2006). Poor variety prevents children from combining materials and exploring new problems to solve. Open-ended materials such as water, paint, dough, sand, and building materials lead to more divergent thinking among children. Closed materials such as puzzles, form boards, and tracing patterns prompt convergent responses. Youngsters who have both divergent (more than one response is correct) and convergent (only one response is correct) experiences become more adept at both types of problem solving (Bodrova & Leong, 1996; Gordon & Browne, 2007).

Logical Thought

Constructing relationships among objects through ordering, grouping, measuring, and counting are significant intellectual tasks in which young children engage. The physical environment can support children's development of logical thought through the kinds of materials offered to children. Examples are sets of materials that are similar but vary by one or more properties—miniature vehicles that are the same size and shape but different colors, paint brushes that vary in width, rocks that vary in weight, and so on (Hohmann & Weikart, 2002). Pretend play experiences are a particularly good source of logical thinking practice. As children pretend, they engage in symbolic representation through role playing, object substitution, object invention, drawing, and writing (Kostelnik et al., 2007). The most sophisticated forms of pretend play come about when children participate in an enriched environment containing multiple props and in physical space that encourages the flow of children from one pretend play area (e.g., a house) to another (e.g., a garage or post office) (Leong, 2007; Petrakos & Howe, 1996).

LANGUAGE DEVELOPMENT

Oral Language

Oral language is a strong predictor of vocabulary and literacy development (Strickland, 2007). The more children hear language directed at them personally and the more they talk to others, the better. Thus early childhood settings need to be organized so children have opportunities to talk with mature language users and with peers about many things, hour after hour, day after day (Risley & Hart, 2006). The same benefits do not occur in environments where children simply sit and listen most of the time or ones in which children have few opportunities to converse with peers and adults in individual or small-group interactions. To promote oral language development, most early childhood classrooms are arranged in small activity areas in which children spend a significant portion of the day interacting freely and talking much of the time. While verbally rich interactions may take place anywhere in such classrooms, there is evidence that the pretend play area is most likely to produce mature language (Leong, 2007). As was true for logical thinking, the most advanced language usage takes place in extended pretend play centers that include more than one pretend setting, such as a house and also a post office or grocery story.

Literacy and Print Concepts

Children's exposure to print during the early childhood years is significantly correlated to literacy development (Soderman & Farrell, 2008). Researchers have written extensively about the importance of creating print-rich environments, in which children have extensive exposure to books, meaningful print in every corner of the room, and storytelling experiences every single day (Soderman & Farrell, 2008). Teachers are advised to have a book area and to include books in every activity center in the classroom—books on machines, transportation, and building in the block area; cookbooks and home construction books in the pretend play area; books about artists, color, and design in the art area; number books and books about nature in the math and science area.

PHYSICAL DEVELOPMENT

Physical Activity

Besides the obvious fact that young children are still maturing physically, today's concerns about childhood obesity make physical development an important focus of early education programs (Leppo, Davis, & Crimm, 2000). In addition, there is clear evidence that physical inactivity leads to boredom (Ginsberg & Wlodkowski, 2000). Consequently, early childhood programs need to encourage movement rather than inhibit it. This involves arranging classrooms to allow for easy access from one interest area to another and creating spaces where children can engage in gross motor activity not only outside, but also indoors (Payne & Isaacs, 2007). Such areas might not be large enough to contain a full-scale climber or accommodate wheel toys, but could provide enough room for children to throw beanbags, balance on a walking beam, jump, or dance.

The Essence of the Research

Findings like those above have led to standard elements in early childhood program design such as

- an emphasis on child-created décor,
- child-scaled furnishings,
- visual cues to promote independence and decision making,
- recommended square footage minimums for classrooms and outdoor spaces,
- varied and plentiful materials for children to choose and use,
- recommendations regarding color, light, sound, ventilation, and temperature,
- rooms arranged in activity centers that address different developmental domains and that accommodate varying numbers of people.

The research also helps us identify certain telltale behaviors that signal that the physical environment is not working well for children and adults. These signs are summarized in Box 13.1.

Box 13.1

Warning Signs That the Physical Environment Is Problematic

The following behaviors signal that the physical environment is not working well for children and teachers.

Children

- Wander aimlessly around or have difficulty finding something to do that interests them
- Frequently run in the classroom
- Repeat the same activities over and over again
- Become frustrated because materials are lost or broken or because activities are too difficult for them to handle on their own
- Continually fight over materials and space
- Use materials destructively
- Yell
- Crawl under tables and shelves
- Consistently depend on adults to reach for things or do things for them

Teachers

- Continually complain about children's behavior
- Have to shout to get children's attention
- Lose track of what children are doing and where children are
- Feel uncomfortable working with individual children or children in small groups even for a little while (Koralek, Colker & Dodge, 1993), pp. 66–73.

To gain more insights into how problems like these could be alleviated or avoided altogether, consider the fundamentals of environmental planning.

FUNDAMENTALS OF ENVIRONMENTAL PLANNING

What Is the Ideal Early Childhood Classroom?

It has to be a good place to live in day after day, to learn in, and just to be . . .

Imagine a room with natural light streaming in the windows, shadows dancing on the floors and walls, and a richly textured world of different shapes and sizes of furniture—with places to work, eat, and just sit and snuggle. An early childhood classroom is one part home, one part child laboratory for exuberant and messy little scientists, [artists and engineers], one part stage that transforms itself daily, and one part gallery. . . . It is a workroom and library and a place to eat, drink and be merry. It is a room with different places to be just like in your house—places that look, sound and feel different—There is a door to the outside, that wonderful place with sun and shade and grass. It is not a room dominated by tables and chairs and the uniform glare of fluorescent lights and gleaming tile. No, this place feels like home. (Greenman, 2005, p. 164)

Design Basics

Supportive early childhood settings come in all shapes and sizes. Some classrooms were originally designed for young children, while many are located in space initially created for other purposes. The best are not always the most costly. Every functional space, however, begins with teachers and principals thinking about safety, health, comfort, convenience, aesthetics, flexibility, and organization (Curtis & Carter, 2003; Kostelnik et al., 2007).

Safety

In early childhood education, "Safety is job one!" Safe environments are those in which obvious hazards have been removed and chances of serious injury are minimized. In such places, children move about freely to explore and attempt new challenges. Adults remain vigilant, but also are free to relax and interact with the children rather than having to constantly police the setting in order to prevent accidents and harm.

Vigorous attention to safety does not mean depriving children of opportunities to challenge themselves physically or to learn how to use age-appropriate tools. Forbidding children to run on the playground or to use child-size scissors may avoid immediate risk, but keeps children from learning ways to explore their world and gain increasing mastery under the watchful eye (and helping hands) of caring adults. The design of the classroom, therefore, must balance safety with children's developmental urges to take on reasonable challenges and acquire new skills.

Health

Healthy environments are ones in which the chances of contracting or spreading illness are reduced (Aronson, 2002). When designing the ideal classroom, designers take into account the need for hygienic practices related to diapering, toileting, food handling, handling of blood and other body fluids, and hand washing. Sanitizing toys and equipment must be easy to carry out. Wall and floor coverings as well as furnishings must be safe for children to chew on, use, and navigate. Childcare licensing regulations in every state and National Association for the Education of Young Children (NAEYC) accreditation guidelines spell out many specifics of how to maintain children's health and physical well-being. Go to the tools section at the back of this book to find **Tool G: Early Childhood Safety and Health Checklist**. This checklist provides examples of typical safety and health practices both indoors and outdoors, and will be a useful resource for planning and maintaining healthy environments.

The way teachers and learners feel about space is vital to learning. Convenience, safety and comfort all help with focus. (Primary school principal)

Comfort and Convenience

Both children and adults need to feel comfortable to perform at their best (Evans, 2006) As noted earlier in this chapter, density, materials, color, sound, and light all contribute to whether or not a physical space is comfortable (Koralek et al., 1993). Designing the space so participants can get what they need conveniently also minimizes fatigue and the tension that comes with things not being at hand or not fitting quite right. For instance, food allergy cards, the refrigerator, small plastic pitchers, and paper cups need to be near where snack and lunch are served; the sink needs to be near where children are finger painting; and some counters need to be the right height for children, while others need to be higher for adults to use comfortably.

Aesthetics

Attractive environments promote children's and teachers' sense of well-being and ease with one another (Bogle & Wick, 2005; Warner & Sower, 2005). Such places are lovely, exciting, and serene. They appeal to the senses. The recent Report from the National Summit on School Design (Bogle & Wick, 2005, p. 6) advocates considering home as a template for school. Homelike elements include such things as using natural materials throughout the building and in the materials and furnishings children use, designing appropriate-scaled elements, locating restrooms near instructional areas, avoiding long sterile hallways, providing friendly and welcoming entries, and creating enclosed backyards. While suggestions like these make common sense, too often early childhood classrooms in the United States are filled with hard plastic furnishings, bright fluorescent lights that stay on all day, vivid primary colors everywhere, and an overabundance of items from school supply catalogues that are overstimulating (Curtis & Carter, 2003). It is common for classrooms to be overcrowded with furniture, large cartoonlike figures on the bulletin boards, and commercial materials that contribute to an unrelenting sameness from one room to the next. Consider the typical circle time carpet as a case in point.

> **A Matter of Taste**
>
> What sort of carpet would you put in your living room or family room, or any place you inhabit for long days, day after day? Bright red or green with lots of primary colored lines and shapes? A carpet that tells a story? A psychedelic mosaic? Very few of us, even the children of the 1960s or the disco generation of the 1970s, would think of it. Why would we then inflict them on children? Garish rugs with numbers, letters, patterns or pictures are often laid on top of brightly colored floors or carpets, and then to add to the visual assault, are often covered with brightly colored plastic. Rugs that purport to teach actually have very little educational value (Greenman, 2005, p. 182).

The more we can do to reduce the institutional nature of early childhood classrooms the better. Children need access to educational settings we ourselves would find pleasing to be in all day. They deserve attractive furnishings, diverse textures and spaces, and real art on the walls. Many objects found at home—flowers in vases, comfortable and varied furniture, real dishes and tools, collections of natural materials or treasured objects—are often missing from the center or school (Tarr, 2001). However, such things should be common features in early childhood classrooms to promote children's sense of belonging and connection to the classroom setting.

Flexibility

High-quality physical environments are flexible, not static (ACNielsen, 2004). Room arrangements vary with the needs of the children, and the same space may be arranged differently from one time to another depending on program goals. Furniture is movable and can be adapted in different ways. Materials and equipment are rotated periodically to keep things interesting.

Organization

Effective early childhood settings reflect children's need for order and predictability. Visually order is communicated by

- creating distinct areas within the room in which different kinds of activities and work occur,
- defining individual activity areas using visual and acoustic boundaries,
- making clear pathways to and from the different areas in the room, and
- providing materials near the places in which those items are to be used.

PHYSICAL REQUIREMENTS OF ACTIVITY-BASED INSTRUCTION

Early childhood settings need to include space for playing or working, food preparation, eating, resting, toileting, group storage, and storing people's personal belongings. Good environmental design addresses all of these functions. However, the most distinctive spatial feature of early childhood classroom design is the use of activity-based interest areas to support children's unique learning styles as well as relevant curricular goals.

> Young children need space that is arranged and equipped to support active learning, independence, and decision making. They need space to use materials, explore, create, and solve problems; space to spread out, move around, and talk freely about what they are doing; space to work alone and with others; space to store their belongings and display their inventions; and space for adults to join them in support of their intentions and interests (Hohmann & Weikart, 2002, p. 111).

Clearly, early childhood classrooms must support a range of activity choices (e.g., art, blocks, language arts), differing forms of human interaction (e.g., solitary, small group, and large group), and different activity types (e.g., explorations, guided discovery, problem solving, discussion, demonstration, and direct instruction). Consequently, some activity spaces must be large, and some must be much smaller. A few will be so specialized that only a narrow range of activities can take place in them (e.g., listening center and water table). Other locations will serve multiple functions, accommodating one kind of activity for part of the day (small-group block building on the rug) and a different type of activity later (whole-group circle time on the rug).

Furnishings and floor and wall space necessary for each of the typical centers you might find in an early childhood classroom are described in **Tool H: Physical Requirements of Small-Group Activity Centers,** found at the back of this book. This chart illustrates how programs can begin with minimum materials and gradually upgrade each activity area to reach an optimal state. It offers a handy resource for teacher and administrative planning.

Besides having the appropriate space, a well-designed classroom has small-group activity centers. Well-designed classrooms are characterized by each of the variables outlined in Table 13.1.

Table 13.1 Characteristics of Well-arranged Activity Areas in Early Childhood Classrooms

Spatial Separation	There are low walls, screens, and furniture, or changes in floor levels define each center and separate one from the other.
Visual Connections	It is possible to see multiple centers from various parts of the room.
Groupings	Similar activity areas are clustered together (e.g., book area and writing center; blocks and pretend play; science and sand/water table).
Convenience	Activity areas are located near necessary physical resources (e.g., art area near sink, listening center near electrical outlet).
Size	Each activity center is an appropriate size for the activity it offers.
Pathways	Children can move from one center to another easily and without interrupting the work or play of other children.
Locations	Noisy and quiet areas are in different parts of the room. Active areas are separated from less-active ones.
Seating	There is a variety of seating (chairs, pillows, and floor space) among the overall array of centers.
Surfaces	There are appropriate surfaces for children's play/work (tables, counters, carpeted areas, tile floors).
Flexibility	The furnishings in each center are flexible enough to allow changes in arrangement.
Storage	Appropriate places for storing children's materials are in or near each center so they are accessible and easy to select and put away.
Display	Shelves, counters, and wall space are available for children to display their work. Children's work is displayed at their eye level.

Source: Adapted from Sanoff (1995).

Calculating How Many Activities to Provide During Center Time Each Day

Each small-group activity area has the capacity to absorb a certain number of children. For instance, a large set of unit blocks may provide enough materials for four to six children to interact comfortably. The listening center, with just two headphones, has just have enough space for two children to be at once. To prevent waiting or arguments over too few materials, it is recommended that teachers plan approximately one and a half spaces per child (Marion, 2007). An example of how this might work for a group of twenty preschoolers is offered in Table 13.2.

Table 13.2 Activity Slots Available in the Willow School State-Funded Preschool During Free-Choice Time

Number of children in the class $= 20$

Activity slots needed $= 20 \times 1.5 = 30$

Area	*Materials*	*Potential Activity Slots Available*
Art area	Open art materials	2
	Easel	2
	Blocks	4 to 5
Language arts	Books	2
	Listening center	2
	Writing area	2
	Flannel board	2
Math & Manipulatives	Number bingo	3
	Puzzles	2
	Open math materials	2
Sand/water		3
Science/collections	Examining worms	3
Pretend play	House and grocery store	4 to 6
Woodworking	Closed today	

Total Number of Activity Slots = 33 to 36

EQUIPPING EARLY CHILDHOOD CLASSROOMS

Adults walking into an early childhood classroom for the first time are often struck by how small everything is—the low tables and chairs, short sinks, and tiny toilets create a miniature world that may seem quaint and not too serious to those unfamiliar with it. In reality, the furnishings and supplies found in early childhood classrooms are as important to student learning and take as much care to select as those found in any school at any level from elementary to higher education. Every item has a purpose. Every item can either support or detract from program goals. Well-chosen materials contribute to high-quality learning; poorly chosen, inappropriate, or missing items undermine children's education. The goal in equipping each classroom is to enhance learning in every developmental domain and to make it possible for children to work independently and in cooperation with others. Refer to **Tool I: Early Childhood Education Classroom Equipment List** in the tools section of this book for a rudimentary list of items that contribute to a well-rounded, developmentally appropriate early childhood program.

Sturdy Multipurpose Materials Are a Good Investment

The equipment presented in **Tool I: Early Childhood Education Classroom Equipment List** is generic. The items can be used across developmental domains or subjects and for many different learning experiences. The broad nature of the equipment makes it suitable for children of varying abilities, backgrounds, and ages. If teachers and principals select high-quality durable products, items like unit blocks can last twenty years or longer, which makes them a good long-term investment.

Target Certain Curricular Goals Through Special Purchases

To supplement the fundamental materials outlined above, early childhood educators also collect some materials specifically designed to highlight certain curricular goals such as cultural diversity. These objects are infused throughout the program. A teacher might, for example, add the following special materials to the basic items described in Tool I for art and music, blocks, and pretend play.

❑ *Art and music*   ❑ Crayons, paper, and paint in different skin-tone colors

          ❑ Art and music examples of cultures represented by the children

          ❑ Art tools and musical instruments of varying culture groups in the community

❑ *Blocks*   ❑ People figures representing varying cultures, abilities, and ages

          ❑ Vehicles of varying cultures; traffic signs in children's home languages

❏ Books showing cultural differences in buildings and building materials

❏ Varied building materials (wood, bricks, and thatch)

❏ *Pretend* ❏ Multiracial female and male dolls, housekeeping dishes, utensils and food
Play   packages reflecting different cultures; dress-up clothes that include items from
           varying cultures; large pieces of fabric representing the cultures of children's
           families that children can use for a variety of purposes; child-sized disability aids
           such as walkers, crutches, or eyeglasses with the lenses removed.

Additional Dimensions That Influence Equipment Selection and Classroom Design

Classroom materials and room arrangements vary along five key dimensions that effect children's experiences in early childhood classrooms (Prescott, 2008). These dimensions are

1. softness or hardness,

2. open or closed,

3. simple or complex,

4. individual or social, and

5. high mobility or low mobility.

The individual elements (e.g., soft versus hard) involved in each dimension are neither positive nor negative. Well-designed classrooms include some of each. These dimensions are further defined in Table 13.3

Table 13.3   Physical Dimensions of Materials and Space That Need to Be Considered

Key Dimension	*Element*	*Definition*	*Examples*
Softness or hardness Degree to which objects are responsive to human manipulation and variation	Softness	Malleable objects that respond to a person's touch Objects that provide tactile sensory stimulation	Finger paints Clay Sand Water Carpets Pillows Fabric furniture Curtains Textile wall hangings Grass outdoors
	Hardness	Inflexible objects	Furniture made of wood, plastic, or metal Tile floors Asphalt or cement outdoors

(Continued)

Table 13.4 (Continued)

Key Dimension	Element	Definition	Examples
Open or closed Degree of flexibility in object's use	Open	Objects that can be manipulated in a variety of ways No one right way to use it	Paints Sand Water Clay Large and small blocks, Collage materials Dress-up clothes
	Closed	Objects that can be manipulated only one way in order to work	Puzzles Board games Models
Simple or complex Capacity of object to sustain child's attention/involvement	Simple	Single materials	Sand Water Clay Blocks
	Complex	Single materials to which other objects or props have been added to increase interest	Sand with sifters Water with pitchers Clay with cookie cutters Blocks with small vehicles and traffic signs
Individual or social Degree of privacy and control over one's own territory	Individual	Spaces that afford some sense of privacy, opportunities to think and to be on one's own or with only one or two other persons at a time, opportunities to use objects without interruption or without having to share	Child's cubby Tent made from a table and sheet Rocking chair in book area "Hiding place" under the forsythia bush outside
	Social	Spaces that accommodate groups and allow easy entry, experiences that involve many children at once	Block area Dress-up area Sandbox Water table Group time

Key Dimension	Element	Definition	Examples
High mobility or low mobility Degree of freedom child has to move around	High mobility	Activities and spaces that encourage child to use whole body	Dancing Running Hopping Climbing Riding tricycles
	In between		Block building Dress-up
	Low mobility	Activities and spaces that require child to be still	Sitting for a story Sitting at snack Sitting at the art table

Source: Prescott, 2008; Kostelnik et al., 2007.

Overarching Principle

Developmentally appropriate early education environments include both facets of each dimension as well as things that fall in between. An overarching principle regarding the environment however, is that the younger the child and the longer the child's day in the program, the **more** the environment should emphasize softness, openness, simple materials that gradually become more complex, places and opportunities for individual activity, and high mobility.

Putting It All Together

As you can see, there is a lot to think about when it comes to creating physical environments that support early learning. To help you determine to what extent the classrooms in your program are designed effectively, refer to **Tool J: Indoor Environment Checklist**, found in the tools section of this book. This checklist incorporates the environmental propositions described earlier in this chapter, research on the relationship between the physical environment and child development and learning, and the fundamentals of environmental planning. This list also takes into account age-appropriate, individually appropriate, and culturally appropriate program practices. It is useful for a planning tool. It can also be used to determine what facets of the checklist are reflected in your environment and what elements you might wish to develop in the future.

Sample Room Arrangements

Many of the criteria outlined in **Tool J: Indoor Environment Checklist** are illustrated in the sample room arrangements presented in Figures 13.1 and 13.2

Figure 13.1   Learning Setting With Loft

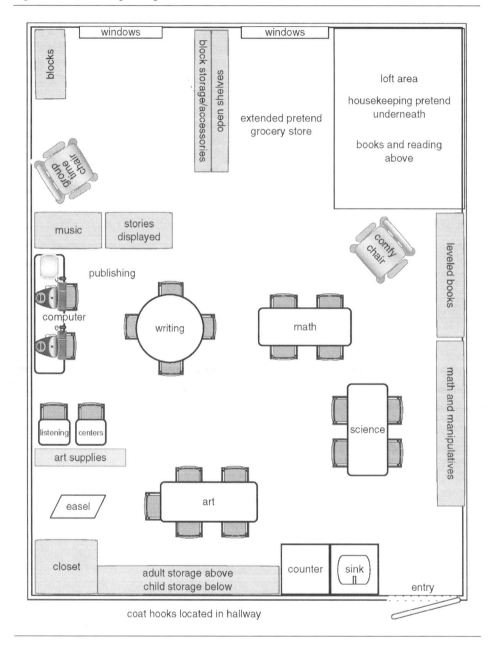

Figure 13.2   Early Learning Setting

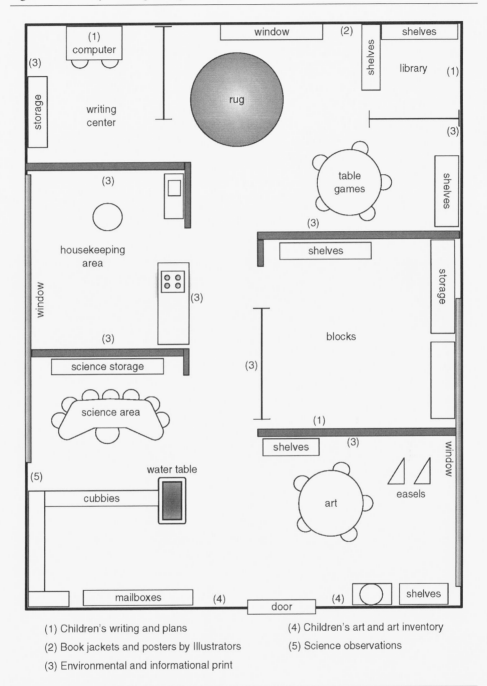

(1) Children's writing and plans

(2) Book jackets and posters by Illustrators

(3) Environmental and informational print

(4) Children's art and art inventory

(5) Science observations

THE GREAT OUTDOORS!

Investigating an anthill
Making it to the top of the climber
Running and chasing friends
Examining a fallen leaf, an acorn, or a caterpillar
Playing hide and seek among the lilac bushes
Digging in the sand

These are some of the wonderful things children can experience outdoors. Because outdoor time has been found to be so essential to child development and learning, national accreditation and most state licensing guidelines require that a fenced outdoor play area be made available to young children at each center or school. This area must provide at least seventy-five square feet of space per child and must include equipment and materials suitable for children below five-years of age. It is expected that young children will have access to outdoor activity regularly (NAEYC, 2005).

In early childhood education, outdoor time is more than just letting children run around and let off steam: it is also an opportunity to expand the learning environment into the natural world. What children learn there has the potential to encompass all areas of development and all areas of the curriculum. Consequently, designing outdoor environments requires the same care and consideration that we traditionally reserve for physical environments bound by four walls and a roof.

Most of the indoor environment design principles discussed earlier in this chapter hold true for playgrounds and other outdoor learning spaces as well. Safety, health, comfort, convenience, aesthetics, flexibility, organization, density, materials, color, light, and sound must all be considered in planning for the outdoors. Similarly, dimensions such as hard or soft, open or close, simple or complex, individual or social, and high mobility or low mobility are applicable to outdoor materials and equipment. And, just like inside, open-air spaces are best thought of as consisting of small-group activity centers that are spread out over the available outdoor play space.

In its well-illustrated publication, *Learning with Nature Idea Book*, the National Arbor Day Foundation (2007, p. 5) suggests that some combination of several of the following activity areas be used to create outdoor play environments:

- Entry to the play yard
- An open area for large-motor activities
- A climbing or crawling area
- A messy materials area
- A building area
- An art area
- A music and movement area
- A garden or pathway through plantings
- A gathering area
- A storage area
- A digging area
- A sand area
- A wheeled-toy area
- An area for swings or slide

While many programs do not have enough outdoor space to address every one of these areas in a single location, most could design or readjust their playgrounds to encompass a reasonable mix of a few. One such example is illustrated in Figure 13.3. The playground depicted can accommodate approximately thirty children at a time. This design is in keeping with the growing trend in early childhood education to reconnect children with nature.

The outdoor design depicted in Figure 13.3 could serve as a valuable extension of any indoor classroom or as the basis for a fully functioning outdoor classroom. In some states, such as California, Texas, and Virginia, the climate is such that increasing numbers of early learning programs are creating outdoor classrooms for young learners in which the majority of the daily schedule occurs outside. Often, the curriculum is designed around nature concepts such as plants, animals, the earth, and water. Other kinds of learning occur, too, related to math, reading, social studies, and art. In every case, the natural world provides a valuable resource for childhood learning.

Figure 13.3 Sample Plan

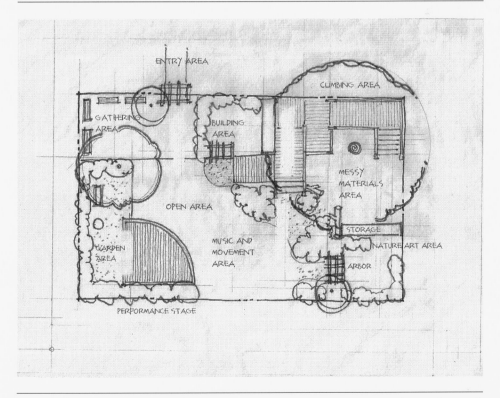

Source: Reprinted with permission from the Arbor Day Foundation and Dimensions Educational Research Foundation (2007). *Learning with Nature Idea Book: Creating Nurturing Outdoor Spaces for Children,* Lincoln, NE: Cuppens, V., Rosenow, N., Wike, J. p. 44.

Today's Children Are at Risk of Being Sedentary and Nature Free

Unfortunately, there is strong evidence that children in the United States (and all over the world, for that matter) are having fewer opportunities to freely enjoy the outdoors at home, at school, or at the center (Davis, 2005; National Arbor Day Foundation, 2007). This is happening because today's young children are spending increasing amounts of time in front of the television or computer screen. When they are outside, it is often within the confines of a structured activity like a sports league of some sort. Concerns over academic achievement have led to up to 40 percent of U.S. elementary schools eliminating recess (Axtman, 2004). Adult worries about safety and their disinterest in being outside with the children have further eroded children's time outdoors playing, exploring, and simply "messing about". This has led to an increase in child obesity due to inactivity, less time for unstructured peer interaction, and children expressing fears and misconceptions about natural phenomena such as wind, rain, wildflowers, trees, and birds (Hoffert & Sandberg, 2000; Sobel, 1996). By designing outdoor environments that provide children with spaces for vigorous play as well as opportunities to observe and interact with nature and with friends, we are helping to minimize the negative impacts of these trends.

Working With Limited and Existing Space

At this point, you might be thinking, "We have limited space" or "Our playground consists of the standard swings, slides, and blacktop" or "We have constrained financial resources." While it is true that some outdoor spaces need a complete overhaul, usually that is not the case. Instead, current environments can be redesigned to accommodate the needs of young children as described here. Besides raising funds for a new or revised playground, here are a few simple strategies principals may adopt immediately:

- Evaluate the playground and select one or two new areas to include from those listed above. Choose areas that do not require much fiscal capital to install. Elicit help from parents as necessary to create the new spaces.
- Eliminate some of the plastic equipment purchased for children's use outdoors. Introduce more natural objects for children to explore and play with (boxes of pine cones, seedpods, collections of seeds, stones, or shells, and so on). Focus on materials indigenous to your area.
- Add open-ended portable equipment and materials that children can use as they wish (e.g., bales of hay, wheels, tires and utility spools, shovels, diggers, garden gloves, wood scraps and planks, barrels, buckets, wheelbarrows). Add a storage place for these things so adults do not have to haul them in and out each day.
- Encourage teachers and staff to take traditional indoor materials outside (art supplies, books, magnifying glasses, and so on).
- Talk with staff about ways in which they might take advantage of the entire outdoor environment available to the program—not just the playground, but also the sidewalk and grounds around the school, city parks, nearby fields, and so on.
- Encourage staff to take children outdoors daily.

Pitfalls to avoid are presented in Box 13.2.

Box 13.2

Twelve Common Mistakes in Designing Playgrounds and
Children's Outdoor Environments

1. Not following the Americans with Disabilities Act (ADA) guidelines for outdoor spaces that apply to all new construction and renovations

2. Relying on a playground equipment manufacturer to design the outdoor space rather than working with a designer or outdoor consultant with expertise in early childhood design

3. Choosing equipment that does not match the developmental needs of young children

4. Creating outdoor space that only addresses children's gross motor skills

5. Creating outdoor spaces that ignore children's gross motor needs

6. Not planting trees, bushes, and other plants in the outdoor area

7. Creating flat open spaces without concern for variations in elevation or creating well-defined areas for different kinds of play

8. Putting all your money into climbing equipment while ignoring other types of physical activity, varied forms of play, and all areas of development for all children

9. Not considering outdoor storage

10. Not including teachers, family members, and children in the design process

11. Underbudgeting for the outdoor environment

12. Treating the outdoor environment as an afterthought rather than as an integral part of the overall education program.

Source: Curtis & Carter, 2003; White Hutchinson Leisure and Learning Group, 2007.

PRINCIPALS' ROLES

Creating Optimal Early Learning Environments

1. Become familiar with the basic elements of the physical environment outlined in this chapter.

2. Consult with early childhood experts when designing new space or renovating space for early childhood programs.

3. Include family members and staff in the design process.

4. Make sure to incorporate the outdoor environment as integral in planning the overall physical environment.

5. Become familiar with and follow local and district guidelines regarding appropriate physical environments for young children.

6. Encourage teachers and staff members to use **Tool G: The Early Childhood Safety and Health Checklist** twice annually to monitor health and safety practices indoors and out. Require that scores be reported to the principal and superintendent as appropriate. This will signal the importance of the expectation. Acknowledge classrooms that are maintaining high safety standards. Ensure that immediate attention is given to classrooms whose scores fall at thirty-five points or below.

7. Require that the early childhood program create a long-range plan for upgrading the learning environment in each classroom using the physical requirements for small-group activity centers delineated in **Tool H: Physical Requirements of Small-Group Activity Centers**.

8. When developing new early childhood programs in the school or district, refer to **Tool I: Early Childhood Education Classroom Equipment List** for guidance regarding necessary materials and furnishings.

9. Determine to what extent the early childhood environment takes into account adult needs. Make adjustments as necessary.

10. Observe early childhood classrooms periodically with the physical environment in mind. Use the Guidelines for Well-Arranged Activity Centers in Early Childhood Classrooms (Table 13.1) or **Tool J: Indoor Environment Checklist** to guide your observations.

11. Ensure that early childhood programs in your jurisdiction incorporate adequate time for children to be physically active.

12. Ensure that classroom and outside environments allow for children to be under adult supervision at all times.

13. Become a champion in the effort to create aesthetically pleasing, homey environments for young children in your school or district.

14. Resist efforts to reduce recess and curtail children's time outdoors.

15. Promote the notion of creating outdoor environments that address whole child learning.

16. Consult additional resources for further details about how to design and evaluate effective early childhood settings. Some examples include Curtis and Carter (2003) DeBord, Moore, Hestenes, Cosco, and McGinnis (2005) Greenman (2005) Harms, Clifford, and Cryer (2007a, 2007b) and the National Arbor Day Foundation (2007).

14

Early Childhood Education

Funding

When principals and superintendents describe their concerns about early childhood education, they often report the challenges of funding. Given competing demands for limited resources, what will be sacrificed to make room for new programs?

Instead of approaching early childhood education as a problem of "What must we sacrifice?" the approach must be "What do we gain?" Fortunately, there is an emerging body of literature that documents the benefits realized from investments in early childhood education.

Principals are in the role of key communicator in a school.

> Public and private support for high-quality early childhood education is growing and principals of elementary schools need to be ahead of the trend. More than 40 states now provide some funding for pre-K programs, and several are committed to include all children whose parents want to enroll them. Principals across the country are becoming more involved with early childhood programs—leading comprehensive pre-K programs in their school buildings or creating new links with many types of pre-K programs in their communities. Getting to know children and their families long before they enroll in first grade is becoming part of the elementary school principal's responsibility. (National Association of Elementary School Principals [NAESP], 2005b, p. v)

A primary role for the principal is to serve as an advocate and spokesperson for early childhood education. This advocacy role should come naturally to an elementary principal since quality early childhood education results in school readiness. The evidence is clear regarding the benefits to children and society of early childhood education. When young children are ready for school, everyone wins. The children are the first beneficiaries, of course, but parents gain, society gains, the economy gains, schools save, states save, and the schools thrive. School readiness is everyone's concern!

Issues of concern in providing early childhood education reflect the constant struggles of the "haves and the have-nots." Quality early childhood education is costly. Many parents cannot afford to pay for early childhood education. Nonpublic programs may not have the resources to pay for qualified staff members. Children in these programs may not have the same learning opportunities that are available to those who can pay for high-quality experiences provided by highly qualified staff members. Yet, the evidence indicates high-quality early childhood programs ultimately save tax dollars (Nebraska Department of Education, 2005). A number of states are moving toward providing incentives or scholarships to children who attend quality-rated child care and prekindergarten (preK) programs. Minnesota, for example, has a pilot program funded by the Minnesota Early Learning Foundation; $4,000 follows children to those programs who have voluntarily participated in the quality rating program—Parent Aware (2008).

The stability of funding is a constant concern.

> Many schools are feeling the pinch of the government's budgeting shortfalls. Add to that the many communities who have turned down levies and tax increases for public school funding and the struggle to find an adequate source of funding becomes even more difficult. (NAESP, 2007, para 2)

FUNDING SOURCES

How to pay for early childhood education is a frequently voiced concern of administrators. The response varies from state to state and district to district. Each state's response to early childhood funding is unique. State spending varies due to differences in costs of delivering early childhood education based on local conditions such as cost of living, existing infrastructure, and demographic factors. For instance, Oklahoma has created a preK program that is seen as part of the education system. "Augenblick says this is the most logical method of providing more state money for preschool" (Education Writers Association, 2008, p. 2).

State spending varies as federal and local funding sources contribute to the costs of early childhood education. Some states rely on federal funding sources such as Title I; some states use local funding sources including tuition paid by parents (National Institute for Early Education Research [NIEER], 2006). Table 14.1 provides a summary of state sources of funding for preK programs.

Table 14.1   Sources of State Funding

Revenue Types	Number of States
General revenues	25
General revenues through school funding formula	13
No general revenues	3
No state-funded preK program	9
Lottery revenues	3
Public-private partnership	6
Gaming revenues	1
Tobacco tax	2
Tobacco settlement funds	1
Total	63

Source: Stone (2008), p. 2.

*Iowa will fund preK through the school funding formula beginning in fiscal year 2009.

**Total number equals sixty-three due to states using multiple funding streams.

HISTORY OF FEDERAL FUNDING

The history of federal financing of child care in the United States is linked to crises such as the Great Depression and World War II, and societal trends and issues such as poverty, and the increasing number of working mothers.

> The first federal investment in child care was made in 1933, primarily to provide government paid jobs for thousands of teachers, nurses, cooks, janitors, and carpenters rendered unemployed by the Depression. Child care services were also seen as beneficial for children and jobless parents. . . . In 1933, the WPA emergency nursery schools were funded at $6 million, and by 1938, over $10.7 million in federal funds had been spent. Between 44,000 and 72,000 children ages two to five were enrolled in any one year. . . . By 1943, with unemployment waning and the WPA abolished, many of the WPA centers had closed. (Cohen, 1996, pp. 28–29)

U.S. involvement in World War II led to the next wave of federal funding for child care:

In 1940, Congress passed the Lanham Act, which authorized federal grants and/or loans to public or private agencies for the maintenance and operation of public works, later interpreted by the administrative decree to mean child care facilities in war impacted areas. In July 1942, Congress authorized the use of $6 million of the waning WPA appropriation for child care facilities for children of working mothers rather than just mothers on home relief. (Cohen, 1996, p. 29)

From 1942 to 1946, the Lanham Act served children of all ages, subsidies were provided for all children, and funds helped parents work and promoted children's development (Cohen, 1996).

Societal factors including poverty, the working poor, and the increasing number of divorces, female-headed households, and middle-class wage-earning women led to greater attention to childcare needs. Parental employment and the percentage of working mothers brought greater public support for the need for child care (Cohen, 1996).

Table 14.2 Percentage of Distribution of Children from Birth Through Age Five and Not Yet in Kindergarten

Mother's Employment Status	Percentage of All Children Birth to Five Years Old	At Least One Weekly Nonparental Care Arrangement
35 or more hours per week	35 percent	85 percent
Less than 35 hours per week	21 percent	69 percent
Looking for work	8 percent	45 percent
Not in the labor force	36 percent	32 percent

Source: NCES, 2005.

Education is a state responsibility. However, the federal government funds specific education programs supported by the government. "The federal government's role as a source of revenue has changed little since 1970. The percentage of a local school budget contributed by the federal government is usually less than 10 percent" (W. Cunningham & Cordeiro, 2006, p. 332).

"Schools are primarily funded through the revenues generated from property, consumption, and state income taxes" (W. Cunningham & Cordeiro, 2006, p. 331). Federal, state, and local governments generate revenue through taxation and fees.

Taxes are assessed based on what you own, spend and earn. Fees are payments for services you use or transactions you make. . . . State-sponsored gambling is in essence a fee charged for the purchase of a lottery ticket. . . . Fees are smaller sources of revenue for government than are taxes. States and communities find that lotteries and "sin" taxes (e.g., on cigarettes or gambling) are far more popular than taxes on income or property. (Mitchell, Stoney, & Dichter, 2001, p. 10)

Mitchell and colleagues (2001) report thirty-seven states have lotteries and at least ten states have legalized casino gambling. Florida and Georgia fund preschool programs with their state lottery proceeds.

Income taxes are major revenue sources for the federal government, and significant revenue sources for states with income taxes. According to Mitchell and colleagues (2001), approximately 35 percent of state revenue is from sales taxes and a third of state revenue is from income taxes. Approximately 90 percent of local revenue is from property taxes.

STATE FUNDING

Each state has its own system of funding. In Minnesota, as in most states, the state constitution charges the legislature with responsibility for public schools:

The stability of a republican form of government depending mainly upon the intelligence of the people, it is the duty of the legislature to establish a general and uniform system of public schools. The legislature shall make such provisions by taxation or otherwise as will secure a thorough and efficient system of public schools throughout the state. (Constitution of the State of Minnesota, article XIII, § 1)

Often, the systems are complex and have an interesting history of development. A familiar concept in school funding is the foundation program that refers to the established minimum financial support that a district receives for each enrolled student. School districts are reimbursed by the state on an average daily membership (ADM) or average daily attendance (ADA) basis. The amount of per pupil allotment may be affected by factors such as

the local fiscal effort, the number of special, vocational, and bilingual education students, and the number of students from families below the poverty level. . . . Other approaches include a flat-grant model, power-equalizing plan, guaranteed tax base plan, and a weighted-student model. Several states use more than one method for financing schools. (W. Cunningham & Cordeiro, 2006, p. 333)

According to NAESP (2006a), there are more that 1 million children enrolled in preK programs. Average state spending per child enrolled in 2005–06 was $3,482, a figure that included federal TANF (Temporary Assistance for Needy Families) directed toward preschool at states' discretion. In 2006–07, "Total state spending for prekindergarten initiatives reached $3.27 billion . . . state governments spent more than $250 billion on grades K–12. Thus, states spent about one penny on preschool education for every $1 spent on K–12" (NIEER, 2006, p. 10). Special education costs are included in K–12 costs; smaller class sizes, increased staff, and partial day programs are included in preschool costs. These factors influence comparisons of the costs of preschool and K–12 education (NIEER, 2006).

"At least 42 states provide funding for pre-kindergarten education, with much of this money going to public schools" (NAESP, 2006a, p. 1).

> There is no perfect formula to determine ideal state spending amounts for publicly funded preschool. . . . The ideal spending amount hinges on the cost of providing prekindergarten. This cost can vary significantly according to state-level factors such as geography and population density, the cost of living, and the existing infrastructure available to support preschool services. The amount of state funding needed for prekindergarten may be reduced when it is possible to tap into additional federal and local funding sources. . . . States vary tremendously in the amount of funding they obtain from these additional sources, and as a result state spending alone is not always indicative of the program's total level of funding. (NIEER, 2006, p. 23)

Many children's initiatives such as Head Start and Title I are discretionary programs. According to Friedman, these discretionary programs are "vulnerable at both the federal and state levels as legislators look for funds to pay for tax cuts and budget deficits" (Friedman, 2004, p. 9).

Head Start Promotes School Readiness

The Head Start program was announced by Lyndon B. Johnson in May 1965 as part of his "War on Poverty," with $96 million in funding to help disadvantaged preschoolers (Tyack, Lowe, & Hansot, 1984). Head Start offers preschool education and other services to young children from families in poverty to prepare them for school and life (Behrman, 1996). In 2005–06, the federal government spent $6.8 billion to serve 11 percent of the nation's four-year-olds and 7 percent of the nation's three-year-olds. Head Start programs operate for a minimum of three and a half hours per day. In recent years, a greater proportion of children enrolled in Head Start have received full-day services. The federal Head Start program provided $7,287 per child during fiscal year 2005, roughly double the average state spending per child in state-funded preschool. Head Start offers a wide range of comprehensive services, including health screening and referrals, meals, and parenting support. Head Start teachers are not required to have a four-year degree, and their salaries are currently about half the average salary of K–12 teachers (NIEER, 2006).

Tables 14.3 and 14.4 display state spending for early childhood. Table 14.3 shows complete rankings by state for spending per child enrolled. Table 14.4 shows the total spending and per child spending for each state, and includes the inflation-adjusted change in total and per child spending from 2005–06 to 2006–07. As Table 14.4 indicates, there is tremendous diversity in the size of state preschool budgets.

Table 14.3   Rankings of State PreK Resources Per Child Enrolled

Resources Rank	State	$ Per Child Enrolled in PreK	State Spending Per Child in K–12	Difference in PreK and K–12 Spending
1	New Jersey*	$9,854	$5,260	$4,594
2	Oregon	$7,932	$4,803	$3,129
3	Minnesota	$7,203	$8,769	−$1,566
4	Connecticut	$7,101	$5,426	$1,675
5	Delaware	$6,261	$8,680	−$2,419
6	Washington	$5,886	$6,961	−$1,075
7	Pennsylvania	$5,080	$4,305	$775
8	Louisiana	$5,012	$4,829	$183
9	Arkansas	$4,836	$3,731	$1,105
10	West Virginia	$4,529	$6,735	−$2,206
11	Alabama	$4,216	$4,518	−$302
12	Tennessee	$4,061	$3,410	$651
13	Georgia	$3,977	$4,501	−$524
14	Michigan	$3,934	$7,278	−$3,344
15	North Carolina	$3,892	$5,350	−$1,458
16	Massachusetts	$3,619	$6,004	−$2,385
17	New York	$3,512	$6,947	−$3,435
18	Virginia	$3,396	$4,604	−$1,208
19	Oklahoma	$3,364	$3,917	−$553
20	California	$3,341	$6,413	−$3,072
21	Illinois	$3,298	$3,204	$94
22	Nevada	$3,116	$2,417	$699
23	Wisconsin	$3,108	$6,625	−$3,517
24	Colorado	$3,056	$4,277	−$1,221
25	Lowa	$2,929	$4,225	−$1,296
26	Texas	$2,653	$3,234	−$581
27	Missouri	$2,632	$2,975	−$343
28	Kansas	$2,554	$5,699	−$3,145
29	Nebraska	$2,482	$3,128	−$646
30	Vermont	$2,439	$12,149	−$9,710

(Continued)

Table 14.3 (Continued)

Resources Rank	State	$ Per Child Enrolled in PreK	State Spending Per Child in K–12	Difference in PreK and K–12 Spending
31	Kentucky	$2,398	$5,195	−$2,797
32	Ohio	$2,345	$5,290	−$2,945
33	Arizona	$2,296	$3,521	−$1,225
34	New Mexico	$2,269	$7,187	−$4,918
35	Florida	$2,163	$3,993	−$1,830
36	Maine	$1,793	$5,037	−$3,244
37	Maryland	$1,787	$4,428	−$2,641
38	South Carolina	$1,085	$4,676	−$3,591
No Program	Alaska	$0	$6,957	NA
No Program	Hawaii	$0	$8,578	NA
No Program	Idaho	$0	$4,414	NA
No Program	Indiana	$0	$5,412	NA
No Program	Mississippi	$0	$4,122	NA
No Program	Montana	$0	$4,148	NA
No Program	New Hampshire	$0	$4,706	NA
No Program	North Dakota	$0	$3,334	NA
No Program	Rhode Island	$0	$4,233	NA
No Program	South Dakota	$0	$2,995	NA
No Program	Utah	$0	$3,613	NA
No Program	Wyoming	$0	$6,547	NA

Source: Barnett, Hustedt, Hawkinson, & Robin, 2006.

Note: For details about how these figures were calculated, see Methodology section and Roadmap to State PreK pages.

*State per-child spending in New Jersey appears to be higher for state prekindergarten programs than for K–12 education, but in fact this is not the case in the districts that offer state preK. More than 80 percent of state prekindergarden enrollment is in Abbott districts, which also have a K–12 state aid payment nearly 3 times the statewide average per child.

Table 14.4 State Preschool Spending During 2005–2006 and Changes from 2004–2005

State	Total State Preschool Spending			State Spending Per Child		
	Total State Preschool in Spending 2005–2006	Change in Total Spending From 2004–2005 to 2005–2006, Nominal Dollars	Change in Total Spending From 2004–2005 to 2005–2006, Adjusted Dollars	State Spending Per Child in 2005–2006	Change in Spending Per Child From 2004–2005 to 2005–2006, Nominal Dollars	Change in Spending Per Child From 2004–2005 to 2005–2006, Adjusted Dollars
Alabama	$4,326,050	$1,035,00	$827,664	$4,216	$830	$617
Alaska	$0	$0	$0	$0	$0	$0
Arizona	$12,258,488	$728,174	$1,764	$2,296	$13	–$131
Arkansas	$57,157,279	$13,265,579	$10,500,402	$4,836	$125	–$172
California	$266,018,034	$1,588,094	–$15,070,992	$3,341	$123	–$80
Colorado	$37,770,856	$10,663,270	$8,955,492	$3,056	–$22	–$215
Connecticut	$52,490,190	$3,870,654	$807,623	$7,101	$438	$18
Delaware	$5,278,300	$375,100	$66,198	$6,261	$445	$78
Florida	$229,100,000	$229,100,000	$229,100,000	$2,163	$2,163	NA
Georgia	$289,894,973	$13,894,973	–$3,493,027	$3,977	$78	–$167
Hawaii	$0	$0	$0	$0	$0	$0

(Continued)

Table 14.4 (Continued)

State	Total State Preschool Spending			State Spending Per Child		
	Total State Preschool Spending in 2005–2006	Change in Total Spending From 2004–2005 to 2005–2006, Nominal Dollars	Change in Total Spending From 2004–2005 to 2005–2006, Adjusted Dollars	State Spending Per Child in 2005–2006	Change in Spending Per Child From 2004–2005 to 2005–2006, Nominal Dollars	Change in Spending Per Child From 2004–2005 to 2005–2006, Adjusted Dollars
Idaho	$0	$0	$0	$0	$0	$0
Illinois	$237,950,581	$21,454,076	$7,814,796	$3,298	$318	$130
Indiana	$0	$0	$0	$0	$0	$0
Iowa	$6,800,000	–$87,531	–$521,445	$2,929	–$249	–$450
Kansas	$13,728,825	$3,783,145	$3,156,567	$2,554	$746	$632
Kentucky	$51,600,000	$0	–$3,250,800	$2,398	–$6	–$158
Louisiana	$69,115,436	$12,981,839	$9,445,422	$5,012	$477	$192
Maine	$3,744,583	–$91,419	–$333,087	$1,793	–$204	–$330
Maryland	$43,269,366	$0	–$2,725,970	$1,787	–$64	–$180
Massachusetts	$62,789,962	–$5,810,038	–$10,131,838	$3,619	–$1,229	–$1,534

Michigan	$84,850,00	$1,163,300	−$4,108,962	$3,934	$568	$356
Minnesota	$19,022,975	$1,922,975	$845,675	$7,203	$$274	−$162
Mississippi	$0	$0	$0	$0	$0	$0
Missouri	$12,129,270	$1,519,401	$850,980	$2,632	$378	$236
Montana	$0	$0	$0	$0	$0	$0
Nebraska	$3,680,471	$1,583,471	$1,451,360	$2,482	$519	$395
Nevada	$3,032,172	$135,589	−$46,896	$3,116	$349	$175
New Hampshire	$0	$0	$0	$0	$0	$0
New Jersey	$455,843,248	$23,495,292	−$3,742,629	$9,854	$549	−$37
New Mexico	$4,444,507	$3,424,607	$3,360,353	$2,269	−$307	−$469
New York	$254,950,090	$8,527,112	−$6,997,536	$3,512	−$36	−$260

(Continued)

Table 14.4 (Continued)

| State | Total State Preschool Spending | | | State Spending Per Child | | |
	Total State Preschool in Spending 2005–2006	Change in Total Spending From 2004–2005 to 2005–2006, Nominal Dollars	Change in Total Spending From 2004–2005 to 2005–2006, Adjusted Dollars	State Spending Per Child in 2005–2006	Change in Spending Per Child From 2004–2005 to 2005–2006, Nominal Dollars	Change in Spending Per Child From 2004–2005 to 2005–2006, Adjusted Dollars
North Carolina	$59,257,237	$9,879,866	$6,769,092	$3,892	–$166	–$422
North Dakota	$0	$0	$0	$0	$0	$0
Ohio	$19,002,195	–$48,866,727	–$53,142,469	$2,345	–$3,980	–$4,379
Oklahoma	$112,352,971	$5,673,803	–$1,046,985	$3,364	$0	–$212
Oregon	27,650,000	$950,000	–$732,100	$7,932	$308	–$173
Pennsylvania	$39,430,989	$14,884,024	$13,337,565	$5,080	$601	$319
Rhode Island	$0	$0	$0	$0	$0	$0
South Carolina	$21,832,678	–$2,000,000	–$3,501,459	$1,085	–$289	–$375
South Dakota	$0	$0	$0	$0	$0	$0
Tennessee	$35,000,000	$25,000,000	$24,370,000	$4,061	$728	$518

Texas	$483,709,332	$5,709,332	–$24,404,668	$2,653	–$54	–$225
Utah	$0	$0	$0	$0	$0	$0
Vermont	$9,595,209	$555,185	–$14,337	$2,439	–$49	–$205
Virginia	$38,518,874	$3,264,939	$1,043,941	$3,396	–$24	–$240
Washington	$34,194,952	$2,103,525	$81,765	$5,886	$278	–$76
West Virginia	$40,511,010	$6,011,010	$3,837,510	$4,529	$206	–$67
Wiscosin	$69,612,500	$8,400,000	$4,543,613	$3,108	$43	–$150
Wyoming	$0	$0	$0	$0	$0	$0
50 states	$3,271,913,604	$380,087,621	$197,902,582	$3,482	–$138	–$372

Source: Barnett, W. S., Hustedt, J. T., Hawkinson, L. E., Robin, K. B. (2006). The State of Preschool 2006: State Preschool Yearbook. Rutgers, New Jersey: The National Institute for Early Education Research.

LOCAL FUNDING

The primary local funding source for public schools is the local property tax.

> The property tax is a function of three variables: the tax base, the assessment practice, and the tax rate. The tax base includes all taxable property in the district except that owned by the federal government, public hospitals, state parks, churches, and nonprofit entities, which are not taxable. (W. Cunningham & Cordeiro, 2006, p. 335)

Private funding sources for early childhood include parent fees, local employers, national corporations, and foundations. The number of local school districts with foundations is increasing. Between 3,500 and 5,000 of the 16,000 school districts in the United States have established foundations to raise money for local schools.

> [Foundations] registered with PEN [The Public Education Network]—about 80—serve 11 million children, 21% of the nation's total enrollment. These foundations are in 16,700 schools, 18% of all schools, and serve seven of the nation's 10 largest districts. (C. Johnson, 2004, p. 1)

The main purpose of a foundation is to solicit funds on behalf of a district or school system from individuals and companies. "Foundations are separate entities, usually nonprofit companies that file for 501 (c)(3) status. They have their own board and governance rules" (C. Johnson, 2004, p. 1). Foundations are designed to address long-term funding needs. "The typical local education foundation has an annual revenue of $630,000. In 2002, local education foundations raised $190 million from various sources" (C. Johnson, 2004, p.1). Donations to foundations are usually tax deductible and provide versatility and flexibility for achieving long-range goals. Public awareness of school needs is increased through a foundation.

Principals need to work with the governance of the foundation. This requires an investment of time as well as the ability to identify the funding needs and the long-term goals for the school. The principal must be able to articulate these goals to the foundation governance and the community. Principals have to understand where dollars are going; communicate this information to parents, teachers, and the community; represent the interests of children and the school; and be a constant and visible supporter of the foundation (C. Johnson, 2004).

Principals should seek the designated principal seat on the foundation board. As a member of the board, the principal has greater information about the foundation's work and is in an influential position. If a foundation is not in place, the administrator who assumes leadership in the formation of a foundation should follow these steps:

- Organize a leadership team to explore the formation of a foundation
- Identify the purposes and goals of the foundation
- Identify the steps to the creation of the foundation
- Obtain 501(c) (3) status and authorization to transact business

- Comply with all applicable state and federal laws
- Review procedures with the school attorney
- Communicate with stakeholders
- Describe the purposes, goals, and needs that will be met by a foundation to the public
- Clarify if the foundation should be a short-term money raiser or a long-term friend raiser, or both
- Recruit a financial advisor to the board
- Describe the process used to establish the foundation to the public
- Engage in continuous public relations concerning the work of the foundation
- Measure accomplishment of goals (W. Cunningham & Cordeiro, 2006; Thayer & Short, 1994; G. Zierdt, personal communication, March 14, 2008)

Although establishing a foundation requires a considerable investment of time, the long-term benefits to the students and school are enduring. Foundations offer new resources from untapped funding sources and opportunities for new initiatives.

START-UP COSTS

Initial cost considerations for early childhood education include personnel, space, transportation, furnishings, and instructional materials. Principals and superintendents need to build on their expertise in these areas to meet the special requirements of an early childhood setting.

Personnel costs are the greatest expense of a school. Identifying space in a school is an ongoing administrative issue. One of the unique concerns in early childhood programs is identifying appropriate learning spaces for young children. Chapter 13 includes a description of the essentials in adapting space to meet the learning needs, hygiene needs, and height requirements of the early childhood population.

New construction costs for facilities that meet the specialized requirements of the preschool population vary by geographic area. Identifying architects who are experienced in the design of the specialized educational space is frequently a challenge. Costs of construction reflect the quality of the proposed facility and the expenses that accumulate as construction errors occur due to lack of familiarity with the design requirements. Identifying professionals who have expertise in design and construction of education facilities is an essential task in controlling costs (Passantino, 1994).

Although principals typically have experience with purchasing equipment and consumable materials for the elementary classroom, the following examples provide information specific to the early childhood classroom.

Table 14.5 includes average costs for an early childhood classroom based on the floor plan identified as Table 13.1 (in Chapter 13). These costs include the expenses of equipment and consumable materials. Some of the costs are high, and may cause sticker shock. Some items are consumable and will need to be replaced annually. Other items will last for many years depending on the quality of the items purchased.

Table 14.5   Average Costs for an Early Childhood Classroom

Equipment	*Total Costs*
Art supplies	$1,437.46
Blocks	$4,234.78
Language arts	$1,811.26
Math and manipulatives	$559.23
Music	$666.78
Physical	$256.83
Pretend play	$1,646.98
Sand and water	$388.82
Science and Collections	$173.14
Woodworking	$272.85
Total	$11,448.13

Source: Constructive Playthings & Kaplan Early Learning Co. http://www.kaplanco.com/classroom-furniture.asp and http://www.constplay.com/family/default.htm. Retrieved December 9, 2007.

These Web sites provide a comprehensive array of price ranges for equipping early childhood classrooms by state and type of classroom. Table 14.6 provides examples of the price ranges.

Table 14.6   Sample Price Ranges for Early Childhood Classroom by State and Type

Multicultural Classroom	$7,295.33
North Carolina preK classroom	$7,726.10
Alabama preK classroom	$7,726.10
Los Angeles preK classroom	$8,368.40
Illinois preK classroom	$9,767.20
Connecticut preK classroom	$11,945.30
Georgia preK classroom	$13,663.00
Florida preK beyond centers and circle time	$16,303.85
Three-year-old classroom	$21,685.15
Four-year-old classroom	$26,225.70

Source: http://www.kaplanco.com/resources/ListItems.asp. Retrieved December 9, 2007.

ADMINISTRATOR VOICES

Following are the observations of superintendents, a nonpublic school principal, and a school business manager concerning funding early childhood programs.

A Superintendent's Perspective

Funding early childhood education can be challenging, but rewarding. To be successful, you MUST think outside the box. Be creative. Be persistent. Don't just think pre-school, but think daycare, as well.

Look to your state Teen Pregnancy Prevention and/or Teen Parenting Programs. The problem here is that funding dries up if the program is successful but you will have received start-up money and the program will be off to a good start. If you are creative, these programs may also serve children of other parents within your community, as well as teen parents.

Most states have a department or division of state government serving children, youth and families. Also check with state departments of health. Frequently, these departments have Child Care Assistance funds for daycare and/or preschool assistance, as well as grants. Call around. Get to know these resources and personnel.

Utilize your school or district IDEA-B Preschool funds. Often these funds support center-based preschool programs in the schools. While special needs children are the primary group served, other children can be served in the same classroom through reverse inclusion. That way, both groups of children benefit and learn from each other, and you are able to provide pre-school services to children who do not qualify for special education services.

Leverage the K–12 resources that already exist in your building or district. This means rooms, educational materials, utilities, child nutrition programs (to pay for breakfast and lunch), and transportation (if your route buses have seatbelts, you can provide free transportation on your regular route buses). Federal Title I funds can definitely be used for preschool programming. This money can usually be used to run the program, but since it is "soft" money, that's a little risky. Better to use these funds as start-up. Pre-K is a national program and available in most states. The Pre-K program will pay for start-up, personnel and other program costs.

Get to know your budgets intimately! You need to know much more than the bottom line. How much? What fund? Where can the funds be spent? Where are they being spent now? How can I combine funds to create a quality program?

Look at partnerships with local community colleges and/or businesses. Community colleges that teach childcare need a lab experience for students. Your quality preschool may be just the ticket. The college may be willing to help with the expense of creating that quality preschool. Businesses will frequently be willing to help with the expense of creating a childcare/preschool program as a perk for employees with children and as a way of keeping employees at work. Local Head Start facilities may also be available for shared use.

School districts with Native American or military students receive Impact Aid money from the federal government. Basically, this money is to compensate the district for the negative tax base that occurs when the federal government owns property within the school district boundaries, such as military bases or Indian reservations. Impact Aid dollars are not restricted and can be made available to fund early childhood programs. Another pot of money generated by Native American students is JOM (Johnson O'Malley). These funds may flow to the local school district or to the local tribal government. How they are spent is determined by a formalized parent group. Again, there are very few restrictions on how this money can be spent.

If all else fails, round up your parents of small children (and especially, round up the small children) and show up at the next town hall meeting to ask for a tiny increase in gross receipts tax. That tiny increase can amount to a very large sum of money to fund your daycare/preschool. A town hall filled with screaming babies and toddlers can be quite convincing! (Dr. Kaye Peery, Superintendent, Zuni Public School District, NM, personal communication, February 27, 2008)

Polansky, a superintendent, states,

[F]unding has become an intricate part of district and school management. . . . In many cases, schools must put up an "open for business" sign. . . . Schools will have to compete with private day-care providers. Are preschool programs educationally sound, providing the students fewer transitions? Can they be an economic "cash cow"? Effective preschool programs will enhance feeder programs, engage parents at early ages and offer community outreach to a population that is politically strong. Funds can be used for schoolwide initiatives. In addition research suggests that the experience of children in the first four years has a strong influence on their future development. (W. Cunningham, & Cordeiro, 2006, p. 338)

A Nonpublic School Principal's Perspective

There is no doubt of the numerous benefits of early childhood education. We see it play out every year in our school with many of our preschoolers moving on to our kindergarten. The difference between the attendees from our preschool or even another preschool program against those who have not attended any type of preschool program is significant . . . as is their progress throughout the year.

In our venue, preschool programs were added in the last twenty to twenty-five years as a method of recruitment and service to the clientele we wished to attract to the local Catholic School. Holy Family School has found the preschool program, now in its twenty-first year, to be a growth area for our school, as well as a financially independent and profitable program. Parents are often more ready and willing to pay the tuition rates with our preschool program than our K–8 program. No doubt because any infant or toddler care center is going to charge "something" to take care of pre-school age children—the rates and quality of program can be quite diverse. We certainly believe the growth our program has seen and the financial stability is a product of the quality offered. We have also found that offering a diverse length of day and variety of program types has enhanced our enrollment. (Peggy Croy, Principal, Holy Family School, Danville, IL, personal communication, March 18, 2008)

A Business Manager's Perspective

A conversation with a school business manager provides a reminder of what administrators need to know.

- Be familiar with the state funding streams. Know what's available in your state.
- Get to know the personnel in the state department of education. Let them know what you are trying to accomplish in your school district so that when new or special grants become available you are notified of the opportunity dollars.
- Get to know the legislators—your local representatives as well as the education committee members. Provide them with information and facts they can use to advocate for early childhood legislation and funding.
- Collaboration is the key to making it work.
- For collaboration to work, all parties need to put the money on the table. This is the only way to make more of the resources that are available.
- Look in your own community and determine what will work.
- You have to make the investment up front to get the returns down the road.
- When you get the "push back" sign from the private early childhood providers, remind everyone that the public schools are not in competition with the programs that are paid for by those who can afford private early childhood education.
- Pay attention to the small grants or soft money that may be available. These funds allow an early childhood innovation to begin and be tested to see if it should be fully implemented.
- Most anyone can find a way to do it (fund early childhood programs)! (Sandra K. Rosenboom, Business Manager, Crete Public School, Crete, NE, personal communication, March 12, 2008)

PRINCIPALS' ROLES

Funding

The principal's and superintendent's roles in providing funding for early childhood programs begin with being able to voice the talking points of funding early childhood programs.

1. Get to know your legislators. The legislators count on school leaders to be conduits of education facts and figures. Show them you are the "go to" person for information (that you are well-read in the current literature, know the local and state context, and provide data, data, and more data!). Through the legislators comes the legislation and funding to support early childhood education. According to Augenblick's report (2001, p. 2), "states provide nearly half the funding for all public education."

Enlisting support of the governor and the governor's staff is another aspect of building support for early childhood education. Get to know your legislators; they will count on you for the facts. Share the benefits of early childhood education with them. Ask for increased funding for early childhood education.

Keep in mind that governors attend the annual meetings of the National Governors Association and legislators attend the annual meetings of the National Conference of State Legislatures. At these meetings, information about education topics is exchanged. Be alert to information shared at these national meetings that may assist in the advocacy for early childhood education. Keeping up with the neighbor (states) is a national pastime. As an example, on January 15, 2008, Governor Jodi Rell of Connecticut held an Early Childhood Summit titled, "Investing in the First 1,000 Days." This summit recapped the accomplishments in their state's early childhood initiative and future projects that have been set in motion with her bold State of the State Address of 2005: "All Connecticut children born beginning in 2006 will enter kindergarten healthy, eager to learn, and ready for school success, and will demonstrate academic mastery in 4th grade." To achieve this end, Governor Rell has been at the center of the Connecticut Early Childhood Investment Initiative. Governor Rell created the Early Childhood Research and Policy Council to develop a multiyear plan to shape Connecticut's investment to improve school readiness for all children (ecpolicycouncil.org).

2. Understand your state's school finance formula. Odden and Picus (2008) describe a school district's success in expanding a half-day kindergarten program to a full-day program because the district leaders understood the state's school finance system and doubled the length of the kindergarten program and realized a fiscal surplus through the change.

3. Understand how to maximize public funding streams. State general funds, local district funds, Head Start, Title I, Even Start, grant funds, and other funds may be available to fund aspects of early childhood education.

4. Become entrepreneurial: think outside the box. "We can no longer rely on traditional funding sources. It is the entrepreneurial administrators who will find funds that best meet the needs of their schools and programs" (W. Cunningham & Cordeiro, 2006, p. 339).

5. Get the facts about early childhood and share them with the stakeholders. Report the educational and economic benefits of early investment in early childhood education. Report the number of children in early childhood programs in your district. Report the indicators of the impacts early childhood education has had in student achievement.

Funding Web Sites and Resources

www.cbpp.org. Center on Budget and Policy Priorities Web site. The article by Fremstad (July 28, 2003), "State fiscal relief funds do not address the need for substantial increases in child care funding," is pertinent to early childhood funding.

www.clasp.org. The Web site for the Center for Law and Social Policy. The article "Myths about the Adequacy of Current Child Care Funding" is pertinent to early childhood funding.

http://economicdevelopment,cce.cornell.edu. Cornell University Web site provides links to state and local studies on the economic impact of the early care and education industry.

http://www.ecs.org/clearinghouse/27/24/2724.htm. The Education Commission of the States, state-funded preK profiles.

http://www.ecs.org/ecsmain.asp?page=/html/IssuesEL.asp. Education Commission of the States. Prekindergarten Quick Facts, 2003.

http://www.fpg.unc.edu/~NCEDL/PAGES/cq.cfm. Executive summary of the report "The Children of the Cost, Quality, and Outcomes Study Go To School."

http://www.smartstart-nc.org/overview/main.htm. Smart Start.

http://www.trustforearlyed.org. Trust for Early Education.

http://www.trustforearlyed.org/. David and Lucile Packard Foundation.

http://www.pewtrusts.com/ideas/index.cfm?page=20&name=Strategies&issue=26. Pew Charitable Trusts. "Starting Early Starting Strong" (Shore, 2002).

http://instruction.aaps.k12mi.us/aabond/EarlyChildhood.htm. This Web site gives an example of "new construction" of early childhood facilities and other site renovations communicated to the community—seeing their dollars in action month by month.

Foundations

Dana Foundation

Since 1991, the Dana Foundation's Education Grants Program has focused on disseminating implementation of well-tested innovations that have the potential to strengthen public school education in American, especially for students in their early years (NAESP, 2006b, p. 2).

Early Childhood Funders' Collaborative

The Early Childhood Funders' Collaborative (ECFC) is an affiliation of individuals who serve as staff at foundations or corporate giving programs that have substantial grantmaking portfolios in early childhood care and education (Friedman, 2004, p. 19).

Annenberg Foundation

The Annenberg Foundation is a private foundation with interests in early childhood education in relation to public education at the primary level (NAESP, 2006b, p. 1).

Action Summary

15

N ow that you have read the book, here are the actions you should take *to GET IT RIGHT!*

CHAPTER 1. EARLY CHILDHOOD EDUCATION: AN EXPANDING ENTERPRISE!

- ✓ Know the benefits of early childhood education—academic, social, and fiscal.
- ✓ Rethink K–12 education to include prekindergarten programs as the foundation for later learning.
- ✓ Make a conscious decision to create a school culture that values early childhood education.
- ✓ Provide others with information about the value of early childhood education.

CHAPTER 2. QUALITY MAKES *ALL* THE DIFFERENCE!

- ✓ Move from the awareness level to the knowledge level of the administrative pyramid by reading early childhood literature, visiting early childhood programs, and talking to community experts in early childhood education.
- ✓ Make quality your focus as you observe early learning classrooms for which you are responsible.

✓ Apply principles of high quality in all preschool to Grade 3 (P–3) classrooms.

✓ Use quality as a fundamental criterion for program decision making.

✓ Expand your expertise in early childhood education.

CHAPTER 3. BREAKING NEW GROUND: GETTING INVOLVED IN EARLY CHILDHOOD EDUCATION

✓ Become an insider, rather than an outsider in early childhood circles.

✓ Promote communication among early childhood programs.

✓ Include other school personnel and decision makers in explorations of early childhood education.

✓ Find someone to serve as a culture broker or early childhood champion for you and others in the school and district.

✓ Demonstrate your alignment with early childhood core values.

✓ As you acquire more knowledge about early childhood education, gradually take on some characteristics of the role of culture broker or early childhood advocate yourself.

✓ Help subculture group members find common ground around which to develop early learning initiatives.

CHAPTER 4. EARLY CHILDHOOD EDUCATION: STAKEHOLDERS

✓ Serve as an information conduit.

✓ Promote the educational and economic benefits of early childhood education.

✓ Invest time in early childhood education.

✓ Identify early childhood education resources.

✓ Anticipate resistance to early childhood education.

✓ See a variety of perspectives, and experiences in early childhood education discussions.

✓ Enlist support for early childhood education.

✓ Involve all stakeholders in early childhood education.

✓ Give voice to stakeholders.

CHAPTER 5. DEVELOPMENTALLY APPROPRIATE PRACTICE

✓ Know what developmentally appropriate practice (DAP) is, and refer to DAP when talking about early childhood programs with staff.

✓ Encourage all of the prekindergarten programs under your supervision, including kindergarten, to achieve National Association for the Education of Young Children (NAEYC) accreditation.

✓ Periodically arrange staff meetings and provide inservice sessions that include all early childhood personnel in your building, school, or district, regardless of each person's source of funding.

✓ Initiate conversations in which teachers and administrators together explore notions of age appropriateness, individual appropriateness, and social and cultural appropriateness.

✓ Observe early childhood programs with the mutually agreed on goal of focusing on DAP. Encourage peer observations focused on DAP. Engage in conversations with teachers privately and in small groups regarding classroom observations.

✓ Recognize that teachers who are moving toward adoption of DAP will demonstrate behaviors related to DAP and developmentally inappropriate practice (DIP) as they make the transition to new teaching practices.

✓ Help teachers recognize their progress in DAP-related knowledge and skills.

✓ Engage in goal setting with staff related to DAP; model the adoption of personal goals relative to DAP.

CHAPTER 6. WHAT PRINCIPALS NEED TO KNOW ABOUT HOW YOUNG CHILDREN DEVELOP AND LEARN

✓ Hire teachers and direct supervisors of early childhood programs who have formal training in child development and specialized knowledge of childhood learning birth to age eight.

✓ Attend at least one professional development activity annually that focuses on early childhood education or early development and learning.

✓ Read the NAEYC journal *Young Children* to keep up with emerging trends in child development and learning.

✓ When making program decisions, use the principles of development and learning outlined in this chapter as benchmarks against which to determine if policies and practices are appropriate for young children.

✓ Watch young children in action in classrooms and outdoors—identify behaviors indicative of child development and learning in a variety of domains.

✓ Work with staff members, parents, and others to identify the dispositions you would like young children to develop in your program.

✓ Create opportunities for early childhood teachers to examine how well their daily plans and practices support child development and learning.

✓ Create mechanisms whereby early childhood education plans and programs are examined to determine how well they

    ○ address all developmental domains and sensitive areas of development,

    ○ support challenge and mastery as part of the learning process,

    ○ enhance children's forward movement through the learning sequences

    ○ accommodate multiple intelligences, and

    ○ address knowledge, skills, feelings, and dispositions.

✓ Adjust staffing schedules to ensure that each child has one or more consistent adults with whom they interact every day.

✓ Monitor programs to ensure that children have materials and opportunities to engage in hands-on activities, space to move about safely and freely, and time to freely interact with peers and adults.

✓ Provide inservice training for staff regarding child development and learning and provide opportunities for continuing education in child development. Pay particular attention to new findings in brain growth development.

✓ Sponsor family education events centering on child development and learning topics.

✓ Create opportunities for parents and other family members to discuss with program staff how their child is developing and how she learns best.

✓ Take the initiative to talk about the importance of child development and learning with members of school boards, community groups such as Rotary, and parents.

✓ Take corrective action to bring program policies into greater alignment with child development and learning principles as necessary.

CHAPTER 7. EARLY CHILDHOOD CURRICULUM

✓ Become familiar with the state's prekindergarten learning standards.

✓ Get to know the early childhood personnel in your state department of education who can serve as resources to you and personnel in your programs.

✓ Observe accredited early childhood programs in the community to better understand how they are approaching the curriculum.

✓ Arrange opportunities for P–3 personnel to visit one another's programs, exchange relevant information, and plan joint activities.

✓ Meet periodically with early childhood staff to discuss curriculum issues. Convey high expectations for children's learning while advocating for DAP.

✓ Regularly observe the early childhood programs in your school or district. Do more than simply "breeze in"—stop and watch for at least twenty minutes to get a better idea of how the program really works.

✓ Meet periodically with early childhood staff to discuss curriculum issues.

✓ Periodically review the written curriculum plans for the early childhood classrooms in your school.

✓ Determine scheduling and equipment needs for the early childhood programs in your school or district.

✓ Work with community professionals, in-house early childhood personnel, district-level administrators, teachers, and families to create formal transition programs that ensure close contact among Head Start programs, preschools, childcare programs, and the public schools.

✓ Develop committees and task forces to align learning expectations P–3.

✓ Encourage the use of a bottom-up approach to curriculum development and reform, rather than a top-down approach in which the highest grades drive the entire curriculum development process.

✓ Share information with families and community members about the holistic, seamless nature of young children's learning from preschool through the later grades.

✓ Become an advocate for developmentally appropriate curricula P–3 with community decision makers.

CHAPTER 8. LEARNING CENTERS AND CLASSROOM ROUTINES

✓ Observe teachers and staff implementing learning centers.

✓ Discuss with teachers what materials, furnishings, and further knowledge or skills they need to carry out learning centers effectively.

✓ Talk with teachers and staff about how they are using daily routines to address curricular goals.

✓ Observe to what extent routines and the daily schedule support curricular goals and expectations.

✓ Determine scheduling and equipment needs for the early childhood programs in your school.

CHAPTER 9. ASSESSING YOUNG CHILDREN'S LEARNING

✓ Support teachers in using systematic child observation as a primary assessment strategy.

✓ Coordinate prekindergarten assessment goals with the early learning standards in your state.

✓ Provide opportunities for staff development in early childhood assessment.

✓ Involve students in monitoring their own learning in age-appropriate ways.

✓ Support teachers in using assessment data to benefit each child through curriculum adjustments or instruction that is more individualized.

✓ Make your assessment practices and policies, and the rationale for them, known to parents and other stakeholders within the community.

✓ Include parents in the assessment process.

✓ Publicly share demographic characteristics of your learning population and general outcomes.

✓ Protect children from inappropriate testing methods and errors in judgment that can result when unreliable or nonvalid tools are used.

CHAPTER 10. EARLY CHILDHOOD EDUCATION: FAMILY INVOLVEMENT

✓ Assess the welcoming aspects of the school.

✓ Consider the experiences and feelings families bring to school.

✓ Consider the experiences and feelings teachers bring to working with families.

✓ Identify the potential barriers to family involvement in the child's education.

✓ Reduce barriers to family involvement in the child's education.

✓ Establish a family resource room in the school.

✓ Provide information about community resources in the family resource room.

✓ Provide opportunities for family involvement in the school that are linked to the child's learning experiences.

✓ Communicate with families in multiple modes continuously.

✓ Provide strategies families can use to increase their involvement with their child's learning.

✓ Encourage and facilitate two-way communication between families and teachers.

✓ Greet the families whenever possible when they come to the classroom or at program events.

✓ Remember: Hospitality calls for coffee and treats!

CHAPTER 11. EARLY CHILDHOOD TEACHERS

✓ Keep early childhood teachers (regardless of funding stream) involved in school conversations and part of school planning.

✓ Treat all early childhood teachers as you would teachers at other grade levels (eligible for school awards, allocated planning time, invitations to inservice events, and school celebrations).

✓ Become actively involved in recruiting and choosing early childhood personnel. Establish specific goals and strategies aimed at choosing high-quality early childhood staff as part of school improvement plans.

✓ Adapt personnel policies to take into account the special circumstances involved in early childhood education that may not be typical of the later elementary grades (e.g., additional time and pay for lesson planning or making home visits).

✓ Take the lead in talking about and advocating for DAP, provide appropriate curricula, classroom equipment, and assessment materials to teachers and staff.

✓ Encourage teachers to use a variety of teaching strategies, from exploration to direct instruction.

✓ Look for the following signs that teachers are addressing the cycle of learning and teaching in the zone of proximal development:

    ○ Offering children open-ended activities
    ○ Working with small groups of children
    ○ Encouraging exploration
    ○ Offering children a wide range of materials
    ○ Offering feedback, providing information, asking relevant questions to enhance inquiry
    ○ Making practice opportunities available
    ○ Giving children chances to generalize

✓ Provide administrative support to improve early childhood practices (e.g., visit classrooms, carry out classroom observations, arrange regular feedback from peers and supervisors, conduct regular evaluations).

✓ Use the daily Tool C: Daily Literacy Checklist and Tool D: Daily Numeracy Checklist to guide classroom observations and conversations with teachers about literacy and numeracy.

✓ Recognize and reward effective teaching.

CHAPTER 12. FINDING AND KEEPING GOOD TEACHERS

✓ Play an active role in selecting early childhood teachers and staff.

✓ Encourage interview teams to observe teacher candidates working with young children.

✓ Refer to Tool F: Sample Interview Questions for Teacher Candidates, for ideas of what to cover in the interview phase of the selection process.

✓ Provide ongoing opportunities for teachers to engage in professional development and continued growth or challenge in the job. Help staff connect to training programs and the fiscal support they need to advance their education.

✓ Take advantage of teachers' intrinsic motivators (seeing children progress, relationships with children and families, respect of coworkers, efficacy in their work).

✓ Recognize factors that prompt teacher frustration(isolation, poor work environments, long hours, inferior status, low pay).

✓ Help early childhood staff navigate the school bureaucracy in order to achieve their goals for children and families.

✓ Advocate for stable staffing, smaller class sizes, and lower child-to-staff ratios.

CHAPTER 13. PHYSICAL ENVIRONMENTS THAT SUPPORT EARLY LEARNING

✓ Become familiar with the basic elements of the physical environment outlined in this chapter.

✓ Consult with early childhood experts when designing new space or renovating space for early childhood programs.

✓ Include family members and staff in the design process.

✓ Make sure to incorporate the outdoor environment as integral to education in planning the overall physical environment.

✓ Become familiar with and follow local and district guidelines regarding appropriate physical environments for young children.

✓ Encourage teachers and staff to use Tool G: The Early Childhood Safety and Health Checklist twice annually to monitor health and safety practices indoors and out.

✓ Require that the early childhood program create a long-range plan for upgrading the learning environment in each classroom.

✓ When developing new early childhood programs in the school or district, refer to Tool I: Early Childhood Education Classroom Equipment List for guidance regarding necessary materials and furnishings.

✓ Determine to what extent the early childhood environment takes into account adult needs.

✓ Observe early childhood classrooms periodically with the physical environment in mind.

✓ Ensure that early childhood programs in your jurisdiction incorporate adequate time for children to be physically active.

✓ Ensure that classroom and outside environments allow for children to be under adult supervision at all times.

✓ Become a champion in the effort to create aesthetically pleasing and homey environments for young children in your school or district.

✓ Resist efforts to reduce recess and curtail children's time outdoor.

✓ Promote the notion of creating outdoor environments that address whole child learning.

✓ Consult the following resources for further details about how to design and evaluate effective early childhood settings: Curtis and Carter (2003); Greenman (2005); Harms et al. (2007a, 2007b); DeBord et al., (2005); National Arbor Day Foundation (2007).

CHAPTER 14. EARLY CHILDHOOD EDUCATION: FUNDING

✓ Get to know your legislators.

✓ Understand your state's school finance formula.

✓ Understand how to maximize public funding streams.

✓ Become entrepreneurial—think outside the box.

✓ Get the facts about early childhood and share them with the stakeholders.

Resources
Tool A

Learning Center Checklist

Part I

Take at least twenty minutes to observe in the classroom. Observers also may talk with adults and children to determine if certain criteria (e.g., repetition) are met.

Put a check by each item you see in the classroom:

❏ Center activities address specific educational goals.

❏ Goals are aligned with state early learning standards.

❏ Goals address individual children's interests and needs.

❏ Centers include both planned activities and unplanned activities: materials children can use on their own.

❏ Center activities are flexible and accommodate children's varying abilities and interests.

❏ Teachers simplify or extend activities in accordance with children's learning needs.

❏ Teachers plan a variety of center-based activities that address all areas of development.

❏ Center-based activities are repeated during the year.

❏ Teachers use each learning center to address different areas of the curriculum.

❏ Teachers use learning centers to integrate instruction across disciplines.

❏ Centers are designed so children can use them with minimal adult guidance.

❏ Teachers use learning center time as instructional time.

❏ Learning centers encompass a range of activity types.

❏ Teachers use learning center time to observe, document, and assess children's learning.

Total number of items checked = _____

Part II

Put a check by each item you see in the classroom:

- ❏ Children rotate through centers on a fixed timetable or wander and are not meaningfully engaged.
- ❏ Learning center time is too short for meaningful engagement.
- ❏ Too few centers are offered or so many centers are available teacher cannot monitor them meaningfully.
- ❏ Centers have no clear link to educational goals.
- ❏ Centers lack variety of materials and flexibility.
- ❏ Centers address only one or two areas of development.
- ❏ Adults fail to support children in center activities or are busy doing other things.

Total number of items checked = _____

Scoring Directions

Add the total number of items checked in Part I. Subject from this total the number of items checked in Part II. This will yield a total score.

Scoring Key

14 to 11 = good use of learning centers

10 to 8 = some improvements needed

Below 7 = much improvement needed

Tool B

Key Instruments Used
Nationally for Evaluation of Children
in Early Childhood Education Programs

Instrument	Purpose	Age	Skill Areas Tested	Method
Basic School Skills Inventory	Inform instruction	4–6.11	Basic knowledge, language and communication skills, literacy, math, classroom behavior	Direct child assessment (DCA)
Battelle Developmental Inventory	Screening	Infant–7.11	Cognitive, social-emotional, language skills, child health, physical development	DCA; teacher observation; parent interview
Bracken Basic Skills Concept Scale–R (BBCS-R)	Academic readiness	2.6–7.11	Cognitive, language, math, social emotional, school readiness	DCA
California Preschool Social Competency Scale	Social adjustment in classroom	Preschool-age children	Social-emotional, school adjustment, attitude	Teacher observation
Child Observation Record	Planning instruction; documenting child progress	2.6–6	Initiative, social relations, creative representation, movement and music, language and literacy, mathematics, science	Teacher observation
Color Bears and Counting Bears	Knowledge of colors and counting ability	3–5	Early literacy, numeracy	DCA
Creative Curriculum Developmental Continuum for Ages three–five Assessment	Inform instruction; track child outcomes; conduct research	3–K	Cognitive development, general knowledge, social emotional, child health, physical development, language and communication	Teacher observation
Comprehensive Test of Phonological Processing (CTOPP)	Screening; tracking child outcomes; conducting research	5–24.11	Language and communication skills	DCA
Developmental Observation Checklist System	Screening; tracking child outcomes	0–Grade 1	Language and communication skills, cognitive, social emotional, motor development	Parent report

(Continued)

(Continued)

Instrument	Purpose	Age	Skill Areas Tested	Method
Developmental Observation Checklist System	Screening; tracking child outcomes	0–Grade 1	Language and communication skills, cognitive, social emotional, motor development	Parent report
Developing Skills Checklist (DSC)	Plan instruction	4–6	Language and communication, visual auditory, math, memory, printing and writing, social emotional, fine and gross motor	DCA; teacher observation; parent observation
Developmental Indicators for Assessment of Learning–3 (DIAL-3)	Screening; inform instruction	3–Grade 2	Social emotional, health and physical, language and communication, self-help concepts	DCA
Expressive One-Word Picture Vocabulary Test (EOWPVT)	Screening; monitoring growth; evaluating program effectiveness	2–18.11	Language and communication skills	DCA
Get it! Got it! Go!	Monitoring change	30–66 months	Literacy skills	DCA
Get Ready to Read	Screening	4–4.11	Literacy skills	DCA
Learning Accomplishments Profile–R (LAP-R)	Inform instruction; track progress	36–72 months	Cognitive, language, self-help, motor and movement, social skills	DCA
Oral and Written Language Scale (OWLS)	Screening; inform instruction; conduct research	3–21	Cognitive development, language and communication, literacy skills	DCA
Peabody Picture Vocabulary Test-III	Screening; tracking child outcomes; conduct research	2.6–17.11	Cognitive development, receptive vocabulary	DCA
Preschool Comprehensive Test of Phonological Processing (Pre-CTOPP)	Phonological awareness, phonological memory, phonological access	3–5	Early literacy skills	DCA
Pre-Language Assessment Scales (Pre-LAS 2000)	Measuring oral language proficiency and preliteracy skills	4–Grade 3	Cognitive development, language and communication, literacy skills	DCA

Preschool and Kindergarten Behavior Scales (PKBS)	Screening; inform instruction; conduct research	3–6	Social emotional development	Rating scale
Preschool Language Scale (PLS-4)	Screening	0–6.11	Expressive and receptive language	DCA
Receptive One-Word Picture Vocabulary Test (ROWPVT)	Ability to understand spoken and written vocabulary of others	0–Grade 4 (plus)	Language communication	DCA
Social Skills Rating System (SSRS)	Screening, inform instruction, track child outcomes, conduct research	3–K	Social emotional, academic competence	Rating scale
Story and Print Concepts	Assess basic story concepts, print concepts, mechanics of reading	3–5	Language, communication skills, general knowledge, awareness	DCA
Teacher-Child Rating Scale (T-CRS)	Screening	K–Grade 3	Social emotional	Rating scale
Woodcock-Johnson III	Screening; inform instruction; track child outcomes; conduct research	2–90 (plus)	Cognitive development, math, general knowledge, language, literacy skills, overall child development	DCA
Work-sampling System	Inform instruction; track child outcomes	3–Grade 6	Cognitive development, math, general knowledge, social emotional, child health, physical, language	Observation and notation

Source: Brown et al. (2007).

Tool C

Daily Literacy Checklist: Preschool Through Grade 3

Every day teachers do the following:

- ❏ Structure a thoughtful balance of activities daily to enhance three major areas of literacy: oral language, writing, and reading
- ❏ Read aloud to children at least once daily, using both narrative and information text and teaching several concepts of print each time
- ❏ Model a variety of writing skills, using teacher-modeled writing activities (such as morning message, group writing exercises, predictable charts, naming the attributes of objects, guessing the letters to make a word or phrase, and so forth)
- ❏ Have children work in their journals, producing illustrations and related writing based on individual skill levels
- ❏ Encourage children to use developing literacy skills for real purposes: to communicate with others, to obtain information, and to read for enjoyment
- ❏ Design and maintain at least two engaging literacy-focused learning centers during learning center time, making sure at least one circle time has a literacy focus
- ❏ Conduct a small-group miniworkshop on literacy skills, teaching some aspect of the alphabetic principle, phonemic awareness, letter-sound association, letter-grapheme association, comprehension, or concept of print
- ❏ Use children's names, familiar songs, nursery rhymes, poems, and finger plays to teach literacy skills and concepts such as alliteration, rhyming, and letter sounds
- ❏ Have at least one brief conversation with each child to develop rapport, learn what each child is interested in, and extend the children's oral language skills
- ❏ Provide plenty of opportunities for children to talk and work together cooperatively in small groups
- ❏ Model and encourage good communication skills such as complete sentences, good eye contact, clear speech, and correct grammar
- ❏ Make sure classrooms are clean, well organized, and structured so that children can easily and independently access and return literacy-related materials.
- ❏ Create print rich environments in which children read, respond to, and create meaningful print
- ❏ Employ useful assessment skills to make sure children are learning; include periodic vocabulary and language assessments, teacher-developed checklists of desired outcomes, dated work samples for comparison, and child self-appraisal forms and checklists
- ❏ Belong to professional organizations, read about effective literacy strategies that other teachers are using, and attend conferences to keep up to date on latest research findings about teaching and learning in language arts

Source: Soderman et al. (2006); Soderman & Farrell (2008). These guidelines were created by Anne K. Soderman, PhD, Professor Emeritus, Michigan State University. Used with permission.

Tool D

Daily Numeracy Checklist: Preschool Through Grade 3

Every day teachers do the following:

- ❐ Provide a rich variety of informal, integrated opportunities as well as formal activities for children to think mathematically
- ❐ Limit time spent on doing mathematics as an isolated activity; integrate mathematical tools and problems into a variety of learning centers
- ❐ Provide various kinds of paper-and-pencil opportunities for children to practice writing numbers, recording thought processes, and communicating mathematical ideas
- ❐ Help children see mathematical thinking as part of the learning of other subject areas by pointing out mathematical connections as children engage in reading, social studies, science, music, or art activities
- ❐ Encourage mathematical play in make-believe and real-life contexts such as shopping and cooking, making tools like play money and measuring cups part of the play environment
- ❐ Make available everyday objects like buttons, beans, and blocks for children to count, recognize how many, and consider questions of greater than and less than
- ❐ Post number words and numerals around the classroom and encourage children to make connections between number words and numerals and to the numbers of objects they represent
- ❐ Create opportunities for children to sort, classify, and order a wide array of objects in a variety of ways
- ❐ Design activities where children are asked to recognize, describe, and extend different kinds of patterns
- ❐ Model situations that involve adding and subtracting using objects, pictures, and symbols and have children do the same
- ❐ Give children opportunities to recognize, name, build, draw, compare, and sort two- and three-dimensional objects
- ❐ Encourage children to measure with conventional tools like measuring cups, rulers, and scales as well as nonconventional units of the same size laid end to end, like paper clips or blocks
- ❐ Ask children to pose questions and gather data about themselves and their surroundings and represent the data using pictures, objects, and graphs
- ❐ Discuss future events with children as likely or unlikely
- ❐ Assess children's mathematical understandings in multiple ways, including performance tasks, interviews, and observation

Source: National Council of Teachers of Mathematics (2001); Clements, Sarama, & DiBiase (2004). These guidelines were created by Ruth Heaton, PhD, University of Nebraska, Lincoln. Used with permission.

Tool E

Guidelines for Structuring Informative On-Site Observations

Before the Observation

- ❏ Determine who will observe the candidate.
- ❏ Determine what you are looking for.
- ❏ Choose when to observe. Learning center time or outdoor time are often the easiest for teachers, children, and candidates to accommodate.
- ❏ Allow at least two hours total from arrival of the candidate to departure.
- ❏ When dealing with multiple candidates, schedule them individually, for approximately the same time on different days to create similar conditions for each one.
- ❏ Schedule observations as close together as possible over the course of a week so memories stay fresh from the first to the last.
- ❏ Create a simple rating form or checklist to evaluate the candidate's performance. Typical categories (followed by more specific subcategories) include
  - personal demeanor,
  - interactions with children,
  - interactions with adults,
  - teaching skills,
  - problem-solving or guidance skills, and
  - professionalism.
- ❏ Determine what information to provide candidates in advance. Typical information includes
  - program materials outlining the philosophy and goals for the program, and
  - rationale for the observation, age of the children, some characteristics of the children and families, when the observation will take place in the daily routine, what area of the room the observation will involve, expectations for what to bring or what to prepare, who will be observing, and how long the observation will last.

❐ Before the candidate arrives, make sure to discuss all arrangements with teachers, and let children know a guest will be coming to their class to interact with them.

❐ When the candidates arrives,
- make sure someone escorts him to the classroom and makes appropriate introductions.
- give the candidate a brief tour of the room.
- allow the candidate to have a twenty- to thirty-minute warm-up period to become familiar with the children and routines prior to carrying out a specific activity or working more independently with the children.

During the Observation

❐ Rate each behavior included on the checklist.

❐ Add written comments to provide examples.

❐ Write as objectively as possible.

❐ Look for strengths as well as any areas of concern.

After the Observation

❐ Thank the candidate.

❐ Give the candidate a graceful exit from the classroom.

❐ Provide the candidate with an opportunity to share impressions with someone on the search committee or program staff.

❐ Gather the observations or provide an opportunity for observers to share their ratings and comments.

Tool F

Sample Interview Questions for Teacher Candidates

Background and Philosophy

1. What experiences have you had working with young children and their families?
2. What strengths do you bring to this position?
3. What areas of professional development are you still working on?
4. How has your education affected your work with children and families?
5. Describe your philosophy of early childhood education.
6. What are three important beliefs you have about young children's development and learning? How do these beliefs influence your work with children and families?

Curriculum

7. What would be the daily schedule in your classroom? Start your description in the morning when the children arrive and end when they go home.
8. What would a typical math activity look like for three-year-olds? For five-year-olds? For seven-year-olds?
9. How might you adapt your math activity for a five-year-old who is hearing impaired, uses a walker, or has a visual disability?
10. How would you address literacy in your classroom?
11. Should reading be taught in the preschool and kindergarten? If your answer is no, at what level should it be taught instead? If your answer is yes, what will reading instruction look like?
12. Give an example of an activity you carried out with young children in the past and what the children learned from it. How did you know the children were learning?
13. Describe three different ways you could use blocks to promote children's learning.
14. What kinds of materials and equipment would you expect to have in your classroom?
15. Describe the selection of activity areas children could choose from in your classroom?
16. What are things we might **not** see in your classroom?

Child Guidance

17. What would you do if it was cleanup time and a child refused to cleanup?
18. How would you handle an argument over a stethoscope between two children, each claiming, "I had it first."

19. What is your philosophy about child guidance in the classroom? How does that philosophy translate into action?

20. Describe a time when you had to follow through on a limit with a child. What was the situation? What did you do? What was the child's response?

21. Describe everything you would do if one child bit another.

22. What would you do if a child had a seizure in your classroom?

23. How do you support children making friends?

Assessment

24. How do you know what children are learning in your classroom?

25. What kinds of records will you keep related to children's learning?

26. Describe two means of assessment with which you have experience. What have you learned from using these tools?

27. How do you balance assessing what children are learning with teaching and interacting with children in the classroom?

28. How will you communicate to families what children are learning?

Working With Families

29. What experiences have you had working with parents and other family members?

30. Describe an example of a time in which you interacted effectively with a family.

31. What do you think is the role of parents and families in children's schooling?

32. What might you do to support children's transition from home to the early childhood program? From the early childhood program to kindergarten? From kindergarten to first grade? From second grade to third grade?

33. What strategies might you use in working with children and families who do not speak English?

34. How might you answer a parent who asks, "What does play have to do with learning?"

35. How would you respond if a family came to you and gave you permission to paddle a child if he was naughty at school?

36. How might you involve family members in children's learning? In school?

Working in a Team

37. What experiences have you had with team teaching?

38. What responsibilities would you give an aide in your classroom?

39. What if you and your assistant teacher had very different ideas about how to approach teaching children to read?

40. What would you do if you saw your assistant teacher reprimand a child harshly?

Tool G

Early Childhood Safety and Health Checklist

Classroom: _____ Date of Observation: _____

Scoring Key   1 Functioning Well   0 Needs Attention

Posted Items in Each Classroom

_____ The current daily schedule

_____ An attendance sheet (filled in each day)

_____ Weekly menus; allergies and special dietary needs noted in writing and individuals in charge of food preparation notified

_____ Diagram showing exits for evacuation during fire drills

_____ Earthquake and other emergency procedures

_____ Classroom and playground safety procedures (also discussed with children and documented)

_____ Emergency telephone numbers (near a phone)

_____ CPR and first aid posters

_____ Instructions on how to wash hands (near sinks for staff and children)

_____ Diapering procedures (near diapering area if diapering is needed)

Classroom

_____ A first aid kit is visibly available and appropriately stocked.

_____ Staff wear latex gloves when changing diapers, providing first aid, or coming in contact with body fluids.

_____ Staff use serving gloves when preparing snacks and meals.

_____ The classroom is equipped with one or more working flashlights

_____ If there is a refrigerator in the classroom, there is a working thermometer inside (not in the door).

_____ Each exit from the classroom is clearly identified with an EXIT sign.

_____ Toothbrushes are covered, have children's names written on toothbrush handle and cover, and are stored in proper holder.

_____ Items to which children need access for hygiene such as tissues, paper towels, sponges, hand washing soap, and so on are stored within reach and are readily available to the children.

_____ Teacher and adult assistants know where to locate and how to use a fire extinguisher.

_____ Sharp-edged objects such as knives, adult scissors, or paper cutters are stored out of reach of children.

_____ Flammable items and cleaning supplies as well as other potentially dangerous materials such as bleach, soap concentrate, ammonia products, and disinfectants are stored in a locked cabinet away from food items and out of the reach of children.

_____ Hot objects such as hot plates, electric frying pans, popcorn poppers, or portable ovens are stored out of children's reach and supervised carefully during cooking experiences.

_____ There is no microwave located in the classroom.

_____ All electrical outlets are capped unless in use.

_____ Electrical cords are not frayed and do not dangle where they could pose safety hazards.

_____ Extension cords are not strung together and are used only temporarily.

_____ Furniture has no sharp edges or corners at or near children's eye level.

_____ All shelves in the classroom are sturdy and secure.

_____ Floor areas near sinks are kept clean and dry.

_____ Countertops and shelves are free of clutter.

_____ Classroom toys are in good repair.

_____ Toys are stored safely on shelves (not on floor or in pathways where they can be a tripping hazard).

_____ Items on high shelves are secure and earthquake safe (e.g., bottles, heavy objects).

Medical

_____ All medication is properly labeled with child's name, name of medication, and dosage.

_____ Medications are under lock and key and out of the reach of children.

_____ Medications to be kept cold are refrigerated.

Outdoors

_____ Outdoor play area is securely fenced and gates are secured.

_____ Outdoor play equipment surfaces are smooth and splinter free. There is no dangerous hardware (e.g., open "s" hooks or protruding bolt seals) and no sharp edges.

_____ There is cushioning material (wood chips, mulch, sand, pea gravel, or safety-tested rubber) at least twelve inches deep under playground equipment (e.g., exposed concrete footing, tree stumps, or rocks).

_____ No objects or obstructions are under or around outdoor play equipment where children might fall.

_____ Outdoor play area is free from broken glass and debris.

_____ Outdoor equipment includes no frayed cables, no worn ropes, and no chains that could pinch.

_____ Elevated surfaces, like platforms and ramps, have guardrails to prevent falls.

_____ Spaces that could trap children, such as openings in guardrails or between ladder rungs, measure less than 3.5 inches or more than 9 inches.

_____ Outdoor toys are in good repair.

_____ Children are supervised outdoors at all times.

_____ **Total Score**

41 to 45	❏ Functioning well
36 to 40	❏ Needs immediate attention
35 and below	❏ Serious cause for concern

Suggestions/Comments

Adapted from forms created by Davis-Morgan-Summit Early Childhood Programs Davis School District, Farmington, Utah, and The Consumer Product Safety Commission, Washington, DC. Retrieved October 20, 2008, from http://www.davis.k12.ut.us/district/earlychildhood/files/249B49FD33324342895C5913451F89DB.pdf

Tool H

Physical Requirements of Small-Group Activity Centers

Center	Degree of Development	Furnishings, Floor, and Wall Space
Art	Minimum	Low tables accommodating three–five children
	Upgraded	Individual easels, storage for art materials nearby, drying rack, display areas, easy-to-clean floor
	Optimal	Individual and group work areas, low sink available to children, natural lighting
Blocks	Minimum	Floor space for individual and group block building, secluded from classroom traffic
	Upgraded	Shelving to store blocks and block accessories, space defined by shelves, shelves labeled to enhance choice and cleanup
	Optimal	Carpeted area to reduce noise, located near pretend play to enhance interactions between the two areas
Language Arts	Minimum	Private area away from classroom traffic, visible from other activity areas, books and listening devices within children's reach
	Upgraded	Soft horizontal areas for reading individually and in groups, table for writing, accessible book displays, means to store children's writing from one day to the next
	Optimal	Changes in surface levels to create nooks for reading, movable and comfortable furniture for reading, writing and word processing, computer, wall space to display children's writing, natural lighting and view to outdoors
Math and Manipulatives	Minimum	Individual area for quiet exploration, low table accommodating three to five children
	Upgraded	Comfortable space for working on the floor, individual and group work spaces, accessible storage, materials stored in bins labeled with pictures
	Optimum	Ample writing surfaces and display space, close proximity to science area
Music	Minimum	Large group space located away from quiet areas
	Upgraded	Sound-absorbing wall and floor surfaces, CD player and CDs available to children
	Optimum	Display and storage of instruments and materials that create sound, some instruments accessible to children

(Continued)

(Continued)

Center	Degree of Development	Furnishings, Floor, and Wall Space
Physical/ Active	Minimum	Adequate floor space for four to five children to move around without bumping into each other, separated from quiet areas, access to plug for CD player
	Upgraded	Portable equipment that can be varied to promote challenge and gradual mastery, noise-reducing soft floor covering (carpet or tumbling mat), accessible storage for small props or objects (balls, scarves, and so on)
	Optimum	Fixed and modular equipment that lends itself to diverse arrangements and increasing complexity, maneuverable by children
Pretend Play	Minimum	Space adequate for small-group play with props accessible to children
	Upgraded	Space defined by play equipment, props, and storage units; ceiling that allows hanging props; area separated from quiet areas; noise-reducing carpet
	Optimum	Child access to moveable props and furnishings that can be added to area by their choice, changes in floor levels and ceiling height; windows and views to the outdoors; enough space to support two scenarios (e.g., house plus airport, house plus grocery store); adjacent to block area to promote interactions between the two areas
Sand/Water	Minimum	Small-group activity space with table to support tubs for sand or water play, easy-to-clean floor
	Upgraded	Sand/water table with easy access from all sides, accessible storage for accessories
	Optimum	Child access to water sink, close to science area, waterproof and slip-proof surfaces, natural lighting, access to protected outdoor area
Science/ Collections	Minimum	Low table accommodating three–five children
	Upgraded	Areas for group and individual work, accessible storage for wide array of materials, shelves labeled with pictures, access to sink, natural lighting
	Optimum	Space in which experiments can be kept multiple days, display space, close proximity to math and sand/water areas; views and access to outdoors
Woodworking	Minimum	Work space to accommodate two children and an adult located away from major traffic areas, portable storage for scrap materials and tools
	Upgraded	Work space to accommodate four children and an adult, stored items accessible to children, display space
	Optimum	Storage and display space define area, tools visible to children on labeled shelves or board, multiple bins of soft wood available in different sizes, space to glue wood as well as hammer/saw wood, space to leave projects to "set"

Source: Adapted from *Creating Environments for Young Children,* by H. Sanoff, 1995, Lake Worth, FL: Humanics. Copyright 1995. Adapted with permission of the author.

Tool I

Early Childhood Education Classroom Equipment List

Art

- Two easels per sixteen to twenty children
- Paint shirts or smocks
- Materials for cleanup (newspaper to cover tables, sponges, drying rack, and so on)
- Assorted paints (tempera paint, finger paint, watercolors)
- Assorted papers (newsprint, construction paper, oak tag, manila, tissue, wax)
- Cookie sheets or large plastic trays on which children may finger paint or use other messy materials
- Art chalk (softer than blackboard chalk), water-soluble markers
- Glue, paste, and glue sticks
- Modeling dough and clay
- Paint brushes—assorted sizes and shapes
- Paint containers with lids
- Rollers, sponges for printing
- Tape (transparent and masking tape)
- Assorted scissors, hole punches, staplers
- Craft sticks, wood scraps, cardboard scraps, paper plates
- Pipe cleaners, straws
- Yarn, ribbon, string
- Paper tubes, old magazines, bits of wrapping paper
- Small cardboard boxes of various shapes and sizes
- Unused toothbrushes
- Buttons, sequins, beads, feathers
- Natural objects (leaves, acorns, small stones, seeds, and so on)
- Picture books showing art, art objects attractively displayed, art prints on walls

Blocks

- Wooden unit blocks (as large a set as possible—200+ block set is a good size for a group of sixteen to twenty children), large hollow blocks, cardboard blocks, ramps
- Shelves to store accessories and blocks by shape
- Plastic or wooden figures, animals, vehicles, street signs, doll furniture
- Paper and markers for making signs, masking tape, carpet tape in various colors
- Wooden train tracks and trains
- Hats (construction, police, fire, and so on), highway maps
- Picture books showing roads, buildings, towns, construction workers, fire, police, and safety workers

Language Arts

- Books, books, and more books (varied by subject and reading level: representative of different ethnic groups, genders and people of different ages and abilities; picture books, storybooks, poetry, expository books, reference books)
- Story reenactment materials: flannel boards with accessories, finger puppets, simple props associated with a particular story, story cards, and photographs
- Listening center with CDs and books
- Assorted paper and writing tools
- Computer
- Comfortable seating

Math and Manipulatives

- Assorted puzzles
- Wooden and plastic construction sets
- Pattern blocks with design sheets, attribute blocks, colored inch cubes
- Cuisenaire rods, Unifix cubes, peg boards, geo boards
- Objects to sort, count, and sequence (rocks, shells, small vehicles, buttons, and so on)
- Numerals, counting mats
- Estimating jar
- Assorted counting and matching games

Music

- Assorted recorded music of many different kinds, moods and origins
- CD player
- Plastic hoops
- Scarves (colored, chiffon, net, and so on), streamers
- Rhythm sticks, tambourines, jingle bells, sand blocks, maracas, drums

Physical

- Fine motor: beads to string or snap, small construction toys, varied writing implements, child-sized scissors, doll clothes, or dress-up things to button, zip, or snap
- Gross motor: balls, ladders, walking beams that vary in size, height, and weight (e.g., a wide walking beam that is low to the ground; a higher beam that is also more narrow), a hurdle that can be raised as children become more adept at jumping over the bar or a ball suspended on a rope that can be raised or lowered to make swinging at the ball easier or more difficult as circumstances require

Pretend Play

- Child-sized kitchen furniture, doll bed, clothes rack, drawers or shelves for storing accessories, nonbreakable mirrors
- Dress-up clothes and accessories for children, varied in color, size, ethnic representation, and attractive to boys and girls
- Dolls, doll clothes

- Play dishes, pots and pans, plastic food models
- Assorted cardboard food containers
- Recipe books, telephone books, picture books of family life
- Changeable or expandable space (to become an airplane, a store, and so on) with props to support such play like a steering wheel, child-sized chairs to use as passenger seats, cash registers, store front, and so on

Sand/Water

- Sand/water table, smocks or waterproof aprons
- Clear plastic tubing, water wheels, sieves, measuring cups, plastic animals and people, small boats, plastic dolls

Science and Collections

- Materials to investigate
- Materials from nature (shells, rocks, leaves, and so on)
- Human-made objects that vary by texture, color, shape, density, weight, and so on
- Assorted plants (vines, succulents, flowering plants)
- Small animals (fish, gerbils or hamsters, snake, hermit crab, worms, and so on)
- Magnets
- Specimens for display that children can touch
- Investigative tools
- Magnifying glasses
- Assorted scales and measuring devices (rulers, measuring spoons, measuring cups, and so on)
- Levers, pulleys, inclined planes
- Containers of varied sizes
- Heat source (e.g., hot plate—to be used with supervision)
- Prisms, colored paddles
- Recording devices—paper, pencils, journals, audio recorders, digital camera
- Science books—picture books, reference books

Woodworking

- Assorted pieces of soft wood (pine works well, but avoid hard woods and pressure-treated lumber), wood scraps
- Wood glue
- Two hammers (sixteen ounces or less) for sixteen to twenty children, common nails
- Two screw drivers, common screws
- Small cross-cut saw
- Brace and bit
- Clamps of varying sizes
- Child-sized woodworking bench
- Two or three pairs of safety goggles
- Books showing tools and people working with tools; books showing wood sculptures and wooden objects

Tool J

Indoor Environment Checklist

A well-designed early childhood classroom meets each of the following criteria:

Appearance

- ☐ The room is safe, clean, comfortable, smells good, and provides access to fresh air.
- ☐ A variety of lighting is used; natural light is available.
- ☐ Colors on walls, furniture, and floor coverings are soft, warm, and neutral.
- ☐ The environment has an aesthetic, homey feeling.
- ☐ The classroom is orderly and uncluttered.
- ☐ Classroom materials and decorations reflect the backgrounds, experiences, and identities of the children and families served.
- ☐ The environment is filled with children's creations (words, pictures, constructions) and representations of their work (photographs, documentation boards, experience stories).

Materials

- ☐ Living plants, animals, and fish, and lovely art objects are displayed.
- ☐ Materials are in plentiful supply so that multiple children can use them and so children have choices about the materials they select.
- ☐ Materials change frequently enough that the environment remains fresh and interesting over the year.
- ☐ Materials meant for children are easily accessible and logically organized.
- ☐ Materials not meant for children are kept out of reach and out of sight.
- ☐ The environment contains many soft elements and some hard ones.
- ☐ Children have access to many open materials and some closed ones.
- ☐ Some activity areas feature simple materials and include accessories that add complexity.
- ☐ Familiar and novel materials are available so children can make connections between past experiences and new ones.
- ☐ Furnishings and equipment are in good repair and are complete so as to be safe and provide meaningful learning opportunities.
- ☐ Most furniture is child sized; some adult-sized furniture is also available.

Storage

☐ Each child has a place to keep personal belongings.

☐ There is adequate storage for adult materials and materials the children are not using; surfaces (such as tops of tables and shelves as well as countertops) are free of clutter.

Room Arrangement

☐ The setting provides appropriate space for playing and working, eating, food preparation, resting, toileting, group storage, and storage of personal belongings.

☐ The classroom is divided into attractive clearly defined interest areas.

☐ There are spaces in the room where children can work on their own, in small groups, and in larger groups.

☐ There is a comfortable space where the whole group can gather.

☐ Activity areas and pathways permit ease of movement through the room; children can get from place to place without interrupting each other.

☐ The room is designed so teachers can easily maintain a global overview of the room even while working with individual or small groups of children.

☐ Accommodations are made for messy play (ex., smocks, tile floor).

☐ Space, materials and furnishings are adapted so children with disabilities can be involved in all parts of the room.

☐ Children and adults have access to a water source for cleanup and to maintain good hygiene.

☐ Adult areas are separated from areas in which children participate.

Source: See Dodge, 2003; Hohman & Weikart (2002); Kostelnik et al. (2007).

References

Ackerman, D., & Barnett, W.S. (2005). *Prepared for kindergarten: What does "readiness" mean?* New Brunswick, NJ: National Institute for Early Education Research, Rutgers University.

ACNeil. (2004). *Best practices in school design* (Report to the ministry of education). Wellington, New Zealand: Author.

American Association of Colleges of Teacher Education (AACTE). (June, 2004). *The early childhood challenge: Preparing high quality teachers for a changing society.* Washington, DC: Author.

American Humane Association (2006). *American humane fact sheet. America's children: How are they doing?* Alexandria, VA: Author.

Amrein-Beardsley, A. (2007, September). Recruiting expert teachers into hard-to-staff schools: Recovering student achievement one-step at a time, 40–44.

Armbruster, B. B., & Osborn, J. (2001). *Put reading first: The research building blocks for teaching children to read kindergarten through Grade 3.* Urbana-Champaign: Center for the Improvement of Early Reading Achievement (CIERA), University of Illinois.

Armstrong, T. (2006). *The best schools: How human development research should inform educational practice.* Alexandria, VA: Association for Supervision and Curriculum Development.

Aronson, S. (2002). *Healthy young children: A manual for programs* (4th ed.). Washington, DC: National Association for the Education of Young Children.

Arthur, L., & Makin, L. (2001). High-quality early literacy programs. *Australian Journal of Early Childhood 26*(2), 19.

Augenblick, J. (2001, July). *The status of school finance today* (ECS Issue Paper: Education Finance in the States: Its Past, Present and Future). Denver, CO: Education Commission of the States.

Axtman, K. (2004). Recess backlash: Parents say it pays to play. *Christian Science Monitor,* November 18, p. 3.

Bailey, D. B., Jr. (2002). Are critical periods critical for early childhood education? The role of timing in early childhood pedagogy. *Early Childhood Research Quarterly, 17,* 281–284.

Banks, J., Cochran-Smith, M., Moll, L., Richert, A., Zeichner, K., LePage, P., et al. (2005). Teaching diverse learners. In L. Darling-Hammond & J. Bransford (Eds.), *Preparing teachers for a changing world* (pp. 232–274). San Francisco: Jossey-Bass.

Barnett, W. S., Hustedt, J. T., Hawkinson, L. E., & Robin, K. B. (2006). *The state of preschool 2006: State preschool yearbook.* Rutgers, NJ: The National Institute for Early Education Research.

Barnett, W. S., & Yarosz, D. J. (2007). *Who goes to preschool and why does it matter?* New Brunswick, NJ: National Institute for Early Education Research.

Baum, S., Viens, J., & Slatin, B. (2005). *Multiple intelligences in the elementary classroom: A teacher's toolkit.* New York: Teachers College Press.

Begley, S. (1996, February 19). Your child's brain. *Newsweek,* 55–62.

Behrman, R. E. (Ed.). (1996). Financing child care. *Future of Children 6*(2), 1–163.

Bell, S. H., & Quinn, S. (2004). Clarifying the elements of challenging behavior. In S. H. Bell, V. Carr, D. Denno, L. J. Johnson, & L. R. Phillips (Eds.), *Challenging behaviors in early childhood settings* (pp. 1–19). Baltimore: Paul H. Brookes.

Berk, L. (2007). *Child development* (7th ed.). Boston: Allyn & Bacon.

Biddle, B. J., & Berliner, D. C. (2002, February). Small class size and its effects. *Educational Leadership, 59*(5), 12–23.

Bjorklund, D. F. (2005). *Children's thinking: Cognitive development and individual differences.* Belmont, CA: Wadsworth Publishing.

Bodrova, E., & Leong, D. (1996). *Tools of the mind: The Vygotskian approach to early childhood education.* Upper Saddle River, NJ: Merrill/Prentice Hall.

Bogard, K., Traylor, F., & Takanishi, R. (2007). *Teacher education and preK outcomes: Are we asking the right questions?* Foundation for Child Development, New York. Retrieved October 1, 2007, from http://www.fcd-us.org/

Bogle, R. E., & Wick, C. P. (2005). *Report from the National Summit on School Design.* Washington, DC: The American Architectural Foundation and the Knowledge Works Foundation.

Boileau, P. L. (2003). *Family night out: An afterschool program.* Stevens Point: University of Wisconsin. (ERIC Document (E479351)

Bowman, B. T., Donovan, M., & Burns, S. M. (2001). *Eager to learn: Educating our preschoolers.* Washington, DC: National Research Council, National Academy of Sciences.

Bransford, J. D., Brown, A. L., & Cocking, R. R. (2000). *How people learn: Brain, mind, experience and school committee on developments in the science of learning.* Washington, DC: National Academy Press.

Bredekamp, S. (2006). Staying true to our principles. *Educating Young Children 12*(2), 10–14.

Bredekamp, S., & Copple, C. Eds. (1997). *Developmentally appropriate practice in early childhood education.* Washington, DC: National Association for the Education of Young Children.

Brock, B., & Grady, M. L. (1995). *Principals in transition: Tips for surviving succession.* Thousand Oaks, CA: Corwin.

Brock, B., & Grady, M. L. (2004). *Launching your first principalship: A guide for beginning principals.* Thousand Oaks, CA: Corwin.

Bronfenbrenner, U. (1974). Is early intervention effective? *Teachers College Record, 76*(2), 279–303.

Brown, G. (2003). *What it takes to support school readiness: Building collaborative partnerships.* Raleigh, NC: North Carolina Partnership for Children.

Brown, G., Scott-Little, C., Amvake, L., & Wynn, L. (2007). *A review of methods and instruments used in state and local school readiness evaluation* (Issues and Answers Report, RE 22007–No. 004). Washington, DC: U.S. Department of Education, Institute of Education Sciences, National Center for Education Evaluation and Regional Assistance, Regional Educational Laboratory Southeast. Retrieved on July 6, 2008, from http://ies.ed.gov/ncee/edlabs

Caruso, J. M., & Fawcett, M. T. (2007). *Supervision in early childhood education: A developmental perspective* (3rd ed.). New York: Teachers College Press.

Center for Comprehensive School Reform and Improvement (The Center). (2005, August). *Meeting the challenge of involving parents in school.* [Newsletter]. Washington, DC: Author.

Center for Comprehensive School Reform and Improvement (The Center). (2006, September). *What schools want parents to know.* [Newsletter]. Washington, DC: Author.

Center on Education Policy. (2006). *A public education primer.* Washington, DC: Author.

Center on Education Policy (2007). *Why we still need public schools: Public education for the common good.* Washington, DC: Author.

Chaiklin, S. (2003). The zone of proximal development in Vygotsky's analysis of learning and instruction. In A. Kozulin, B. Gindis, V. Ageyev, & S. Miller (Eds.). *Vygotsky's educational theory and practice in cultural context* (pp. 39–64). Cambridge, England: Cambridge University Press.

Chavkin, N., & Gonzalez, D. (1995). *Forging partnerships between Mexican American parents and the schools.* Charleston, WV: ERIC-Cress.

Children's Defense Fund (CDF). (2004). *State of America's children: 2004.* Washington, DC: Author.

Children's Defense Fund (CDF). (2006). *State of America's children: 2005.* Washington, DC: Author.

Chipman, M. (1997). Valuing cultural diversity in the early years: Social imperatives and pedagogical insights. In J. P. Isenberg, & M. R. Jalongo (Eds.). *Major trends and issues in early childhood education: Challenges, controversies and insights* (pp. 43–55). New York: Teacher's College Press.

Christensen, D. (2007, September 1). *21st century learning begins now!* Keynote address, Administrator Days. Kearney, NE: Nebraska Department of Education.

Christie, J. F. (2008). The scientifically based reading research approach to early literacy instruction. In L. M. Justice & C. Vukelich (Eds.), *Achieving excellence in preschool literacy instruction* (pp. 25–40). New York: Guilford Press.

Clayton, M. K., Forton, M. B., Doolittle, L., & Lord, J. (2001). *Classroom spaces that work.* Greenfield, MA: Northeast Foundation for Children.

Clements, D., Sarama, J., & DiBiase, A. (Eds.). (2004). *Engaging young children in mathematics: Standards for early childhood mathematics education.* Mahweh, NJ: Lawrence Erlbaum Associates.

Click, P., & Karkos, K. A. (2008). *Administration of programs for young children.* Clifton Park, NY: Delmar/Thomson.

Cohen, A. J. (1996). A brief history of federal financing for child care in the United States. *Future of Children Financing Child Care, 6*(2), 26–40.

Colbert, J. (1997). Classroom design and how it influences behavior. *Early Childhood News, 9*(3), 22–29.

Connecticut State Board of Education. (2006). *The Connecticut framework: Preschool curriculum framework.* Hartford, CT: Connecticut State Department of Education Bureau of Early Childhood Education and Social Services.

Cooper, A. (2002). *Collaborative leadership: A forum on universal prekindergarten.* New York: Early Childhood Strategic Group Resource Center.

Copley, J. V. (2003). Assessing mathematical learning: Observing and listening to children. *Child Care Information Exchange, 107*(2), 47–50.

Copple, C., & Bredekamp, S. (2006). *Basics of developmentally appropriate practice: An introduction for teachers of children 3 to 6.* Washington, DC: National Association for the Education of Young Children.

Council of Chief State School Officers (CCSSO). (2003). *Early childhood education assessment consortium: Building a system for successful early learners.* Washington, DC: Author. Available at http://www.ccsso.org/projects/scass/projects/early_childhood_assessment_consortium/publications_and_products/3002.cfm

Cox, M., Phillips, D. & Pianta, R. (2002, March 13). *National Institute of Child Health and Human Development: Study of early child care and youth development.* Paper presented at the Society for Research in Child Development, Washington, DC.

Cunha, F., & Heckman, J. (2007, September 9–10). *Investing in disadvantaged young children is good economics and good public policy.* Paper presented at the Telluride Economic Summit on Early Childhood Investment, Telluride, CO.

Cunningham, B., & Watson, L. W. (2002). Recruiting male teachers. *Young Children, 57*(6), 10–15.

Cunningham, W. G., & Cordeiro, P. A. (2006). *Educational leadership: A problem-based approach* (3rd ed.). Boston: Pearson.

Curtis, D., & Carter, M. (2003). *Designs for living and learning. Transforming early childhood environments.* St. Paul, MN: Redleaf Press.

Darling-Hammond, L., Banks, J., Zumwalt, K., Gomez, L. Sherin, M. G., Griesdorn, J., et al. (2005). Educational goals and purposes: Developing a curricular vision for teaching. In L. Darling-Hammond & J. Bransford (Eds.), *Preparing teachers for a changing world* (pp. 169–200). San Francisco: Jossey-Bass.

Davis, K. (2005). *Creating outdoor environments for learning and fun: The early childhood module series.* Bloomington: Indiana's University Center for Excellence on Developmental Disabilities.

DeBord, K., Moore, R. C., Hestenes, L. L., Cosco, N. G., & McGinnis, J. R. (2005). *Preschool outdoor environment measurement scale (POEMS).* Greensboro: North Carolina State University and the University of North Carolina Greensboro. Available at http://www.poemsnc.org/poems.html

Dickinson, D. K., & Tabors, P. (Eds.). (2001). *Building literacy with language: Young children learning at home and school.* Baltimore: Paul H. Brookes.

Dinos, L. (2004, December). Early childhood centers. *School Planning and Management, 12*(43), 34–35.

Dodge, D. T. (2003). *The creative curriculum for early childhood.* Washington, DC: Teaching Strategies.

Douglas-Hall, A., & Chau, M. (2007). *Basic facts about low-income children birth to age 6.* New York: National Center for Children in Poverty, Columbia University.

Dunn, L., & Kontos, S. (1997). What have we learned about developmentally appropriate practice? *Young Children, 52*(5), 4–13.

Early, D. M., Maxwell, K. I., Burchinal, M., Bender, R. H., Ebnks, C., Henry, G. T., et al. (2007). Teacher's education, classroom quality, and young children's academic skills: Results from seven studies of preschool programs. *Child Development, 78,* 558–580.

Edwards, C. P., Churchill, S., Gabriel, M., Heaton, R., Jones-Branch, J., Marvin, C., (2007). Students learn about documentation throughout their training program. *Early Childhood Research and Practice, 10*(2). Available at http://ecrp.uiuc.edu/v9n2/edwards.html

Egertson, H. (2008, June). Assessment in early childhood: A primer for policy and program leaders. *The State Education Standard,* 28–34.

Eliason, C., & Jenkins, L. (2007). *A practical guide to early childhood curriculum.* Upper Saddle River, NJ: Merril/Prentice Hall.

Elkind, D. (2006). "Young children learn in a diff . . ." In R. Andrews, M. Biggs, & M. Seidel (Eds.), *The Columbia World of Quotations* (p. 5). New York: Columbia University Press.

Elkind, D. (2007). *The power of play.* Cambridge, MA: Da Capo Press.

Epstein, A. S. (2007). *The intentional teacher: Choosing the best strategies for young children's learning.* Washington, DC: National Association for the Education of Young Children.

Epstein, J. L. (1988). How do we improve programs for parent involvement? *Educational Horizons, 66*(2), 58–59.

Epstein, J. L., & Salinas, K. C. (2004). Partnering with families and communities. *Educational Leadership, 61*(8). 12–18.

Evans, G. W. (2006). Child development and the physical environment. *Annual Reviews in Psychology, 57,* 423–451.

Feine, R., Greenberg, M., Bergsten, M. Carl, B., Fegley, C., & Gibbons, L. (2002). *The Pennsylvania early childhood quality settings study.* Harrisburg, PA: Governor's Task Force on Early Care and Education.

Fleck, F. (2005). *What successful principals do!* Poughkeepsie, NY: Richard H. Adin Freelance Educational Services.

Fleer, M., & Raban, B. (2005). *Literacy and numeracy that counts from birth to five years: A review of the literature.* Melbourne, Australia: Early Childhood Learning Resources, Department of Education, Science and Training.

Freiberg, H. J., & Driscoll, A. (2005). *Universal teaching strategies.* (3rd ed.). Boston: Allyn & Bacon.

Fremstad, S. (2003, July 28). *State fiscal funds do not address the need for substantial increases in child care funding.* Washington, DC: Center on Budget and Policy Priorities.

Friedman, D. E. (2004, October). *The new economics of preschool: New findings, methods, and strategies for increasing economic investments in early care and education.* (Report prepared for the Early Childhood Funders' Collaborative). Available at http://www.earlychildhoodfinance.org/handouts/FriedmanArticle.doc

Froebel, F. (2003). *The education of man* (W. N. Hailmann, Trans.). New York, London: D. Appleton Century. (Original work published 1887.)

Fromberg, D. P. (2002). *Play and meaning in early childhood education.* Boston: Allyn & Bacon.

Fronczek, V. (2004). The International Play Association (IPA): Promoting the child's right to play. *Children, Youth and Environments, 14*(2).

Frost, J. L., Worthman, S., & Reifel, S. (2004). *Play and child development.* Upper Saddle River, NJ: Merrill/Prentice-Hall.

Fukkink, R. G., & Lont, A. (2007). Does training matter? A meta-analysis and review of caregiver training studies. *Early Childhod Research Quarterly, 23*(3), 294–311.

Fullan, M. G. (1991). *The new meaning of educational change.* New York: Teachers College Press.

Galinsky, E. (2006). *The economic benefits of high-quality early childhood programs: What makes a difference?* (Report prepared for the Committee of Economic Development). Washington, DC: Committee of Economic Development.

Garbarino, J. (2006). *See Jane hit: Why girls are growing more violent and what we can do about it.* New York: Penguin Group.

Gardner, H. (1993). *Multiple intelligences: The theory in practice.* New York: Basic Books.

Geertz, C.(2000). *Interpretations of cultures.* New York: Basic Books Classics.

Gestwicki, C. (1997). *The essentials of early education.* Clifton Park, NY: Thomson/Delmar Learning.

Gestwicki, C. (2007). *Developmentally appropriate practice, curriculum and development in early education.* Albany, NY: Delmar.

Gill, N. G. (2007). Goodbye, Mr. and Mrs. Chips. *Education Week, 26*(43), 33.

Ginsberg, M. B., & Wlodkowski, R. J. (2000). *Creating highly motivating classrooms for all students: A schoolwide approach to powerful teaching with diverse learners.* San Francisco: Jossey-Bass.

Gonzalez-Mena, J., & Widmeyer-Eyer, E. D. (2006). *Infants, toddlers and caregivers.* Mountain View, CA: Mayfield Publishing.

Good, R. H., & Kaminski, R. A. (2002). *Dynamic indicators of basic early literacy skills: Administration and scoring guide.* Eugene: University of Oregon.

Gordon, A. M., & Browne, K. W. (2007). *Beginning essentials in early childhood education.* Albany, NY: Delmar/Thomson.

Greenman, J. (2005). *Caring spaces, learning places: Children's environments that work.* Redmond, WA: Exchange Press.

Groark, C. J., Mehaffie, K. E., McCall, R. B., & Greenberg, M. T. (2007). *Evidence-based practices and programs for early childhood care and education.* Thousand Oaks, CA: Corwin.

Gruendel, J. M. (2004, April). *Achieving equitable education for all students: Legal, institutional and activist strategies.* Paper presented at the National Conference for Community and Justice Quarterly Forum, Hartford, CT.

Gullo, D. F. (2006). *K today: Teaching and learning in the kindergarten year.* Washington, DC: National Association for the Education of Young Children.

Halliday, M. A. K. (2006). *The language of early childhood: The collected works of M. A. K. Halliday Vol. 4* (J. J. Webster Ed.). London: Continuum International Publishing Group.

Harms, R., Clifford, R. M., & Cryer, D. (1998). *Early childhood environment rating scale* (Rev. ed.). New York: Teachers College Press.

Harms, T., Clifford, R., & Cryer, D. (2007a). *Early childhood environment rating scale.* Carrboro, NC: Frank Porter Graham Child Development Institute. Available at http://www.fpg.unc.edu/~ecers/

Harms, T., Clifford, R., & Cryer, D. (2007b). *School-age care environment rating scale.* Carrboro, NC: Frank Porter Graham Child Development Institute. Available at http://www.fpg.unc.edu/~ecers/

Harris, S. (2005). *Best practices of award-winning elementary school principals.* Thousand Oaks, CA: Corwin.

Hart, B., & Risley, T. R. (1995). *Meaningful differences in the everyday experience of young American children.* Baltimore: Paul H. Brookes.

Hart, C. H., Burts, D.C., & Charlesworth, R. (1997). Integrated developmentally appropriate curriculum: From theory to research to practice. In C.H. Hart, D.C. Burts, & R.Charlesworth (Eds), *Integrated curriculum and developmentally appropriate practice: Birth to age 8* (1–27). Albany: State University of New York Press.

Hart, C. H., Burts, D. C., Durland, M. A., Charlesworth, R., DeWolf, M., & Fleege, P. O. (1998). Stress behaviors and activity type participation of preschoolers in more or less developmentally appropriate classrooms: SES and sex differences. *Journal of Research in Childhood Education, 12*(2), 176–196.

Harvard Family Research Project. (2006b, Spring). *Family involvement makes a difference* (Issue Report No. 1). Cambridge, MA: Harvard Graduate School of Education.

Heckman, J. J., & Masterov, D. V. (2007). *The productivity argument for investing in young children.* A lecture given as the T.W. Schultz Award Lecture at the Allied Social Sciences Association annual meeting, Chicago, January 5–7. Retrieved November 17, 2008, at http://jenni.uchicago.edu/human_inequality/papers/Heckman_final_all_wp_2007-03-22c_jsb.pdf

Helburn, S. W. (1995). *Cost, quality and child outcomes in child care centers: Technical report.* Denver: Department of Economics, University of Colorado at Denver.

Hiebert, E. H., & Mesmer, H. A. E. (2006). Perspectives on the difficulty of beginning reading texts. In D. K. Dickinson, & S. B. Neuman (Eds.), *Handbook of early literacy research: Vol. 2* (pp. 395–405). New York: Guilford Press.

Hill, P. S. (1941). Kindergarten. In *The American Educator Encyclopedia*. Wheaton, MD: The Association of Childhood Education International.

Hinkle, D. (2000). *School involvement in early childhood*. Washington, DC: Office of Educational Research and Improvement, U.S. Department of Education.

Hodgkinson, H. B. (2006). *The whole child in a fractured world*. Alexandria, VA: Association for Supervision and Curriculum Development.

Hoffert, S., & Sandberg, J. (2000). *Changes in American children's time 1981–1997*. (CEEL Working Paper 013-00). Detroit, MI: Center for the Ethnography of Everyday Life. Retrieved June 24, 2007, from http://ceel.psc.isr.umich.edu/pubs

Hohmann, M., & Weikart, D. (2002). *Educating young children*. Ypsilanti, MI: High/Scope Educational Research Foundation.

Horowitz, F. D., Darling-Hammond, L. and Bransford, J. (2005). Educating teachers for developmentally appropriate practice. In L. Darling-Hammond & J. Bransford (Eds.), *Preparing teachers for a changing world* (pp. 88–125). San Francisco: Jossey-Bass.

Howes, C., & Sanders, K. (2006). Child care for young children. In B. Spodek & O. N. Saracho (Eds.), *Handbook of research on the education of young children* (pp. 375–391). Mahwah, NJ: Lawrence Erlbaum Associates.

Howes, C., James, J., & Ritchie, S. (2003). Pathways to effective teaching. *Early Childhood Research Quarterly, 18*(1), 104–120.

Huffman, L. R., & Speer, P. W. (2000). Academic performance among at-risk children: The role of developmentally appropriate practices. *Early Childhood Research Quarterly, 15*, 167–184.

Hymes, James L., Jr. (1994). *The child under six*. Englewood Cliffs, NJ: Prentice Hall.

International Association for the Evaluation of Educational Achievement. (2008). *Pre-primary project*. Retrieved February 2, 2008, from http:// www.iea.nl/ppp.html

International Reading Association (IRA). (2005). *Literacy development in the preschool years: A position statement of the International Reading Association*. Newark, DE: Author.

Jacobson, L. (1999, September 15). Tensions surface in public-private preschool plans. *Education Week, 5*.

Jacobson, L. (2006, August). *Financing early education*, Washington, DC: National Education Writers Association. Retrieved March 17, 2008, from http://www.ewa.org/files/docs/prek%20finance&20brief.pdf

Jago, Z. E., & Tanner, K. (1999). *The influence of the school facility on student achievement*. Unpublished honors paper, College of Education Research Abstracts and Reports, University of Georgia, Athens, GA.

Jezewski, M. (1995). Staying connected: The core of facilitating health care for homeless persons. *Public Health Nursing, 12*(3), 203–210.

Johnson, C. (2004, February). Funding through foundations. *National Association of Elementary School Principals Communicator, 27*(6), 1, 7. Retrieved June 23, 2006, from http://www.naesp.org/ContentLoad.do?contentId=1149& action=print

Johnson, J. A. (2007). *Finding your smile again: A child care professional's guide to reducing stress and avoiding burnout*. St Paul, MN: Redleaf Press

Jorde-Bloom, P. (1997). *A Great Place to Work: Improving conditions for staff in young children's programs*. Washington, DC: National Association for the Education of Young Children.

Jung, M., Kloosterman, P., & McMullen, M. B. (2007). Young children's intuition for solving problems in mathematics. *Young Children, 62*(5), 50–56.

Justice, L. M., & Vukelich, C. (2008). *Achieving excellence in preschool literacy instruction*. New York: Guilford Press.

Kagan, S. L., & Kauerz, K. (2006). Making the most of kindergarten: Trends, policies and issues. In D. F. Gullo (Ed.), *K today: Teaching and learning in the kindergarten year* (pp. 161–170). Washington, DC: National Association for the Education of Young Children.

Kahn, P., & Kellert, S. (2002). *Children and nature: Psychological, sociocultural, and evolutionary investigations*. Cambridge, MA: MIT Press.

Kansas State Department of Education. (2003). *Kansas curricular standards for mathematics education*. Topeka, KS: Author. Available at http://www.ksde.org/Default.aspx?tabid=141

Karoly, L. A., Kilburn, M. R., & Cannon, J. S. (2005). *Early childhood interventions: Proven results, future promise*. Santa Monica, CA: RAND Corporation.

Katz, L. (1994, November). *Family and culture*. Paper presented at the National Conference for the National Association for the Education of Young Children, Washington, DC.

Katz, L. (2008). Another look at what young children should be learning. *Exchange* (April/March), 53–56.

Katz, L. G. (1990, October). Should preschoolers learn the three R's? *Parents Magazine, 65*(10), 206.

Katz, L. G., & Chard, S. (2000). *Engaging Children's Minds: The project approach*, 2nd ed. Stamford, CT: Ablex.

Kentucky Department of Education (2006). *Building a strong foundation for school success: Kentucky's early learning standards*. Available at http://www.education.ky.gov/KDE/Instructional+Resources/Early+Childhood+Development/Building+a+Strong+Foundation+for+School+Success+Series.htm

Koralek, D. G., Colker, L. J., & Dodge, D. T. (1993). *The what, why and how of high-quality early childhood education: A guide for on-site supervision.* Washington, DC: National Association for the Education of Young Children.

Kostelnik, M. J. (1998). Misconstructing developmentally appropriate practice. *Early Years: The North American Issue* (Spring), 19–26.

Kostelnik, M. J. (2006, April). *Lessons I've learned on the way to the future.* Keynote address, MidWest AEYC Conference, Omaha, NE.

Kostelnik, M. J. (2008, January 23). *Value of early education: P–3.* Paper presented at Governor's Summit on Expanded Learning Opportunities, Lincoln, NE.

Kostelnik, M. J., Soderman, A. K., & Whiren, A. P. (2007). *Developmentally appropriate curriculum: Best practices in early childhood education* (4th ed.). Upper Saddle River, NJ: Pearson.

Kostelnik, M. J., Whiren, A. W., Soderman, A. K., & Gregory, K. M. (2009). *Guiding children's social development and learning.* Clifton Park, NY: Thomson/Delmar Learning

Kovalik, S. J., & Olsen, K. D. (2001). *Exceeding expectations: A user's guide to implementing brain research in the classroom.* Seattle, WA: Books for Educators.

Krogh, S., & Morehouse, P. (2008). *The early childhood curriculum: Inquiry learning through integration.* Boston: McGraw-Hill.

Lackney, J. A., & Jacobs, P. J. (2002). *Teachers as placemakers: Investigating teachers' use of the physical learning environment in instructional design.* Madison: University of Wisconsin, School of Engineering, School Design Research Studio. (ERIC# ED463645)

Lee, V. E., & Burkham, D. T. (2002). *Inequality at the starting gate: Social background differences in achievement as children begin school.* Washington, DC: Economic Policy Institute.

Leong, D. (2007, February 27). *Dramatic play . . . So much more than fun: How play contributes to the development of self-regulation/executive function.* Presentation to the National Association for the Education of Young Children Taskforce on Developmentally Appropriate Practice, Washington, DC.

Leppo, M. I., Davis, D., & Crim, B. (2000). The basics of exercising the mind and the body. *Childhood Education, 76*(3), 142–147.

Lewis-Moreno, B. (2007, June). Shared responsibility: Achieving success with English-language learners. *Phi Delta Kappan, 88*(10), 772–775.

Lockwood, A. T. (2008). *The principal's guide to afterschool programs: Extending student learning opportunities.* Thousand Oaks, CA: Corwin.

Lunenburg, F., & Irby, B. (2006). *The principalship: Vision to action.* Belmont, CA: Thomson Higher Education.

Lynch, R. (2007). *Enriching children, enriching the nation: Public investment in high-quality prekindergarten.* Washington, DC: Economic Policy Institute.

Makin, L. (2003). Creating positive literacy learning environments in early childhood. In N. Hall, J. Larson, & J. Marsh (Eds.). *Handbook of early childhood literacy* (pp. 327–337). London: Sage.

Mapp, K. L. (2002, April 1–5). *Having their say: Parents describe how and why they are involved in their children's education.* Paper presented at the Annual Meeting of the American Educational Research Association, New Orleans, LA.

Marcon, R. (1999). Differential impact of preschool models on development and early learning of inner-city children: A three-cohort study. *Developmental Psychology, 35,* 358–375.

Marcon, R. (2002). Moving up the grades: Relationship between preschool model and later school success. *Early Childhood Research and Practice, 4*(1).

Marcon, R. (2003). Reply to Lonigan commentary. *Early Childhood Research and Practice, 5*(1).

Marion, M. (2007). *Guidance of Young Children,* (7th ed.). Upper Saddle River, NJ: Merrill/Prentice Hall.

Maryland State Department of Education. (2004, February). *A parent's guide to achievement matters most: Maryland's plan for preK–12 education.* Baltimore: Author.

Marzano, R. J. (2003). *What works in schools: Translating research into action.* Alexandria, VA: Association for Supervision and Curriculum Development.

Marzano, R. J. (2007). *The art and science of teaching: A comprehensive framework for effective instruction.* Alexandria, VA: Association for Supervision and Curriculum Development.

Maslow, A. H. (1943). A theory of human motivation. *Psychological Review 50,* 370–396.

Maxim, G. W. (2003). *Dynamic social studies for elementary classrooms* (7th ed.). Upper Saddle River, NJ: Merrill/Prentice Hall.

Maxwell, L. E. (2000). A safe and welcoming school: What students, teachers, and parents think. *Journal of Architectural and Planning Research, 17*(4), 271–282.

McAfee, O., Leong, D. J., & Bodrova, E. (2004). *Basics of assessment: A primer for early childhood education.* Washington, DC: National Association for the Education of Young Children.

McCaslin, J. M. (2004). *Developmentally appropriate practice: A case study of mentoring for teacher change.* Unpublished master's thesis, Louisiana State University, Baton Rouge.

McKee, J. S. (1990). Children's nature and understanding their development. In J. S. McKee (Ed.), *The developing kindergarten: Programs, children and teachers* (pp. 69–119). Lansing: Michigan Association for the Education of Young Children.

Mellor, S. (2007). Australian education review # 50. Australian Council for Educational Research, Camberwell, Victoria.

Miller, J. L., & Wang, C. (2008). *Apple or cherry?* Documentation record collected at the Ruth Staples Child Development Laboratory School, University of Nebraska–Lincoln.

Mills, P. E., Dale, P. S., Cole, K. N., & Jenkins, J. R. (1995). Follow-up of children from academic and cognitive preschool curricula at age 9. *Exceptional Children, 61*(4), 378–393

Missouri Department of Elementary and Secondary Education. (2001). *Project construct and developmentally appropriate practice: How children benefit.* Columbia, MO: Author.

Mitchell, A., Stoney, L., & Dichter, H. (2001). *Financing child care in the United States: An expanded catalog of current strategies, 2001 ed.* North Kansas City, MO: Ewing Marion Kauffman Foundation.

Montessori, M. (2002). *The Montessori method.* Mineola, NY: Dover Publishing. (Original work published in 1912)

Montie, J. E., Xiang, Z., & Schweinhardt, L. (2006). Preschool experience in 10 countries: Cognitive and language performance at age 7. *Early Childhood Research Quarterly, 21,* 313–331.

Morgan, G. G., & Fraser, J. (2007). Professional development and higher education systems to develop qualified early childhood educators. In C. J. Groark, K. E. Mehaffie, R. B. McCall, & M. T. Greenberg (Eds.), *Evidence-based practices and programs for early childhood care and education* (pp. 159–180). Thousand Oaks, CA: Corwin.

Morrison, G. S. (2007). *Early childhood education today* (10th ed.). Upper Saddle River, NJ: Pearson.

National Arbor Day Foundation. (2007). *Learning with nature idea book.* Lincoln, NE: Author.

National Association for the Education of Young Children (NAEYC). (1996b). *Guidelines for preparation of early childhood professionals.* Washington, DC: Author.

National Association for the Education of Young Children (NAEYC). (1997). *Developmentally appropriate practice in early childhood programs serving children from birth through age 8: A position statement of the National Association for the Education of Young Children.* Washington, DC: Author.

National Association for the Education of Young Children (NAEYC). (2002). *Developmentally appropriate practice in early childhood programs.* (S. Bredekamp & C. Copple, Eds.). Washington, DC: Author.

National Association for the Education of Young Children (NAEYC). (2003). *Preparing early childhood professionals: NAEYC's standards for programs.* Washington, DC: Author.

National Association for the Education of Young Children (NAEYC). (2005). *Early childhood learning standards and accreditation criteria: The mark of quality in early childhood education.* Washington, DC: Author.

National Association for the Education of Young Children (NAEYC). (2006). *Research and reports in ECE: National Association for the Education of Young Children: Partnering for success: Community approaches to early learning.* Retrieved June 3, 2006, from http://www.naeyc.org/ece/research.asp

National Association for the Education of Young Children (NAEYC). (2008). *Developmentally appropriate in early childhood programs serving children from birth through age 8. Position statement.* Washington, DC: Author.

National Association for the Education of Young Children and the National Association of Early Childhood Specialists in State Departments of Education (NAEYC/NAECS/SDE). (2003, November). *Early childhood curriculum, child assessment, and program evaluation: Building an accountable and effective system for children birth through age eight. A joint position statement.* Washington, DC: Author.

National Association of Elementary School Principals (NAESP). (1998). *Early childhood education and the elementary principal: Standards for quality programs for young children.* Alexandria, VA: Author.

National Association of Elementary School Principals (NAESP). (2005). *Leading early childhood learning communities: What principals should know and be able to do.* Alexandria, VA: Author.

National Association of Elementary School Principals (NAESP). (2006a). *Early childhood funding.* Retrieved June 23, 2006 from http://www/naesp.org/search/Search.do;jsessionid=B286164C865A

National Association of Elementary School Principals (NAESP). (2006b). *Grants and funding hot links.* Retrieved June 3, 2006 from http://www.naesp.org/ContentLoad.do?contentId=917&action

National Association of Elementary School Principals (NAESP). (2006c). *Leading early childhood learning communities: What principals should know and be able to do.* Alexandria, VA: Author.

National Association of Elementary School Principals (NAESP). (2006d). *Principals lead the way for preK–3: Early investment, strong alignment, better results.* New York: NAESP Foundation for Child Development. Retrieved March 18, 2008, from http://www.naesp.org/ContentLoad.do?contentId=1928

National Association of Elementary School Principals (NAESP). (2007). *Leading early childhood learning communities: What principals should know and be able to do.* Alexandria, VA: National Association of Elementary School Principals.

National Center for Education Statistics (NCES). (2000). *Special analysis 2000: Entering kindergarten: A portrait of American children when they begin school.* Washington, DC: U.S. Department of Education.

National Center for Family and Community Connections with School (NCFCCS). (2002). *A new wave of evidence: The impact of school, family, and community connections on student achievement.* Austin, TX: Southwest Educational Development Laboratory.

National Child Care Information and Technical Assistance Center (NCCIC). (2008). *Family, friend, and neighbor child care: National initiatives and resources.* Fairfax, VA: Author. Retrieved, at http://www.nccic.org/poptopics/kithandkin.html

National Council of Teachers of Mathematics. (2001). Principles and standards for school mathematics. Reston, VA: Author.

National Education Association (NEA). (2004). *Are males on the road to extinction?* [NEA News Release for National Teacher Day 2004.] Washington, DC: Author.

National Education Association (NEA). (2008). *Professional pay.* Retrieved March 14, 2008, from http://www.nea.org/pay/maps/teachermap.html

National Institute for Early Education Research (NIEER). (2002, February 5). *Preschool for all: Investing in a productive and just society.* Washington, DC: Author.

National Institute for Early Education Research (NIEER). (2006). *The State of Preschool: 2005 State Preschool Yearbook.* New Brunswick: The State University of New Jersey.

National Institute for Early Education Research (NIEER). (2007). *The State of Preschool: 2006 State Preschool Yearbook.* New Brunswick: The State University of New Jersey.

National Institute for Early Education Research (NIEER). (2008, March 19). *The state of preschool 2007: State preschool yearbook.* Rochester NJ: Rutgers University Graduate School of Education.

National Institute of Child Health and Human Development (NICHD). (2002). Early child care and children's development prior to school entry: Results from the NICHD study of early child care. Early child care research network. *American Educational Research Journal, 39,* 133–164.

National Women's Law Center. (2008, February). *The reality of the workforce: Mothers are working outside the home.* Available from http://www.nwlc.org/pdf/WorkingMothersMarch2008.pdf

Nebraska Department of Education (2005). *Nebraska early learning guidelines for ages 3 to 5.* Lincoln, NE. Author.

Nelson, B. G. (2006). Where are the men? *Principal 85*(5), 3–5.

Nelson, R. F. (2004, December). The transition to kindergarten. *Early Childhood Education Journal 32*(3), 187–190.

Nelson, R. R., Cooper, P., & Gonzales, J. (2007). *Stepping stones to literacy: What works clearinghouse.* Washington, DC: Institute of Education Sciences, U.S. Department of Education.

Neugebauer, R. (2007, October). Formal education Part 3, *ExchangeEveryDay.* Retrieved October 2, 2007, from http://www.childcareexchange.com/eed/news_print.php?news_id=1825

Neugebauer, R., & Neugebauer, B. (2005). *Staff challenges.* Redmond, WA: Exchange Press.

Neuman, S. B. (2007).Changing the odds. *Educational Leadership, 65*(2), 16–21.

Neuman, S. B., & Roskos, K. A. (1993). *Language and literacy learning in the early years.* New York: Harcourt, Brace, Jovanavich College Publishers.

Neuman, S. B., & Roskos, K. (2005). Whatever happened to developmentally appropriate practice in early literacy? *Young Children, 60*(4), 22–26

New Zealand Ministry of Education. (2003). He Whàriki Màtauranga mò ngà Mokopuna o Aotearoa: Early childhood curriculum (pub. in English). Wellington, New Zealand: Ministry of Education Learning Media Division.

Nieto, S. (2007). *Affirming diversity: The sociopolitical context of multicultural education,* 3rd ed. New York: Longman.

No Child Left Behind Act of 2001. Publ. L. No. 107–110. Sect. 9101(32), 115 Stat. 1425 (2002). Retrieved September 15, 2006, from http://www.ed.gov/policy/elsec/leg/esea02/pg107.html#sec9101

O'Connell, J. (2005, January 24). *Preschool for all: A first-class learning initiative.* Annual address from the California Superintendent of Public Instruction on the status of education in California, Sacramento.

Odden, A., & Picus, L. (2008). *School finance: A policy perspective* (4th ed.). New York: McGraw-Hill.

Odom, L. L., Wolery, R., Lieber, J., & Horn, E. (2002). *Widening the circle: Including children with disabilities in preschool programs.* New York: Teachers College Press.

Paley, V. G. (1981). *Wally's stories: Conversations in the kindergarten.* Cambridge, MA: Harvard University Press.

Parent Aware. (2008). *What is Minnesota's Parent Aware rating tool?* Retrieved March 14, 2008, http://www.parentawareratings.org

ParentLink. (2008). http://www.parentlink.net/html/ContentBase/Content/Home

Passantino, R. J. (1994). Preschool comes to school: Design concerns of preschool facilities. *School Business Affairs, 60*(1), 26–30.

Payne, V. G., & Isaacs, L. (2007). *Human motor development: A lifespan approach* (6th ed.). New York: McGraw-Hill.

Peisner-Feinberg, E. S., Burchinal, M. R., Clifford, R. M., Culkin, M. L., Howes, C., Kagan S. L., et al. (2000). *The children of the Cost, Quality, and Outcomes Study go to school: Technical report.* Chapel Hill: University of North Carolina at Chapel Hill, Frank Porter Graham Child Development Center.

Peña, D. C. (2000). Parent involvement: Influencing factors and implications. *Journal of Educational Research, 94*(1), 42–54.

Peske, H. E., & Haycock, K. (2006). *Teaching inequality: How poor and minority students are shortchanged on teacher quality.* Chicago: Education Trust.

Peterson, K. D., & Peterson, C. A. (2006). *Effective teacher evaluation. A guide for principals.* Thousand Oaks, CA: Corwin.

Petrakos, H., & Howe, N. (1996). The influence of the design of the dramatic play center on children's play. *Early Childhood Research Quarterly,* 11, 63–77.

Phillips, D., Mekos, D., Scarr, S., McCartney, K., & Abbott-Shimm, M. (2000). Within and beyond the classroom door: Assessing quality in child care centers. *Early Childhood Research Quarterly, 15*(4), 475–496.

Pianta, R., Cox, M. J., & Snow, K. L. (2007) *School readiness and the transition to kindergarten in the era of accountability.* Baltimore, MD: Paul H. Brookes Publishing Company.

Picard, C. J. (2006). Need for statewide preschool program. Louisiana Department of Education. Retrieved October 15, 2008 from www.doe.state.la.us/DOE/news/super/preschool

Pipher, M. (2002). *The middle of everywhere: The world's refugees come to our town.* New York: Harcourt.

Prescott, E. (2008, March/April). The physical environment: A powerful regulator of experience. *Exchange, 2,* 34–37.

Public Policy Forum. (2007). *Research on early childhood education outcomes.* Milwaukee, WI: Author.

Raikes, H., Torquati, J., Hegland, S., Raikes, A., Scott, J., Messner, L., et al. (2004). Studying the culture of quality: A holistic approach to measuring characteristics of the workforce and child care quality in four Midwestern states. In I. Martinez-Beck & M. Zaslow (Eds.), *Early childhood professional development and training and children's successful transition to elementary school* (pp. 164–184). New York: Brooks.

Ramey, S. L., & Ramey, C. T. (2006). Early educational interventions: Principles of effective and sustained benefits from targeted education programs. In D. K. Dickinson & S. B. Neuman, *Handbook of early literacy research* (pp. 445–459). New York: Guilford Press.

Ricken, R. (2007). *Mastering the balance of the principalship: How to be a compassionate and decisive leader.* Thousand Oaks, CA: Corwin.

Rinaldi, C. (1994). *In dialogue with Reggio Emilia: Listening, researching and learning.* London: Routledge Falmer.

Risley, T. R., & Hart, B. (2006). Promoting early language development. In N. F. Watt, C. Ayoub, R. H. Bradley, J. E. Puma, & W. A. LeBouef (Eds.), *The crisis in youth mental health: Critical issues and effective programs: Vol. 4, Early intervention programs and policies* (pp. 83–88). Westport, CT: Praeger.

Robles de Melendez, W. (2007). *Teaching young children in multicultural classrooms: Issues, concepts and strategies* (2nd ed.). Albany, NY: Delmar.

Rolfe, H. (2005). *Men in childcare* (Occupational segregation working paper, Series # 35). Manchester, UK: National Institute of Economic and Social Research.

Rosman, E., Kass, D., & Kirsch (2006). *High-quality preschool: The key to crime prevention and school success in Iowa.* Washington, DC: Fight Crime: Invest in Kids.

Salinger, T. (2006). Policy decisions in early literacy assessment. In David K. Dickinson & Susan B. Neuman, *Handbook of Early Literacy Research: Vol. 2* (pp. 427–444). New York: Guilford Press.

Sanoff, H. (1995). *Creating environments for young children.* Lake Worth, FL: Humanics.

Scelfo, J. (2007, September 27). Come back Mr. Chips. *Newsweek,* p. 44.

Schweinhart, L. J., Barnes, H. V., & Weikart, D. P. (1993). *Significant benefits: The High/Scope Perry Preschool Study through age 27* (Monographs of the High/Scope Educational Research Foundation, 10). Ypsilanti, MI: High/Scope Press.

Schweinhart, L. J., Montie, J., Xiang, Z. Barnett, W. S., Belfield, C. R., & Nores, M. (2005). *Lifetime effects: The High/Scope Perry Preschool Study through age 40* (Monographs of the High/Scope Educational Research Foundation, 14). Ypsilanti, MI: High/Scope Press.

Shellenbarger, S. (2006). Work & Family: High teacher turnover can affect preschoolers. *Wall Street Journal,* August 31.

Shepard, L., Kagan, S. L., & Wurtz, E. (1998). *Principles and recommendations for early childhood assessments.* Washington, DC: National Educational Goals Panel.

Shonkoff, J. P., & Phillips, D. A. (Eds.). (2000). *From neurons to neighborhoods: The science of early childhood development.* Washington, DC: National Academy Press.

Shore, R. (1997). *Rethinking the brain: New insights into early development.* New York: Families and Work Institute.

Shore, R. (2002, December). *Starting early, starting strong.* Washington, DC: The Pew Charitable Trusts. Retrieved November 14, 2008, from http://www.earlychildhoodmichigan.org/articles/2-03/Pew12-02.htm

Slentz, K. L., & Krogh, S. L. (2001b). *Teaching young children: Context for learning.* Mahwah, NJ: Lawrence Erlbaum Associates.

Smart, M. S., & Smart, R. C. (1982). *Children: Development and relationships.* New York: Macmillan.

Smith, A. B. (1992). Early childhood educare: Seeking a theoretical framework in Vygotsky's work. *International Journal of Early Years Education, November*(1), 10–36.

Smith, B. J. (2002). *The collaborative planning outreach project: Building comprehensive early childhood systems*. Denver: Colorado University Center for Collaborative Educational Leadership.

Sobel, D. 1996). *Beyond ecophobia: Reclaiming the heart in nature education*. Great Barrington, MA: The Orion Society.

Soderman, A. K., & Farrell, P. (2008). *Creating literacy-rich preschools and kindergartens*. Boston: Pearson.

Soderman, A. K., Gregory, K. S., & McCarty, L. T. (2006). *Scaffolding emergent literacy: A child-centered approach for preschool through grade 5*. Boston: Allyn & Bacon.

Spiegel, Alix (Writer). (2008, February 21). Old-fashioned play builds serious skills. In *Morning Edition* [Radio broadcast]. Washington, DC: National Public Radio. Retrieved March 28, 2008, from http://www.npr.org/templates/story/story.php?storyId=19212514

Steele, F. (1980). Defining and developing environmental competence. *Advances in Experiential Social Processes, 2*, 225–244.

Steiner, J., & Whelan, M. S. (1995). *For the love of children: Daily affirmations for people who care for children*. St. Paul, MN: Redleaf Press.

Stipek, D. (2004, May 23). In praise of good teachers. *San Francisco Chronicle*, p. E-5.

Stone, D. (2008). Dollars and sense: A review of economic analyses of preK. preK Now, Washington, DC. Retrieved March 7, 2008, from http://www.preknow.org/documents/FundingtheFuture_Feb2008.pdf

Strickland, D. (2007, March 4). Findings from the National Literacy Panel's providing a focus for early language and literacy development. 16th National Conference on Family Literacy, Orlando, FL.

Strickland, D. S., & Shanahan, T. (2004). Laying the groundwork for literacy. *Educational Leadership, 61*(2), 74–77.

Stronge, J. H. (2002). *Qualities of effective teachers*. Alexandria, VA: Association for Supervision and Curriculum Development.

Stuber, G. M. (2007a). Centering your classroom: Setting the stage for engaged learners. *Young Children, 62*(4), 58–60.

Stuber, G. S. (2007b). *Of primary interest: Centering your classroom and setting the stage for engaged learners. Beyond the journal: Young children on the Web*. Washington, DC: National Association for the Education of Young Children. Retrieved March 16, 2008, from http://journal.naeyc.org/btj/ 200707/BTJPrimaryInterest.asp

Sylwester, R. (1996). *A celebration of neurons*. Alexandria, VA: Association for Supervision and Curriculum Development.

Tarr, P. (2001, May). Aesthetic codes in early childhood education: What art educators can learn from Reggio Emilia. *Art Education 54*(3), 33–39.

Taylor, B. J. (2002). *Early childhood program management: People and procedures*. Upper Saddle River, NJ: Merrill/Prentice Hall.

Thayer, Y., & Short, T. (1994). New sources of funding for the twenty-first-century school. *NASSP Bulletin 78*(566), 6–15.

Thegen, K., & Weber, L. (2002). *Family support: A solid foundation for children*. Raleigh, NC: Partnership for Children.

Trawick-Smith, J. (2009). *Early childhood development: A multicultural perspective*, 4th ed. Upper Saddle River, New Jersey: Merrill/Prentice Hall.

Trister Dodge, D. (2004). Early childhood curriculum models: Why, what and how programs use them. *Child Care Information Exchange*. January/February, 71–75.

Tyack, D., Lowe, R., & Hansot, E. (1984). *Public schools in hard times: The great depression and recent years*. Cambridge, MA: Harvard University Press.

Udell, T., Deardorff, P., Glasenapp, G., & Norris, D. (2001). *Developmentally appropriate practice*. Monmouth: Teaching Research Institute, Western Oregon University.

United Nations Educational, Scientific and Cultural Organization (UNESCO). (2005). *The quality imperative* (Education for All Global Monitoring Report). Paris: Author.

United Nations Educational, Scientific and Cultural Organization (UNESCO). (2007). *Strong foundations: Early childhood care and education* (Education for All Global Monitoring Report). Paris: Author.

United Way. 2008. *Our work in education*. Alexandria, VA: Author. Retrieved March 16, 2008, from http://www.unitedway.org/sb6/index.cfm

U.S. Census Bureau. (2006). *Current Population Survey, 2006 annual social and economic supplement*. Washington, DC: Author.

U.S. Department of Education (2004). *Parental involvement: Title I, part A: Non-regulatory guidance*. Washington, DC: Government Printing Office. Retrieved September 15, 2006, from http://www.ed.gov/programs/titleiparta/parentinvguid.doc#_Toc70481096

U.S. Department of Health and Human Services (DHHS). (2003). *Easing the transition from preschool to kindergarten: A guide for early childhood teachers and administrators*. Washington, DC: Head Start Information and Publication Center.

U.S. Department of Health and Human Services (DHHS). (2007). *National child care information center. Selected state early learning guidelines on the Web*. Washington, DC: Administration for Children and Families. Retrieved July 30, 2007, from http://www.nccic.org/pubs/goodstart/elgWebsites.html

U.S. Department of Labor. (2007). *Occupational outlook handbook*. Washington, DC: Bureau of Labor Statistics. www.bls.gov

Vandell, D. L., & Wolfe, B. (2000). *Child care quality: Does it matter and does it need to be approved?* Washington, DC: U.S. Department of Health and Human Services.

Vandivere, S., Moore, K. A., & Zaslow, M. (2000). *Children's family environment: Findings from the National Survey of America's Families: Snapshots of America's families II.* Washington, DC: Urban Institute and Child Trends.

VMAssociates. (2002). *How to start intergenerational programs in communities.* Winsor Mill, MD: Ready at Five Partnership.

Warden, C. (2008, July 26). *Talking and thinking floorbooks.* Keynote address, NeAEYC, Lincoln, NE.

Warner, L., & Sower, J. (2005). *Educating young children: Preschool through primary grades.* Needham Heights, MA: Allyn & Bacon.

Wat, A. (2007). *Dollars and sense: A review of economic analyses of pre-K.* Washington, DC: Pre-K Now.

Weaver, R. (2003) *The face of the American teacher.* Address to the National Education Association Annual Conference, New Orleans, LA, July 1.

Weinstein, C. S. (1987). Designing preschool classrooms to support development: Research and reflection. In C. S. Weinstein & T. G. David (Eds.). *Spaces for children: The built environment and child development* (pp. 159–186). New York: Plenum Press.

Weinstein, C. S., & Mignano, A., Jr. (2007). *Elementary classroom management: Lessons from research and practice* (4th ed.). New York: McGraw-Hill.

White Hutchinson Leisure and Learning Group, Kansas City, MO, 2007. Creating sustainable environments for young children. Institute on Creating Sustainable Environments for Young Children, Nebraska City, NE.

Whitebook, M. (2003). *Early education quality: Higher teacher qualifications for better learning environments: A review of the literature.* Berkeley: Institute of Industrial Relations, Center for the Study of Child Care Employment, University of California.

Whitebook, M., Sakai, I., & Howes, C. (1997). *NAEYC accreditation as a strategy for improving child care quality.* Washington, DC: National Center for the Early Childhood Work Force.

Wien, C. A. (2004). *Negotiating standards in the primary classroom: The teacher's dilemma.* New York: Teachers College Press.

Willis, S. (2002). Crossing borders, learning to count. *Australian Educational Researchers, 19*(2), 115–130.

Wilson, K. M. (2008, January 24). *Research-based emerging and early literacy instruction.* Paper presented at the Nebraska Department of Education Research to Practice Early Childhood Conference, Omaha, NE.

Wiltz, N. W., & Klein, E. L. (2001). What do you do in child care? Children's perceptions of high and low quality classrooms. *Early Childhood Research Quarterly, 16*(2), 209–236.

Zigler, E., & Styfco, S. (Eds.). (2004). *The Head Start debates.* Baltimore: Paul H. Brookes.

Index

Page references followed by *fig* indicate an illustrated figure; followed by *t* indicate a table; followed by *b* indicate a box.

CORWIN

A SAGE Company

The Corwin logo—a raven striding across an open book—represents the union of courage and learning. Corwin is committed to improving education for all learners by publishing books and other professional development resources for those serving the field of PreK–12 education. By providing practical, hands-on materials, Corwin continues to carry out the promise of its motto: **"Helping Educators Do Their Work Better."**

naesp™ National Association of Elementary School **Principals**

*Serving All Elementary &
Middle Level Principals*

The mission of the National Association of Elementary School Principals is to lead in the advocacy and support for elementary and middle level principals and other education leaders in their commitment for all children.